D1027273

# A DECADE OF NEUROPEPTIDES:
# PAST, PRESENT, AND FUTURE

ANNALS OF THE NEW YORK ACADEMY OF SCIENCES
*Volume 579*

# A DECADE OF NEUROPEPTIDES: PAST, PRESENT, AND FUTURE

*Edited by George F. Koob, Curt A. Sandman, and Fleur L. Strand*

*The New York Academy of Sciences*
*New York, New York*
*1990*

Copyright © 1990 by the New York Academy of Sciences. All rights reserved. Under the provisions of the United States Copyright Act of 1976, individual readers of the Annals are permitted to make fair use of the material in them for teaching or research. Permission is granted to quote from the Annals provided that the customary acknowledgment is made of the source. Material in the Annals may be republished only by permission of the Academy. Address inquiries to the Executive Editor at the New York Academy of Sciences.

Copying fees: For each copy of an article made beyond the free copying permitted under Section 107 or 108 of the 1976 Copyright Act, a fee should be paid through the Copyright Clearance Center, Inc., 21 Congress St., Salem, MA 01970. For articles of more than 3 pages the copying fee is $1.75.

⊚ The paper used in this publication meets the minimum requirements of American National Standard for Information Sciences—Permanence of Paper for Printed Library Materials, ANSI Z39.48-1984.

Cover (paper edition): Schematic of two separate, time-dependent gestational effects of ACTH on neuromuscular development (see page 72).

### Library of Congress Cataloging-in-Publication Data

A Decade of neuropeptides : past, present, and future / edited by
George F. Koob, Curt A. Sandman, and Fleur L. Strand.
    p.  cm. — (Annals of the New York Academy of Sciences, ISSN
0077-8923 ; v. 579)
    Papers presented at the Tenth Annual Winter Neuropeptide
Conference held in Breckenridge, Colo. on Jan. 16–20, 1989.
    Includes bibliographical references.
    ISBN 0-89766-563-5 (alk. paper). — ISBN 0-89766-564-3 (pbk. :
alk. paper)
    1. Neuropeptides—Congresses. I. Koob, George F. II. Sandman,
Curt A. III. Strand, Fleur L. IV. Winter Neuropeptide Conference
(10th : 1989 : Breckenridge, Colo.) V. Series.
    [DNLM: 1. Neuropeptides—congresses. W1 An626YL v. 579 / WL 104
D3415 1989]
Q11.N5 vol. 579
[QP552.N39]
500 s—dc20
[599'.0188]
DNLM/DLC
for Library of Congress
        89-14280
        CIP

**B-B**
*Printed in the United States of America*
**ISBN 0-89766-563-5 (cloth)**
**ISBN 0-89766-564-3 (paper)**
**ISSN 0077-8923**

ANNALS OF THE NEW YORK ACADEMY OF SCIENCES

Volume 579
February 28, 1990

# A DECADE OF NEUROPEPTIDES: PAST, PRESENT, AND FUTURE [a]

Editors and Conference Chairs
GEORGE F. KOOB, CURT A. SANDMAN, AND FLEUR L. STRAND

Conference Coordinator
DEBRA EDWARDS

## CONTENTS

[a] The papers in this volume were presented at the Tenth Annual Winter Neuropeptide Conference entitled "A Decade of Neuropeptides: Past, Present, and Future" held in Breckenridge, Colorado on January 16–20, 1989.

## Part V. Molecular Biology: The Future of Neuropeptide Research

## Financial assistance was received from:

- ABBOTT LABORATORIES
- E. I. DU PONT DE NEMOURS AND COMPANY
- ELI LILLY AND COMPANY
- G. D. SEARLE AND COMPANY
- HOFFMANN-LA ROCHE, INC.
- JANSSEN PHARMACEUTICALS
- MONSANTO
- PFIZER, INC.
- SCHERING CORPORATION
- THE COUNCIL FOR TOBACCO RESEARCH—USA, INC.
- THE UPJOHN COMPANY

The New York Academy of Sciences believes it has a responsibility to provide an open forum for discussion of scientific questions. The positions taken by the participants in the reported conferences are their own and not necessarily those of the Academy. The Academy has no intent to influence legislation by providing such forums.

# Preface

## The Winter Neuropeptide Conference

The first Winter Neuropeptide Conference (WNPC) was organized by Curt Sandman, Lyle Miller, and Abba Kastin in the summer of 1976 as the Bicentennial Neuropeptide Conference. Most of the scientific participants (including Fleur Strand) in the small but growing area presented at the first conference, and the proceedings are contained in two published volumes. The first "legitimate" WNPC was in Copper Mountain, Colorado in 1979, organized by Sandman and Miller, and was an outgrowth from and a satellite of the Winter Conference on Brain Research. The WNPC moved to Breckenridge, Colorado in 1981 and has since remained there, often being referred to as "The Breckenridge Conference." The tenth year of the conference marks the passage of fourteen years, and it is remarkable that a number of investigators who contributed to the first volumes also contributed to the present one (Beckwith, Dunn, Kastin, Sandman, Strand, and Walker). In addition, several of the participants have remained active and continue to contribute to this important field.

## Overview

This volume presents an overview of the extraordinary development of the field of neuropeptide research over the past decade, as well as of present and future directions. The tone for this is well set in the introductory lecture by the keynote speaker, Abba Kastin, who points out the many difficulties in the birth of the neuropeptide decade and how some traditional concepts of hormone action, dosage, binding, and route of administration have had to be severely modified. This theme is extended in Part I by Marvin Brown, who discusses the great diversity of neuropeptides, both natural and synthetic, their evolutionary similarity and diversity, and peptide-induced integration of complex systems, including the central nervous system

Neuropeptides are considered as regulatory agents in the next series of detailed papers. The interaction between the neuroendocrine and immune systems, volume transmission as a means of peptide distribution, and neuropeptides as growth regulating factors are topics that emphasize the global significance of neuropeptides in the normal and pathological integration of physiological functions. The question of specificity versus redundancy of many neuropeptides is raised. Do neuropeptides merely induce permutations in the neuronal environment that permit interaction with other more specific regulators, or does each neuropeptide have a specific function?

Neuropeptides play different biological roles in the developing, adult, and aging organism. In Part II, using the opioid neuropeptides as an example, several papers examine the changing role of neuropeptides at various life stages, a longitudinal view of neuropeptide function that yields important insights into the multidimensional functions of neuropeptides.

Neuropeptide regulation of autonomic function is another indication of the neuropeptides' widespread importance. In Part III interactions between neuropeptides, neurotransmitters, and the autonomic system are discussed in terms of cardiovascular changes and neuropeptide distribution within the spinal cord. The localization of neuropeptides in afferents to and within sympathetic preganglionic neurons indicates that neuropeptide regulation of sympathetic outflow may be at the level of the spinal cord. Sympathetic activity may also be modulated in a complex manner by the midline raphe and parapyramidal region of the ventral medulla.

Recent behavioral studies are associated with the development of model systems underlying behavioral effects of neuropeptides, especially corticotropin-releasing factor (CRF), opiomelanocortins, and vasopressin (VP). In Part IV CRF is evaluated as a stress peptide; a model of the behavioral actions of vasopressin is generated from intracellular recordings of the hippocampal slice; and growth hormone-releasing factor (GRF) is shown to have centrally mediated stimulatory effects on food intake that can be viewed as complementing GRF's pituitary effects of growth hormone release. In addition, 1-des-amino-8-D-arginine vasopressin (DDAVP) is indicated to have effects on learning and memory in healthy young adults that are dependent on variables that may be important in developing and understanding of the actions of vasopressin on human memory. While the behavioral effects of the neuropeptide galanin are not as thoroughly studied, galanin and acetylcholine coexist in neurons of the basal forebrain and galanin may be an inhibitory modulator of cholinergic function. The functional significance of this coexistence of a "classical" neurotranmitter and a neuropeptide is investigated through behavioral studies on learning and memory. The results indicate that galanin may be an inhibitory modulator of cholinergic function.

In the last section of this *Annal* (Part V) several techniques are presented and applied to elucidate the molecular biology of neuropeptides. A new method for *in situ* hybridization histochemistry is described that provides a higher degree of cellular resolution than radiolabeled or other nonradiolabeled techniques. The regulation of the substance P gene expression and the structure-function relationship of one of the tachykinin receptors is shown using a nuclease protection assay. The novel technique, subtractive cloning, permits the comparison of gene expression and related functions in any two cell populations. These approaches may lead to the discovery of new neuropeptides, peptide receptors, or peptide effector systems.

*Fleur L. Strand*
*Curt A. Sandman*
*George F. Koob*

# A Decade of Changing Perceptions about Neuropeptides

ABBA J. KASTIN, WILLIAM A. BANKS, AND

JAMES E. ZADINA

*Veterans Administration Medical Center*
*University of New Orleans*
*and*
*Tulane University School of Medicine*
*1601 Perdido Street*
*New Orleans, Louisiana 70146*

## HISTORY

The plenary lecture of the tenth anniversary meeting of the annual Winter Neuropeptide Conference provides an opportunity to reflect upon the background of neuropeptides. When the first neuropeptide meeting was conceived, it was difficult to believe that enough investigators had worked with peptides to provide speakers for such a gathering. It was even more improbable to think that the meeting would foreshadow a time when half a dozen scientific journals would deal exclusively with peptides. Furthermore, one would hardly have expected that in only the first six years of one of those journals, over 65 peptides and their fragments and analogs would be reported to have central nervous system (CNS) effects.[1]

The prevalent mood about neuropeptides in the scientific community at the time the first meeting was being organized was one of skepticism. It recalls a time two decades ago when the question of the possible existence of hypothalamic peptides controlling pituitary function was a subject of ridicule; an able investigator who had been president of national and international scientific societies compared them in print with the Loch Ness monster.

During the next decade, when the first neuropeptide meeting was being conceived, similarly prominent investigators were astounded to learn that we believed that hypothalamic peptides could act ''upwards'' on the brain as well as ''downwards'' on the pituitary. Our introduction of the terms ''extra-endocrine'' and ''extra-pituitary'' for actions of hypothalamic and pituitary peptides was considered to be as presumptuous as was the related concept that peripherally administered peptides could directly affect the brain. Even among the investigators who had been providing evidence for CNS effects of peptides for several years, this issue was avoided. It seemed to take what were then the bold titles of ''Peripheral Administration of Hypothalamic Peptides Results in CNS Changes'' in one review[2] and ''CNS Effects of Peripherally Administered Brain Peptides'' in another review[3] to finally legitimize what investigators in the field had been finding for several years. After these reviews, the issue of whether neuropeptides injected peripherally without long-acting vehicles could affect the brain was seldom raised again. Instead, skepticism shifted from whether peptides could act on the brain to whether this action was a direct one exerted by intact peptides crossing the blood-brain barrier (BBB).

### Blood-Brain Barrier and Peptides

The first direct chemical evidence that a small amount of neuropeptide could cross the BBB in intact form was provided in 1976.[4] Previous studies usually involved peripheral

1

injection of a radioactively labeled peptide and measurement of the resulting counts in the brain or else injection of an unlabeled peptide and measurement of the resulting immunoreactivity in the brain by radioimmunoassay. Those studies, unlike the study in 1976,[4] did not establish that the measured increase was due to the intact peptide. Alternative methods by which peripherally administered peptides could act on the brain were acknowledged, but we felt the challenge remaining was to show that neuropeptides could cross in intact form.[5,6]

Most of the prevalent feelings were strongly against the possibility that intact peptides crossed the BBB and were based on unsupported opinions rather than on substantive data. With one major exception, there was essentially no convincing evidence against peptides entering the brain. This exception was provided by a group that worked with an otherwise useful method that was not sensitive enough for detection of the entry of peptides. Unfortunately, the main investigator was vociferous at meetings and prolific in writing articles aimed at promulgating his misconception that the BBB excludes peptides. This group now believes that peptides do cross the BBB, but their attitude is reminiscent of the phases of scientific discovery attributed to J. B. S. Haldane. Haldane described the first phase of the reaction to an unorthodox discovery as the feeling that the results are worthless nonsense. His last-described phase deals with the mistaken feeling within the scientific community that it was the disbeliever who made the initial discovery.

It is easy to see how some investigators might have been fooled by their own data generated with an inappropriate method. Determination of penetration of a peptide across the BBB is usually made by measurement of material appearing in the brain after peripheral administration. Several methods can be used to determine transport of a peptide across the BBB. However, if the peptide injected peripherally is being actively transported out of the brain, measurement of residual material in the brain might show little peptide left there and hence result in the mistaken impression that no penetration into the brain ever occurred.

It is now known that peptides can be transported both into and out of the brain by saturable and nonsaturable mechanisms.[7,8] Where saturable transport mechanisms do not occur, the lipophilicity of the peptides is the major determinant of their direct membrane penetration of the BBB.[9,10] This penetration does not involve generalized pinocytosis or leakage around the endothelial cells whose tight junctions are the principal constituents of the BBB. Injected material remaining in the intravascular space of the brain can be measured with vascular markers such as albumin and red blood cells. It is difficult, unless cerebrospinal fluid is assessed, to rule out the possibility that a substance considered to penetrate into the brain may only be binding to receptors on the luminal side of the BBB.

The method we first used to demonstrate saturable transport out of the brain is not subject to these limitations since it involves a decrease in material remaining in the brain. Tyr-MIF-1 (Tyr-Pro-Leu-Gly-NH$_2$) is the endogenous brain peptide most frequently used in studies of carrier-mediated transport of peptides out of the brain. None of the constituent parts of the peptide compete for its selective transport and even D-Tyr-MIF-1 is ineffective. Essentially the only competing peptides are opiates. This is intriguing, since Tyr-MIF-1 has antiopiate activity.

## Antiopiate Peptides

The discovery of the enkephalins provided a powerful stimulus to much of the peptide field. In our laboratory, also, it stimulated the performance of experiments designed to support two new concepts. For the first, we showed that opiate peptides could exert actions not involving analgesia and pain.[3,11,12] This was an extension of our concept of the multiple actions of brain peptides.[13] For the second, we showed that there are antiopiate neuropeptides that can serve to balance the opiate peptides.[14,15] Evidence has accumulated from a number of laboratories in favor of each of these concepts that initially were also greeted with skepticism. It will be of interest to see whether these concepts also eventually suffer the fate of either being considered well known at the time of their controversial introductions or discovered by one of their original opponents.

Synthetic naloxone is a potent opiate antagonist, but any endogenous antiopiate system is likely to act more like a "fine tuner" than like a powerful antagonist.[15,16] Using Tyr-MIF-1 as the prototype, we showed that the antiopiate system can function differentially under various environmental conditions to ensure that the organism's responses to its perception of the immediate environment are appropriate and specific.[16] The antagonism of opiate, but not non-opiate, stress-induced analgesia by MIF-1 and Tyr-MIF-1 has been found in both vertebrates and invertebrates.[17-21] Antiopiate effects of Tyr-MIF-1 have been shown during development in rodents[22] and in human lymphocytes.[23] MIF-1 has also shown antiopiate effects in humans.[24] During our recent isolation of Tyr-MIF-1 from bovine brain tissue,[25] we observed the presence of three other structurally similar peptides and a possible precursor whose sequences have yet to be determined. They could represent a family of antiopiate peptides related to Tyr-MIF-1, to be added to the other peptides with antiopiate properties.[15]

The mechanism by which the antiopiate effect of neuropeptides is exerted is not known. Tyr-MIF-1 can bind to classical mu opiate receptors. However, given its low ($\mu$M) affinity and, therefore, the relatively high concentrations of peptide required to occupy these receptors, it is more likely that the major locus of action of Tyr-MIF-1 is its own binding site. This site, to which the milk-derived opiate peptides casomorphin and morphiceptin can also bind, is a high (nM) affinity site. Recently, we have demonstrated that the number of binding sites for Tyr-MIF-1 in rat brain changes during addiction.[26] These results show that binding sites for an endogenous antiopiate peptide may play a role in tolerance and dependence. Tyr-MIF-1 also augments GABA-induced benzodiazepine binding.[27,28] Although MIF-1 can exert antiopiate activity, it does not bind to the opiate receptor[29] or to the Tyr-MIF-1 site,[30] nor does it compete with Tyr-MIF-1 for transport out of the brain.[31,32] The antidepressive activity of MIF-1 and Tyr-MIF-1 can be blocked by dopamine receptor antagonists,[33] but the antiopiate activity of these peptides may not be affected by dopamine antagonists (unpublished results with John Britton). MIF-1 can, nevertheless, block dopamine receptor supersensitivity in the brain[34,35] and can modify dopamine behavior in the absence of overt changes in the binding of striatal dopamine D1 and D2 receptors.[36]

Although there could be a role for MIF-1 and Tyr-MIF-1 in the complex interactions that may exist among depression, pain, and benzodiazepines, this role is unlikely to be simple. It would emphasize, however, the older concept of the multiple actions of a peptide.[13] Unfortunately, the current tendency among funding agencies to encourage only that research designed to investigate mechanisms for known phenomena may inhibit the search for new phenomena.

Some of the many other concepts involving neuropeptides for which a mechanism is lacking are mentioned next. They should not be ignored just because they are not understood. Howard Cosell is supposed to have said that you need not put your hand in a blender to ensure that it is working; more appropriate might be the saying that you need not know how a television set works in order to use it.

## *"Rediscovered" Concepts*

There are several concepts that have been known for more than a decade in the peptide field that are frequently rediscovered with each new neuropeptide. As the influence of the neuropeptides is found to extend throughout the body, groups of investigators who have never worked with peptides but who have been concentrating on a different area or organ find themselves drawn into the peptide field. Unfamiliar with previous work with other "older" peptides, some of these investigators are amazed to find that their new peptide has some of the same characteristics as the "older" peptides. Here are some examples.

The half-life of a small peptide in blood is very short, but this may have little to do with its duration of action. Many pharmacologists, especially in the pharmaceutical industry, seem to be stuck in the old rut of thinking that a drug's half-life in blood must correlate with its duration of action. The short half-time disappearance of a peptide with longer-lasting effects was well illustrated by work done with MIF-1 in the rat[37,38] and man[39] a decade and a half ago. It is to be expected that the "new" peptides will have durations of action exceeding their short half-lives.

Peptides can exert inverted-U shaped dose-response curves. This can be seen as a more potent effect of a lower dose as well as by paradoxical effects of different doses. In 1971 this was observed with MIF-1 in the rat[40] and later with the same peptide in depressed human subjects.[41] Subsequently, it has been observed with peptides such as DSIP,[42] CCK-related caerulein,[43] substance P,[44,45] and β-endorphin.[46]

Peptides administered during the perinatal period can exert long-term effects. Originally described with steroids, this phenomenon was applied to peptides more than a decade ago. Effects of peptides injected during the neonatal period have been found in the adult rat with TRH,[47] MSH,[48,49] ACTH,[50,51] enkephalin,[52] β-endorphin,[22] morphiceptin,[22] Tyr-MIF-1,[22] vasopressin,[53,54] and substance P.[55] Not yet "rediscovered" for many of the "newer" peptides, it can be predicted that this will occur and should provide much useful information even before the mechanisms are fully elucidated.

## SUMMARY

The last decade has seen rapid growth in research with neuropeptides. During this time, we have been actively developing several concepts including the highly controversial one that peptides can cross the blood-brain barrier in intact form. One of the endogenous brain peptides used as a prototype for that concept, Tyr-MIF-1, also was used for the concept of the existence of endogenous antiopiate neuropeptides. As has been true for most novel developments in science, these concepts, as well as some older ones, were met with a great deal of skepticism when first suggested. Eventually, however, amnesia concerning the difficulties initially encountered with the introduction of new concepts occurs, with their subsequent "rediscovery" made easier.

## REFERENCES

1. ZADINA, J. E., W. A. BANKS & A. J. KASTIN. 1986. Central nervous system effects of peptides, 1980–1985: A cross-listing of peptides and their central actions from the first six years of the journal *Peptides*. Peptides 7: 497–537.
2. KASTIN, A. J., D. H. COY, A. V. SCHALLY & L. H. MILLER. 1978. Peripheral administration of hypothalamic peptides results in CNS changes. Pharmacol. Res. Commun. 10: 293–312.
3. KASTIN, A. J., R. D. OLSON, A. V. SCHALLY & D. H. COY. 1979. CNS effects of peripherally administered brain peptides. Life Sci. 25: 401–414.
4. KASTIN, A. J., C. NISSEN, K. NIKOLICS, K. MEDZIHRADSZKY, D. H. COY, I. TEPLAN & A. V. SCHALLY. 1976. Distribution of [³H]α-MSH in rat brain. Brain Res. Bull. 1: 19–26.
5. KASTIN, A. J., L. A. WADE, D. H. COY, A. V. SCHALLY & R. D. OLSON. 1980. Peptides and the blood-brain barrier. *In* Brain and Pituitary Peptides. W. Wuttke, A. Weindl, K. H. Voigt & R. R. Dries, Eds. 71–78. Karger. Munich.

6. KASTIN, A. J., R. D. OLSON, E. FRITSCHKA & D. H. COY. 1981. Neuropeptides and the blood-brain barrier. *In* Cerebral Microcirculation and Metabolism. J. Cervos-Navarro & E. Fritschka, Eds. 139–145. Raven Press. New York, NY.
7. BANKS, W. A. & A. J. KASTIN. 1987. Saturable transport of peptides across the blood-brain barrier. Life Sci. **41:** 1319–1338.
8. BANKS, W. A. & A. J. KASTIN. 1988. Interactions between the blood-brain barrier and endogenous peptides: Emerging clinical implications. Am. J. Med. Sci. **31:** 459–465.
9. BANKS, W. A. & A. J. KASTIN. 1985. Peptides and the blood-brain barrier: Lipophilicity as a predictor of permeability. Brain Res. Bull. **15:** 287–292.
10. BANKS, W. A. & A. J. KASTIN. 1985. Permeability of the blood-brain barrier to neuropeptides: The case for penetration. Psychoneuroendocrinology **10:** 385–399.
11. PLOTNIKOFF, N. P., A. J. KASTIN, D. H. COY, C. W. CHRISTENSEN, A. V. SCHALLY & M. A. SPIRTES. 1976. Neuropharmacological actions of enkephalin after systemic administration. Life Sci. **19:** 1283–1288.
12. KASTIN, A. J., E. L. SCOLLAN, M. G. KING, A. V. SCHALLY & D. H. COY. 1976. Enkephalin and a potent analog facilitate maze performance after intraperitoneal administration in rats. Pharmacol. Biochem. Behav. **5:** 691–695.
13. KASTIN, A. J., R. D. OLSON, C. A. SANDMAN, A. V. SCHALLY & D. H. COY. 1981. Multiple independent actions of neuropeptides on behavior. *In* Endogenous Peptides and Learning and Memory Processes. J. L. Martinez, R. A. Jensen, R. B. Messing, H. Rigter & J. L. McGaugh, Eds. 563–577. Academic Press. New York, NY.
14. KASTIN, A. J., R. D. OLSON, R. H. EHRENSING, M. C. BERZAS, A. V. SCHALLY & D. H. COY. 1979. MIF-1's differential actions as an opiate antagonist. Pharmacol. Biochem. Behav. **11:** 721–723.
15. GALINA, Z. H. & A. J. KASTIN. 1986. Existence of antiopiate systems as illustrated by MIF-1/Tyr-MIF-1. Life Sci. **39:** 2153–2159.
16. GALINA, Z. H. & A. J. KASTIN. 1988. Differential activity of the endogenous antiopiate Tyr-MIF-1 after various intensities of stress. Neurosci. Lett. **84:** 312–316.
17. GALINA, Z. H. & A. J. KASTIN. 1985. MIF-1 antagonizes warm-, but not cold-water stress-induced analgesia: Dissociation from immobility. Peptides **6:** 1109–1112.
18. GALINA, Z. H. & A. J. KASTIN. 1987. Tyr-MIF-1 attenuates antinociceptive responses induced by three models of stress-analgesia. Br. J. Pharmacol. **90:** 669–674.
19. TESKEY, G. C. & M. KAVALIERS. 1985. Prolyl-leucyl-glycinamide reduces aggression and blocks defeat-induced opioid analgesia in mice. Peptides **6:** 165–167.
20. KAVALIERS, M. & M. HIRST. 1986. Inhibitory influences of MIF-1 (PLG) and Tyr-MIF-1 (YPLG) on aggression and defeat-induced analgesia in mice. Peptides **7:** 1007–1010.
21. KAVALIERS, M. 1987. MIF-1 and Tyr-MIF-1 antagonize morphine and opioid but not non-opioid stress-induced analgesia in the snail, Cepaea nemoralis. Peptides **8:** 1–5.
22. ZADINA, J. E., A. J. KASTIN, P. K. MANASCO, M. F. PIGNATIELLO & K. L. NASTIUK. 1987. Long-term hyperalgesia by neonatal β-endorphin and morphiceptin is blocked by neonatal Tyr-MIF-1. Brain Res. **409:** 10–18.
23. STRIMAS, J. H., D. S. CHI & A. J. KASTIN. 1987. Brain peptide reverses effect of morphine on human lymphocytes. Peptides **8:** 1165–1167.
24. EHRENSING, R. H., A. J. KASTIN & G. F. MICHELL. 1984. Antagonism of morphine analgesia by prolyl-leucyl-glycinamide (MIF-1) in humans. Pharmacol. Biochem. Behav. **21:** 975–978.
25. HORVATH, A. & A. J. KASTIN. 1989. Isolation of Tyr-MIF-1 from bovine brain tissue. J. Biol. Chem. **264:** 2175–2179.
26. ZADINA, J. E., A. J. KASTIN, L. J. GE, H. GULDEN & K. J. BUNGART. 1989. Chronic, but not acute, administration of morphine alters antiopiate (Tyr-MIF-1) binding sites in rat brain. Life Sci. **44:** 555–561.
27. MILLER, L. G., A. J. KASTIN & D. J. GREENBLATT. 1987. Tyr-MIF-1 augments benzodiazepine receptor binding in vivo. Pharmacol. Biochem. Behav. **28:** 521–524.
28. MILLER, L. G., A. J. KASTIN & R. B. ROY. 1987. Effects of Tyr-MIF-1 and MIF-1 at the GABA$_A$ receptor chloride channel site. Brain Res. Bull. **19:** 743–745.
29. LUCIANO, M. G., J. E. ZADINA, A. J. KASTIN & D. H. COY. 1981. Mu and delta opiate receptors in rat brain are affected by GTP but not by MIF-1. Brain Res. Bull. **7:** 677–682.

30. ZADINA, J. E., A. J. KASTIN, E. F. KRIEG & D. H. COY. 1982. Characterization of binding sites for N-Tyr-MIF-1 (Tyr-Pro-Leu-Gly-NH$_2$) in rat brain. Pharmacol. Biochem. Behav. **17:** 1193–1198.
31. BANKS, W. A. & A. J. KASTIN. 1984. A brain-to-blood carrier-mediated transport system for small, N-tyrosinated peptides. Pharmacol. Biochem. Behav. **21:** 943–946.
32. BANKS, W. A., A. J. KASTIN, A. J. FISCHMAN, D. H. COY & S. L. STRAUSS. 1986. Carrier-mediated transport of enkephalins and N-Tyr-MIF-1 across blood-brain barrier. Am. J. Physiol. **251:** E477–E482.
33. PULVIRENTI, L. & A. J. KASTIN. 1988. Blockade of brain dopamine receptors antagonizes the anti-immobility effect of MIF-1 and Tyr-MIF-1 in rats. Eur. J. Pharmacol. **151:** 289–292.
34. CHIU, P., G. RAJAKUMAR, S. CHIU, R. L. JOHNSON & R. K. MISHRA. 1985. Mesolimbic and striatal dopamine receptor supersensitivity: Prophylactic and reversal effects of L-prolyl-L-leucyl-glycinamide (PLG). Peptides **6:** 179–183.
35. BHARGAVA, H. N. 1984. Effects of prolyl-leucyl-glycinamide and cyclo(leucyl-glycine) on the supersensitivity of dopamine receptors in brain induced by chronic administration of haloperidol to rats. Neuropharmacology **23:** 439–444.
36. KOSTRZEWA, R. M., T. G. WHITE, J. E. ZADINA & A. J. KASTIN. 1989. MIF-1 attenuates apomorphine stereotypies in adult rats after neonatal 6-hydroxydopamine. Eur. J. Pharmacol. **163:** 33–42.
37. REDDING, T. W., A. J. KASTIN, R. M. G. NAIR & A. V. SCHALLY. 1973. The distribution, half-life, and excretion of $^{14}$C and $^3$H-labeled L-prolyl-L-leucyl-glycinamide in the rat. Neuroendocrinology **11:** 92–100.
38. KASTIN, A. J., C. NISSEN, T. W. REDDING, R. M. G. NAIR & A. V. SCHALLY. 1974. Delayed disappearance of $^{14}$C-labeled-Pro-Leu-Gly-NH$_2$ from the blood of hypophysectomized rats. Neuroendocrinology **16:** 36–42.
39. REDDING, T. W., A. J. KASTIN, D. GONZALEZ-BARCENA, D. H. COY, Y. HIROTSU, J. RUELAS & A. V. SCHALLY. 1974. The disappearance, excretion, and metabolism of tritiated prolyl-leucyl-glycinamide in man. Neuroendocrinology **16:** 119–126.
40. PLOTNIKOFF, N. P., A. J. KASTIN, M. S. ANDERSON & A. V. SCHALLY. 1971. DOPA potentiation by a hypothalamic factor, MSH release-inhibiting hormone (MIF). Life Sci. **10:** 1279–1283.
41. EHRENSING, R. H. & A. J. KASTIN. 1978. Dose-related biphasic effect of prolyl-leucyl-glycinamide (MIF-1) in depression. Am. J. Psychiatr. **135:** 562–566.
42. KASTIN, A. J., G. A. OLSON, A. V. SCHALLY & D. H. COY. 1980. DSIP-More than a sleep peptide? Trends Neurosci. **3:** 163–165.
43. ELLINWOOD, E. H., JR., W. J. K. ROCKWELL & N. WAGONER. 1983. A caerulein-sensitive potentiation of the behavioral effects of apomorphine by dibutyryl-cAMP. Pharmacol. Biochem. Behav. **19:** 969–971.
44. NARANJO, J. R., F. SANCHEZ-FRANCO & J. DEL RIO. 1982. Blockade by Met-enkephalin antiserum of analgesia induced by substance P in mice. Neuropharmacology **21:** 1295–1299.
45. SCHLESINGER, K., D. U. LIPSITZ, P. L. PECK, M. A. PELLEYMOUNTER, J. M. STEWART & T. N. CHASE. 1983. Substance P enhancement of passive and active avoidance conditioning in mice. Pharmacol. Biochem. Behav. **19:** 655–661.
46. GORDON, C. J., A. H. REZVANI & J. E. HEATH. 1984. Role of β-endorphin in the control of body temperature in the rabbit. Neurosci. Behav. Rev. **8:** 73–82.
47. STRATTON, L. O., C. A. GIBSON, K. G. KOLAR & A. J. KASTIN. 1976. Neonatal treatment with TRH affects development, learning, and emotionality in the rat. Pharmacol. Biochem. Behav. **5**(Suppl. 1): 65–67.
48. BECKWITH, B. E., C. A. SANDMAN, D. HOTHERSALL & A. J. KASTIN. 1977. Influence of neonatal injections of α-MSH on learning, memory and attention in rats. Physiol. Behav. **18:** 63–71.
49. BECKWITH, B. W., R. K. O'QUIN, M. S. PETRO, A. J. KASTIN & C. A. SANDMAN. 1977. The effects of neonatal injections of α-MSH on the open field behavior of juvenile and adult rats. Physiol. Psychol. **5:** 295–299.
50. NYAKAS, C., G. LEVAY, J. VILTSEK & E. ENDROCZI. 1981. Effects of neonatal ACTH administration on adult adaptive behavior and brain tyrosine hydroxylase activity. Dev. Neurosci. **4:** 225–232.

51. SAINT-COME, C., G. R. ACKER & F. L. STRAND. 1985. Development and regeneration of motor systems under the influence of ACTH peptides. Psychoneuroendocrinology **10:** 445–459.
52. KASTIN, A. J., R. M. KOSTRZEWA, A. V. SCHALLY & D. H. COY. 1980. Neonatal administration of Met-enkephalin facilitates maze performance of adult rats. Pharmacol. Biochem. Behav. **13:** 883–886.
53. HANDELMANN, G. E., J. T. RUSSELL, H. GAINER, R. ZERBE & M. BAYORH. 1983. Vasopressin administration to neonatal rats reduces antidiuretic response in adult kidneys. Peptides **4:** 827–832.
54. HANDELMANN, G. E. & S. C. SAYSON. 1984. Neonatal exposure to vasopressin decreases vasopressin binding sites in the adult kidney. Peptides **5:** 1217–1219.
55. HANDELMANN, G. E., J. H. SELSKY & C. J. HELKE. 1984. Substance P administration to neonatal rats increases adult sensitivity to substance P. Physiol. Behav. **33:** 297–300.

# Peptide Biology:
# Past, Present, and Future

MARVIN R. BROWN

*Autonomic Physiology Laboratory*
*Departments of Medicine and Surgery*
*University of California, San Diego Medical Center*
*225 Dickinson Street*
*San Diego, California 92103*

## INTRODUCTION

Over the past 20 years, a large number of biologically active peptides with molecular weights (MW) between 1 and 5 K have been recognized to exist within biological tissues and fluids. Whether there exists a unique modal distribution of peptides within this MW range has not been proved. There is an impression, however, that peptides of this size constitute a generic class of substances that may play important roles as regulators of cellular function.[1-3] The explanation for this phenomenon may be that peptides of this size possess the optimum structural requirements to participate as secreted ligands that specifically bind to cellular receptors and elicit biological responses. Alternatively, peptides of this size may exist because of some mechanistic characteristic of peptide synthesis. That is, peptides of this size may be produced because they are made more efficiently than smaller or larger peptides.

The isolation and characterization of peptides has occurred at a rapid rate because of the development of refined methods of chemical and biological assay, peptide purification, peptide and nucleotide sequence determination, and molecular biotechnology. Strategies for peptide characterization have been based on purification schemes guided by detection of biological or chemical activity, followed by peptide sequence analysis. Alternatively, peptide structures have been deduced by knowledge of RNA or DNA sequences. Isolation of peptides based on knowledge of a biological activity present in an extract of tissue or fluid has the advantage that a putative function exists at the time of sequence determination. Thus, a rationale exists for the isolation and characterization of a particular peptide. It is well recognized, however, that peptides isolated on the basis of one biological action have, upon subsequent investigation, been found to elicit a host of initially unsuspected biological effects. Peptides isolated on the basis of chemical characteristics, such as presence of a C-terminal alpha-amide, or peptides whose structures have been deduced from DNA or RNA sequences generally have no known biological function. In these cases, a search ensues to find a function or role for these peptides in the systems from which their structures were derived (*e.g.*, calcitonin gene-related peptide). Isolation of peptides without knowledge of biological activity removes bias for biologists who determine the physiological significance of peptides. The nature of the search for biological actions of new peptides is primarily determined by the interest and resources of the investigator involved.

The initial naming of a peptide may bias future studies regarding determination of its biological significance. Although some peptide nomenclature reflects historical information, names that imply specific actions may lead to the belief of nonexistent boundaries regarding the function of a particular peptide. Peptide names such as bombesin, derived from its source of isolation, the frog, *Bombina bombina*, may result in retardation of

8

scientific investigation on the basis of aesthetics.[4] In addition, characterization of peptide sequences that are members of structurally related peptide families is regarded with less interest than new unique structures. There is reason to believe that enormous bias exists on the part of peptide chemists and biologists regarding the importance of any particular peptide based on the natural history of the peptide and the research focus of the investigator.

Whether there are unique characteristics of peptide sequence or conformation from which predictions can be made regarding function has not been determined. The concept that peptides contain encoded information corresponding to a kind of intercellular communication language that provides predictable types of integrated cellular and organ responses will be discussed below.

The issue of peptide function largely remains an unanswered question. Although most peptides have been tested and found to exhibit biological actions, the physiological significance of these actions remains uncertain. The diverse actions of peptides to influence the functional biology of animals forms the basis on which to develop a powerful pharmacology. Irrespective of what their physiology may turn out to be, unique biological actions of peptides may lead to the development of many new therapeutic substances useful in man and animals.

Peptides are predominantly distributed in the nervous system and gut of most animals, and in the skins of amphibians. The significance of these patterns of distribution is uncertain. One possibility is that these structures and their interfacing with the environment comprise the most highly developed areas of information processing and exchange. Although many actions and putative roles of peptides in the brain and gut exist,[1-3] the role of peptides in amphibian skin remains a mystery. Within the brain, the anatomic localization of peptides is most notably associated with those regions concerned with neuroendocrine and autonomic regulation.[5] In fact, the only peptides present in the brain that have proven physiological functions are oxytocin and vasopressin, released from the posterior pituitary, and the peptides that regulate anterior pituitary hormone release.

In light of the large number of peptide structures now known, it is reasonable to begin to formulate hypotheses regarding the significance of their existence. One possibility is that all translated and processed peptides play important roles in biology and that, given enough time, scientists will identify these roles. Alternatively, it may be more reasonable to postulate that not all peptides play physiologic roles during all stages of ontogeny and/or phylogeny. Some peptides may be functional and others may be functionless, and thus the latter may be tolerated either within specific cellular systems or in the whole organism. Tolerated peptides, their receptors, postreceptor transduction mechanisms, and the biological responses that they are capable of promoting may form the basis for successful molecular, cellular, and systems reclamation important in evolution. If all the peptides present in the brain play physiologic roles in an animal's neurobiology, we will need new ways of considering the function of the nervous system and methods to study a system with so many transmitters and/or neuromodulators. Thus, the characterization of all these peptides may be in a similar situation to physics, where it has been pointed out that the number of elementary particles is not only excessive in number, but may not lead to an understanding of higher level functions.[6] This subject, of course, is a part of the overall issue of whether reduced parts of a system at any level of organization, from the atom to behavior, can be reassembled to understand the whole. Understanding any particular system may be achieved using methods that evaluate performance of that intact unit. The characteristics and operation of isolated parts, however, may be of little value in the context of the whole system. This does not deny that there may be organizational processes not yet understood that will provide a mechanism by which information derived through reductionism can be reconstructed to understand the whole. In fact, one of the primary hypotheses presented in this paper is that peptides may be involved in this integrative or dynamic construction process. The quest for these organizing principles in complex systems is one of central importance in biology.

Synthetic chemistry has provided biologists with replicas of peptides that have enabled evaluation of their functions. The availability of these peptides and methods to measure them has led to the recognition that a major role of peptides is to function as mediators of intercellular communication. The possibility that peptides play important roles as intracellular messengers is also worthy of consideration; however, this concept has not been evaluated. From a whole organism standpoint, one of the most important aspects of the biology of peptides is that they may provide the basis for coordination of disparate cellular activities into grouped systems with emergent properties (see below). In such, they may carry information that constitutes the dynamic glue that allows multicellular/organ systems with complex functions to perform in a coordinated fashion.

### Properties of Peptides

Although peptides exhibit many unique properties, this discussion will be limited to the following four subjects: 1) proximity of peptides to genetic regulation; 2) diversity of peptide structures; 3) distribution of peptide receptors that results in the ability to coordinate complex systems; and 4) mechanisms by which peptides transmit information in the central nervous system (CNS).

#### Proximity to Genetic Regulation

Peptides, as opposed to other classes of regulators of cellular function, *e.g.*, steroids, catecholamines, etc. are more proximal to genomic regulation. This relationship may in fact explain the large number of peptide structures present in animals, *i.e.*, cells are efficient at making proteins. The synthesis of catecholamines or steroids, for example, requires multiple enzymes and is a more complex process than the synthesis of peptides. The temporal consequence of genomic control of peptide synthesis to biological action is probably most evident during development. Under most circumstances, genomic control of regulatory peptide production probably ensures the existence of a repository of stored peptide, and thus transcriptional and translational events may be relatively unimportant in determining the dynamics of peptide participation in the regulation of cellular activities. Regulation of peptide release is probably the dynamic determinant of peptide action. This is especially true in short time domain systems where changes of genetic expression operate with longer latencies of response than highly dynamic release processes. Thus, although the genetic basis and regulation of peptide synthesis are extremely important issues, it is unlikely that they will lead to an elucidation of the function of peptides in biological systems. The exception to this conclusion is the usefulness of methods to specifically regulate peptide synthesis by preventing transcription or translation (see below).

#### Diversity of Peptide Structures

It is apparent that great diversity of both peptide and peptide receptor structures exists. The basis for this diversity of peptide structure results from regulation of gene expression, splicing of RNA, and regulation of translation and posttranslational processing. Of these processes, splicing and posttranslational processing will be briefly discussed. Alternative processing of nuclear RNA (nRNA) that results in mRNA encoding for different peptides is illustrated by the calcitonin gene products. Rosenfeld and Evans demonstrated that nRNA derivative from the calcitonin gene may be alternatively spliced, yielding mRNAs that encode for either calcitonin or calcitonin-gene-related peptide (CGRP).[7] It was originally hypothesized that different cells, e.g., brain versus thyroid C-cells, might exhibit some relative specificity in these processing patterns. Thus, splicing offers a means to enhance the diversity of translated peptide structure. In the case of CGRP and calcitonin, it is noteworthy that these peptides probably represent tandem duplicated gene products within the calcitonin gene. The positioning of the disulfide bridges and other structural homologies support this conclusion. Despite these homologies, CGRP, in contrast to calcitonin, does not affect calcium metabolism, but does exert potent effects on the gastrointestinal and cardiovascular systems.[8,9]

Posttranslational processing of peptides is an area of importance and of growing interest. TABLE 1 lists some of the major types of posttranslational processing events. Glycosylation, sulfonation and hydroxylation are not as common in small peptides as in proteins. Primary and secondary cleavage, pGlu formation and C-terminal alpha-amidation play important roles in determining peptide structure. Propeptide conversion enzymes act upon propeptide structures to produce small peptides that may remain unchanged or undergo further processing within or outside the cell of origin. pGlu and C-terminal alpha-amidation are structural characteristics that are commonly found in peptides. Fisch-

**TABLE 1.** Posttranslational Processing of Peptides

| Type of Processing | Enzyme |
| --- | --- |
| 1. Primary and secondary cleavage | propeptide conversion enzymes (PCE) |
| 2. pGLU formation | glutamyl cyclase (J. Spiess) |
| 3. C-Terminal alpha-amidation | peptidylglycine alpha monooxygenase (PAM) (Eipper and Mains) |
| 4. Glycosylation | — |
| 5. Sulfonation (TYR) | — |
| 6. Hydroxylation (LYS-GLY) | — |

er and Spiess have recently characterized an enzyme that is involved in pGlu formation.[10] In addition, Eipper et al. have reported the characterization of a peptidylglycine alpha-monooxygenase enzyme that cleaves C-terminal glycine residues resulting in the formation of a C-terminal alpha-amide.[11] Each of these processing events leads to diversity of peptide structure.

Structural diversity of peptides can be contrasted with structural similarity exemplified by the existence of peptide families. Structurally related peptides are thought to result from gene duplication.[12] Subsequent point mutations have resulted in the divergence of structures to varying degrees. Structurally related peptides may exhibit similar functions, e.g., somatostatin-14 and somatostatin-28 (inhibition of growth hormone, insulin, and glucagon), or they may exhibit divergence of function, e.g., gastrin (stimulates gastric acid secretion) and cholecystokinin (stimulates exocrine pancreas and gallbladder). Of interest is the example of structurally related peptides between species and evaluation of the divergence of their functions. An intriguing example of the divergence of function of structurally related peptides is that of endothelin-related peptides. Endothelin is a 21-amino acid-containing peptide isolated from the culture media of vascular endothelial cells.[13] Endothelin is a potent vasoconstrictor and has recently been reported to act as a positive inotrope on the heart.[14] It has been suggested that endothelin may mediate the actions of several vasoactive substances to elicit vascular smooth muscle contraction.[13]

Endothelin is structurally related to two peptides, sarafotoxin, a peptide present in snake venom, and apamin, a peptide present in bee venom.[15,16] These structurally related peptides exhibit divergence of function between species. A poison present in snake or bee venom may be a regulator of cardiovascular function in animals. It is unknown whether sarafotoxin is present in blood vessels analogous to endothelin. An important question is whether or not in man and other animals endothelin may be released in sufficient quantities to act like a snake venom to produce coronary vasoconstriction, A-V block, and cardiac arrest and death.[15] This is an example on a molecular level of the cooptation of existing structures for a specific function. This situation is similar to those described by Stephen Jay Gould in other areas of biology.[17]

*Peptide-Induced Integration of Complex Systems*

Peptides act through cellular receptors, recruit G proteins, activate second messengers such as cyclic nucleotides and phosphorylate proteins, and change membrane ion fluxes to bring about changes of cellular function.[18] These peptides mediate changes of single function and those that result in initiation of more complex cellular and organ responses that translate to the functioning of entire systems and behaviors.

A popular subject in science today is to question how components of a biological system, when assembled, result in the emergence of properties not predicted by knowledge of its individual parts. One such mechanism may be through the diverse and anatomically disparate actions of peptides and other intercellular transmitters. It is well recognized that for many peptides there exist collections of biological effects that result from the actions of these peptides on many different cellular systems. For instance, angiotensin-II (A-II) has the following actions: it increases behavioral acquisition of water, increases vasopressin and aldosterone secretion, facilitates the action of norepinephrine, and produces vasoconstriction.[19] Each of these actions occurs by virtue of an interaction of A-II with a receptor present on different cells of different organ systems. Atrial natriuretic peptide (ANP), in contrast to A-II, acts independently upon the same sites that A-II does, but exhibits diametrically opposed actions.[20] Many examples of this complex coordination exist, *e.g.*, LRF initiates ovulation but also stimulates libido; insulin acts on different cellular sites to coordinate deposition of nutrients following a meal; and corticotropin releasing factor coordinates the neuroendocrine and autonomic nervous system responses to stress.[3] These examples serve to demonstrate the emergent properties of peptides, *i.e.*, peptides mediate the coordinated responses of complex systems, responses that as a whole are not predicted by their individual parts.

*Peptide Transmission of Information within the Central Nervous System*

On the basis of molecular size, biological action, and anatomical studies, peptides have been noted to be, in principle, capable of acting as neurotransmitters through synaptic arrangements, as paracrine substances acting on neighboring cells, or as hormones capable of being delivered to and acting upon sites distal to their origin. The latter possibility that peptides may be delivered to anatomically distant sites by diffusion has gained interest.[21] Fuxe has formalized this concept into a term called volume transmission.[22] The profound anatomic mismatch that exists in the brain between peptides and their putative receptors supports this concept.[23,24] Furthermore, for some peptides the relationship between distribution of terminal fields and sites of biological action exhibits a no less profound mismatch.[21] Perivascular streaming of substances through brain parenchyma may provide a facilitated means of transport of peptides.[25] The only argument against the possibility of delivery of peptides by diffusion within the central nervous sytem is that such a process has not actually been measured. Extreme methodologic hurdles will need to be crossed before such evidence exists.

### Future Developments Necessary to Understand the Biological Roles of Peptides

The rich peptide pharmacology that has unfolded over the past 20 years is ripe for testing for its relevance to physiology. Unfortunately, this task is made difficult by the complexity of the organism and questions to be answered, as well as by limitations of methodology. Following the simplistic concept of Koch's postulates leads one to immediately recognize at least some of the obvious developmental requirements that will be needed to adequately assess the physiologic role of peptides in biological systems.

### Regulation of Peptide Synthesis and Release

In the next few years, molecular biotechnology will hopefully be developed that will allow biologists to selectively manipulate the transcriptional, translational, and posttranslational events that lead to generation of a particular peptide in a specific anatomic cellular site. For instance, the ability to shut off corticotropin releasing factor (CRF) expression within neurons of the central nucleus of the amygdala would be an unprecedented and powerful tool for studying the role of CRF within that brain area. Alternatively, perhaps more powerful and important, would be the development of methods to selectively modify the secretion of a peptide. Such a method should ideally be rapid in onset, reversible, and devoid of nonspecific effects. To date, this goal has not been reached. The closest approximation has been the use of capsaicin and cysteamine to study the physiology of substance P and somatostatin, respectively. Capsaicin depletes cellular stores of substance P in primary sensory neurons.[26] This methodology has been used to demonstrate a physiologic role of substance P in this system.[26] Cysteamine depletes cellular stores and inhibits the synthesis of somatostatin.[27] Through the use of cysteamine, brain somatostatin has been demonstrated to be involved in the regulation of adrenal epinephrine and pituitary vasopressin secretion.[28,29] Despite the successful use of capsaicin and cysteamine as tools for studying substance P and somatostatin, these substances are not without problems and controversy concerning their use.

### Measurement of Peptide Release In Vivo

Measurements of peptides in discrete brain areas using radioimmunoassay or immunocytochemistry are useful; however, they are severely limited by sensitivity, specificity, and ability to test dynamic changes. In situ collection methods, especially the use of in vivo microdialysis, may provide useful techniques, although these methods are extremely laborious.[30] In vivo electrochemistry for peptides has been of little value. Evaluation of peptide synthesis using incorporation of labelled amino acids may be useful for studying peptide dynamics in some circumstances.[31] These methods may not be useful as reflecting peptide release in short time domain systems. Future development of probes capable of dynamic sensing of the release of peptides within a discrete region may solve many of our problems.

*Receptor Characterization*

Two areas in receptor characterization would provide methods that would extend our current investigational ability. First would be the isolation and biochemical characterization of individual peptide receptors. This would aid a variety of investigations including, but not being limited to, the following: 1) study of the interactions between ligands and receptors to aid in analog design; 2) evaluation of receptor interaction with postreceptor proteins; and 3) development of antibodies against receptors to facilitate receptor localization and their use to inhibit ligand binding to receptors as a tool for studying physiology.

The second area of receptor characterization will be to develop methods that can identify and segregate the functionally significant peptide receptors in the brain from those that may be artifact, receptors not coupled to postreceptor events, or receptors in transit. The apparent difficulties in showing functional changes of brain peptide receptors under different physiologic conditions or following the sustained administration of their respective ligand may result from the inability to measure functionally relevant receptors.

**TABLE 2.** Peptide Receptor Antagonists

| |
|---|
| Opiates |
| Vasopressin $V_1$ and $V_2$ |
| Oxytocin |
| LRF |
| CRF |
| GRF |
| CCK |
| Bradykinin |
| Angiotensin-II |
| Bombesin |
| Substance P |
| PTH |

*Peptide Analog and Antagonist Development*

Receptor antagonists have provided powerful tools in the study of numerous biologically important ligands such as catecholamines, histamine, acetylcholine, and others. TABLE 2 is a list of peptides for which receptor antagonists have been characterized. The potency and specificity of these peptide antagonists varies; however, these analogs have been important in the development of an understanding of the biology of their respective peptide agonists. Development of peptide antagonists has largely been an empirical effort directed at optimization of regions of peptide binding while eliminating those residues involved in the generation of intrinsic activity. Several investigators have analyzed peptide confirmation with the aim of predicting changes in structure that might result in higher receptor affinity and/or intrinsic activity.[32]

An ultimate goal in peptide analog design is to characterize predictable ways to synthesize nonpeptide ligands that act as agonists or antagonists by binding to peptide receptors. The future of pharmacotherapeutics based on actions through peptide receptors will depend on the success of this venture. Such an achievement will provide ligands capable of binding to specific peptide receptors in or outside the brain, based on their controlled entrance into the brain resulting from differences in analog size, charge, or other physiochemical characteristics.

An extension of analog development is the coupling of peptides to cytotoxic agents. Conjugate of peptides to toxins such as ricin or gelonin may result in products that are capable of binding to and destroying cells possessing a particular receptor type.[33,34] These compounds can be used as functional antagonists to prevent the action of a peptide, and also as tools to identify brain cellular elements that contain these receptors and to determine the neuroanatomic relationship of these sites to other cell structures.


## CONCLUSION


In addition to the development of new methods, future efforts in the study of peptide biology should include development of a conceptual framework in which peptides are thought to operate. It may be that these new pictures of peptide biology will be necessary before current and future facts can be seen in a different perspective.[35]

Peptide biology has reached a point in its developmental history that allows the formulation of general concepts regarding their chemistry, cellular mechanisms of action, and general roles as transmitters of intercellular information. It will, as in all areas of science, be important to use information derived from reductionist analysis to form a method of predictable constructionalism that leads to an understanding of the role of peptides in biology.


## REFERENCES

1. BLOOM, F. E., ED. 1980. Peptides: Integrators of Cell and Tissue Function. Raven Press. New York, NY.
2. KRIEGER, D. T., M. J. BROWNSTEIN & J. B. MARTIN, Eds. 1983. Brain Peptides. John Wiley & Sons. New York, NY.
3. BROWN, M. R. & L. A. FISHER. 1984. Brain peptides as intercellular messengers. J. Am. Med. Soc. **251:** 1310–1315.
4. ANASTAS, A., V. ERSPAMER & M. BUCCI. 1971. Isolation and structure of bombesin and olytensin, two analogs active peptides from the skins of the European amphibians, *Bombina* and *Alytes*. Experientia **27:** 166–167.
5. PALKOVITS, M. 1988. Distribution of neuropeptides in the brain: a review of biochemical and immunohistochemical studies. *In* Peptide Hormones: Effects and Mechanism of Action. A. NEGRO-VILLAR & P. M. CONN, Eds. Vol. 1: 3–67. CRC Press. Boca Raton, FL.
6. FEYNMAN, R. P. 1987. *QED*. Princeton University Press. Princeton, NJ.
7. ROSENFELD, M. G., J-J. MERMOD, S. G. AMARA, L. W. SWANSON, P. E. SAWCHENKO, J. RIVIER, W. W. VALE & R. M. EVANS. 1983. Production of a novel neuropeptide encoded by the calcitonin gene via tissue-specific RNA processing. Nature **304:** 129–135.
8. FISHER, L. A., D. O. KIKKAWA, J. E. RIVIER, S. G. AMARA, R. M. EVANS, M. G. ROSENFELD, W. W. VALE & M. R. BROWN. 1983. Stimulation of noradrenergic sympathetic outflow by calcitonin gene-related peptide. Nature **305:** 534–536.
9. LENZ, H. J., J. E. RIVIER & M. R. BROWN. 1985. Biological actions of human and rat calcitonin and calcitonin gene-related peptide. Regul. Pept. **12:** 81–89.
10. FISCHER, W. H. & J. SPIESS. 1987. Identification of a mammalian glutaminyl cyclax converting glutaminyl into pyroglutenyl peptides. Proc. Natl. Acad. Sci. USA **84:** 3628–3632.
11. EIPPER, B. A., R. E. MAINS & C. C. GLENTOBSKI. 1983. Identification in pituitary tissue of a peptide alpha-amidation activity that acts on glycine-extended peptides and requires molecular oxygen, copper, and ascorbic acid. Proc. Natl. Acad. Sci. USA **80:** 5144–5148.
12. MILLER, W. L., J. D. BAXTER & N. L. EBERHARDT. 1983. Peptide hormone genes: structure

and evolution. *In* Brain Peptides. D. KRIEGER, M. J. BROWNSTEIN & J. B. MARTIN, Eds. 16–78. John Wiley and Sons. New York, NY.

13. YAMAGISAWA, M., H. KURIHARA, S. KIMURA, Y. TOMOBE, M. KOBAYASHI, Y. MITSUI, Y. YAZAKI, K. GOTO & T. MASABI. 1988. A novel potent vasoconstrictor peptide produced by vascular endothelial cells. Nature **332:** 411–415.

14. ISHIKAWA, T., M. YANAGISAWA, S. KIMURA, K. GOTO & T. MASAKI. 1988. Positive inotrope action of novel vasoconstrictor peptide endothelin on guinea pig atria. Am. J. Physiol. (Heart Circ. Physiol.) **24:** H970–H973.

15. KLOOG, Y., I. AMBAR, M. SOKOLOVSKY, E. KOCHVA, Z. WOLLBERG & A. BDOLAH. 1988. Sarafotoxin, a novel vasoconstrictor peptide: phosphomositide hydrolysis in rat heart and brain. Science **242:** 268–270.

16. HABERMANN, E. 1972. Bee and wasp venoms. Science **177:** 314–322.

17. GOULD, S.J. 1982. The Panda's Thumb. W. W. Norton. New York, NY.

18. BLOOM, F.E. 1988. Neurotransmitters: past, present and future directions. FASEB J **2:** 32–41.

19. PHILLIPS, M. I., S. M. GALLI & E. M. RICHARDS. 1988. Central actions of angiotensin II. *In* Peptide Hormones: Effects and Mechanism of Action. A. NEGRO-VILLAR & P. M. CONN, Eds. **Vol 1:** 219–258. CRC Press. Boca Raton, FL.

20. ATLAS, S. A. 1986. Atrial natriuretic factor: a new hormone of cardiac origin. Rec. Prog. Horm. Res. **42:** 207–249.

21. BROWN, M. R. 1986. Corticotropin releasing factor: central nervous system sites of action. Brain Res. **399:** 10–14.

22. FUXE, K. 1989. This volume.

23. HERBENHAM, M. & S. MCLEAN. 1986. Mismatches between receptor and transmitter localizations in the brain. *In* Quantitative Receptor Autoradiography. C. A. BOAST, E. C. O. SNOWHILL & C. A. ALTER, Eds. 137–171. Alan R. Liss. New York, NY.

24. SHULTS, C. W., R. QUIRION, B. CHRONWALL, T. N. CHASE & T. L. O'DONOHUE. 1984. A comparison of the anatomical distribution of substance P and substance P receptors in the rat central nervous system. Peptides **5:** 1097–1128.

25. RENNELS, M. L., T. F. GREGORY, O. R. BLAUMANIS, K. FUJIMOTO & P. A. GRADY. 1985. Evidence for a perivascular fluid circulation in the mammalian central nervous system, provided by the rapid distribution of tracer protein throughout the brain from the subarachnoid space. Brain Res. **226:** 47–63.

26. BURKS, T. F., S. H. BUCK & M. S. MILLER. 1985. Mechanisms of depletion of substance P by capsaicin. Fed. Proc. **44:** 2531–2534.

27. ARIMURA, A. & S. SZABO. 1982. Selective depletion of somatostatin in rat brain by cysteamine. Brain Res. **240:** 178–180.

28. BROWN, M. R., L. FISHER, R. T. MASON, J. RIVIER & W. VALE. 1985. Neurobiological actions of cysteamine. Fed. Proc. **44:** 2556–2560.

29. BROWN, M. R., M. MORTRUD, R. CRUM & P. SAWCHENKO. 1988. Role of somatostatin in the regulation of vasopressin secretion. Brain Res. **45:** 212–218.

30. WESTERINK, B. H. C., G. DAMSMA, H. ROLLEMA, J. B. DeVRIES & A. S. HORN. 1987. Scope and limitations of *in vivo* dialysis: a comparison of its application to various neurotransmitter systems. Life Sci. **41:** 1763–1776.

31. CAMERON, J. L. & J. D. FERNSTROM. 1986. Effects of cysteamine administration on the *in vivo* incorporation of [35S]cysteine into somatostatin-14, somatostatin-28, arginine vasopressin, and oxytocin in rat hypothalamus. Endocrinology **119:** 1292–1297.

32. HAGLER, A., D. OSGATHORPE, P. DAUBER-OSGUTHORPE & J. HEMPEL. 1985. Dynamics and conformational energetics of a peptide hormone: vasopression. Science **227:** 1309–1315.

33. OELTMANN, T. N. & E. C. HEATH. 1979. A hybrid protein containing the toxic subunit of ricin and the cell-specific subunit of human chorionic gonadotropin. J. Biol. Chem. **254:** 1022–1028.

34. STIRPE, F., S. OLSNES & A. PHIL. 1980. Gelonin, a new inhibitor of protein synthesis, nontoxic to intact cells. J. Biol. Chem. **255:** 6947–6952.

35. ELDREDGE, N. & S. J. GOULD. 1972. Punctuated equilibria: an alternative to phyletic gradualism. *In* Models in Paleobiology. T. J. M. SCHOPF, Ed. 82–115. Freeman, Cooper and Co. San Francisco, CA.

# Bidirectional Communication between the Neuroendocrine and Immune Systems

## Common Hormones and Hormone Receptors

DOUGLAS A. WEIGENT, DANIEL J. J. CARR, AND
J. EDWIN BLALOCK

*University of Alabama at Birmingham*
*Department of Physiology and Biophysics*
*UAB Station*
*Birmingham, Alabama 35294*

## INTRODUCTION

The immune and neuroendocrine systems appear to communicate with each other by virtue of common signal molecules (hormones) and common receptors.[1] A growing body of evidence has shown that hormones can modulate immune system functions and that lymphokines can influence neuroendocrine tissues.[2] The important aspects of common signals and receptors is that the immune and neuroendocrine systems can relay information within as well as between one another. Thus, the immune system has receptors and senses noncognitive stimuli (bacteria, viruses, antigens, etc.) that are not recognized by the central nervous system. This information is then relayed to the neuroendocrine system by lymphocyte-derived hormones and a physiologic change results. On the other hand, central nervous system recognition of cognitive stimuli results in hormonal information being conveyed to and recognized by hormone receptors on lymphocytes, resulting in immunologic changes. This report will review: (1) The evidence for production of neuroendocrine hormones by leukocytes, (2) the evidence for shared receptors on cells of the immune and neuroendocrine systems, (3) the effect of neuroendocrine hormones on leukocyte functions, and (4) the effect of lymphokines and monokines on neuroendocrine tissue.

### The Production of Neuroendocrine Hormones by Leukocytes

A summary of the production of hormones produced by cells of the immune system which have been observed in our laboratory are shown in TABLE 1. The following section describes in greater detail those hormones which are common to the immune and neuroendocrine systems.

#### ACTH, Endorphins and Enkephalins

To date, the most thoroughly studied neuroendocrine hormones produced by leukocytes are the proopiomelanocortin (POMC)-derived peptides. Recent reviews discuss the authenticity in the production of these neuroendocrine hormones by cells of the immune system (immunocyte).[1,3,4] Evidence supporting leukocyte-derived corticotropin (ACTH)

17

and endorphins includes biological activity, molecular weight, antigenicity, identical retention times on a reverse phase high pressure liquid chromatography column, and responsivity to the hypothalamic releasing hormone, corticotropin releasing hormone, as well as the negative feedback inhibitor, dexamethasone (synthetic glucocorticoid). In addition, immunocytes possess and actively transcribe and translate the POMC mRNA which specifies the production of ACTH and endorphins (among others).[5,6] Recently, amino acid sequence of murine leukocyte-derived ACTH shows it to be nearly identical to pituitary-derived ACTH (Smith, Galin, LeBoerd, Coppenhaver, Harbour, and Blalock, submitted for publication). Collectively, the data suggest the production of bona fide POMC-derived peptides by immunocytes. These observations have led us to investigate the potential for other neuroendocrine hormones being produced by leukocytes.

*TSH*

Thyrotropin (TSH) was the second *de novo* synthesized neuroendocrine peptide hormone to be found in the immune system.[7] Unlike ACTH and endorphines which are either constitutively made or induced by virus or lipopolysaccharide, lymphocytes produce TSH

**TABLE 1.** Neuroendocrine Hormones Produced by Cells of the Immune System

| Hormone | Mol. Wt. (Daltons) | Lymphocyte Origin (Ref.) |
|---|---|---|
| Thyroid-stimulating hormone | 28,000 | 7 |
| Follicle-stimulating hormone | 29,000 | 2 |
| Luteinizing hormone | 29,000 | 16,18 |
| Prolactin | 23,000 | 15 |
| Growth hormone | 22,000 | 14 |
| Adrenocorticotropic hormone | 4,500 | 1,3,4 |
| β-lipotropin | 9,500 | 1,3,4 |
| Endorphins | 2–4,000 | 1,3,4 |
| Chorionic gonadotropin | 58,000 | 10 |

in response to staphylococcal enterotoxin A (SEA). In this study, the lymphocyte-derived TSH was shown to bear a marked resemblance to pituitary TSH in terms of its glycoprotein nature, immunogenicity, molecular mass, and subunit structure. In addition, leukocytes have been shown to respond to thyrotropin releasing hormone (TRH) by producing TSH, suggesting TSH to be an endogenous regulator of an immune response.[8] Specifically, TSH has previously been shown to enhance antibody production *in vitro*.[9] TRH treatment of leukocytes augments the production of antibody and such potentiation can be blocked by antisera to the TSH β-chain.[8] Recently, TSH β-chain mRNA has been isolated from leukocytes and has been found to be similar in size to pituitary TSH β-chain mRNA, 0.7 kilobases (Harbour, Kruger, Coppenhaver, Smith, and Meyer, submitted for publication).

*Chorionic Gonadotropin*

Our previous studies showing that cells of the immune system produce specific hormone peptides in response to unique immunogenic stimuli prompted us to examine what, if any, hormones are being produced during an allogeneic response. Chorionic gonadotropin (CG) production, as monitored by immunofluorescence with antibody to CGβ, paralleled the blastogenic response of a mixed lymphocyte reaction (MLR).[10] On day 5, significant immunofluorescence from the cells of the MLR, but not the control cells, was observed when they were stained with antisera to the β subunit of human chorionic gonadotropin (hCG). This immunofluorescence was not seen when the cells were stained with other hormones or when the cells were stained with antiserum to hCG-β after mitogenic stimulation with Con A, SEA, or phytohemagglutinin. It is unclear at present why mitogens do not induce irCG; however, one possibility would be that mitogens produce a signal that suppresses CG production. Besides antigenicity, leukocyte-derived CG appears to be similar to placental CG in terms of bioactivity and structure.[10] Given that during pregnancy, which essentially represents an allograft, implantation and development of the fetus depends on sufficient CG levels[11] and that lymphocytes infiltrate the area surrounding the blastocyst prior to and during the implantation,[12] a potential role for leukocyte-derived CG during pregnancy is suggested. The concept has been supported by the recent observations which show that unknown factors secreted by stimulated lymphocytes affect steroidogenesis in rat granulosa cells.[13]

*Growth Hormone*

Most recently, we have obtained strong evidence that leukocytes produce and secrete growth hormone (GH).[14] Previous to our studies, it was shown that concanavalin A caused the production of prolactin (PRL) and GH/PRL-related RNAs.[15] We have confirmed these studies by using RNA slot blot analysis where we have detected specific GH mRNA in the cytoplasm of leukocytes. Additional studies designed to address the size of the mRNA by Northern blot hybridization have identified a 1.0 kilobase polyadenylated RNA in the cytoplasm of leukocytes. Protein purification studies reveal that leukocyte-derived, affinity-purified GH migrates with a molecular weight of 22 kilodaltons which corresponds to the molecular weight of pituitary-derived GH. Moreover, affinity-purified, leukocyte-derived GH could displace [$^{125}$I]-GH binding to GH receptors on leukocytes.[4] In addition, leukocyte-derived GH is biologically active in that it was shown to stimulate growth of the Nb 2 rat lymphoma cell line (dependent on GH for proliferation).[14] Taken together, these results infer GH to be yet another hormone produced by cells of the immune system. The broad distribution of irGH producer cells secreting GH including lymphoid tissues isolated from peripheral blood, spleen, thymus, and bone marrow suggests that they circulate throughout the body and are ubiquitous in lymphoid tissue.

*Luteinizing Hormone*

Previous immunofluorescence studies indicated that leukocytes stained positive for gonadotropic hormones.[2] A follow-up investigation revealed that a LH-like molecule was produced by cells of the immune system in response to luteinizing hormone releasing hormone (LHRH).[16] Analysis of the LH-like molecule revealed it to be a 35-kilodalton glycoprotein, recognizable by monospecific antisera to the LH β-chain, possess specific bioactivity like pituitary LH, and be elicited by LHRH. Confirmation of these findings has recently occurred. Specifically, by employing the reverse hemolytic plaque assay[17] to study LH production by individual splenocytes, it was determined that LHRH caused a time- and dose-dependent increase in LH production.[18] Additionally, the optimal dose of LHRH ($10^{-8}$ M) correlates closely to that observed with gonadotrophs (cells in the pituitary responsive to LHRH) and the response parallels gonadotroph-like desensitization at higher LHRH levels.[18] Due to the kinetics in the release of LH by leukocytes, it would appear that LH is not released from stores, but rather is actively synthesized *de novo*. In summary, cells of the immune system actively synthesize neuroendocrine peptide hormones either constitutively or upon induction. It is tempting to speculate that their production by leukocytes may have an impact on the physiology of other organ systems which respond to neuroendocrine hormones.

### Neuroendocrine Peptide Hormone Receptors in the Immune System

Much evidence has accumulated to suggest that the neuroendocrine system can influence immune function. Many of the early studies were performed *in vivo* and as such did not delineate direct from indirect hormonal effects. Direct effects are most easily studied by effects of peptide hormones on *in vitro* correlates of immune functions (see next section for details). Thus, the presence of neuroendocrine hormone receptors on immune cells and their regulation represents an important and fascinating area of investigation to better understand bidirectional communication. A summary list is shown in TABLE 2 for both the hormone receptors and releasing hormone receptors identified on immune cells. The following section describes the molecular characteristics of several neuroendocrine peptide hormone receptors on immune cells.

**TABLE 2.** Neuroendocrine Hormone Receptors on Immune Cells

| Pituitary Hormone Receptor | Ref. | Hypothalamic Releasing Hormone Receptor | Ref. |
|---|---|---|---|
| Corticotropin | 19,23 | Corticotropin | 34,35 |
| Opioid | 19,24–27 | Growth Hormone | 14,submitted |
| Growth hormone | 33 | Thyrotropin | 8 |
| Prolactin | 33 | | |
| Substance P | 33 | | |
| Vasoactive intestinal peptide | 33 | | |

### ACTH Receptors

In addition to producing ACTH, cells of the immune system also possess ACTH receptors. Thus, binding studies have shown that mouse spleen cell populations have two binding affinities for ACTH, one a high-affinity ($K_d$ 0.1 nM) and the other a low-affinity ($K_d$ 4.8 nM) receptor.[19] These seem to correspond in $K_d$ to high- ($K_d$ 0.25 nM) and low- ($K_d$ 10 nM) affinity receptors on rat adrenal cells.[20] Recently, by the application of a novel methodology based on the molecular recognition theory,[21] an antibody was synthesized which recognized an ACTH receptor.[21] The antibody was used as an affinity absorbant for the purification of ACTH receptor from Y-1 adrenal cells which was shown to be composed of four polypeptide chains of 83, 64, 52, and 22 kilodaltons.[22] The ACTH binding site was located on the 83-kilodalton chain. Similar experiments were then done with peripheral blood mononuclear cells and a similar if not identical receptor was observed (unpublished observations). Like adrenal cells, one pathway by which ACTH mediates its effects upon receptor activation in leukocytes is through the stimulation of adenylate cyclase and subsequent rise in cyclic AMP levels.[23] Our conclusion from the above experiments is that there is bidirectional communication between the immune and neuroendocrine systems through ACTH by virtue of their sharing a common set of structurally identical signal molecules (hormones) and receptors.

*Opioid Receptors*

Binding sites on leukocytes for endogenous opioid peptides (enkephalins, endorphins, and dynorphins) (of mu, delta, and kappa classes) have also been described. Stereospecific, high-affinity binding sites for mu-type (*e.g.*, dihydromorphine),[24] delta-type (enkephalins)[19,25] and kappa-type (U-69,593)[26] ligands have all been described to exist on immunocytes. Recently, employing the delta-specific, affinity ligand, cis-( + )-3-methylfentanylisothiocyanate, a delta-class opioid receptor has been specifically labeled.[27] Gel electrophoresis and autoradiography suggests the receptor migrates at a molecular weight of 58 kilodaltons. Similar results have also been observed analyzing receptors isolated from neuroendocrine tissue.[28] Secondary pathways upon opioid receptor activation have also been studied. Two intracellular pathways investigated include the cAMP and ionic conductance systems. cAMP levels are reduced by opioid peptides in a naloxone-reversible (opioid receptor antagonist) fashion in neural[29] and immune[30] tissues. Additionally, potassium conductance pathways are affected by endogenous opioid peptides in neural[31] and immune[32] cells. Collectively, these results illustrate a biochemical and physicochemical similarity between opioid receptors of the immune and neuroendocrine systems.

*Other Neuroendocrine Peptide Hormones*

Numerous other neuropeptide receptors have been described on cells of the immune system including prolactin, vasopressin, growth hormone, oxytocin, vasoactive intestinal peptide, thyrotropin, and substance P, a topic which has recently been reviewed by Bost.[33] It is anticipated that analysis of the biochemical characteristics of these receptors on cells of the immune system with their neuroendocrine counterparts will find them to possess similar traits.

*Releasing Hormones*

From previous investigations, it has been shown that leukocytes can specifically respond to releasing hormones such as corticotropin releasing hormone (CRH).[34] In fact, CRH receptors have been mapped to various regions of the spleen including the marginal zones but are absent in the periarteriolar and peripheral follicular white pulp regions.[35] Other releasing hormone receptors that leukocytes appear to possess include TRH[8] and growth hormone releasing hormone (GHRH)[14] receptors. The binding of GHRH to leukocytes is specific and of high affinity (Kd = $10^{-8}$ M, Guarcello *et al.*, submitted).

Collectively, all of the above data and observations would seem to point to a biochemical basis for bidirectional communication between the immune and neuroendocrine systems. Put most simply, these two systems contain and use the same set of signal molecules in the form of hormones, lymphokines, and monokines for inter- and intrasystem communication and regulation. Furthermore, they harbor the same array of receptors for the shared ligands. With time, it seems that the two systems will be further interwoven with respect to shared ligands and receptors.

## The Effect of Neuroendocrine Hormones on Leukocyte Functions

The observations of neuroendocrine peptide hormones and hormone receptors in the immune system raised the possibility that these peptides may also function as immunoregulatory agents (*i.e.*, lymphokines). A selected list of some of the effects of neuroendocrine hormones is shown in TABLE 3 and reveals that neuroendocrine hormones do in fact act as lymphokines and influence numerous immune reactions. The following section describes in greater detail the effect of neuroendocrine hormones on leukocyte functions.

*ACTH*

It is clear that ACTH acts on the immune system in part through the stimulation of glucocorticoid secretion by the adrenal cortex. Glucocorticoids in turn have an immuno-suppressive effect. While steroid hormones are important in immunoregulation,[36] more recently, it has been shown that ACTH can also directly modulate the immune response. For example, ACTH has been shown to suppress antibody production as measured by *in vitro* plaque-forming cell assays,[19] suppress interferon $\gamma$ (IFN-$\gamma$) production by T lymphocytes,[3] and block IFN-$\gamma$-induced activation of macrophages to a tumoricidal state.[37] Thus, ACTH is able to modulate the function of each of the principal cell types within the immune system.

**TABLE 3.** Summary of Effects of Neuroendocrine Hormones on Immune Cells

| Hormone | Effect | Ref. |
|---|---|---|
| ACTH | suppress antibody production | 19 |
|  | suppress lymphokine production | 3,37 |
| Opioid peptides | suppress antibody production | 19 |
|  | stimulate NK activity | 37 |
|  | enhance cytotoxic T cell generation | 37 |
|  | stimulate monocyte chemotaxis | 37 |
| TSH | enhance antibody production | 61,62 |
| GH | enhance cytotoxic T cell | 42 |
|  | enhance T cell colony formation | 43 |
| CG | inhibit NK and T cell cytotoxicity | 46,47 |
|  | inhibit T cell mitogenesis and MLC | 46,47 |
| Substance P | stimulate T cell proliferation | 49 |
|  | enhance IgA production | 48 |
| Somatostatin | inhibit T cell proliferation | 49 |
| VIP | inhibit T cell proliferation | 49 |
|  | inhibit T cell migration | 49 |
| AVP | replace IL-2 requirement | 3 |

*Endorphins and Enkephalins*

The endogenous opioid peptides also influence the functions of cells within the immune system. One aspect of the immunoregulatory activity of endorphins is that even though the $\alpha$, $\gamma$, and $\beta$ forms have identical amino termini, they have different immu-nomodulatory functions.[3] For instance, Johnson *et al.*[19] showed that $\alpha$-endorphin, as well as [met] and [leu]-enkephalins, but not $\beta$- or $\gamma$-endorphins were potent suppressors of antibody production and this suppression could be blocked by the opiate antagonist, naloxone. Endorphins and/or enkephalins have also been shown to enhance natural killer cell activity and the generation of cytotoxic T lymphocytes, stimulate monocyte chemo-taxis, and augment the production of IFN-$\gamma$ by lymphocytes, which has been reviewed.[38] The numerous immune parameters affected by the endogenous opioids suggest their importance as mediators in immune homeostasis.

*Growth Hormone*

Growth hormone is another pituitary hormone that was initially recognized as having profound effects on the immune system. Baroni and co-workers were the first to call attention to the immunodeficiency of hereditary pituitary recessive dwarf mice of Snell-Bagg strain.[39] These animals are characterized by early involution of the thymus, hypocellularity in peripheral lymphoid organs, and impaired immune responses. Dwarf mice can be normalized immunologically by GH treatment. Spleen cells from hypophysectomized mice show a persistent depression of the immune reactivity to antigen *in vitro*.[40] Furthermore, spleen natural killer cell activity was observed to be reduced in hypophysectomized mice which showed recovery after GH treatment.[41] In mixed cultures of mouse lymphocytes, insulin, but not GH, was necessary for the generation of the blastogenic response. However, the presence of GH early on during a 5-day culture allowed for the generation of cytotoxic T lymphocytes.[42] In humans, it has been observed that nanogram quantities of GH potentiate colony formation by normal human T cells, which is species specific.[43] Patients with GH deficiency have increased proportions of suppressor/cytotoxic T lymphocytes and surface immunoglobulin-bearing B lymphocytes.[44] Collectively, these results suggest that GH may influence both the proliferation of T lymphocytes as well as their terminal differentiation into effector cells.

*Chorionic Gonadotropin*

Current models of pregnancy suggest that maternal immunologic recognition of the blastocyst and production of effector factors that mediate suppression of subsequent immune responses are necessary components of successful pregnancy.[45] Interestingly, CG could be one such suppressor factor since it has been shown to inhibit cytotoxic T cell and NK cell activity, T cell mitogenesis, and mixed lymphocyte reactions.[46,47] One mechanism for this effect might be through the ability of CG to induce suppressor cell activity.[47] Thus, on the basis of our previous data showing lymphocytes produce a biologically active CG-like molecule, leukocytes and their products appear to be a key ingredient in promoting fertility. While we do not know the cell surface antigens that elicit the CG production, they are likely to be located in or close to the Dr or Ia region, since these control the MLR.

*Other Neurohormones*

Immunomodulation by neurohormones is not limited to the above-described peptides but also includes substance P, somatostatin, TSH, vasoactive intestinal peptide (VIP), and arginine vasopressin (AVP) among others. These molecules can affect antibody[48] and/or lymphokine production, degranulation of mast cells or basophils, migration of lymphocytes, and/or delayed-type hypersensitivity reactions and other cell-mediated immune responses (for review, see Payan *et al.*[49] and Blalock[3]).

**The Effect of Lymphokines and Monokines on Neuroendocrine Tissue**

The existence of signals originating in the immune system to bring about neuroendocrine responses has only very recently begun to be evaluated. We believe that a wide range of immune cell products will eventually be described which will help us understand bidirectional communication. The following section describes in greater detail the effect of lymphokines and monokines on neuroendocrine tissue.

### Interferon

Interferons (IFN) were perhaps the first products of immune cells that were observed to have a hormonal function. For example, IFN was shown to cause an ACTH-like increase in steroid production by adrenal cells, induce melanin synthesis by melanoma cells much like α-melanocyte-stimulating hormone, and demonstrate opioid-like effects.[50] A more recent and perhaps related finding is the ability of human IFN-α to block a naloxone-induced withdrawal reaction in morphine-addicted rats.[51] Collectively, these observations seem to leave little doubt that this lymphokine/monokine has many hormonal activities.

### Interleukins

The interaction of IFN with the immune and neuroendocrine systems and the influence neuroendocrine hormones have on IFN is not limited to this one product of the immune system. IL-1 is present in the brain and has endogenous pyrogen activity.[52] IL-2 has also recently been shown to cause an elevation in circulating ACTH and cortisol levels during clinical testing.[53] In this case, the action of IL-2 may well be on the pituitary gland, since this lymphokine can cause POMC production and release from pituitary tumor cells and corticotrophs.[54]

### Other Lymphokines and Monokines

Another hormone-like substance produced by monocytes, hepatocyte-stimulating factor (HSF or IFN-β), has been shown to have corticotropin-releasing activity on AtT 20 cells.[55] Interestingly, the production of HSF by monocytes is inhibited by the synthetic glucocorticoid, dexamethasone, suggesting a possible feedback loop between HSF production and the end product of the corticotropin pathway, glucocorticoids. Thus, the functional association and interaction of the hormones produced by the neuroendocrine and immune systems leaves little doubt that common elements can be perceived by both systems.

Finally, numerous organisms contain substances which resemble vertebrate neuropeptides.[56] These include neurotensin, insulin, somatostatin, ACTH, β-endorphin, and calcitonin from organisms such as E. coli, Candida and tetrahymena. It is intriguing to speculate that the release of neuropeptide-like molecules from these infectious agents may lead to altered neuroendocrine and immune function that serve to allow the agent to survive in the host.

### SUMMARY

The results reviewed here support a molecular basis for bidirectional communication between the immune and neuroendocrine systems. The main findings can be summarized as follows: First, cells of the immune system can synthesize biologically active neuroendocrine peptide hormones. Second immune cells also possess receptors for many of

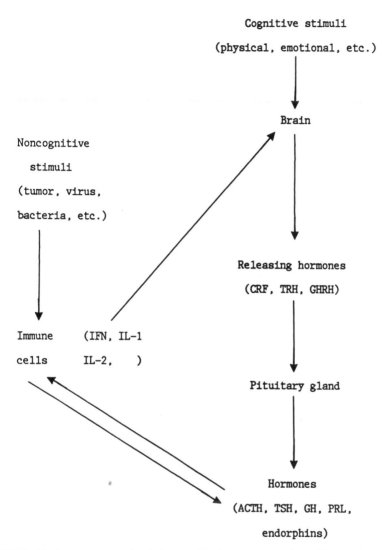

**FIGURE 1.** The immune system: the sixth sense. The immune system is sensitive to stimuli not perceived by the nervous system such as bacteria and viruses. Upon activation, cells of the immune system synthesize and secrete monokines and lymphokines as well as neuroendocrine hormones. The monokines and lymphokines can act on other immunocytes as well as neural components such as the brain. The neuroendocrine hormones may assume immunoregulatory or neuroendocrine regulatory roles depending on their concentration and circulation half-lives. Likewise, the brain's perception of cognitive stimuli can modify immune homeostasis through the activation of the hypothalamus-pituitary axis ultimately leading to the release of various neuroendocrine peptides which interact with specific receptors found on immunocytes. IFN = interferon, IL-1 = interleukin-1, IL-2 = interleukin-2, ACTH = corticotropin hormone, TSH = thyrotropin, GH = growth hormone, PRL = prolactin, CRF = corticotropin-releasing hormone, TRH = thyrotropin-releasing hormone, GHRH = growth-hormone-releasing hormone.

these peptides. Third, these same neuroendocrine hormones can influence immune function; and fourth, lymphokines can influence neuroendocrine tissues. The interesting conceptual advance is the idea that the immune system may serve as a sensory organ. Thus, the immune system may sense stimuli that are not recognized by the central or peripheral nervous system. These stimuli are termed noncognitive and include bacteria, viruses, tumors and antigens (FIG. 1). The recognition of such stimuli is converted into information in the form of lymphokines, monokines, and hormones and a message received by neuroendocrine tissues. On the other hand, nervous system recognition of stimuli can also be converted into chemical signals that can be relayed to immune cells resulting in physiological changes (FIG. 1). On this basis, we predict that the pathophysiology associated with infectious agents may be related to the types and amounts of hormones produced by the immune system.

## REFERENCES

1. WEIGENT, D. A. & J. E. BLALOCK. 1987. Immun. Rev. **100:** 79–108.
2. BLALOCK, J. E. 1984. J. Immunol. **132:** 1067–1070.
3. BLALOCK, J.E. 1984. Prog. Allergy **43:** 1–13.
4. CARR, D. J. J., D. A. WEIGENT & J. E. BLALOCK. 1989. Drug Des. Del. **4:** 187–195.
5. LOLAIT, S. J., J. A. CLEMENTS, A. J. MARKWICK, C. CHENG, M. MCNALLY, A. I. SMITH & J. W. FUNDER. 1986. J. Clin. Invest. **77:** 1776–1779.
6. WESTLEY, H. J., A. J. KLEISS, K. W. KELLEY, P. K. Y. WONG & P. H. YUEN. 1986. J. Exp. Med. **163:** 1589–1594.
7. SMITH, E. M., M. PHAN, T. E. KRUGER, D. H. COPPENHAVER & J. E. BLALOCK. 1983. Proc. Natl. Acad. Sci. USA **80:** 6010–6013.
8. KRUGER, T. E. & J. E. BLALOCK. 1989. J. Immunol. **142:** 744–747.
9. KRUGER, T. E. & J. E. BLALOCK. 1986. J. Immunol. **137:** 197–200.
10. HARBOUR-MCMENAMIN, D., E. M. SMITH & J. E. BLALOCK. 1986. Proc. Natl. Acad. Sci. USA **83:** 6834–6838.
11. CASPER, R. F., E. WILSON, J. A. COLLINGS, S. E. BROWN & J. A. PARKER. 1983. Lancet **2:** 1191–1193.
12. BOYD, D. J. & W. J. HAMILTON. 1970. *In* The Human Placenta. Heffer. Cambridge, UK.
13. GOROSPE, W. C. & B. G. KASSON. 1988. Endocrinology **123:** 2462–2471.
14. WEIGENT, D. A., J. B. BAXTER, W. E. WEAR, L. R. SMITH, K. L. BOST & J. E. BLALOCK. 1988. FASEB J. **2:** 2812–2818.
15. HEISTAND, P. C., P. MEKLER, R. HORDMANN, A. GRIEDER & C. PERMMONGKOL. 1986. Proc. Natl. Acad. Sci. USA **83:** 2599–2603.
16. EBAUGH, M. J. & E. M. SMITH. 1987. Fed. Proc. **46:** 7811.
17. NEILL, J. D. & J. S. FRAWLEY. 1983. Endocrinology **112:** 1135–1137.
18. BLALOCK, J. E. & O. COSTA. 1989. Ann. N.Y. Acad. Sci. **564:** 261–266.
19. JOHNSON, H. M., E. M. SMITH, B. A. TORRES & J. E. BLALOCK. 1982. Proc. Natl. Acad. Sci. USA **79:** 4171–4174.
20. MCILHINNEY, R. A. J. & D. SCHULSTER. 1975. J. Endocrinol. **64:** 175–184.
21. BOST, K. L., E. M. SMITH & J. E. BLALOCK. 1985. Proc. Natl. Acad. Sci. USA **82:** 1372–1375.
22. BOST, K. L. & J. E. BLALOCK. 1986. Mol. Cell. Endocrinol. **44:** 1–9.
23. JOHNSON, E. W., J. E. BLALOCK & E. M. SMITH. 1988. Biochem. Biophys. Res. Commun. **157:** 1205–1211.
24. LOPKER, A., L. G. ABOOD, W. HOSS & F. J. LIONETTI. 1980. Biochem. Pharmacol. **29:** 1361–1365.
25. AUSIELLO, C. M. & G. RODA. 1984. Cell Biol. Int. Rep. **8:** 97–106.
26. CARR, D. J. J., B. R. DECOSTA, C. -H. KIM, A. E. JACOBSON, V. GUARCELLO, K. C. RICE & J. E. BLALOCK. 1989. J. Endocrinol. **122:** 161–168.
27. CARR, D. J. J., B. DECOSTA, C. -H. KIM, A. E. JACOBSON, K. C. RICE & J. E. BLALOCK. 1988. Cell. Immunol. **116:** 44–51.

28. CARR, D. J. J., B. DeCOSTA, A. E. JACOBSON, K. L. BOST, K. C. RICE & J. E. BLALOCK. 1987. FEBS Lett. **224:** 272–276.
29. KLEE, W. A. & M. NIRENBERG. 1976. Nature **263:** 609–612.
30. CARR, D. J. J., K. L. BOST & J. E. BLALOCK. 1988. Life Sci. **42:** 2615–2624.
31. SIMONDS, W. F. 1988. Endocr. Rev. **9:** 200–212.
32. CARR, D. J. J., J. K. BUBIEN, W. T. WOODS & J. E. BLALOCK. 1988. Ann. N.Y. Acad. Sci. **540:** 694–697.
33. BOST, K. L. 1988. Prog. Allergy **43:** 68–83.
34. SMITH, E. M., W. J. MEYER, A. C. MORRILL & J. E. BLALOCK. 1986. Nature **321:** 881–882.
35. WEBSTER, E. L. & E. B. DeSOUZA. 1988. Endocrinology **122:** 609–617.
36. CUPPS, T. R. & A. S. FAUCI. 1982. Immunol. Rev. **65:** 133–155.
37. KOFF, W. C. & M. A. DUNEGAN. 1985. J. Immunol. **135:** 350–354.
38. CARR, D. J. J. & J. E. BLALOCK. 1986. A molecular basis for bidirectional communication between the immune and neuroendocrine systems. *In* Progress in Immunology VI. B. Cinader & R. G. Miller, Eds. 619–629. Academic Press. Orlando, FL.
39. BARONI, C. D., N. FABRIS & G. BERTOLI. 1969. Immunol. **17:** 303–314.
40. GISLER, R.H. & L. SCHENKEL-HULLIGER. 1971. Cell. Immunol. **2:** 646–657.
41. SAXENA, Q. B., R. K. SAXENA & W. H. ADLER. 1982. Int. Arch. Allergy Appl. Immunol. **67:** 169–174.
42. SNOW, C. E. 1985. J. IMMUNOL. **135:** 776s–778s.
43. MERCOLA, K. E., M. J. CLINE & D. W. GOLDE. 1981. Blood **58:** 337–340.
44. GUPTA, S., S. M. FIKRIG & M. S. NOVAL. 1983. Clin. Exp. Immunol. **54:**87–90.
45. BERCZI, I., E. NAGY, S. L. ASA & K. KOVACS. 1983. Allergy **38:** 325.
46. FUCHS, T., L. HAMMARSTROM, C. I. SMITH & J. BRUNDIN. 1982. J. Reprod. Immunol. **4:** 185–190.
47. RICKETS, R. M. & D. B. JONES. 1985. J. Reprod. Immunol. **7:** 225–232.
48. STANISZ, A. M., D. BEFUS & J. BIENENSTOCK. 1986. J. Immunol. **136:** 152–156.
49. PAYAN, D. G., J. P. McGILLIS & E. J. GOETZL. 1986. Adv. Immunol. **39:** 299–323.
50. BLALOCK, J. E. & C. HARP. 1981. Arch. Virol. **67:** 45–49.
51. DAFNY, N. & C. REYES-VASQUEZ. 1985. Immunopharmacology **9:** 13–17.
52. FONTANA, A., E. WEBER & J. M. DAYER. 1984. J. Immunol. **133:** 1696–1698.
53. LOTZE, M. T., L. W. FRANA, S. O. SHARROW, R. J. ROBB & S. A. ROSENBERG. 1985. J. Immunol. **134:** 157–166.
54. BROWN, S. L., L. R. SMITH & J. E. BLALOCK. 1987. J. Immunol. **139:** 3181–3183.
55. WOLOSKI, B. M. R. N. J., E. M. SMITH, W. J. MEYER, III, G. M. FULLER & J. E. BLALOCK. 1985. Science **230:** 1035–1037.
56. LeROITH, D., C. ROBERTS, JR., M. A. LESNIAK & J. ROTH. 1986. Experentia **42:** 782–788.

# On the Role of Neuropeptide Y in Information Handling in the Central Nervous System in Normal and Physiopathological States

## Focus on Volume Transmission and Neuropeptide Y/α2 Receptor Interactions[a]

K. FUXE,[b] L. F. AGNATI,[c] A. HÄRFSTRAND,[b] M. ZOLI,[c]
G. von EULER,[b] R. GRIMALDI,[c] E. MERLO PICH,[c] B. BJELKE,[b]
P. ENEROTH,[d] F. BENFENATI,[c] A. CINTRA,[b] I. ZINI,[c] AND
M. MARTIRE[e]

*[b]Department of Histology and Neurobiology*
*Karolinska Institutet*
*Box 60400*
*S = 104 01 Stockholm, Sweden*
*[c]Department of Human Physiology*
*University of Modena, Modena, Italy*
*[d]Department of Biochemistry*
*Huddinge Hospital, Huddinge, Sweden*
*[e]Department of Pharmacology*
*Catholic University, Rome, Italy*

## INTRODUCTION

We have for many years been involved in the analysis of the role of neuropeptide Y (NPY) in central cardiovascular and neuroendocrine regulation[1-14] as well as of the interactions between NPY and α2 receptors in the pre- and postsynaptic membranes of the NPY/adrenaline (A) costoring terminals of the central nervous system (CNS).[15-18]

In the present article we will focus on three topics. First, we will present a quantitative neuroanatomical analysis of the relationship between pre- and postsynaptic features of NPY immunoreactive (IR) neuronal systems of the rat brain, giving support to the view that NPY plays an important role in volume transmission in brain in view of the functional and topological mismatches demonstrated between the NPY receptors and NPY IR terminals.[19,20] Volume transmission has been defined as an electrochemical transmission using the extracellular fluid as a pathway for chemical and electrical signals in the CNS.[21-23] Second, we will review our results on NPY/α2 receptor interactions and how they are altered in brain ischemia. Third, we will summarize the evidence showing that the ability of NPY to interact with catecholamine (CA) transmission lines in the CNS underlies many of its neuroendocrine and cardiovascular actions. All the results taken

[a]This work has been supported by Grant 04X-715 from the Swedish Medical Research Council, by a grant from L. Osterman's Foundation, by a grant from Knut and Alice Wallenberg's Foundation, and by a grant from the Swedish Stroke Foundation.

together indicate a role of NPY both in wiring and volume transmission in the CNS at the synaptic, local circuit, and network level.[19,24,25]1

## COMPUTER ASSISTED MORPHOMETRICAL AND MICRODENSITOMETRICAL ANALYSIS OF CENTRAL NEUROPEPTIDE Y NEURONS. FOCUS ON THE RELATIONSHIP BETWEEN PRE- AND POSTSYNAPTIC FEATURES OF NEUROPEPTIDE Y IMMUNOREACTIVE NEURONAL SYSTEMS OF THE RAT BRAIN

### *Distribution of NPY Immunoreactive Nerve Cell Bodies and Their Content of Glucocorticoid Receptor Immunoreactivity*

There exists a widespread distribution of NPY IR cell bodies in the cerebral cortex including the hippocampal formation, where NPY immunoreactivity (IR) is found in nonpyramidal neurons present in practically all layers.[26,27] As shown by in situ hybridization these NPY IR perikarya also appear to contain NPY mRNA (FIG. 1) Scattered NPY IR nerve cell bodies are also found all over the neostriatum.[28] Large numbers of the NPY IR neurons of the cerebral cortex and the neostriatum costore somatostatin IR and many of them also appear to be GABAergic.[29,30]

We have recently found that the vast majority of these NPY IR perikarya including those within the reticular thalamic nucleus lack glucocorticoid receptor (GR) IR.[31]

In contrast, the densely packed NPY IR cell group present within the medial parvocellular part of the arcuate nucleus (FIG. 1) projecting into *inter alia* the paraventricular and dorsomedial hypothalamic nuclei[26,32,33] all appear to contain strong GR IR.[31,34] It should also be underlined that the vast majority of the NPY/PNMT (phenylethanolamine-N-methyl-transferase) costoring neurons of the C1, C2 and C3 groups of the rostral medulla oblongata[35-39] contain strong GR IR.[40] The same is also true for the NPY/ noradrenaline (NA) costoring neurons of group A1 in the caudal ventrolateral medulla and in the locus coeruleus.[34,40]

Taken together these results indicate that the central NPY neurons are differentially regulated by glucocorticoids. Thus, the arcuate NPY neurons and the NPY/A and NPY/ NA costoring neurons of the medulla and pons represent those which are directly influenced by glucocorticoids.

Adrenalectomy (14 days) has also been shown to produce reductions of NPY IR and NPY mRNA levels within the locus coeruleus.[17,24] Dexamethasone treatment (1 mg/kg, i.p., once daily) for 2 weeks in adrenalectomized rats increased NPY mRNA levels in the locus coeruleus and especially in the arcuate nucleus, indicating a direct stimulating influence of glucocorticoids on gene expression of NPY. Furthermore, a discrete depletion of NPY IR has been demonstrated after a 14-day adrenalectomy in the medial preoptic area.[17,24] Adrenalectomy and subsequent treatment with glucocorticoids have also been found to influence coexistence of NPY and PNMT IR in nerve terminals of the hypothalamus.[41]

In addition, evidence also indicates that gonadal steroids regulate discrete NPY levels within the hypothalamus, suggesting a facilitatory role of progesterone and estogen in the ovariectomized rats and of testosterone in the castrated male rat in their control of NPY synthesis and release.[42,43] These effects of gonadal steroids were predominantly exerted in the arcuate nucleus and in the ventromedial hypothalamic nucleus. Thus, the possibility exists for a direct control by both gonadal steroids and glucocorticoids of the NPY arcuate neurons.

*On the Relationship of NPY IR Nerve Terminals and High Affinity NPY Binding*
*Sites in the CNS of the Rat Brain*

High affinity NPY receptors have been demonstrated in the CNS of mammals and shown to be regulated by inorganic cations and guanyl nucleotides.[44-47] Receptor autoradiographical studies have demonstrated high densities of NPY receptors within, *e.g.,* the superficial layers of the cerebral cortex, the olfactory tubercle, the claustrum, the lateral septal area, and many thalamic nuclei, such as the laterodorsal thalamic nucleus, intermediate dorsal interanteromediate thalamic nuclei, the centrolateral nucleus and the

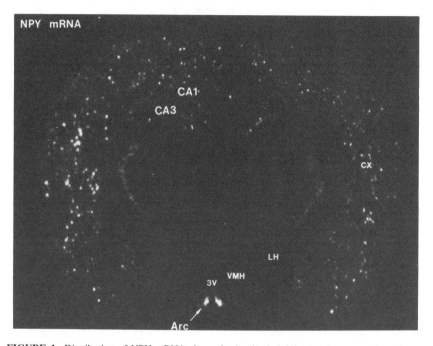

**FIGURE 1.** Distribution of NPY mRNA shown by in situ hybridization in a coronal section at Bregma −2.3 mm. Strong labelling is shown in scattered spots all over the cerebral cortex (CX) and in the arcuate (Arc) nucleus. A $^{35}$S-NPY cRNA probe (480 bp) was used (Aronsson *et al.*, in preparation). CA1,3 = CA1,3 fields of Ammon's horn; LH = lateral hypothalamus; VMH = ventromedial hypothalamic nucleus; 3V = third ventricle.

reuniens nucleus (FIGS. 3,4,5,6).[2,17,48,49] High densities have also been demonstrated in cardiovascular regions of the medulla oblongata such as the nucleus tractus solitarius (nTS), the area postrema, as well as in the inferior olive and the substantia gelatinosa of the spinal nucleus of the trigeminal nerve.[50,51]

In our analysis of the NPY IR nerve terminal distribution of the high affinity NPY receptors, mismatches between these two features of NPY transmission have been demonstrated.[19,20] Both a topological and a functional mismatch has been found (FIGS. 2,7,8 vs FIGS. 4,5,6). The topological mismatch is characterized either by the failure to demonstrate high affinity binding sites for the transmitter in an area rich in nerve terminals

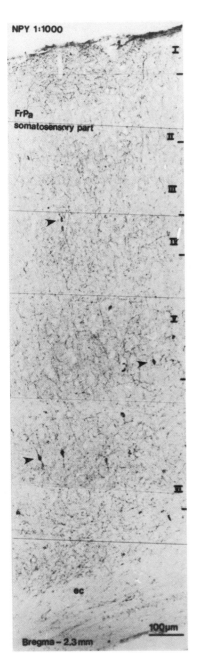

**FIGURE 2.** A coronal section of the somatosensory part of the frontoparietal cortex (FrPa) at Bregma −2.3 mm, showing nerve terminal plexa with NPY IR in all cortical layers and scattered NPY IR perikarya (some are indicated with *arrowheads*) in most layers. The six cortical layers are indicated to the *right* and capsula externa (ec) at the lower part of the picture.

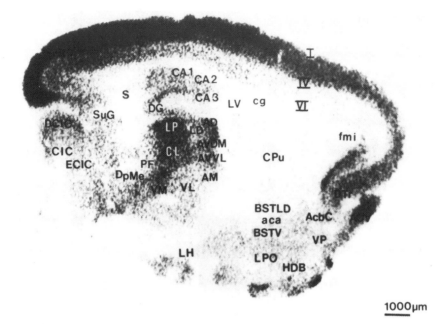

**FIGURE 3.** Visualization of $^{125}$I-NPY binding (0.5 nM) shown in a 14-μm sagital section of the rat brain. Lateral level = 1.40 mm. Abbreviations used: I = cortical layer I; IV = cortical layer IV; VI = cortical layer VI; aca = anterior commissure, anterior; AcbC = accumbens nuc, core; AD = anterodorsal thalamic nuc; AOV = anterior olfactory nuc, ventral; AVDM = anteroventral thalamic nuc, dorsomedial; AVVL = anteroventral thalamic nuc, ventrolat; BSTLD = bed nuc stria ter, lat div, dors; BSTV = bed nuc stria ter, ventral div; CA 1–3 = fields CA1–3 of Ammon's horn; cg = cingulum; CIC = central nuc inferior colliculus; CL = centrolateral thalamic nuc; CPu = caudate putamen; DCIC = dorsal cortex inf colliculus; DG = dentate gyrus; DpMe = deep mesencephalic nuc; DTr = dorsal transition zone; ECIC = external cortex inf; fmi = forceps minor corpus callosum; HDB = nuc horizontal limb diagonal band; LD = laterodorsal thalamic nuc; LH = lateral hypothalamic area; LP = lateral posterior thalamic nuc; LPO = lateral preoptic area; LV = lateral ventricle; PF = parafascicular thalamic nuc; S = subiculum; SuG = superficial gray layer sup col; VL = ventrolateral thalamic nuc; VM = ventromedial thalamic nuc; VP = ventral pallidum; Bar = 1000 μm. Nomenclature according to Paxinos and Watson.[52]

for that transmitter, or vice versa the failure to demonstrate nerve terminals for the transmitter in an area where there exist high affinity binding sites for that transmitter.[19,20] The functional mismatch is a situation where either no correlation between the density distribution of the pre- and postsynaptic markers of the chemical transmission can be demonstrated, or where there exists an inverse relationship between the density distribution of the pre- and postsynaptic markers.[19,20] It should be underlined that the topological mismatch phenomenon is highly dependent upon the sensitivity of the techniques used. It is conceivable that by the development of more sensitive procedures more NPY receptors and nerve terminals may be demonstrated. In contrast, the functional mismatch may mainly depend on the reliability of the cytochemical and receptor autoradiographical techniques. This reliability is presently demonstrated for NPY immunoreactivity and receptor autoradiography, since these techniques highly correlate with the results obtained by means of radioimmunoassay and biochemical receptor binding assays, respectively.[19]

Furthermore, the functional mismatch also depends on the set of the chosen areas. The aspects discussed above are illustrated in FIGURE 9.

The analysis of the pre- and postsynaptic features of the NPY neuronal systems has been carried out at the upper pons level, the upper mesencephalic level, the midhypothalamic level and the striatal level (Bregma −8.3, −5.8, −2.8 and 0.7 mm, respectively, according to Paxinos and Watson atlas[52]). Some of the morphological findings are summarized in FIGURES 2,7,8, vs 4,5,6. These figures illustrate the high degree of mismatch existing within the thalamus and hypothalamus with regard to the pre- and postsynaptic features of the NPY neuronal systems. It seems clear when comparing the thalamic and hypothalamic features of the NPY neurons in these preparations that they are almost a mirror image of one another. Thus, within the thalamic midline nuclei and the lateral thalamic nuclei there exist, in most cases, high amounts of high affinity NPY binding sites but very few immunoreactive nerve terminal networks. The same is true, *e.g.*, for the septal area. In contrast, within the hypothalamic regions there exist high amounts of strongly immunoreactive NPY nerve terminal networks but very few high affinity NPY binding sites (dorsomedial hypothalamic nucleus, periventricular hypothalamic nucleus, arcuate nucleus). It should be noted, however, that within the paraventricular thalamic nucleus there exist high concentrations of NPY nerve terminals, which are associated with an almost complete absence of high affinity NPY binding sites. Thus, these figures illustrate the existence of topological mismatches. It is also of substantial interest to note in FIGURES 2 and 4 that the neocortical network of NPY IR nerve terminals is rather evenly distributed all over the six layers of the cerebral cortex, while the high affinity NPY binding sites are concentrated in the outer layers. Few high affinity NPY

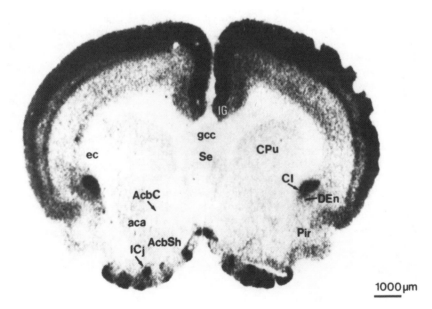

FIGURE 4. Demonstration of [125]I-NPY (0.5 nM) binding in a coronal section of the telencephalon at Bregma level 1.2 mm. Abbreviations used: aca = anterior commissure, anterior; AcbC = accumbens nu, core; AcbSh = accumbens nu, shell; Cl = claustrum; gcc = genu corpus callosum; ICj = islands of Calleja; IG = indusium griseum; Pir = piriform cortex; Se = septal area. Nomenclature according to Paxinos and Watson.[52]

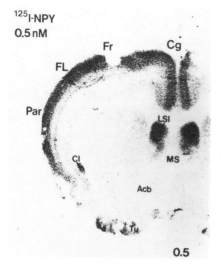

FIGURE 5. Demonstration of [125]I-NPY (0.5 nM) binding in a coronal section of the telencephalon at Bregma level 0.5 mm. A strong binding is found in the superficial layers of cortex, in claustrum (Cl), parts of tuberculum olfactorium (Tu) and in the lateral septal intermediate nucleus (LSI) but not in the medial septal nucleus (MS). Acb = nuc accumbens; Par = parietal cortex; FL = forelimb area of cortex; Fr = frontal cortex area 1–2; Cg = cingulate cortex.

receptors are found in the deep layers (layers 5 and 6). FIGURE 10 demonstrates in a quantitative way the topological and the functional mismatch, which in this case results in an inverse correlation.[19,20]

The presence of topological and functional mismatches has in this case been explained by the existence of volume transmission, by the presence of low affinity NPY binding sites and by the putative presence of subtypes of NPY receptors.[53,54] These concepts are summarized in FIGURE 11. These schemes underline the fact that the NPY neuronal systems may not only operate via a classical synaptic transmission (wiring transmission) but also via a volume transmission. An area in which the volume transmission of NPY dominates (see FIG. 11, lower panel, neuroanatomical area A2) is characterized by the presence of high amounts of high affinity NPY binding sites and relatively low amounts of low affinity NPY binding sites linked to NPY synapses. Thus, in this situation most of the NPY would carry its message via a diffusion in the extracellular fluid to surrounding high affinity binding sites (volume transmission). Instead an area in which the wiring transmission dominates (see FIG. 11, lower panel, neuroanatomical area A1) is characterized by the presence of a low number of high affinity NPY binding sites and a relatively high number of low affinity NPY binding sites linked to the NPY synapses.

This interpretation is based on the assumption that the NPY terminals involved in synaptic contacts[55] are always linked to low affinity NPY binding sites. The state of affinity of the NPY receptors is probably regulated by the guanyl nucleotides.[44]

It will be of special interest to evaluate if the γ2 NPY receptors, which recognize NPY fragments such as NPY (13–36), are mainly localized to areas where, according to the above definition, volume transmission of NPY dominates.

## Effects of Aging on the NPY Neuronal Systems of the Brain

We have in a series of publications demonstrated the high vulnerability of NPY IR to the aging processes.[55,56] Thus, a marked disappearance of NPY IR takes place in many NPY IR perikarya of the C1 and C2 cell groups of the rostral medulla of the 24-month-old male rat compared with a three-month-old male rat, which also leads to disappearance in the number of NPY IR perikarya in these areas. A marked loss of NPY IR also takes place, *e.g.*, in the nerve terminals of the paraventricular hypothalamic nucleus of the 24-month-old male rat. Losses in the number of NPY IR perikarya but not in other peptide perikarya also take place, *e.g.*, in the striatum during the aging process (FIG. 12), where NPY IR is costored with somatostatin IR, and not with CA as in the rostral medulla. In agreement with these results obtained with image analysis, radioimmunoassay determinations have demonstrated in aged male rats the existence of markedly reduced NPY concentrations in many hypothalamic nuclei.[57] These results obtained on NPY in the aging rat brain are of substantial interest also in view of the recent demonstrations that NPY is a major regulator of a large number of behaviors.[57] Thus, NPY appears to enhance memory recall and retention and appears capable of improving memory also in old animals.[58]

### *Effects of Transient Forebrain Ischemia on NPY Immunoreactive Neurons*

The ischemic insult was induced by the permanent occlusion of the vertebral arteries and the transient (30 min) occlusion of the common carotid arteries.[59] The analysis has

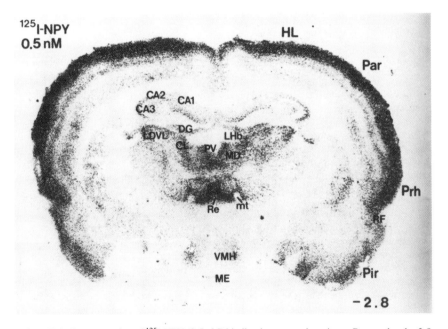

**FIGURE 6.** Demonstration of [125]I-NPY (0.5 nM) binding in a coronal section at Bregma level −2.8 mm. A strong binding is obtained in the superficial cortical layers as well as in parts of the hippocampal formation, mainly CA3 and molecular layer of dentate gyrus (DG) and the thalamic nuclei (*e.g.*, laterodorsal thalamic nucleus, ventrolateral part (LD, VL), nuc reuniens (Re), nuc centralis lateralis (CL) and mediodorsal thalamic nucleus (MD)). Almost no binding is present in lateral habenular nucleus (LHb) and paraventricular thalamic nucleus (PV) and in large parts of hypothalamus. Abbreviations used: mt = mammillo thalamic tract; HL = hindlimb area of cortex; Par = parietal cortex; Prh = perirhinal cortex; Pir = piriform cortex; RF = rhinal fissure; VMH = ventromedial hypothalamic nuc; ME = median eminence.

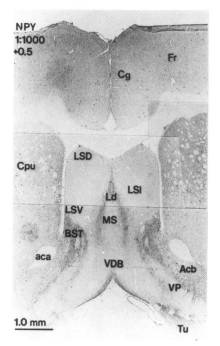

**FIGURE 7.** NPY IR in a coronal section at Bregma level 0.5 mm. The NPY innervation of the cerebral cortex is not seen in this low magnification. A strong NPY IR is present in bed nuc of striae terminalis (BST) and lamboid septal zone (Ld) but very little IR is found in the lateral septal nuclei and in the nuclei of the diagonal band. Bar indicating 1.0 mm. Abbreviations used: Cg = cingulate cortex; Fr = frontal cortex; CPu = nuc caudatus putamen; LSD = dorsal part of the lateral septal nucleus; LSI = intermediate part of the lateral septal nucleus; LSV = ventral part of the lateral septal nucleus; MS = medial septal nucleus; aca = anterior part of the anterior commissure; VDB = nuc of the ventrical limb of the diagonal band; VP = ventral pallidum; Acb = nuc accumbens; Tu = tuberculum olfactorium.

been carried out at various time intervals of reperfusion, but here we will focus on only the seven-day time interval of reperfusion. The NPY neuronal systems were analyzed by means of NPY immunocytochemistry and by means of receptor autoradiography. Relative quantitation of NPY immunocytochemistry was performed by means of the microdensitometrical procedures outlined by Agnati *et al.*[55] A high degree of correlation was observed between immunocytochemical and radioimmunoassay determination of regional NPY IR. Microdensitometrical analysis was used for a quantitative evaluation of the high affinity binding sites in various brain areas.[50,55]

The effects of the transient forebrain ischemia on NPY immunoreactivity in various brain regions are summarized in FIGURE 13. It is shown that NPY immunoreactivity is reduced by about 50% in NPY IR perikarya located within the frontoparietal cortex and within the nucleus caudatus putamen. The NPY nerve terminal systems were analyzed within the arcuate nucleus, the paraventricular and periventricular hypothalamic nuclei and within the paraventricular thalamic nucleus. In all regions except the arcuate nucleus NPY immunoreactivity was reduced by approximately 50%.[19] These results indicate a major action of ischemia on the NPY stores in the majority of the NPY neuronal systems at tel- and diencephalic levels.

The quantitative receptor autoradiographical results obtained on high affinity $^{125}$I-NPY and on $^3$H-paraminoclonidine ($^3$H-PAC) binding sites showed that within the thalamus, the amygdaloid cortex and the frontoparietal cortex the ischemic insult did not affect the density, either of $^{125}$I-NPY or of $^3$H-PAC binding sites.[19] These results indicate a major difference between the sensitivity of the presynaptic versus the postsynaptic features of the NPY neuronal systems to the cerebral ischemia.

## NPY/α2 INTERACTIONS AT THE PRE- AND POSTSYNAPTIC MEMBRANE LEVEL IN NORMAL AND PHYSIOPATHOLOGICAL STATE

### *Studies on Presynaptic Interactions*

In previous work we have been able to show that NPY (1 nM) can enhance the ability of clonidine to inhibit potassium-evoked $^3$H-NA release from synaptosomal preparations of the dorsal medulla of the hypothalamus and of the frontoparietal cortex.[60–62] These results indicate that there may exist high affinity NPY receptors on the nerve terminal membrane of NA and A networks capable of enhancing the α2-autoreceptor function leading to increased inhibition of $^3$H-NA release upon the α2-autoreceptor activation by clonidine (see FIG. 14A). It is of substantial interest that in the spontaneously hypertensive rat a high affinity NPY receptor can no longer modulate the inhibitory effects of clonidine on $^3$H-NA release from synaptosomal preparations of the dorsal medulla.[61] High concentrations of NPY (100 nM) can, however, produce significant enhancement of the

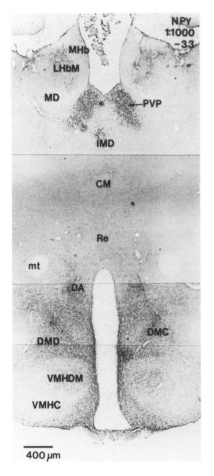

**FIGURE 8.** NPY IR is shown in a coronal section at Bregma level −3.3 mm. A strong IR is present in the posterior part of the paraventricular thalamic nuc (PVP), dorsal hypothalamic area (DA), diffuse part and compact part of the dorsomedial hypothalamic nuc (DMD and DMC) and a collection of NPY IR terminals is seen in dorsomedial part of the ventrohypothalamic nuc (VMHDM) but not in ventral part of the ventromedial hypothalamic nuc (VMHC). Bar indicating 400 μm. Abbreviations used: MHb = medial habenular nuc; LHbM = medial part of lateral habenular nuc; MD = mediodorsal thalamic nuc; IMD = intermediodorsal thalamic nuc; CM = centromedial thalamic nuc; Re = nuc reuniens; mt = mammillothalamic tract.

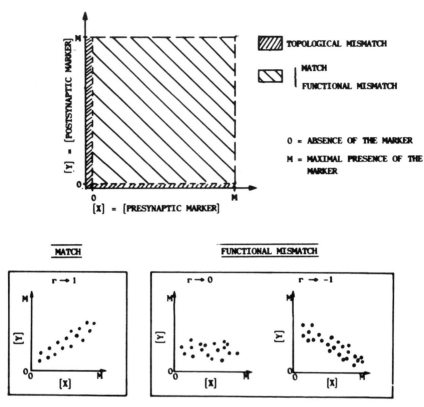

**FIGURE 9.** Schematic representation of the possible relationship between the pre- and postsynaptic markers of a transmitter-identified neuronal system (r = correlation coefficient).

inhibitory effects of clonidine on potassium-evoked $^3$H-NA release (FIG. 14B). Prejunctional effects of NPY have also been observed in sympathetic vascular control.[63] It is of particular interest that the α2 receptors controlling $^3$H-5-HT release in the cerebral cortex, hypothalamus and the medulla oblongata do not appear to be modulated by NPY, at least not in the nanomolar range.[62] Thus, high affinity NPY receptors apparently do not exist adjacent to the α2 receptors on the 5-HT nerve terminal membrane. Furthermore, the results obtained in the spontaneously hypertensive rat open up the possibility that in the nerve terminal membrane of the NA and/or A networks, the NPY receptor may exist in a low affinity state due to an altered regulation of the NPY receptor by guanyl nucleotides.

It seems possible to explain the inhibitory effects of low doses of intraventricularly injected NPY on regional NA turnover within the hypothalamus[10] on the basis of the ability of NPY to enhance the α2 autoreceptor function in discrete hypothalamic NA nerve terminal systems. The fact that with high doses of NPY instead increases in NA utilization were observed in the various hypothalamic NA nerve terminal systems[10] may have several explanations. One possibility is that at low concentrations of NPY, the peptidases involved in forming active NPY fragments[53,54] (*e.g.*, NPY 13–36) have only submaximal occupancy of their catalytic sites leading to increased activation of Y2 NPY receptors vs Y1 NPY receptors. Y2 NPY receptors are known in the peripheral nervous system to inhibit NA release. Instead, with high concentrations of NPY, peptidases involved with the breakdown of NPY may be saturated at their catalytic sites, so that the Y1 NPY receptor stimulation may dominate. Preferential activation of the Y1 receptors may then *inter alia* lead to the increases of NA turnover demonstrated with high doses of NPY.[10]

In view of the fact that NPY is able to enhance the inhibitory effect of clonidine on

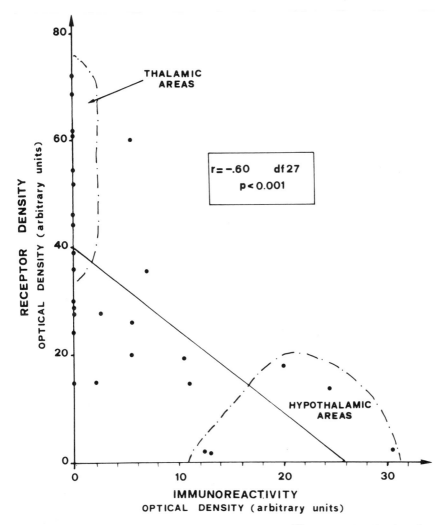

**FIGURE 10.** Correlation between the density of NPY IR and [125]I-NPY binding sites in various regions of the central nervous system. Pearson's correlation coefficient is given. For details on immunocytochemical and autoradiographic procedures see REFERENCES 55 and 17. The quantitation of NPY IR was obtained by means of computer-assisted image analysis. The optical density of NPY IR was shown to be linearly correlated with the content of NPY IR evaluated by means of radio-immunoassay (Agnati *et al.*, in preparation). The low r-value (−0.60) indicates the presence of a strong mismatch between NPY IR and NPY binding in the rat brain.

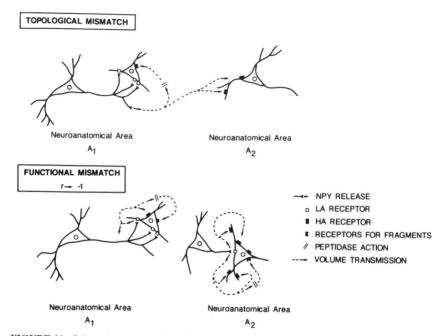

**FIGURE 11.** Schematic representation of a hypothesis to explain the mismatch observed in central neuronal NPY systems. The neurochemical features of the topological (*upper panel*) and functional (*lower panel*) mismatch are given. Abbreviations: HA = high affinity; LA = low affinity.

NA release in the nTS area without affecting NA release itself,[60] it may be suggested that there is an interaction between presynaptic NPY and $\alpha$2 receptors in this region. This putative receptor interaction probably takes place at the synaptic level in view of the demonstration of costorage of NPY and PNMT IR in the nerve terminal networks in this region.[2] Instead, within the cerebral cortex the receptor-receptor interaction probably takes place at the local circuit level, since the cortical NA nerve terminal networks do not contain NPY IR, which instead is present within the scattered NPY interneurons present in all cortical layers (FIGS. 1,2). Thus, the cortical NPY IR neurons may control $\alpha$2 autoreceptor function in the NA afferents from the brain stem and especially from the locus coeruleus. It should be pointed out that the NPY/NA costoring locus coeruleus neurons seem to exclusively project into the hypothalamus.[64] Within the hypothalamus NPY/$\alpha$2 receptor interaction probably takes place both at the synaptic and at the local circuit level.

Also the ability of NPY given intraventricularly to produce biphasic changes in dopamine (DA) turnover in the median eminence in the normal male rat with reductions of DA turnover in low doses and increases of DA turnover in high doses may, *e.g.*, be explained on the basis of preferential Y2 receptor activation in low doses and preferential Y1 receptor activation in high doses.[10] Thus, the arcuate NPY IR nerve terminals, probably regulating indirectly the activity of the tubero infundibular DA neurons via the $\beta$-endorphin systems[24] (see below) may possess Y2 autoreceptors, which are preferentially activated by low doses of NPY.

### Interactions at the Postsynaptic Membrane Level

In previous work we have demonstrated that NPY in the nanomolar range can reduce the affinity of α2 agonist binding sites in membrane preparations of the medulla oblongata.[2,3,15,18] This change is often associated with a small increase in the $B_{max}$ value.[2,3,15,18] These results indicate that high affinity NPY receptors via a receptor-receptor interaction can modulate the characteristics of $\alpha_2$-adrenergic receptors in the medulla oblongata. These α2 receptors are probably mainly located in the postsynaptic membranes. As seen in FIGURE 15 similar results have been obtained in membrane preparations of the hypothalamus. Also in these membrane preparations the α2 adrenergic receptors have been predominantly postsynaptically located. It is shown that NPY (3 nM) reduces the affinity of α2 agonist binding sites, an effect which is associated with an increase in the $B_{max}$ value. However, the dominating actions appear to be a reduction in affinity, which, if present *in vivo*, should lead to reduced α2 receptor function at the postsynaptic level, when using low doses of NPY. Furthermore, autoradiographical studies in the medulla oblongata indicate that clonidine, both *in vivo* and *in vitro*, can reduce the affinity of the [125]I-NPY binding sites in the nTS area.[2,19] Thus, it seems possible that in postsynaptic membranes NPY and α2 adrenergic receptors can reduce the affinity of one another and thus exert antagonistic interactions. Based on experiments of Martire and colleagues,[60–62] however, NPY enhances the α2 autoreceptor function, controlling release of [3]H-NA. Therefore, at the presynaptic level an increase in the number of α2 autoreceptors may be the dominating result of the NPY receptor activation.

Of great interest is the fact that these interactions open up the possibility that the costoring NPY/A nerve terminals can switch from an adrenaline-dominated transmission into a transmission dominated by its cotransmitter NPY (FIGS. 16,17). In view of the above discussion indicating a role of NPY in volume transmission[19,20] it would allow the

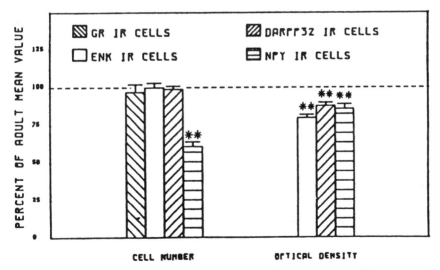

**FIGURE 12.** Quantitative evaluation of the number and relative antigen content of the glucocorticoid receptor (GR), enkephalin (ENK), dopamine and cAMP-regulated phosphoprotein (DARPP-32) and NPY IR profiles present in the adult and old striatum. The y-axis reports the percent of the ratio adult/old for the two parameters (cell number and antigen content) under study. For further details see text. Statistical analysis according to Mann-Whitney U-test, ** = $p < 0.01$.

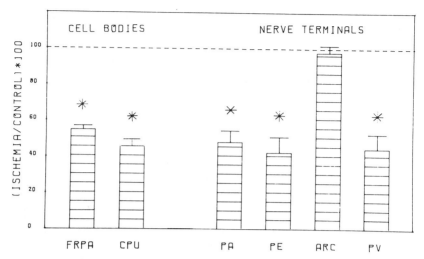

**FIGURE 13.** Morphometrical (cell body count) and microdensitometrical (antigen content) analyses of the effects of transient forebrain ischemia on NPY IR neuronal systems in various regions of the rat brain. The animals (n = 12) were sacrificed 7 days after reperfusion. Means ± SEM are given. The statistical analysis was carried out by Mann-Whitney U-test, ischemic vs control rats. * = $p$ <0.01. Abbreviations: ARC = arcuate nucleus; CPU = caudate putamen; FRPA = frontoparietal cortex; PA = paraventricular hypothalamic nucleus; PE = periventricular hypothalamic nucleus; PV = paraventricular thalamic nucleus.

neuron to change from a wiring transmission, involving A, into a volume transmission, involving NPY and its active fragments, which can *inter alia* also be released to diffuse into the extracellular space to reach distant receptors, producing more prolonged responses. Obviously it must also be considered that interactions between NPY and CA can take place at the network level, which can contribute to the antagonistic interactions observed.

Recent experiments involving intraventricular injections of pertussis toxin[3] have provided evidence for an involvement of a $G_i$ protein in the intramembrane receptor-receptor interactions between NPY and $\alpha$2 adrenoceptors. In agreement, NPY is known to be able to inhibit cAMP accumulation in various tissues including the nTS, which includes a pertussis toxin-sensitive G protein.[65–67] Thus, the modulatory influence of NPY on the $\alpha$2 receptors in membrane preparations were almost completely antagonized by pretreatment with pertussis toxin (FIGS. 18,19).

It must also be pointed out that the ability of NPY to modulate $\alpha$2 adrenergic receptors in membrane preparations of the dorsal medulla from the spontaneously hypertensive rat is abolished[68] indicating that integrative mechanisms within the neuronal membrane involved in cardiovascular regulation are disturbed in the spontaneously hypertensive rat in comparison with the Wistar Kyoto normotensive rat.

Based on these findings on NPY/$\alpha$2 receptor interactions we have now tested if these interactions between NPY and $\alpha$2 adrenergic receptors are disturbed following a transient forebrain ischemia. To begin with we studied whether this interaction between the two receptors also takes place under *in vivo* conditions by infusing NPY (14 ng/h) via osmotic minipumps into the lateral ventricle of awake unrestrained male rats for a period of 7 days.[19] We then studied whether this putative modulation, which takes place in various brain regions following infusion of NPY, is disturbed in the ischemic rats. As seen in

FIGURE 20 it was demonstrated that NPY infused into the lateral ventricle, as described above, is able to reduce the binding of ³H-PAC in various thalamic and amygdaloid nuclei. It is also shown that, at the 7-day time interval after reperfusion, the modulation by NPY *in vivo* on ³H-PAC binding sites is lost. The results also showed that, after transient forebrain ischemia, the basal binding of ³H-PAC and ¹²⁵I-NPY is unchanged in various areas. Instead the interactions between these two transmission lines in various telencephalic and diencephalic areas appear to be impaired.[19]

The results reported above indicate that upon brain ischemia the homeostatic control of the synaptic NPY transmission is lost. In fact, in the face of a marked change in the transmitter stores (see above), no change was detected in the recognition sites. Furthermore, an impairment of the interactions between the two transmission lines (NPY and α2) was shown. This alteration may have profound consequences for the information handling, since it reduces the integrative capabilities of the central nervous system at local circuit and/or synaptic level, which may deeply affect higher brain functions such as learning and memory retrieval.[69,70]

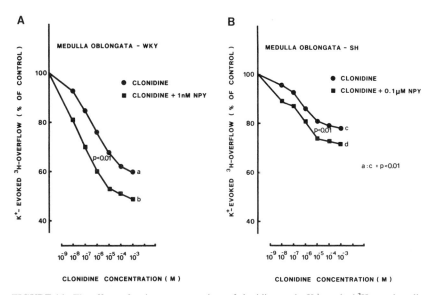

**FIGURE 14.** The effects of various concentrations of clonidine on the $K^+$-evoked ³H-noradrenaline release from synaptosomes of the medulla oblongata of the male (**A**) Wistar-Kyoto (WKY) and (**B**) spontaneously hypertensive (SH) rat in the absence or presence of NPY. For details on the experimental procedure, see Martire *et al.*[61] Total ³H-noradrenaline release is given as means, and is shown in percent of total radioactivity. For calculation of percent inhibition, the value was used which was obtained by subtraction of the value of total basal release ($8.80 \pm 0.60\%$ of total ³H-NA recovered) from the value of total ³H-noradrenaline release ($18.05 \pm 1.20\%$ of total ³H-NA recovered). Jonckheere-Tepstra test for ordered alternatives demonstrated a concentration-related ($p < 0.01$) inhibition of the total ³H-noradrenaline release by clonidine in both WKY and SHR rats. Number of observations for each value is 9. A significant enhancement by NPY of the inhibitory effects of clonidine on ³H-NA release was found both in WKY (1 nM) and in SH (0.1 μM) rats at all concentrations tested of clonidine (Mann-Whitney U-test).

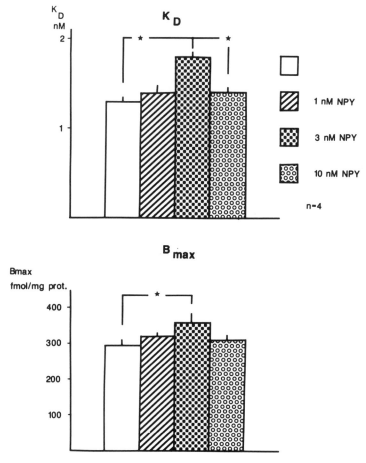

**FIGURE 15.** Effects of various concentrations of NPY on the binding characteristics of $^3$H-paraaminoclonidine ($^3$H-PAC) binding sites in membrane preparations of the hypothalamus of the normal male rat. For details on the binding procedures, see Agnati et al.[15] Means ± SEM are shown. The $K_D$ values and the $B_{max}$ values were obtained from Scatchard analysis. The concentrations of the radioligand ranged from 0.2 to 8 nM. The Dunn test was used in the statistical analysis. * = $p$ < 0.05.

## INTERACTIONS BETWEEN NEUROPEPTIDE Y AND CATECHOLAMINE, ESPECIALLY ADRENALINE, TRANSMISSION LINES IN NORMAL AND PHYSIOPATHOLOGICAL STATES

### Cardiovascular Actions of Centrally Administered NPY

In a number of publications[1,2,4,5,17,49] NPY in subnanomolar amounts has been shown to produce marked and prolonged vasodepressor and bradycardic actions, when given intracisternally or intraventricularly into the α-chloralose anaesthetized or the awake unrestrained male rat, respectively. It was found that NPY is more potent than A and clonidine in producing a lowering of mean arterial blood pressure, while the maximal actions are similar (FIG. 21). An important difference in the awake and unrestrained male rat between A and NPY lies in the ability of NPY to produce a maintained lowering of mean arterial blood pressure compared with A (FIG. 22). These findings open up the possibility that also under physiological conditions NPY released from the costoring NPY/A terminals may have a more prolonged action than A, since it may be more resistent to breakdown. It seems possible that NPY/A costoring terminals may operate via a short-lasting (A) or a long-lasting (NPY) mode by releasing its transmitter and cotransmitter, respectively, to lower mean arterial blood pressure (see above) (see FIG. 17).

In relation to the above discussion it should be underlined, however, that neither the NPY fragment (13–36) nor the free acid of NPY induced a lowering of mean arterial blood pressure, even in high doses[49] (FIG. 23). These results emphasize the specificity in the action of NPY and the involvement of Y1 NPY receptors. The only other NPY-related peptide known to evoke marked and potent vasodepressor actions is peptide YY.[5,49] In high doses bovine pancreatic polypeptide was shown to produce a certain lowering of the mean arterial blood pressure and of heart rate. These results would favor the view that in the CNS the NPY receptors involved in regulation of cardiovascular function are of the Y1 type, since NPY (13–36) was ineffective.[53,54]

It seems likely that the cardiovascular effects of intracisternal and intraventricular

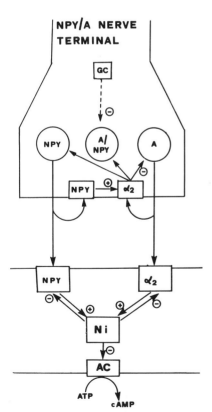

**FIGURE 16.** Possible stimulatory ( + ) and inhibitory ( − ) mechanisms for the adrenaline (A) /NPY costoring neurons. The antagonistic postsynaptic interaction between the NPY and the α2-receptors are indicated. The presynaptic NPY receptor may enhance the presynaptic α2-receptor mechanisms in the medulla oblongata, and NPY may inhibit its own release.

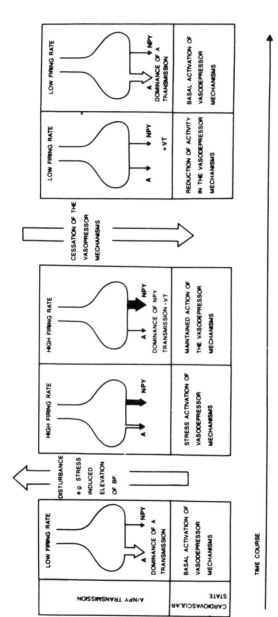

**FIGURE 17.** Schematic illustration of putative A/NPY transmission lines involved in central cardiovascular control. The illustration is in part based on the theory of frequency-dependent chemical coding. In the basal state (*first panel*), the transmission line operates mainly via an adrenergic transmission line (low firing rate). When disturbances occur in the system (*e.g.*, stress) leading to increased blood pressure there is a higher firing rate which activates the NPY transmission line (*second panel*), which inhibits the adrenaline transmission line. The effect (see *third panel*) of this line may be further enhanced by volume transmission (VT). Following the cessation of the vasopressor mechanism a lower firing rate reappears (*fourth panel*) and the system is returned to a basal state (*fifth panel*) with inhibition of the NPY transmission line.

injections of NPY are mediated via high affinity NPY receptors which are reached via a volume transmission mode. It also seems likely that, at least partly, NPY acts via reaching the high density of high affinity NPY receptors located in the cardiovascular subnuclei of the nTS, where the baroreceptor afferents terminate. In addition, the low affinity types of NPY receptors in the nTS may also mediate hypotensive responses, since it has been demonstrated that injections of NPY into the nTS at the level of the caudal area postrema induced hypotensive responses.[71]

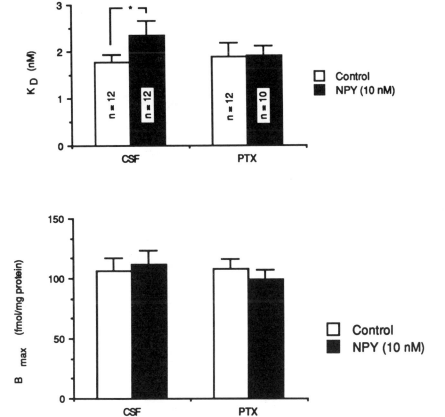

**FIGURE 18.** The effects of NPY (10 nM) on the binding characteristics of $^3$H-paraaminoclonidine (0.2–8 nM) were analyzed in membrane preparations from the dorsal medulla oblongata of the rat. The rats had previously been treated i.v.t. (24 h) with pertussis toxin (PTX, 10 μg/rat) or CSF. Nonspecific binding was defined as the binding in presence of 10 μM (−)noradrenaline. Means ± SEM are shown. Each group was represented by 10–12 rats. * = $p < 0.05$, Wilcoxon two-samples test.

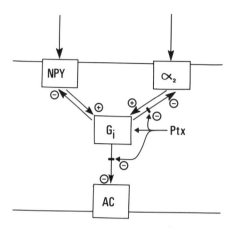

**FIGURE 19.** Intraventricular treatment with pertussis toxin (PTX, 10 μg/rat, 24 h) inhibits the reduced affinity of α2 agonist binding sites in the medulla oblongata caused by NPY (10 nM) receptor activation. Pertussis toxin also inhibits the stimulation of adenylate cyclase (AC). These effects of pertussis toxin suggest the involvement of the inhibitory G protein (G$_i$) in the mediation of this receptor-receptor interaction. Three possible sites of actions are indicated. The binding of α2 agonist sites are not affected by pertussis toxin, whereas the binding of NPY to its receptor is increased.

*Interactions between the NPY and Adrenaline Transmission Line in Cardiovascular Regulation*

Antagonistic interactions have been demonstrated to exist between centrally administered A and NPY with regard to cardiovascular actions.[5,72] As shown in FIGURE 24 NPY and A given together antagonize the vasodepressor actions of one another as seen both when evaluating the peak responses as well as the overall actions (area values). It has also recently been demonstrated by Lightman et al.[73] that when NPY is injected together with

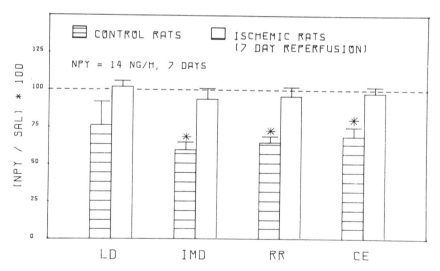

**FIGURE 20.** Effects of transient forebrain ischemia on $^3$H-paraaminoclonidine ($^3$H-PAC) binding sites after chronic NPY i.c.v. infusion (14 ng/h, 7 days). The animals (n = 4) were sacrificed 7 days after reperfusion. Means ± SEM are given. The statistical analysis was carried out by Mann-Whitney U-test, ischemic vs control rats. * = $p$ <0.05. Abbreviations used: LD = laterodorsal thalamic nucleus; IMD = intermediodorsal thalamic nuc; RR = rhomboid and reuniens thalamic nuc; CE = central amygdaloid nuc.

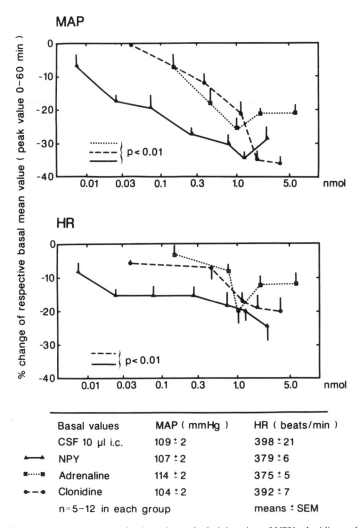

**FIGURE 21.** Maximal responses after intracisternal administration of NPY, clonidine and adrenaline are shown in the α-chloralose anaesthetized rat. Means ± SEM are shown. *P*-values indicate a dose-response relationship. Abbreviations: MAP = mean arterial blood pressure; HR = heart rate.

NA into the nTS it can substantially diminish the hypotensive action induced. Taken together these results give a functional correlate to the neurochemical evidence reported above that the NPY and α2 receptors may antagonize the affinity of one another in the postsynaptic membranes.

A pertussis toxin-sensitive G protein seems to be involved in mediating the cardiovascular actions of NPY, since prior intraventricular injections of pertussis toxin block the vasodepressor actions of NPY and also clonidine.[3] Thus, G proteins appear to play a

# MAP

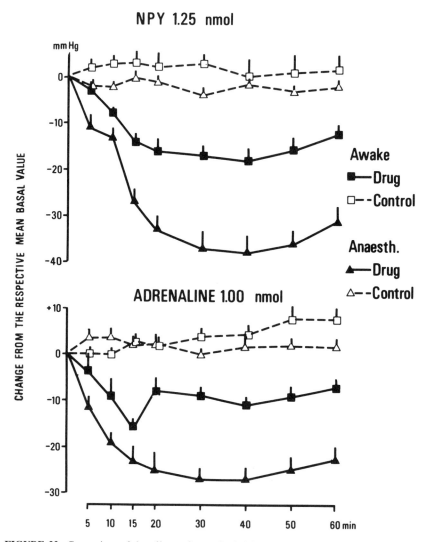

**FIGURE 22.** Comparison of the effects of central administration of maximal doses of NPY and adrenaline in the awake freely moving, and in the α-chloralose anaesthetized male rats. The difference in the hypotensive action is marked between awake and anaesthetized animals when considering blood pressure both for NPY and adrenaline while almost a similar response in heart rate is observed especially for NPY. Note the sustained peak action of NPY in the awake animals, which is not observed after adrenaline administration in the awake rat. Means ± SEM are shown. MAP = mean arterial blood pressure.

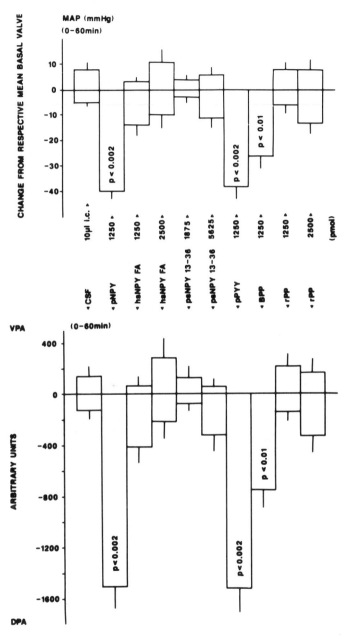

**FIGURE 23.** Cardiovascular effects of intracisternal administration of maximal doses of pNPY and pPYY in the α-chloralose anaesthetized male rat and how they compare with related peptides. Means ± SEM are shown out of 4–6 rats. The absolute change is shown in relation to respective mean basal value. The statistical analysis was performed according to Mann-Whitney U-test. VPA = vasopressor area; DAP = depressor area.

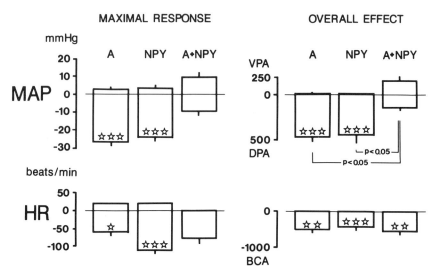

**FIGURE 24.** Interaction between centrally administered NPY and A on mean arterial blood pressure (MAP) and heart rate (HR) in the awake unrestrained male rat. The *left panels* show the maximal responses (peak) and the *right panels* show overall effects on blood pressure and HR responses during the 1 h time period after drug administration. Doses used: A, 0.45 nmol i.v.t.; NPY, 0.25 nmol i.v.t.; A + NPY, 0.45 + 0.25 nmol i.v.t. The basal values were as follows giving MAP in mmHg and HR in beats/min$^{-1}$ (means ± SEM). A, 112 ± 3, 432 ± 12, n = 7 rats; NPY 105 ± 3, 406 ± 9, n = 8 rats; A + NPY, 109 ± 4, 396 ± 18, n = 8 rats. The basal values for the respective mock CSF-treated rats are given together with the respective peak (pressor peak, depressor peak, tachycardic and bradycardic peak for MAP and HR, respectively) and area (VPA, DPA, TAC and BCA) changes induced by the CSF treatment alone. CSF (A, n = 7): 102 ± 12, 388 ± 12 (MAP: 10 ± 3 (pressor peak), −3 ± 1 (depressor peak), 212 ± 85 (VPA), −62 ± 36 (DPA); HR: 39 ± 9 (tachycardic peak), −27 ± 8 (bradycardic peak), 59 ± 27 (TCA), −180 ± 60 (BCA); CSF (NPY, n = 7): 114 ± 2, 405 ± 18 (MAP: 4 ± 1, −7 ± 1, 30 ± 18, −144 ± 46; HR: 42 ± 15, −36 ± 7, 243 ± 174, −204 ± 55); CSF (A + NPY, n = 7): 110 ± 4, 412 ± 20 (MAP: 5 ± 1, 5 ± 1, 10 ± 6, −43 ± 17; HR: 41 ± 15, −40 ± 9, 242 ± 17, −224 ± 68). Abbreviations used: A = adrenaline; NPY = neuropeptide Y; VPA = vasopressor area; DPA = vasodepressor area; TCA = tachycardic area and BCA = bradycardic area. Significances vs respective CSF control group value: * = p <0.05, ** = p <0.02, *** = p <0.002 (Mann-Whitney U-test). *Embracing bars* show significances between groups (Dunn test).

crucial role in NPY transmission in cardiovascular regulation as well as for its integrative actions in the membranes (see above).

*Cardiovascular Actions of NPY in the 80-Week-Old Male Rat*

As seen in FIGURE 25, NPY in a high dose of 1.25 nmoles per rat can induce a significant reduction of mean arterial blood pressure and of heart rate also in the 80-week-old male rat as seen from the analysis of the peak actions and the area values. However, no signs of NPY receptor supersensitivity can be found as a response to the reduced amounts of NPY IR found in many brain areas of the aged animal (see above). If anything, there was a reduced overall vasodepressor effect of NPY on arterial blood pressure in the 80-week-old male rat. In line with these results we have also observed

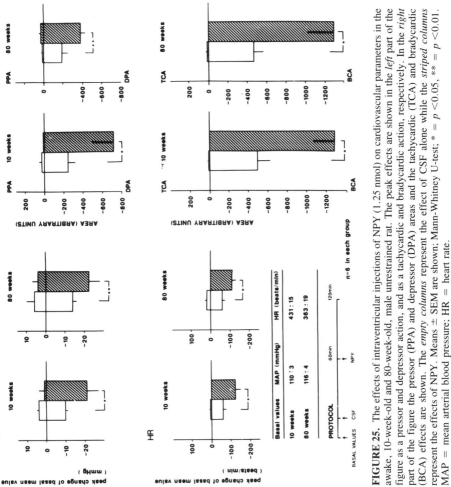

**FIGURE 25.** The effects of intraventricular injections of NPY (1.25 nmol) on cardiovascular parameters in the awake, 10-week-old and 80-week-old, male unrestrained rat. The peak effects are shown in the *left* part of the figure as a pressor and depressor action, and as a tachycardic and bradycardic action, respectively. In the *right* part of the figure the pressor (PPA) and depressor (DPA) areas and the tachycardic (TCA) and bradycardic (BCA) effects are shown. The *empty columns* represent the effect of CSF alone while the *striped columns* represent the effects of NPY. Means ± SEM are shown; Mann-Whitney U-test; * = $p < 0.05$, ** = $p < 0.01$. MAP = mean arterial blood pressure; HR = heart rate.

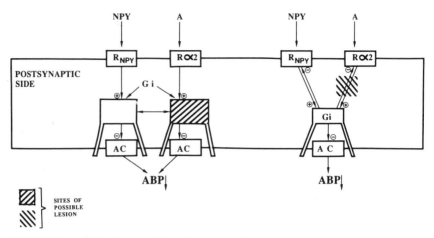

**FIGURE 26.** Possible schemes of the effects of transient forebrain ischemia on the interactions between NPY and $\alpha2$ transmission lines. ABP = arterial blood pressure. The receptors may converge on the same $G_i$ protein (*right*) or operate via separate $G_i$ proteins interacting with each other (*left*).

significantly reduced effects of microinjections of NPY into the paraventricular hypothalamic nucleus in the 24-month-old Sprague-Dawley rat compared with the adult rat (Merlo Pich *et al.* in preparation) as far as an enhancement of food intake. These results underline the view that NPY transmission is severely reduced in the aged brain, which may contribute to the development of hypertension, and the reduced food intake found in senescence.

*Cardiovascular Actions of NPY in the Spontaneously Hypertensive Rat*

The ED50 value of NPY to produce a lowering of mean arterial blood pressure in the spontaneously hypertensive rat is increased by 10 times.[74] The neurochemical results (see above) also indicate a reduced ability of NPY to modulate the $\alpha2$ agonist binding sites in membrane preparations of the dorsal medulla. These results may point to a disturbance of the regulation of the $G_i$ protein in the spontaneously hypertensive rat. Furthermore, an increased breakdown of NPY by peptidases in the spontaneously hypertensive rat compared with the Wistar Kyoto rat may partly explain the results in view of the fact that the lowering of arterial blood pressure by NPY seems to require activation of a Y1 NPY receptor, since fragments such as NPY 13–36 are ineffective.

*Cardiovascular Actions of NPY and Clonidine during a Transient Forebrain Ischemia*

It has recently been found (Grimaldi *et al.*, in preparation) that at the 7-day time interval of reperfusion after a transient forebrain ischemia the cardiovascular effects of centrally administered clonidine in both low and high doses are blocked. Instead the vasodepressor effects of a low dose of centrally administered NPY are, if anything, enhanced (TABLE 1). Based on the neurochemical evidence reported above[19] it seems likely that the $\alpha2$ transmission line is disturbed by a lesion at the level of the $G_i$ protein (see FIG. 26). Due to such a lesion the NPY receptors can no longer modulate the α2 receptor agonist binding sites. The NPY transmission line will, if anything, be enhanced due to a disappearance of the antagonistic interaction between the α2 and the NPY receptors in the postsynaptic membrane. As outlined in FIGURE 26 the α2 and NPY receptors can converge on the same $G_i$ protein or operate via separate $G_i$ proteins interacting with one another. The results open up the possibility that after ischemia the function of NPY/A costoring synapses may still operate via the maintenance of the NPY transmission line in the face of a failure of the α2 transmission line, thus contributing to

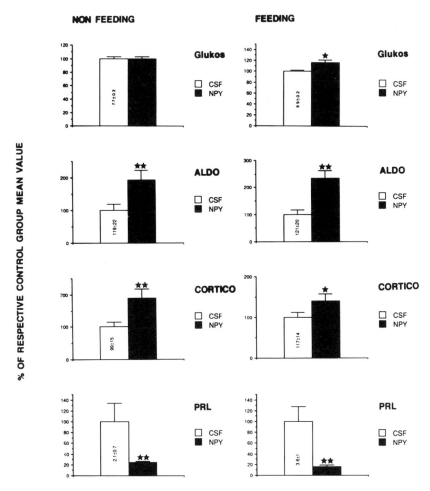

**FIGURE 27.** The effects of intraventricular administration of NPY (1.25 nmol) on serum hormone levels in rats allowed (pellets present in the cages; *right* part of the figure) or not allowed (no pellets present in the cages) to express feeding behavior. Values are expressed in per cent of the respective control group (*open columns*, means ± SEM). The values are expressed in mmol $l^{-1}$ (glucose), pg $ml^{-1}$ (aldosterone, ALDO), nmol $l^{-1}$ (corticosterone, CORTICO) and ng $ml^{-1}$ (PRL). The rats were sacrificed 1 h after NPY administration. In the statistical analysis the Mann-Whitney U-test was used. * = $p < 0.05$; ** = $p < 0.01$.

**TABLE 1.** Comparisons of Cardiovascular Actions of Clonidine and NPY in Ischemic Rats vs Controls[a]

| | Mean Arterial Blood Pressure (Time from Preperfusion)[b] | | | | | | | |
| | 120 min | | 24 h | | 7 days | | 30 days | |
| | C | I | C | I | C | I | C | I |
|---|---|---|---|---|---|---|---|---|
| Clon. 0.37 nmol/5 μl i.v.t. | ↓ | - | ↓ | - | ↓ | - | ↓ | ↓ |
| Clon. 3.7 nmol/5 μl i.v.t. | ↓↓ | - | ↓↓ | ↓ | ↓↓ | - | ↓↓ | ↓↓ |
| NPY 0.25 nmol/5 μl i.v.t. | ↓ | ↓ | ↓ | ↓ | ↓ | ↓↓ | ↓ | ↓ |
| NPY 2.5 nmol/5 μl i.v.t. | ↓↓ | ↓↓ | ↓↓ | ↓↓ | ↓↓ | ↓↓ | ↓↓ | ↓↓ |

[a]Summary of the cardiovascular actions of clonidine and neuropeptide Y (NPY) in brain ischemia according to the Pulsinelli model.

[b]Measurements were made of mean arterial blood pressure (MAP) 120 min, 24 h, 7 days and 30 days after reperfusion. C = control; I = ischemia. One arrow represents a small change and two arrows a large change in MAP.

a cardiovascular regulation. These results show that importance of synaptic redundancy, when the synapse is challenged by a lesion.

### Neuroendocrine Actions of Centrally Administered NPY

In 1982 the first report appeared on the neuroendocrine actions of a NPY-like peptide, peptide YY, which after its intraventricular injection in the male rat produced profound effects of peptide YY on gonadotrophin and growth hormone secretion.[6] In subsequent papers we have shown that in the high nanomolar range NPY and PYY produce inhibitory effects on LH, prolactin and TSH secretion as well as excitatory effects on vasopressin, aldosterone and corticosterone secretion (FIG. 27).[7,8,10,32, see also 11–14] The neuroendocrine actions of high doses of NPY were not modulated by the simultaneous presence of feeding behavior.[49] These results are of interest, since they indicate that the neuroendocrine actions of NPY are not secondary to cardiovascular effects. In fact, NPY-elicited

**TABLE 2.** Effects of a Single Dose of NPY on PRL, LH and TSH Serum Levels after Various Time Intervals[a]

| | Time Min | PRL % | LH % | TSH % |
|---|---|---|---|---|
| CSF 30 μl i.v.t. | 0 | 100 ± 27 | 100 ± 16 | 100 ± 10 |
| NPY 750 pmol i.v.t. | 5 | 16 ± 5* | 67 ± 20 | 67 ± 12 |
| | 60 | 4 ± 1* | 36 ± 13* | 29 ± 4* |
| | 120 | 14 ± 10* | 38 ± 10* | 33 ± 17* |
| | 240 | 92 ± 80 | 356 ± 154* | 58 ± 11* |

[a]The rats were decapitated at 5, 60, 120 and 240 min, and the blood was rapidly collected and taken to RIA. Means ± SEM are shown. The values are expressed in percent of the respective control group mean value. The basal values for the respective hormones are expressed in ng ml$^{-1}$ and were as follows: PRL = 26.4 ± 7.2; LH = 0.17 ± 0.04; TSH = 1.80 ± 0.19. N = 12 rats in each group. A one-way ANOVA in combination with a multiple comparison test was used. In the statistical analysis the comparisons treatment vs control are shown. * = $p < 0.05$.

**TABLE 3.** The Effects of a Single Dose of NPY on PRL, LH, TSH and GH Serum Levels after Various Time Intervals[a]

|  | Time Min | PRL % | LH % | TSH % | GH % |
|---|---|---|---|---|---|
| CSF 30 μl i.v.t. | 0 | 100 ± 43 | 100 ± 8 | 100 ± 13 | 100 ± 15 |
| NYP 7.5 pmol i.v.t. | 5 | 289 ± 18 | 98 ± 11 | 76 ± 8 | 51 ± 27 |
|  | 15 | 1274 ± 969* | 72 ± 12 | 90 ± 16 | 61 ± 27 |
|  | 60 | 52 ± 11 | 120 ± 46 | 118 ± 8 | 99 ± 18 |
|  | 120 | 1399 ± 442* | 108 ± 25 | 113 ± 25 | 100 ± 27 |
|  | 240 | 193 ± 111 | 166 ± 25* | 84 ± 13 | 52 ± 29 |

[a]The rats were decapitated at 5, 60, 120 and 240 min, and the blood was rapidly collected. Means ± SEM are shown. The values are expressed in per cent of the respective control group mean value. The basal values for the respective hormones are expressed in ng ml$^{-1}$ and were as follows: PRL = 14.05 ± 8.46; LH = 0.50 ± 0.05; TSH = 0.75 ± 0.1; GH = 129 ± 30. N = 12 rats in each group. A one-way ANOVA in combination with a multiple comparison test was used. In the statistical analysis the comparisons treatment vs control are shown. * = $p$ <0.05.

feeding behavior counteracts the vasodepressor actions of intraventricularly administered NPY.[4] When analyzing the time course of the inhibitory effects of NPY on LH, prolactin and TSH secretion in the male rat, the peak reduction is observed after 60 min and the effects have disappeared after 4 hours except for the inhibitory effects on serum TSH levels (see TABLE 2). In the lowest doses excitatory effects on prolactin secretion and inhibitory effects on corticosterone and aldosterone secretion were found in the analysis of the intact male rat (see TABLES 3,4) indicating the existence of biphasic dose-response curves.[10] The specificity of the effects of NPY is demonstrated by the fact that the NPY free acid does not produce even in high doses a reduction of LH, prolactin and TSH secretion.[24,49]

As discussed above, the biphasic dose-response curves, in this case seen in the analysis of corticosterone, aldosterone and prolactin secretion in the intact male rat may be explained by the assumption that in low doses NPY preferentially affects the NPY autoreceptors of, *e.g.*, the NPY/CA costoring terminals of the hypothalamus, which may *inter alia* lead to an inhibition of NPY release and an enhancement of the α2 autoreceptor function.[60-62] The preferential activation of the NPY autoreceptors may, as discussed

**TABLE 4.** The Effects of a Single Dose of NPY on Corticosterone, Angiotensin II and Aldosterone Serum Levels after Various Time Intervals[a]

|  | Time Min | Cortico % | Angio. II % | Aldo. % |
|---|---|---|---|---|
| CSF 30 μl i.v.t. | 0 | 100 ± 6 | 100 ± 18 | 100 ± 15 |
| NPY 7.5 pmol i.v.t. | 5 | 106 ± 7 | 131 ± 13 | 132 ± 26 |
|  | 15 | 106 ± 5 | 397 ± 71* | 138 ± 24 |
|  | 60 | 28 ± 8* | 85 ± 21 | 15 ± 8* |
|  | 120 | 92 ± 11 | 93 ± 18 | 66 ± 17 |
|  | 240 | 93 ± 10 | 170 ± 23 | 186 ± 84 |

[a]The rats were decapitated at 5, 60, 120 and 240 min, and the blood was rapidly collected. Means ± SEM are shown. The values are expressed in per cent of the respective control group mean value. The basal values for the respective hormones were as follows: corticosterone = 123.5 ± 11.3 nmol/l; angiotensin II = 20.35 ± 4.46 pg/l; aldosterone = 544.9 ± 81.3 pmol/l. N = 12 rats in each group. A one-way ANOVA in combination with a multiple comparison test was used. In the statistical analysis the comparisons treatment vs control are shown. * = $p$ <0.05.

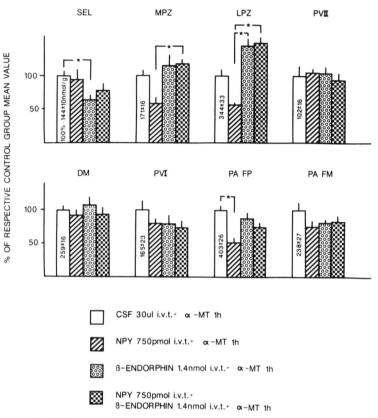

**FIGURE 28.** Effects of β-END and NPY and their combined treatment on regional hypothalamic catecholamine utilization in the male rat. Means ± SEM are shown out of 6 rats. The results are expressed as percentage of the respective CSF + αMT group mean value. In the statistical analysis Wilcoxon test was used, comparing all possible pairs of treatments. * = $p$ <0.05. Abbreviations used: SEL = subependymal layer; MPZ = medial palisade zone; LPZ = lateral palisade zone; P II = posterior periventricular hypothalamic region; DM = dorsomedial hypothalamic nucleus; PV I = anterior periventricular hypothalamic nucleus; PA FP = parvocellular part of the paraventricular hypothalamic nucleus; PA FM = magnocellular part of the paraventricular hypothalamic nucleus; αMT = α-methyltyrosine methylester.

above, be related to an increased formation of the NPY fragments, *e.g.*, NPY 13–36, which preferentially activates the Y2 NPY receptors. Thus, it seems possible that the NPY autoreceptor is of the Y2 type. Obviously, it becomes of importance to analyze the neuroendocrine actions of this NPY fragment.

In previous experiments evidence was obtained that in the higher dose range intraventricularly administered NPY can produce an increase of DA utilization in both the medial and lateral palisade zone of the median eminence. DA is probably released as a prolactin inhibitory factor from the medial palisade zone, and in the lateral palisade zone DA is probably released to inhibit, *e.g.*, the release of LHRH and TRH.[8,10,24,75] In the same experiments it was demonstrated that the NPY-induced increases of DA utilization in the median eminence were associated with marked inhibitory effects on LH, prolactin and TSH secretion in the intact and castrated male rat. Thus, the tuberoinfundibular DA neurons probably participate in mediating at least some of the inhibitory effects of NPY on prolactin, LH and TSH secretion. In the intact, but not in the castrated male rat, biphasic actions of centrally administered NPY have been observed on the tuberoinfundibular DA neurons and on prolactin secretion.[24,75] Thus, in the lowest doses, excitatory effects on prolactin secretion are associated with reductions of DA turnover in the medial and lateral palisade zone of the median eminence. Again the development of such a biphasic response can be explained, at least in part, by the existence of high affinity NPY autoreceptors, which may be of the Y2 type and may be preferentially activated by the low doses of NPY due to the increased formation of NPY fragments relative to NPY itself, leading to activation of the Y2 receptors. Such effects could lead to reduced NPY release and also NA release from the costoring NPY/NA and NPY/A nerve terminals of the hypothalamus. Thus, the effects are opposite to those

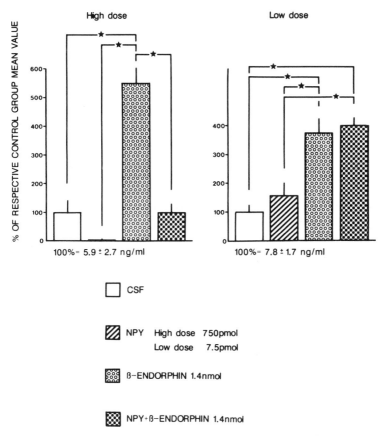

**FIGURE 29.** Effects of NPY and β-endorphin and their combined treatment on serum prolactin levels in the awake unrestrained male rat. Means ± SEM are shown for 6 rats. Doses (indicated in the figure) were given i.v.t. 1 h. The results are expressed as percent of the respective control group mean value. Basal values are given under the respective control column. In the statistical analysis multiple comparisons were performed by means of the Dunn test. * = $p < 0.05$.

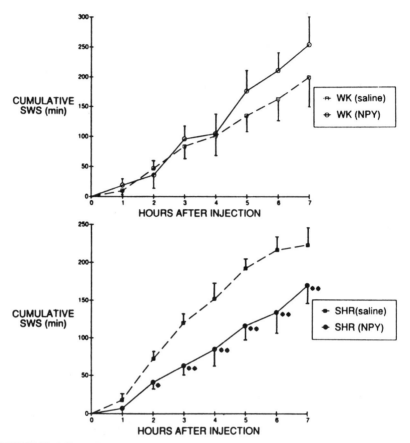

**FIGURE 30.** Effects of i.c.v. injections of NPY on slow wave sleep (SWS) in male spontaneously hypertensive (SH) and normotensive (WK) rats. Values are expressed as the mean cumulative time spent in SWS each hour $\pm$ SEM (* = $p$ <0.05; ** = $p$ <0.01; Tukey's test).

found with higher doses of NPY, in which case $\gamma 1$ receptor activation will dominate due to increased amounts of NPY 1–36 versus the NPY fragments, *e.g.*, NPY 13–36.

As demonstrated by several groups,[11–14] gonadal steroids play a crucial role in the expression of the excitatory actions of NPY on LHRH release. It seems possible that the gonadal steroids may differentially increase the sensitivity of the $\gamma 2$ NPY receptors or that they may increase the activity of the peptidases involved with the formation of active NPY fragments, such as NPY 13–36, which will substantially improve $\gamma 2$ versus $\gamma 1$-NPY receptor activity.

*Interactions between NPY and β-Endorphin Neuronal Systems in Neuroendocrine Regulation*

As seen in FIGURES 28 and 29 a simultaneous injection of β-endorphin and NPY into the lateral ventricles abolishes completely the ability of NPY to reduce DA levels and to increase DA utilization in the medial and lateral palisade zone of the median eminence, whereas the action of β-endorphin to reduce DA utilization in the tuberoinfundibular DA neurons remains completely intact.[16,24] These results could be explained on the basis that the NPY IR terminals at least in part control the tuberoinfundibular DA neurons via their innervation of the β-endorphin IR nerve cell bodies and dendrites in the arcuate nucleus.[16,24] Consequently, when β-endorphin and NPY are simultaneously injected, NPY can no longer exert its action on the tuberoinfundibular DA neurons, since inhibition of endogenous β-endorphin release is of no consequence in view of the presence of exogenously administered β-endorphin. When analyzing the interaction between NPY and β-endorphin in the same experiment with regard to prolactin secretion, NPY is nevertheless capable of counteracting the increase of prolactin secretion induced by β-endorphin. These results suggest that NPY not only inhibits prolactin secretion by

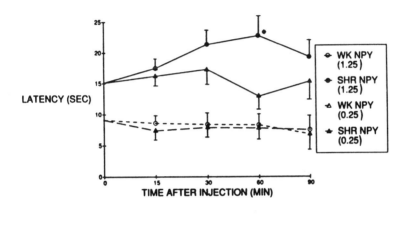

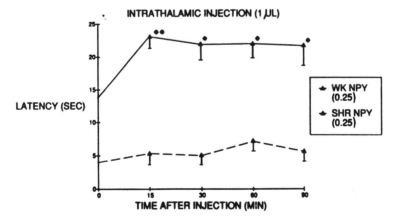

FIGURE 31. Effects of microinjections of NPY on hot-plate latencies in SH and WK rats. Microinjections were performed i.c.v. or intrathalamically via chronically implanted cannulas. Values are expressed as means ± SEM. Statistical analysis was carried out by means of ANOVA for repeated measurements followed by Dunnet test (* = $p$ <0.05; ** = $p$ <0.01, vs basal mean values). The doses used were 0.25 and 1.25 nmoles/rat.

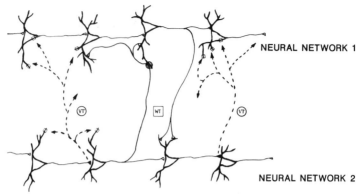

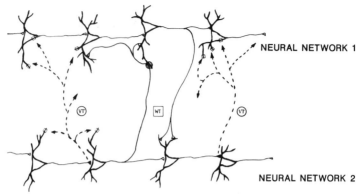 volume transmission          ▲ sites of release of chemical signals for VT

 wiring transmission          □ biological "traps" (e.g. receptors) for VT chemical signals

---ECF pathways                 ◉ sites of possible electrotonic influences

**FIGURE 32.** Schematic representation of the possible WT and VT communication channels among neuronal networks. The sites of release (*black triangles*), extracellular fluid pathways (*broken lines*) and biological traps, *e.g.*, receptors (*open squares*) for VT signals are indicated. The sites of possible electrotonic influences are also indicated with *dashed areas*. *Open triangles* represent sites of classical synaptic (WT) communications.

increasing DA release in the medial palisade zone but also via another unknown mechanism, so that the β-endorphin-induced increase of prolactin secretion can be reduced to normal levels, in spite of the maintained reduction of DA release (FIGS. 28 and 29).

### Effects of Central Administration of NPY on Vigilance and Pain Threshold Especially in Spontaneously Hypertensive Rats

#### Studies on Vigilance

It was early demonstrated that centrally administered NPY can reduce EEG arousal in the male rat.[9,79] In this analysis the interesting observation was also made that in the spontaneously hypertensive rat intraventricular injections of NPY increased EEG arousal instead of reducing it. Thus, as seen in FIGURE 30 NPY significantly reduced the cumulative time spent in slow wave sleep during the first 7 hours after injection of NPY, while opposite effects were observed in the Wistar Kyoto normotensive rat. Also the latency to the first episode of slow wave sleep and REM sleep was significantly increased by NPY injection in the ventricles in the spontaneously hypertensive rat.[9] The dose of NPY used in these experiments was 1.25 nmoles/rat. It seems possible that these alterations in the functional actions of centrally administered NPY can be related to the impairment in the spontaneously hypertensive rat of the reciprocal NPY/CA receptor interactions.[61,68] There may also exist in the spontaneously hypertensive rat an increased formation of active neuropeptide fragments, such as NPY 13–36, which can lead to a preferential activation of the Y2-NPY receptors, which may be involved in behavioral activation.[53]

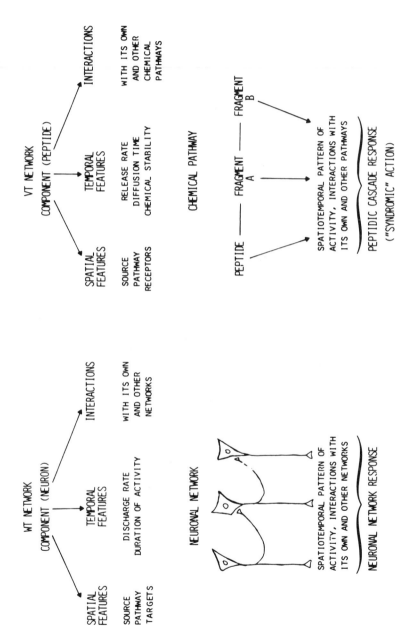

**FIGURE 33.** Schematic representation of the WT and VT networks. While the WT networks rely upon the chemicophysical as well as the structural features of the neurons, the VT networks rely upon the chemical characteristics of the message and the chemicophysical as well as structural features of the extracellular fluid.

*Studies on Pain Threshold*

Recently it has been demonstrated by Merlo Pich *et al.*[9] that stereotaxic microinjections of NPY into the midline thalamic nuclei, known to be involved in central control of pain and arousal,[77] can increase pain threshold preferentially in the spontaneously hypertensive rats in a dose of 0.25 nmoles/rat (see FIG. 31).

These results are of substantial interest in view of the demonstration of a topological mismatch in the thalamus (see above) showing a high density of high affinity NPY receptors and few NPY IR nerve terminals. The effects of intrathalamically injected NPY on pain threshold had a short latency (less than 15 min). These results indicate that the high affinity NPY receptors present in the midline thalamic nuclei in fact are coupled receptors, which are functional and can respond to NPY, released from the few NPY IR nerve terminals present in the thalamus, reaching the high affinity receptors via the extracellular fluid. Also it seems possible that NPY in the cerebrospinal fluid may reach the midline thalamic nuclei via diffusion in the extracellular fluid. In fact, Merlo Pich *et al.*[9] could demonstrate that in 6 times higher doses, NPY given into the lateral ventricle could after a long latency (60 min) increase the pain threshold. Again the failure to demonstrate effects on pain threshold with NPY in Wistar Kyoto rats, in the doses used, may be related to altered NPY/CA receptor-receptor interactions or to an increased formation of biologically active NPY fragments from peptidases, having an increased activity in the spontaneously hypertensive rats (see above). These events might lead to a preferential activation of $\gamma 2$ NPY receptors, or at least to an increase in $\gamma 2$ receptor activation compared to the Wistar Kyoto rat.

## SUMMARY

The NPY neurons play an important role in information handling in the CNS by their ability to interact in both wiring and volume transmission at the network, local circuit and synaptic level (FIG. 32). The importance of NPY/$\alpha 2$ receptor-receptor interactions in cardiovascular, neuroendocrine and vigilance control is emphasized. Alterations in these receptor-receptor interactions take place in the spontaneously hypertensive rats as well as in the ischemic brain, which may have profound consequences for the information handling and contribute to the functional alterations found in these pathophysiological states. Finally, in the aging brain there appears to exist a marked reduction in NPY transmission line, which may affect higher brain functions, such as learning and memory retrieval. The most impressive result is, however, the indications of a role for NPY in volume transmission, where NPY appears to produce syndromic actions via its conversion into biologically active fragments, which may have preferential actions at Y2 NPY receptors (FIG. 33). These syndromic pathways may be altered in the spontaneously hypertensive rat and may be controlled by gonadal steroids and glucocorticoids. Glucocorticoid receptors have been demonstrated in all arcuate NPY neurons and all NA/NPY and A/NPY costoring neurons.

## REFERENCES

1.  FUXE, K., L. F. AGNATI, A. HÄRFSTRAND, I. ZINI, K. TATEMOTO, E. MERLO PICH, T. HÖKFELT, V. MUTT & L. TERENIUS. 1983. Acta Physiol. Scand. **118:** 189–192.
2.  FUXE, K., L. F. AGNATI, A. HÄRFSTRAND, A. M. JANSON, A. NEUMEYER, K. ANDERSSON, M. RUGGERI, M. ZOLI & M. GOLDSTEIN. 1986. *In* Progress in Brain Research. Vol. **68:** 303–320. Elsevier Science Publishers. Amsterdam.

3.  VON EULER, G., K. FUXE, I. VAN DER PLOEG, B. B. FREDHOLM & L. F. AGNATI. 1989. Eur.
    J. Pharmacol. In press.
4.  HÄRFSTRAND, A. 1986. Acta Physiol. Scand. **128:** 121–123.
5.  HÄRFSTRAND, A. 1989. Acta Physiol. Scand. In press.
6.  FUXE, K., K. ANDERSSON, L. F. AGNATI, P. ENEROTH, V. LOCATELLI, L. CAVICCHIOLI, F.
    MASCAGNI, K. TATEMOTO & V. MUTT. 1982. INSERM **110:** 65–86.
7.  FUXE, K., L. F. AGNATI, K. ANDERSSON, P. ENEROTH, A. HÄRFSTRAND, K. TATEMOTO, V.
    MUTT, M. ZOLI, R. GRIMALDI & C. FARABEGOLI. 1984. XVth Int. ISPNE Congress, p. 88.
8.  FUXE, K., L. F. AGNATI, K. ANDERSSON, P. ENEROTH, A. HÄRFSTRAND, M. GOLDSTEIN, B.
    BERNARDI, W. VALE, Z.-Y. YU & J. Å. GUSTAFSSON. 1985. *In* Dopamine and Neuro
    endocrine Active Substances. E. del Pozo & E. Flückiger, Eds. 11–18. Academic Press.
    London.
9.  MERLO PICH, E., M. ZOLI, I. ZINI, F. FERRAGUTI, V. SOLFRINI, M. TIENGO, K. FUXE & L.
    F. AGNATI. 1989. Effects of central administration of neuropeptide Y on vigilance and pain
    threshold in spontaneously hypertensive rats. *In* Advances in Pain Research and Therapy.
    Lipton, Tunks & Zoppi, Eds. Raven Press. New York, NY. In press.
10. HÄRFSTRAND, A., P. ENEROTH, L. F. AGNATI & K. FUXE. 1987. Regul. Pept. **17:** 167–179.
11. KALRA, S. P. 1986. *In* Frontiers in Neuroendocrinology. W. F. Ganong & L. Martini, Eds.
    31–76. Raven Press. New York, NY.
12. KALRA, S. P. & W. R. CROWLEY. 1984. Life Sci. **35:** 1173–1176.
13. MCCANN, S. M., W. YU, O. KHORRAM, S. KENTROTI, E. VIJAYAN & M. ARISAWA. 1988. *In*
    The Brain and Female Reproductive Function. A. R. Genazzani, U. Montemagno, C. Nappi
    & F. Petraglia, Eds. 57–63. The Parthenon Publishing Group. New Jersey, NJ.
14. MCDONALD, J. K., M. D. LUMPKIN, W. K. SAMSON & S. M. MCCANN. 1985. Proc. Natl.
    Acad. Sci. USA **82:** 561–564.
15. AGNATI, L. F., K. FUXE, F. BENFENATI, N. BATTISTINI, A. HÄRFSTRAND, K. TATEMOTO, T.
    HÖKFELT & V. MUTT. 1983. Acta Physiol. Scand. **118:** 293–295.
16. FUXE, K., L. F. AGNATI, M. ZOLI, A. CINTRA, A. HÄRFSTRAND, G. VON EULER, R. GRI-
    MALDI, M. KALIA & P. ENEROTH. 1988. *In* Regulatory Roles of Opioid Peptides. P. Illes &
    C. Farsang, Eds. 33–68. VCH, Weinheim. New York, NY.
17. FUXE, K., A. HÄRFSTRAND, L. F. AGNATI, M. KALIA, B. FREDHOLM, T. SVENSSON, J.-Å.
    GUSTAFSSON, R. LANG & D. GANTEN. 1987. J. Cardiovasc. Pharmacol. **10(12):** 1–13.
18. HÄRFSTRAND, A., K. FUXE, L. F. AGNATI & B. B. FREDHOLM. 1989. J. Neural Transm. In
    press.
19. AGNATI, L. F., M. ZOLI, E. MERLO PICH, F. BENFENATI, R. GRIMALDI, I. ZINI, G. TOFFANO
    & K. FUXE. 1989. NPY receptors and their interactions with other transmitter systems. *In*
    Nobel Conference on NPY. V. Mutt, K. Fuxe, T. Hökfelt & J. Lundberg, Eds. Raven Press.
    New York, NY. In press.
20. ZOLI, M., L. F. AGNATI, K. FUXE & B. BJELKE. 1989. Demonstration of NPY transmitter
    receptor mismatches in the central nervous system of the male rat. Acta Physiol. Scand. In
    press.
21. AGNATI, L. F., K. FUXE, M. ZOLI, I. ZINI, G. TOFFANO & F. FERRAGUTI. 1986. Acta Physiol.
    Scand. **128:** 201–207.
22. AGNATI, L. F., K. FUXE, E. MERLO PICH, M. ZOLI, I. ZINI, F. BENFENATI, A. HÄRFSTRAND
    & M. GOLDSTEIN. 1987. *In* Receptor-Receptor Interactions. A New Intramembrane Integra-
    tive Mechanism. K. Fuxe & L. F. Agnati, Eds. 236–249. MacMillan Press. London.
23. FUXE, K., L. F. AGNATI, A. HÄRFSTRAND, A. CINTRA, M. ARONSSON, M. ZOLI & J.-Å.
    GUSTAFSSON. 1988. *In* Current Topics in Neuroendocrinology, Vol. 8. F. Ganten & D. Pfaff,
    Eds. 1–53. Springer Verlag. Berlin-Heidelberg.
24. FUXE, K., L. F. AGNATI, A. HÄRFSTRAND, P. ENEROTH, A. CINTRA, B. TINNER, E. MERLO
    PICH, M. ARONSSON, B. BUNNEMANN, R. LANG & D. GANTEN. 1989. Studies on the
    neurochemical mechanisms underlying the neuroendocrine actions of neuropeptide Y. *In*
    Nobel Conference on NPY. V. Mutt, K. Fuxe, T. Hökfelt & J. Lundberg, Eds. Raven Press.
    New York, NY. In press.
25. FUXE, K., A. HÄRFSTRAND, L. F. AGNATI, G. VON EULER, T. SVENSSON & B. FREDHOLM.
    1989. On the role of NPY in central cardiovascular regulation. *In* Nobel Conference on NPY.
    V. Mutt, K. Fuxe, T. Hökfelt & J. Lundberg, Eds. Raven Press. New York, NY. In press.

26. CHRONWALL, B. M., D. A. DiMAGGIO, V. J. MASSARI, V. M. PICKEL, D. A. GURRIERO & T. L. O'DONOHUE. 1985. Neuroscience **15:** 1159–1181.
27. DEQUIDT, M. E. & P. C. EMSON. 1986. Neuroscience **18:** 545–618.
28. FUXE, K., L. F. AGNATI, M. ZOLI, A. HÄRFSTRAND, S.-O. ÖGREN, E. MERLO PICH, I. ZINI & M. GOLDSTEIN. 1987. *In* Neurotransmitter interactions in the Basal Ganglia. M. Sandler, C. Feuerstein & B. Scatton, Eds. 31–46. Raven Press. New York, NY.
29. CHRONWALL, B. M., T. N. CHASE & T. L. O'DONOHUE. 1984. Neurosci. Lett. **52:** 213–217.
30. HENDRY, S. H. C., E. G. JONES, J. DEFELIPE, D. SCHMECHEL, C. BRANDON & P. C. EMSON. 1984. Proc. Natl. Acad. Sci. USA **81:** 6526–6530.
31. HÄRFSTRAND, A., A. CINTRA, K. FUXE, M. ARONSSON, A.-C. WIKSTRÖM, S. OKRET, J.-Å. GUSTAFSSON & L. F. AGNATI. 1989. Regional differences in glycocortical receptor immunoreactivity among neuropeptide Y immunoreactive neurons of the rat brain. Acta Physiol. Scand. In press.
32. HÄRFSTRAND, A., K. FUXE, L. F. AGNATI, P. ENEROTH, I. ZINI, M. ZOLI, K. ANDERSSON, G. VON EULER, L. TERENIUS, V. MUTT & M. GOLDSTEIN. 1986. Neurochem. Int. **8:** 355–376.
33. BAI, F. L., M. YAMANO, Y. SHIOTANI, P. C. EMSON, A. D. SMITH, J. F. POWELL & M. TOHYAMA. 1985. Brain Res. **331:** 172–175.
34. FUXE, K., A. CINTRA, A. HÄRFSTRAND, L. F. AGNATI, M. KALIA, M. ZOLI, A.-C. WIKSTRÖM, S. OKRET, M. ARONSSON & J.-Å. GUSTAFSSON. 1987. Ann. N.Y. Acad. Sci. **512:** 362–393.
35. HÖKFELT, T., J. M. LUNDBERG, K. TATEMOTO, V. MUTT, L. TERENIUS, J. POLAK, S. BLOOM, C. SASEK, R. ELDE & M. GOLDSTEIN. 1983. Acta Physiol. Scand. **117:** 315–318.
36. HÖKFELT, T., J. M. LUNDBERG, H. LAGERCRANTZ, K. TATEMOTO, V. MUTT, J. LUNDBERG, L. TERENIUS, B. J. EVERITT, K. FUXE, L. F. AGNATI & M. GOLDSTEIN. 1983. Neurosci. Lett. **36:** 217–222.
37. EVERITT, B. J., T. HÖKFELT, L. TERENIUS, K. TATEMOTO, V. MUTT & M. GOLDSTEIN. 1984. Neuroscience **11:** 443–462.
38. BLESSING, W. W., P. R. HOWE, T. H. JOH, J. R. OLIVER & J. O. WILLOUGHBY. 1986. J. Comp. Neurol. **248:** 285–300.
39. SAWCHENKO, P. E., L. W. SWANSON, R. GRZANNA, P. R. C. HOWE, S. R. BLOOM & J. M. POLAK. 1985. J. Comp. Neurol. **241:** 138–153.
40. HÄRFSTRAND, A., K. FUXE, A. CINTRA, L. F. AGNATI, I. ZINI, A.-C. WIKSTRÖM, S. OKRET, Z.-Y. YU, M. GOLDSTEIN, H. STEINBUSCH, A. VERHOFSTAD & J.-Å. GUSTAFSSON. 1986. Proc. Natl. Acad. Sci. USA **83:** 9779–9783.
41. FUXE, K., L. F. AGNATI, M. ZOLI, A. HÄRFSTRAND, R. GRIMALDI, P. BERNARDI, M. CAMURRI, F. TUCCI & M. GOLDSTEIN. 1985. *In* Quantitative Neuroanatomy in Transmitter Research. L.F. Agnati & K. Fuxe, Eds. pp. 157–174. MacMillan Press, London.
42. CROWLEY, W. R., R. E. TESSEL, T. L. O'DONOHUE, B. A. ADLER & S. P. KALRA. 1985. Endocrinology **117:** 1151–1155.
43. SAHU, A., S. P. KALRA, W. R. CROWLEY, T. L. O'DONOHUE & P. S. KALRA. 1987. Endocrinology **120:** 1831–1836.
44. UNDEN, A. & T. BARTFAI. 1984. FEBS Lett. **177:** 125–128.
45. UNDEN, A., K. TATEMOTO, V. MUTT & T. BARTFAI. 1984. Eur. J. Biochem. **145:** 525–530.
46. SARIA, A., E. THEODORSSON-NORHEIM & J. M. LUNDBERG. 1985. Eur. J. Pharmacol. **107:** 105–107.
47. CHANG, R. S., V. J. LOTTI, T.-B. CHEN, D. J. CERINO & P. J. KLING. 1985. Life Sci. **37:** 2111–2122.
48. MARTEL, J.-C., S. ST. PIERRE & R. QUIRION. 1986. Peptides **7:** 55–60.
49. HÄRFSTRAND, A. 1987. Acta Physiol. Scand. Suppl. 565.
50. HÄRFSTRAND, A., K. FUXE, L. F. AGNATI & F. BENFENATI. 1986. Acta Physiol. Scand. **128:** 195–200.
51. NAKAJIMA, T., Y. YASHIMA & K. NAKAMURA. 1986. Brain Res. **380:** 144–150.
52. PAXINOS, G. & C. WATSON. 1982. Academic Press, New York.
53. SCHWARTZ, T. W. 1989. *In* Nobel Conference on NPY. V. Mutt, K. Fuxe, T. Hökfelt & J. Lundberg, Eds. Raven Press. New York, NY. In press.
54. WAHLESTEDT, C., N. YANAIHARA & Å. HÅKANSON. 1986. Regul. Pept. **13:** 307–318.

55. HENDRY, S. H. C., E. G. JONES & P. C. EMSON. 1984. J. Neurosci. **4:** 2497–2517.
56. AGNATI, L. F., K. FUXE, M. ZOLI, I. ZINI, A. HÄRFSTRAND, G. TOFFANO & M. GOLDSTEIN. 1988. Neurosci. **26:** 461–478.
57. ZOLI, M., L. F. AGNATI, K. FUXE, I. ZINI, E. MERLO PICH, R. GRIMALDI, A. HÄRFSTRAND, M. GOLDSTEIN, A. C. WIKSTRÖM & J.-Å. GUSTAFSSON. 1988. Neuroscience **26:** 479–492.
58. SAHU, A., P. S. KALRA, W. R. CROWLEY & S. P. KALRA. 1988. Endocrinology **125:** 2199–2203.
59. GRAY, T. S. & J. E. MORLEY. 1986. Life Sci. **38:** 389–401.
60. MORLEY, J. E. & J. F. FLOOD. 1989. Effects of NPY on memory processing and ingestive behaviors. *In* Nobel Conference on NPY. V. Mutt, K. Fuxe, T. Hökfelt & J. Lundberg, Eds. Raven Press. New York, NY. In press.
61. PULSINELLI, W. A. & J. B. BRIERLEY. 1979. Stroke **10:** 267–272.
62. MARTIRE, M., K. FUXE, G. PISTRITTO, P. PREZIOSI & L. F. AGNATI. 1986. J. Neural Transm. **67:** 113–124.
63. MARTIRE, M., K. FUXE, P. PISTRITTO, P. PREZIOSI & L. F. AGNATI. 1989. Reduced inhibitory effects of clonidine and neuropeptide Y on $^3$H-noradrenaline release from synaptosomes of the medulla oblongata of the spontaneously hypertensive rat. J. Neural Transm. In press.
64. MARTIRE, M., K. FUXE, P. PISTRITTO, P. PREZIOSI & L. F. AGNATI. 1989. J. Neural Transm. In press.
65. LUNDBERG, J. M., J. PERNOW, K. TATEMOTO & C. DAHLOF. 1985. Acta Physiol. Scand. **123:**511.
66. HÖKFELT, T., V. R. HOLETS, W. STAINES, B. MEISTER, T. MELANDER, M. SCHALLING, M. SCHULTZBERG, J. FREEDMAN, H. BJÖRKLUND, L. OLSON, B. LINDH, L.-G. ELFVIN, J. M. LUNDBERG, J. Å. LINDGREN, B. SAMUELSSON, B. PERNOW, L. TERENIUS, C. POST, B. EVERITT & M. GOLDSTEIN. 1986. Progr. Brain Res. **68:** 33–70.
67. FREDHOLM, B. B., I. JANSEN & L. EDVINSSON. 1985. Acta Physiol. Scand. **124:** 467–469.
68. KASSIS, S., M. OLASMAA, L. TERENIUS & P. H. FISHMAN. 1987. J. Biol. Chem. **262:** 3429–3431.
69. HÄRFSTRAND, A., B. FREDHOLM & K. FUXE. 1987. Neurosci. Lett. **76:** 185–190.
70. AGNATI, L. F., K. FUXE, F. BENFENATI, N. BATTISTINI, A. HÄRFSTRAND, T. HÖKFELT, L. CAVICCHIOLI, K. TATEMOTO & V. MUTT. 1983. Acta Physiol. Scand. **119:** 309–312.
71. AGNATI, L. F., K. FUXE, M. FERRI, F. BENFENATI & S.-O. ÖGREN. 1981. Med. Biol. **59:** 224–229.
72. AGNATI, L. F., K. FUXE, M. ZOLI, C. RONDANINI, S.-O. ÖGREN. 1982. Med. Biol. **60:** 183–190.
73. CARTER, D. A., M. VALLEJO & S. L. LIGHTMAN. 1985. Peptides **6:** 421–425.
74. HÄRFSTRAND, A. & K. FUXE. 1987. Acta Physiol. Scand. **130:** 529–531.
75. LIGHTMAN, S. L., M. VALLEJO & D. A. CARTER. 1989. NPY catecholamine interactions in the central nervous system. *In* Nobel Conference on NPY. V. Mutt, K. Fuxe, T. Hökfelt & J. Lundberg, Eds. Raven Press. New York, NY. In press.
76. HÄRFSTRAND, A., K. FUXE, L. F. AGNATI, D. GANTEN, P. ENEROTH, K. TATEMOTO & V. MUTT. 1984. Clin. Exp. Hypertens. Part A Theory Pract. **6 (10 & 11):** 1947–1950.
77. FUXE, K., A. HÄRFSTRAND, P. ENEROTH, M. ZOLI & L. F. AGNATI. 1988. *In* Frontiers in Gynecological Endocrinology Series. A. R. Genazzani, U. Montemagno, C. Nappi & F. Petraglia, Eds. 45–55. The Parthenon Publishing Group.
78. ZINI, I., E. MERLO PICH, K. FUXE, P. L. LENZI, L. F. AGNATI, A. HÄRFSTRAND, V. MUTT, K. TATEMOTO & M. MOSCARA. 1984. Acta Physiol. Scand. **122:** 71–77.
79. ALBE-FESSARD, D., K. J. BERKLEY, L. KRUGER, H. J. RALSTON & W. D. WILLIS. 1985. Brain Res. Rev. **9:** 217–296.

# Neuropeptides as Neuronal Growth Regulating Factors

## Peripheral Nerve Regeneration and the Development of Sexually Dimorphic and Motor Behavior[a]

FLEUR L. STRAND, ANNABELL C. SEGARRA,
LISA A. ZUCCARELLI, JUNE KUME, AND KENNETH J. ROSE

*Biology Department*
*and*
*Center for Neural Science*
*New York University*
*Room 1009 Main Building*
*Washington Square*
*New York, New York 10003*

Over the last decade, as the number of identified neuropeptides has increased spectacularly, their physiological roles have seemingly come to overlap. Analogs with amino acid sequences that appear to have little similarity to the native molecule still retain comparable functions. Many neuropeptides are described as growth factors: the task for the future is to determine how specific these factors are in terms of tissue substrate, receptor binding, critical periods of action, and interaction with other, perhaps more specific growth regulators, including the sex steroids. This paper will focus on the melanocortins as possible growth factors during ontogeny and regeneration, reviewing the progress made over the previous ten years and introducing new evidence that indicates that the melanocortins are subtle regulators of development, providing the fine control necessary to bring maturing elements into balance. This balance permits the correct chronological integration of intricately functioning systems, from the development of neuronal pathways in the central nervous system to the formation of synaptic contacts in the periphery. Information derived from these developmental studies should be applicable to some extent to processes of regeneration; consequently, it has significant clinical application.

### The Melanocortins

Adrenocorticotropin (ACTH) and melanocyte-stimulating hormone (MSH) are two potent neuropeptides derived from the large polypeptide precursor, proopiomelanocortin (POMC). Also contained within this precursor molecule is the related opiate β-lipotropin, which will not be included in this discussion. POMC is a 29,500 molecular weight peptide synthesized in the anterior and intermediate lobes of the pituitary gland and in various other brain regions, especially the arcuate nucleus of the hypothalamus.[1] The sequential arrangement of ACTH and β-lipotropin in the precursor molecule was first demonstrated by Roberts and Herbert.[2] Recombinant DNA approaches have elucidated the structure of the complete POMC molecule and later studies show that POMC is differently processed

[a]Supported by the Council for Tobacco Research and Biomeasure, Incorporated.

in the anterior and intermediate pituitary lobes, resulting chiefly in the production of ACTH 1–39 by the anterior lobe and α-MSH (ACTH 1–13) by the intermediate lobe.[3] The processing is depicted in FIG. 1.

Both behavioral and neurotrophic studies have demonstrated differences in the potencies of various melanocortin fragments.[4,5] The naturally secreted molecule ACTH 1–39 contains all its bioactivity within the first 24 amino acid sequence: ACTH 1–24 possesses both corticotropic and neurotrophic properties. The synthesis of specific ACTH fragments, such as ACTH 1–10, 4–10, and 11–16, as well as 1–13 (α-MSH) has shown that the corticotropic potency resides in the sequences 11–24 and that the shorter N terminus sequences have varying neurotrophic potencies. The most potent fragment with respect to enhancement of nerve regeneration appears to be α-MSH.[6,7]

Various analogs of the melanocortins also possess neurotrophic potency: the best evaluated of these is Org 2766, a trisubstituted analog of ACTH 4–9 which is relatively resistant to enzymatic degradation and has been shown to be 100–1,000× more potent than ACTH 4–10 in several paradigms.[8–16] Other ACTH 4–10 analogs, such as BIM 22015, are being tested for their comparable potency in these and other paradigms.

### Growth Factors

Peptides that regulate the growth of tissues, whether in a positive or negative manner, are termed growth factors. Many of these factors, such as the epidermal and fibroblast growth factors, exert their main effects on nonneural tissues. The nomenclature for growth factors is often too narrow to describe their wide-ranging effects since they may have separate and different actions depending on their tissue substrate. The multifunctional roles of peptide growth factors is well described by Sporn and Roberts.[17] Our recent work, described later in this paper, indicates that neuropeptides may have separate and different effects on the same tissue depending upon the time in ontogeny when they are administered.

The melanocortins influence a wide range of neural activities, from changes in firing threshold of single brain and spinal neurons to alterations in complex behavioral patterns.[18–20,4] In addition, these POMC derivatives accelerate the maturation of the developing neuromuscular system, enhance the regeneration of peripheral nerve, and influence the pattern by which regenerating motor units are formed.[21] *In vitro* studies have also shown that these peptides encourage neurite outgrowth.[22–25]

Are these specific, distinctive activities designed to augment the growth and development of neurons or are these peptides acting as generalized growth-promoting factors in collaboration with other growth factors? Our studies, and those of other laboratories, clearly show that the melanocortins influence nerve growth and synapse formation during development and regeneration, that these influences may be stimulatory or inhibitory depending on the same time frame of peptide administration, on the dosage and pattern of administration, as well as on the duration of administration, and that slight variations in peptide structure and length may profoundly influence the nature of the response. Similarly, the metabolic state of the organism is important: neuropeptides are well known for their ability to improve the responses of the depressed (hypophysectomized or adrenalectomized), developing, or regenerating system, returning them to normal or near-normal levels, but having little effect upon normal function.[26] Does this indicate a redundancy of message, a fail-safe mechanism or specificity? We shall attempt to answer this after presenting further evidence of neuropeptide influences on neuronal growth.

### Sites of Action of Melanocortin Growth Factors

Nonneuronal growth factors may stimulate or inhibit the proliferation of nonneural cells. However, the effect of the melanocortins on nerve cells usually is to initiate and/or

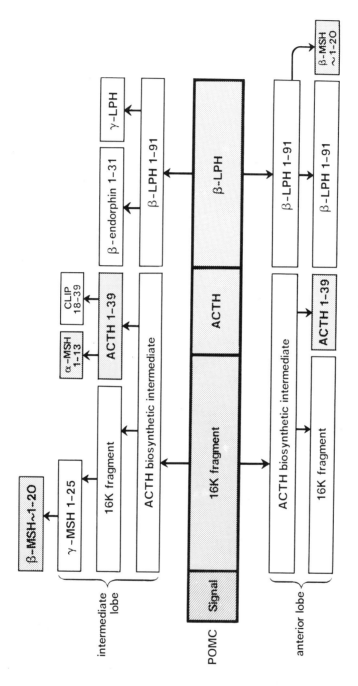

**FIGURE 1.** Processing of proopiomelanocortin (POMC) the precursor for the melanocortins and opiates in the mammalian pituitary gland. Processing occurs by proteolytic cleavage at sites of paired basic amino acids, some of which are shown here as *dark bands*. In both the anterior and the posterior lobes, POMC is processed into an ACTH biosynthetic intermediate and into β-lipotropin (β-LPH). In the anterior lobe, subsequent processing yields the two biologically important products, ACTH 1–39 and β-MSH. In the intermediate lobe, ACTH 1–39 is further processed to yield α-MSH and CLIP (corticotropin-like intermediate peptide). From the 16K fragment, via γ-MSH, β-MSH is derived. This hormone varies in length in different species. (From Strand *et al.*[21])

maintain neurite outgrowth, axonal elongation and maturation, and synapse formation for target cell innervation.

We have studied axonal transport in rat sciatic nerve and found that fast transport essentially is unchanged by endogenous alterations in ACTH, *e.g.*, depletion induced by hypophysectomy or augmentation via adrenalectomy.[27,28] These studies also were unable to show any observable change in transport in regenerating, crushed sciatic nerve. Similarly, administration of ACTH 1–24, ACTH 4–10, or Org 2766 leaves the rate of fast transport unaltered.[27,28] While the overall fast transport rate seems impervious to these endocrine and traumatic manipulations, certain specific growth-associated proteins (GAPs) are found in greater concentrations in developing and regenerating nerves than in mature, healthy nerves.[29] In particular, B-50 protein, a neuron-specific, acidic GAP phosphoprotein, is greatly increased in growth cone membranes and its phosphorylation is affected by ACTH peptides.[30,31] The involvement of the melanocortins with second messenger systems is a fertile field for investigation.

## EVIDENCE FOR MELANOCORTINS AS GROWTH FACTORS IN THE PERIPHERAL NERVOUS SYSTEM DURING ONTOGENY: TIME-DEPENDENT EFFECTS

The melanocortins exert positive maturational effects on the peripheral neuromuscular system if they are administered at certain crucial periods during development. In the rat the neuromuscular system matures during the first two weeks of postnatal life and administration of the noncorticotropic fragments ACTH 4–10 or Org 2766 (10 μg/kg s.c. daily from the day of birth) accelerates the maturational processes, as seen in greater neuromuscular coordination, muscle strength, and faster muscle contraction times.[10,32–35] Recently, however, we have shown there is a similar but far more complex prenatal period of susceptibility to ACTH peptides, and that ACTH 4–10 first (gestation days [GD] 3–12) acts upon the embryonic noninnervated muscle to accelerate its development. Subsequently (GD 13–21), the newly innervated muscle loses its sensitivity to neuropeptide influence and the effect of ACTH 4–10 administration is to depress the nerve that innervates the muscle. Thus, if the peptide treatment continues throughout gestation (GD 3–21), no significant effect is observed on neuromuscular maturation, since the two opposite influences balance one another out. However, postnatal administration of these peptides finds the nerve in a different state of responsiveness, and neuromuscular maturation is accelerated (FIG. 2). It must be emphasized that once the muscle has become innervated it loses forever its sensitivity to these peptides: all responses subsequently are via the nerve.[36] The underlying mechanisms responsible for these changes in responsiveness to neuropeptides are unknown.

There is also a clearly defined period of susceptibility to melanocortin administration when the morphology of the developing neuromuscular junction (nmj) is investigated by quantitative techniques. Nerve sprouting occurs as a normal physiological process during development and in the immature newborn rat each muscle fiber is polyneuronally innervated. Sprouting is increased by peptide administration during the first two weeks of postnatal life, when the developing nmj is most plastic in its responses. ACTH (10 μg/kg s.c. daily from the day of birth) increases nerve terminal branching but a much smaller dose (0.01 μg/kg) of the trisubstituted derivative of ACTH 4–9 (Org 2766) has an earlier and more potent effect, increasing endplate perimeter and nerve terminal branching at both 7 and 14 days of age.[11] It must be noted that this is a strongly dose-dependent effect, since 10 μg/kg of Org 2766 markedly inhibits nerve terminal branching (FIG. 3).

# EVIDENCE FOR MELANOCORTINS AS GROWTH FACTORS IN THE CENTRAL NERVOUS SYSTEM DURING ONTOGENY

## Development of Motor Activity

Our earlier studies on the motor activity of neonatal rats showed that ACTH 4–10 and Org 2766 accelerate the normal appearance of hyperactivity in these young animals, indicating an action on central motor areas as well as on the peripheral neuromuscular system.[10,34] Subsequently, we have shown that there is a marked age-related suscepti-bility to these peptides; one-week-old neonates remain unresponsive to ACTH 4–10, whereas two-week-old rat pups increase their motor activity in response to this peptide.

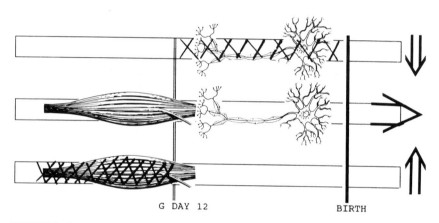

G DAY 12                                        BIRTH

**FIGURE 2.** Selective administration of ACTH 4–10 during gestation. ACTH has two separate, time-dependent gestational effects on neuromuscular development. Given exclusively during G3–G12, the peptide fragment accelerates muscle development directly. Later gestational administration (G13–21) of ACTH 4–10 decelerates muscle development via this peptide's opposing action on the nerve that innervates the muscle. The net effect of totigestational exposure to this stress hormone on development is the appearance of normal neuromuscular maturation seen in control animals. (From Rose and Strand.[36])

## Development of Sexually Dimorphic Behaviors

The organizational effect of hormones on reproduction and mating behavior in the rat is exerted both during gestation and in the neonatal period. While sex steroids clearly play the dominant part in development of the circuitry of neural pathways in the adult male or female sexual behavior, there is much evidence to show that prenatal stress alters sexual differentiation of the offspring.[37–42] We now provide evidence that perinatal administra-tion of the stress-evoked hormone ACTH has profound effects on subsequent male sexual behavior and on other sexually dimorphic behaviors such as salt preference. Of especial interest is the discovery that the nature of the adult response (positive or negative) is dependent upon the time of ACTH administration, *i.e.*, prenatal or postnatal.

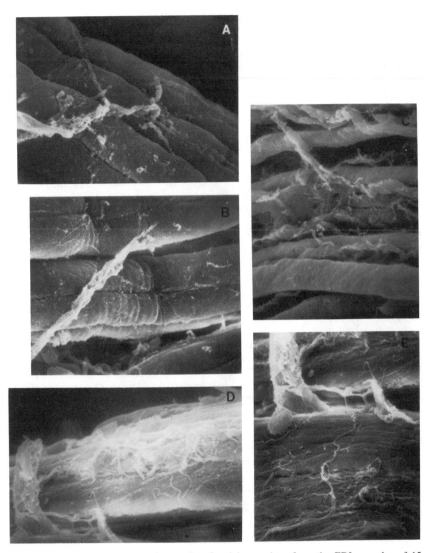

**FIGURE 3.** Scanning electron micrographs of endplate regions from the EDL muscles of 15-day-old rats. (**A**) saline-treated neonate. The nerve can be seen branching into narrower nerve terminals along the muscle fiber. 1881×. (**B**) Org 2766-treated (10 μg/kg) neonate. The nerve terminal shows a marked reduction in branching. 1986×. (**C**) ACTH 4–10-treated (10 μg/kg) neonate showing extensive nerve terminal branching. 1100×. (**D**) Org 2766-treated (0.01 μg/kg) neonate with arborization of nerve terminals. 2750×. (**E**) higher magnification of Org 2766-treated (0.01 μg/kg) neonate showing considerable nerve terminal branching at the endplate. 5775×. Compare with (**B**). (From Frischer and Strand.[11])

## METHODS

Pregnant Sprague-Dawley rats (Taconic Farm) were housed individually and water and Purina rat chow provided ad libitum. The rats were maintained with a 12 h light:12 h dark photoperiod with lights off at 12:00 h. For the prenatal treatment the rats were ordered 3 days pregnant, for postnatal treatment they were ordered 18 days pregnant. The animals were divided into the following treatment groups:

1. *Prenatal treatment.* Dam injected twice daily from gestation day (GD) 14–21 with
   a) saline or b) ACTH 1–24 (0.1 mg/animal i.p.).
2. *Postnatal treatment.* Pups injected daily from day of birth to day 14 with a) saline
   or b) ACTH 1–24 (0.1 mg/animal s.c.).

ACTH 1–24, obtained from Organon, was dissolved in saline and injected in a volume of 0.1 ml/100 g.

Once the pups were born each litter was culled to 5 males and 3 females. From day 10 to day 18 the animals were checked daily for eye opening. At 28 days of age males and females were separated from the mother and housed in groups of the same sex with 3 or 4 animals per cage. When the males attained 63–65 days of age they were tested for sexual behavior.

*Behavioral Tests*

The animals were divided into two main groups: one group consisted of animals tested for sexual behavior; the other group was used for the salt preference tests.

*Sexual behavior tests:* A more detailed description of these tests may be found in Segarra and Strand.[43] Briefly, the males were placed in the testing area and after an adaptation period of 3 min, a sexually experienced, hormonally primed female was presented. The females were rotated between the males approximately every 10 min so that each male was tested with 5 different females during each trial. Each male was tested on 3 separate days. The following behavioral measurements were made for each test:

1. Mount: mount with pelvic thrusting
2. Intromission: mount with vaginal penetration
3. Ejaculation: mount with intromission and a final prolonged thrust
4. Mount latency: time to first mount
5. Intromission latency: time to the first intromission
6. Ejaculation latency: time from first intromission to first ejaculation
7. Postejaculatory interval: time after ejaculation to the first intromission of a new series.

The test was concluded when one of the following occurred:

1. The male failed to mount within 15 min
2. The male mounted but failed to ejaculate in 30 min
3. The male ejaculated twice and initiated a third series of mounts.

*Salt preference*: When the animals reached 55–61 days of age, they were housed individually for one week and offered a choice between two water bottles, one of which contained tap water and the other a 3% sodium chloride solution. Every 24 h the amount of water remaining in the bottles was measured with a graduated cylinder and refilled to 200 ml with fresh solution.

*Dissections*

A week after the behavioral tests were concluded (approximately at 70 days of age) the animals were anesthetized with ether, and blood drawn from the inferior vena cava with a syringe containing EDTA as an anticoagulant and kept on ice until centrifuged. The rats were decapitated with a guillotine and the levator ani muscle and testes removed and weighed. In addition, the testes were prepared for microscopic examination to determine the presence of spermatogenesis.

*Testosterone Levels*

*Radioimmunoassay:* Testosterone levels were determined utilizing the Coat-a-Count Free Testosterone RIA kit from Diagnostic Products. This kit has a sensitivity of up to 0.15 pg/ml. The data reduction was calculated by the conventional RIA techniques of linear regression and logit-log representation with its calibrators.
*Bioassay:* The weights of the testes and the androgen sensitive levator ani muscle were used as a bioassay for adult testosterone levels.

*Brain Neurotransmitter Levels*

The brain was dissected on ice using a "homemade" apparatus. The preoptic area was identified using the Palkovitz Brain Atlas and removed using a 1 mm punch. The brain tissue was stored at $-70°C$. The concentrations of 5-hydroxytryptamine (5-HT or serotonin), 5-hydroxyindolamine acetic acid (5-HIAA), 3,4-dihydroxyphenethylamine (dopamine or DA), and dihydroxyphenylacetic acid (DOPAC) were determined using high performance liquid chromatography (HPLC) with electrochemical detection as described in previous papers.[44,45]

*Statistical Analysis*

The behavioral tests and neurotransmitter concentrations were analyzed by Chi-square, Students *t* test and 2-way ANOVA tests according to the variables under evaluation. RIA levels were compared with the Student *t* test.

## RESULTS

*Sexual Behavior*

*Prenatal treatment:* There was a decrease in the overall sexual performance of sexually experienced males treated prenatally with ACTH (TABLE 1). Of the rats in the prenatal group, 54% of the ACTH males did not ejaculate, compared to 16% of the saline-treated rats.
*Postnatal treatment:* Postnatal treated ACTH males performed as well or better than the postnatal saline males. Once they acquired sexual experience 100% of the males completed two ejaculatory series and initiated a third (TABLE 1).

## Salt Preference

There is a significant difference between saline-treated males and females in their saline solution consumption. Males have a higher overall liquid intake than females ($p = 0.0022$). Males also consume a greater amount of water than females and have a lower saline solution intake. Although males consume more liquid than females, the mean amount of saline solution consumed per day is less, thus the percent of saline solution intake is less.

Prenatal treatment with ACTH abolishes all differences between males and females, except for total liquid consumption which remains higher in males ($p < 0.02$) (FIG. 4a). Males show a decrease in the amount and percent of saline solution intake (FIGS. 4a and 4b).

**TABLE 1.** Percent of Adult Male Rats Treated Pre- or Postnatally with ACTH 1–24 That Exhibited Sexual Behavior

| | n | 2× | 1× | NE | NB |
|---|---|---|---|---|---|
| Prenatal treatment | | | | | |
| Pretrial | | | | | |
| Saline | 19 | 15.8 | 52.6 | 0 | 31.6 |
| ACTH | 13 | 23.1 | 23.1 | 0 | 53.8 |
| Trials 1 & 2 | | | | | |
| Saline | 19 | 68.4 | 5.3 | 10.5 | 15.8 |
| ACTH[a] | 13 | 38.5 | 7.7 | 0 | 53.8 |
| Postnatal treatment | | | | | |
| Pretrial | | | | | |
| Saline | 14 | 28.6 | 42.9 | 0 | 28.6 |
| ACTH | 10 | 40.0 | 30.0 | 0 | 30.0 |
| Trials 1 & 2 | | | | | |
| Saline | 14 | 100 | 0 | 0 | 0 |
| ACTH | 10 | 100 | 0 | 0 | 0 |

*Prenatal treatment* = ACTH 1–24 (0.10 mg/rat/2 × /day). All prenatal injections were administered intraperitoneally. *Postnatal treatment* = the dosage listed above (subcutaneously) once a day, the pups thus receiving half the dosage administered to the pregnant dams. *Pretrial* = males tested as sexually naive males. *Trials 1 & 2* = males tested after acquiring sexual experience. Data expressed as mean ± standard error of the mean. Statistical comparisons by Kolmogorov-Smirnov goodness of fit.

2× = percent males that ejaculated twice.
1× = percent males that ejaculated once.
NE = percent males that did not ejaculate.
NB = percent males that did not mount or intromit.
[a] $p = 0.05$ for ACTH vs saline.

## Testosterone Radioimmunoassay

Plasma testosterone levels were unaffected by perinatal ACTH treatment (Saline = 22.71 ± 3.96; ACTH = 16.08 ± 3.46; values expressed in pg/ml).

## Testosterone Bioassays

Levator ani weight, which is used as a bioassay for circulating testosterone levels, was not affected by prenatal ACTH administration (ratio levator ani/body weight: saline = 0.08 ± 0.004; ACTH = 0.09 ± 0.003).

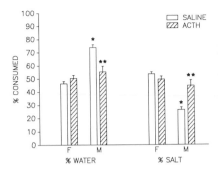

**FIGURE 4a.** Percent of water vs saline solution intake recorded from adult male and female rats treated prenatally with saline or ACTH 1–24 (0.1 mg/animal/2× day). *Saline males significantly different from saline females (*t* test, *p* <0.001). **ACTH males significantly different from saline males (ANOVA, *p* = 0.02).

## Eye Opening

The accelerated eye opening of females as compared to males was evident in both the saline and ACTH groups. Pre- and postnatal treatment with ACTH accelerated eye opening in both the male and female offspring. Postnatal ACTH treatment also accelerated eye opening in both sexes. These data are shown in TABLE 2.

## Interaction with Central Neurotransmitters: Neurotransmitter Concentration in the Preoptic Area

There was an increase in serotonin levels in the preoptic area (POA) of males treated prenatally with ACTH (saline = $2.10 \pm 1.01$; ACTH = $4.60 \pm 0.79$, $p = 0.002$; values expressed as pg/mg of protein). 5-HIAA, DA, and DOPAC concentrations did not vary significantly from the saline controls.

## DISCUSSION

### Sexually Dimorphic Behavior

*Sexual behavior*: Our studies indicate that perinatal administration of ACTH 1–24 alters the process of sexual differentiation in the rat by inducing demasculinization and feminization of the male progeny. Sexual differentiation of the brain in the rat occurs both prenatally and during the first week of postnatal life. Elevated fetal androgen levels during

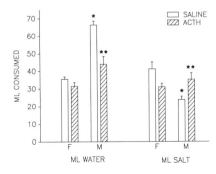

**FIGURE 4b.** Amount of liquid intake (saline solution vs water) recorded from adult male and female rats treated prenatally with saline or ACTH 1–24 (0.1 mg/animal/2× day). *Saline males significantly different from saline females (*t* test, *p* <0.001). **ACTH males significantly different from saline males (ANOVA, *p* = 0.001).

the prenatal period normally result in behavioral development in the male direction.[37,46,47] During the first few days after birth the levels of androgens in the neonate are critical for the development of the male acyclic hypothalamus.[48] McEwen *et al.* point out that masculinization of the brain takes place during the prenatal stage, whereas defeminization occurs during the postnatal period.

Several studies have found a correlation between prenatal manipulation, testosterone levels, and sexually dimorphic behaviors. Ward reported that prenatal stress decreases sexual behavior in the male offspring of rats.[49] Rhees and Fleming reported a decrease in sexual behavior with prenatal ACTH 1–24 administration.[50] In subsequent studies on the pattern of testosterone secretion in the fetus, Ward showed that while in control males testosterone levels peaked at GD 18, this peak was shifted to GD 17 in males that had been stressed prenatally.[51,52]

While we found no changes in adult testosterone levels of the males treated perinatally with ACTH to correspond to the changes in their sexual behavior, this could be attributed to alterations in fetal androgen levels during critical periods of development. Fetal androgen levels could be affected by exposure of the fetus to stress hormones. It is also possible that ACTH may act directly on neuronal circuitry underlying male sexual behavior during the time of heightened neural plasticity.

**TABLE 2.** Day of Eye Opening of Male and Female Rats following Perinatal Treatment with ACTH 1–24[a]

|  | n | Females | Males |
|---|---|---|---|
| Prenatal treatment |  |  |  |
| Saline | 17 | 15.4 ± 0.18 | 16.0 ± 0.19 |
| ACTH | 29 | 13.8 ± 0.27[b] | 14.9 ± 0.26[b] |
| Postnatal treatment |  |  |  |
| Saline | 8 | 15.7 ± 0.33 | 15.8 ± 0.20 |
| ACTH | 16 | 13.8 ± 0.48[c] | 15.0 ± 0.26[c] |

[a]Pre- and postnatal treatment as described in TABLE 1. Data expressed as mean ± standard error. The data were analyzed by ANOVA with sex as a covariant; Newman-Keuls test was used for post-hoc comparison between groups.
[b]Significantly different from saline ($p = 0.0006$).
[c]Significantly different from saline ($p = 0.0001$).

*Salt preference*: This study corroborates previous reports of the existence of sex differences in saline solution intake in adult rats.[53,54] Prenatal ACTH administration increases the volume and percent of saline solution intake in male rats to levels comparable to females. Not only do these males increase their consumption of saline solution, but the volume and percent of water intake is reduced. Thus, the decrease in the overall fluid intake of these males can be attributed exclusively to a decrease in water consumption since saline intake is actually increased. The increase in salt preference in these males can be taken as an index of feminization.

Other studies with prenatal ACTH administration also report feminization of the male progeny as seen by an increase in lordosis behavior.[50]

## Eye Opening

The acceleration of eye opening, an indication of central nervous system (CNS) maturation, caused by pre- or postnatal ACTH treatment provides further evidence of the sensitivity of the developing CNS to the action of this neuropeptide. Earlier studies with neonatal ACTH administration also report an acceleration in eye opening in the male and female progeny.[55]

*Handling Stress*

In a preliminary study, the effect of handling and of the injection procedure on subsequent sexual behavior of the offspring was investigated and reported to have no effect.[43] It is therefore unlikely that the stress of handling the dams is a significant feature in the changed sexual responses of the offspring.

These results emphasize the remarkable plasticity of the brain during sexual differentiation. Perinatal drug manipulation during this developmental period can product alterations which are permanent or at least persist into adulthood. The ontogenetic period most sensitive to ACTH administration appears to be prenatal, as seen by the demasculinization and some feminization of the male progeny. Although feminization is reported to occur mainly during early neonatal life, it appears to be susceptible to environmental cues during the prenatal stage as well. Postnatal administration of ACTH had the inverse effect of prenatal treatment, improving the sexual performance of the male progeny.

Increased levels of the neurotransmitter serotonin in the medial preoptic area are correlated with decreased male copulatory behavior.[56] The elevated serotonin levels in the POA of males prenatally treated with ACTH suggests that their decreased sexual behavior may be partially mediated by this change in serotonin amount.

Thus this study provides further evidence for "localizing" the process of masculinization during the prenatal ontogenetic stage. The effect of hormones, specifically of ACTH, on sexual differentiation of the brain may vary according to the developmental stage when they are administered; the brain substrate may be embryologically competent to some substances at one stage and nonresponsive, or respond in a completely opposite fashion, to these same inductors at other stages.

## EVIDENCE FOR MELANOCORTINS AS GROWTH FACTORS DURING PERIPHERAL NERVE REGENERATION

Nerve sprouting in regeneration occurs as a restorative process. While regeneration is often seen as a recapitulation of ontogeny, there are important differences. Sprouting during development occurs in virgin territory with growing axons innervating muscle fibers to form the original endplates and motor units. During regeneration, however, while previous endplates are selectively reinnervated the muscle fibers that form the reinnervated motor units are differently distributed within the muscle and fewer, larger motor units result. Animals treated with ACTH 4–10 or with Org 2766 following peroneal nerve crush show both qualitative and quantitative improvements in motor unit formation.[34,13] Two types of motor units are produced, many small motor units that are highly resistant to fatigue and some large, stronger motor units. This is in contrast to untreated, regenerating motor units which are typically only large and thus lacking in fatigue resistance and fine control.

One may infer from these results that the melanocortins influence the growth pattern of the reinnervating axons. Consequently, we investigated both the morphology of the reinnervated endplates following nerve crush and the return of motor function, as indicated by an analysis of the walking pattern and the extent of toespread during regeneration.

**TABLE 3.** Effect of Administration of Peptide (10 μg/kg/48 h) on Endplate Parameters from EDL Muscles 15 Days after Sciatic Crush Lesion[a]

| Parameters | Saline | ACTH 4–10 | α-MSH |
|---|---|---|---|
| Nerve terminal branching (μm) | 256.6 ± 4.3 | 336.8 ± 12.5*** | 369.3 ± 17.5*** |
| Perimeter (μm) | 232.0 ± 6.0 | 234.8 ± 5.9 | 255.7 ± 4.7** |
| Area (μm²) | 3501.2 ± 200.3 | 3572.7 ± 188.5 | 4091.9 ± 152.4* |

[a]N = 36. Means (± SEM). *$p < 0.05$; **$p < 0.01$; ***$p < 0.001$. (From Strand et al.[7])

## METHODS

### Animals

Mature male Sprague-Dawley rats (180–200 g) were housed 5 per cage and maintained on a 12 h dark:12 h light cycle and fed rat chow and water ad libitum. All surgeries were performed between 10 a.m. and 12 noon and all injections administered during these times. Surgery was performed under anesthesia with 8% chloral hydrate (0.6 ml/0.1 kg i.p.). The extensor digitorum longus (EDL) muscle was denervated by crushing the ipsilateral sciatic nerve with a #5 Dumont forceps with a uniformly filed tip, producing a 1-mm wide lesion 30 mm from the nerve exit from the spinal cord. For the experiments with BIM 22015, the peroneal nerve was crushed as the nerve enters the muscle. The wound was closed with surgical staples. Immediately after the operation, treatment commenced with the i.p. administration of one of the following:

1. 0.9% saline
2. ACTH 4–10 (10 μg)
3. α-MSH (10 μg)
4. BIM 22015 (10 μg).

The peptides were administered every 48 h until the time of dissection (15 or 21 days after sciatic nerve crush, 7 days after peroneal nerve crush).

### Morphological Techniques

The EDL muscle was fixed in situ and viewed under a light microscope using a combined silver-cholinesterase stain which facilitated the quantitative measurement of morphological parameters. These included total length of nerve terminal branching within the endplate, and the cholinesterase-positive endplate area and perimeter. Experimental preparations were observed with an Olympus BH 100X oil immersion objective (total magnification 1000×) and measurements were performed with a Bioquant image analysis system.

### Statistical Analysis

ANOVA and Newman-Keuls test were used for statistical evaluation. Data are expressed as mean plus or minus standard error of the mean (SEM).

*Locomotor Tests*

The return of motor function was measured in two ways. In sciatic nerve crush experiments, the sciatic function index (SFI) of De Medinaceli *et al.* was used.[57] This index is determined empirically using several gait parameters. Gaits and toespreads were collected by running the animals up a paper-coated, slightly elevated track (76 cm long) after coating their hindfeet with nontoxic paint.

*Toespread*

In the peroneal nerve experiments, the toespread from the first to the fifth digits was measured and expressed as a percentage of recovery as compared to the contralateral, intact side. There were three groups of animals in this experiment: sham operated, peroneal nerve crush plus saline, and peroneal nerve crush plus BIM 22015.

## RESULTS

*Endplate Morphology*

As shown in TABLE 3, treatment with either ACTH 4–10 or α-MSH markedly increases interior branching within the endplate. The effects of α-MSH are more impressive than those of ACTH 4–10. The greater potency of α-MSH is more clearly seen on the other two parameters measured: this neuropeptide also increases the area and perimeter of the endplates, whereas these aspects of endplate structure are unchanged by ACTH 4–10. By 21 days, only the interior branching is still greater in the peptide-treated groups: area and perimeter are the same as in the saline-treated controls.

The ACTH 4–10 analog, BIM 22015 is as effective as the other two neuropeptides in increasing nerve terminal branching within the endplate in the peroneal nerve crush model. However, these effects are seen only at 7 days after nerve crush. Like ACTH 4–10, it has no effect on either endplate area or perimeter (TABLE 4).

*Locomotor Tests*

FIGURE 5 shows the return of motor function following sciatic nerve crush as evaluated by the sciatic function index. There are no significant differences between the peptide-treated (ACTH 4–10 or α-MSH) and saline-treated rats during the first two weeks of regeneration. By 18 days following the crush, ACTH 4–10-treated rats showed an

**TABLE 4.** Effect of Administration of Peptide (10 μg/kg/48 h) on Endplate Parameters from EDL Muscles 7 and 14 Days after Peroneal Crush Lesion[a]

| Parameters | | Saline | BIM 22015 | Sham |
|---|---|---|---|---|
| Nerve terminal | 7d | 231.5 ± 5.7 | 273.8 ± 12.3** | 371.4 ± 12.6 |
| branching (μm) | 14d | 114.4 ± 60.9 | 227.5 ± 50.6 | 460.3 ± 45.4 |
| Perimeter (μm) | 7d | 250.0 ± 5.5 | 247.3 ± 7.7 | 267.8 ± 8.4 |
| | 14d | 257.2 ± 26.8 | 236.8 ± 11.9 | 303.8 ± 7.9 |
| Area (μm²) | 7d | 4048.9 ± 249.5 | 3795.1 ± 203.8 | 4469.5 ± 156.7 |
| | 14d | 3745.7 ± 668.5 | 3188.2 ± 380.7 | 5043.1 ± 331.7 |
| Muscle fiber | 7d | 68.7 ± 1.1 | 71.4 ± 1.4 | 87.2 ± 6.0 |
| diameter (μm) | | n = 6 | n = 8 | n = 5 |

[a]Means ± SEM. ANOVA. **$p = 0.01$ vs saline crush. All values from crushed nerve are significantly different from sham crushed values at $p < 0.05$ (post-hoc tests used were Newman-Keuls and Least Significant Difference).

improvement over the saline- and α-MSH-treated animals. By 21 days, this improvement is also evident in the α-MSH-treated rats.

*Toespread*

In the peroneal nerve crush group, 3 days after sham crush, there is a 94% recovery of the exterior toespread as compared to the 68.4% recovery from crush in the saline-treated animals. At this time there is a significant (ANOVA $p = 0.01$) improvement in toespread recovery from nerve crush in the BIM 22015-treated rats as compared to the saline controls. While there still appears to be superior recovery with BIM 22015 6 days after nerve crush it is no longer significant (ANOVA $p = 0.06$). By 9 days after crush,

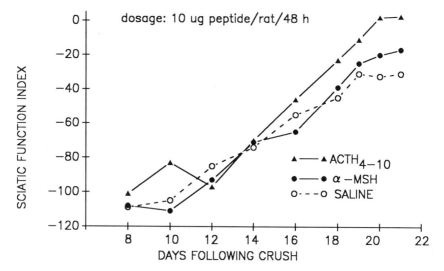

**FIGURE 5.** The return of motor function following sciatic nerve crush as evaluated by the sciatic function index. There are no significant differences between the peptide-treated (ACTH 4–10 or α-MSH) and saline-treated rats during the first two weeks of regeneration. By 18 days following crush, ACTH 4–10-treated rats showed an improvement over the saline- and α-MSH-treated animals. By 21 days, this improvement is also evident in the α-MSH-treated rats.

there is no difference between saline- and BIM 22015-treated animals, and neither group (84.5% and 85.2% respectively) has completely recovered to the level of the toespread of the sham-operated animals (98.5%).

## DISCUSSION

All the melanocortins that we have tested, including the analogs Org 2766 and BIM 22015, increase intraendplate nerve terminal branching, with α-MSH also able to increase endplate area and perimeter. These effects on nerve growth may provide a stronger structural basis for improved neurotransmitter release and fine motor control. Previous studies have demonstrated that the melanocortins accelerate the process of regeneration, that they induce early nerve sprouting and that the reinnervated motor units are more efficient when they have been restructured under peptide control.[58–61,13]

More rapid reinnervation, improved restructuring of motor units, and better motor control in animals that have received melanocortin treatment may underlie the enhanced locomotor ability, as demonstrated by the sciatic function index. The recovery of the toespread distance is also accelerated by BIM 22015, indicating a more rapid innervation of the muscles supplied by the peroneal nerve and consequently, a peptide-induced acceleration of growth of the regenerating axons. As these peptides can hasten motor and sensory recovery effectively only if peptide administration is begun within 48 h after nerve crush they must act on the early growth processes of regeneration.[14,13] As in ontogeny, there are critical periods of plasticity or sensitivity during which the melanocortins exert a growth-promoting, organizational function on growing neurons.

## EVIDENCE FOR MELANOCORTINS AS GROWTH FACTORS DURING CENTRAL NERVOUS SYSTEM REGENERATION

Despite the well-known inability of central neurons to regenerate, there are indications that, given a suitable environment, limited regeneration is possible. This response can be augmented by treatment with the noncorticotropic melanocortins but not by ACTH 1–24 or ACTH 1–39, since they evoke the secretion of corticosteroids which exert a negative effect on neuronal regeneration. This is reviewed in more detail by Strand *et al.*[62]

In the frog, vestibular compensation following unilateral vestibular lesions has been interpreted as indicating collateral sprouting, a process that is enhanced by melanocortin administration. The substitution of the 7-D-phenyl isomer of ACTH 4–10 inhibits the response.[63,64] Postoperative treatment with Org 2766 but not with ACTH 4–10 enhances recovery from septal lesions.[65,66] Both Org 2766 and α-MSH improve reversal learning in rats with bilateral lesions of the parafascicular area.[67] Retention of information following lesions of the frontal cortex in the rat appears to be improved by the ACTH 4–10 analog BIM 22015 (Stein, 1988, personal communication).

Studies of embryonic rat cerebral cells in culture indicate that ACTH 1–24 and ACTH 4–10 increase neuritic density, fasciculation, and the size and number of neuronal aggregates.[22] Similarly, neurons in slices of fetal rat spinal cord show a dose-dependent increase in neurite outgrowth following the addition of either ACTH 4–10 o4 α-MSH to the culture medium.[25] A study of the structure of melanocortin peptides and their ability to increase serotonin uptake by mesencephalic cells in culture, indicates that ACTH fragments up to 1–24, including Org 2766, are effective in culture but that MSH lacks a neurotrophic effect on raphe cells.[23]

## GENERAL CONCEPTS OF PEPTIDE ACTION

At the beginning of the "neuropeptide decade" we believed that each neuropeptide had a specific, identifiable action upon a specific tissue, and that there would be a typical dose response characterized by an increased effect as the dosage was increased. We now perceive the role of neuropeptides to be far more complex. They are found in storage form with other peptides and classical neurotransmitters, with which they may interact. Their functions vary with physiological conditions to such a degree that these variations may be considered to be mechanisms whereby each peptide is regulated by its physiological environment, enabling it to act as a multifunctional regulator itself. A brief review of these variations on the peptide theme follows:

### *Binding of Melanocortins*

If melanocortins act upon different tissues, or upon the same tissues at different times in development, there must be physiological and/or structural variations in the receptors that bind them. Apart from the adrenocortical receptors, and the receptors for ACTH in the hypothalamus, we know little about receptors for ACTH in either the central or peripheral nervous system, let alone receptors for the melanocortin fragments. However, peptide-induced alterations in synaptic membrane dynamics may induce changes in receptor dynamics.[68] ACTH 1–24 inhibits the binding of a muscarinic antagonist to rat brain membranes.[69] Limited labelling of ACTH 4–10 and Org 2766 has been reported in the septal and preoptic areas.[70] The limited binding for Org 2766 to axonal sprouts or glia in the dorsal horn, which is not displaced by naloxone, is specifically affected by nerve crush.[71] It is surprising that the only spinal binding sites for this peptide, which has important effects on motor function, are in the dorsal horns.

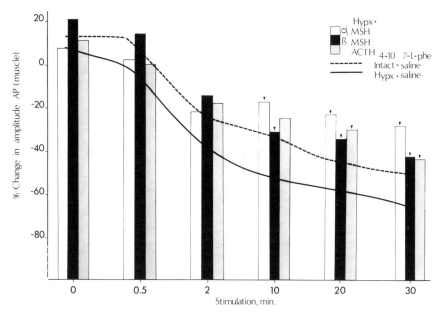

**FIGURE 6.** Hypophysectomy (hypx) depresses muscle action potential (AP) amplitude and increases fatigue in rats during a 30-min period of stimulation. These parameters are restored to normal levels by administration of α-MSH (20 μg/kg), or by β-MSH (10 μg/kg), or by ACTH 4–10 (1 μg/kg). *Black triangles* = $p < 0.05$ vs hypx saline-treated rats. All ACTH 4–10 values differ from saline-treated intact controls at $p < 0.05$. 8 rats per group. Extensor digitalis longus muscle stimulated via deep peroneal nerve *in situ*, monophasic square wave pulses, frequency 10 Hz, duration 0.05 msec, strength 3× maximal. (From Strand et al.[73])

### Structure-Activity and Dosage Relationships of the Melanocortins

The trisubstituted analog of ACTH 4–9, Org 2766 (FIG. 1), has a 100–1000× greater potency than ACTH 4–10 on certain parameters such as behavior and the morphology of the endplate, especially nerve terminal branching.[11,12] On other parameters, such as motor unit reorganization during nerve regeneration, the potency of this analog is the same as that of ACTH 4–10. α-MSH is more potent than the other melanocortins on many aspects of neuromuscular function (FIG. 6).[73,59] For all the melanocortins, there is an inverted U shaped curve for the optimum dosage, with high dosages usually having a markedly inhibitory effect.

The 7-D-phenyl isomer of ACTH 4–10 has opposite effects to the L-isomer on certain behavioral measurements.[8] In tests of neuromuscular efficiency, we have observed that substitution of the D-isomer renders ACTH 4–10 ineffective. Other substitutions in the ACTH 4–10 sequence, such as in BIM 22015, result in a peptide that retains the potency of the other melanocortins on certain parameters but not on others.

## Modes of Administration

Although neuropeptides penetrate the blood-brain barrier poorly, they are effective in such minute quantities that peripheral administration is satisfactory.[74,75] While the amount of peptide needed for intracerebro-ventricular injection is several fold less than that required for peripheral injection, the practical advantages of the latter, and the very small quantities of peptide required even for this route, make peripheral administration preferable for most studies.

It is surprising that there is so little difference in the effective dosage of the melano-cortins whether they are administered by subcutaneous injection every 48 h, by implantation of osmotic minipumps, or by the injection of biodegradable microspheres containing the peptides.[76,14] Less peptide is needed when injections are i.p. rather than s.c. Local application of $\alpha$-MSH to the site of nerve injury using microporous Accurel® tubing, which not only concentrates endogenous neurotrophic factors but also acts as a guide for regenerating axons, also seems to reduce the amount of peptide needed.[77]

## Initiation and Duration of Peptide Treatment

Early treatment with the melanocortins is essential for a successful response during regeneration. For the accelerated recovery of function the injured nerve must be exposed to the melanocortins during the first 8 days following injury, beginning as soon as possible after the actual nerve trauma.[59,78,79,13] The best pattern of melanocortin administration appears to be s.c. or i.p. injections every 48 h.[79,13]

Long-term administration of ACTH 4–10 or Org 2766 indicates a similar sensitivity to the duration of melanocortin treatment: prolonged treatment (3 weeks) reduces the favorable effects on regenerative responses evoked by the first two weeks of therapy.[61,13] For optimal neurotrophic results we recommend that peptide treatment should begin early, be continued on a moderate dosage and injection schedule, and be discontinued prior to the onset of possible detrimental effects.

## Metabolic State

The melanocortins appear to have little if any effect on a normal, healthy, mature neural system. They have profound, stabilizing effects on a metabolically disturbed system, such as seen following hypophysectomy, or adrenalectomy.[80,73,58] Melanocortin effects on developing and regenerating systems have been amply documented in this paper.

## Interaction with Neurotransmitters

Several lines of evidence point to an interaction of the stress-evoked melanocortins with stress-evoked neurotransmitters. This is particularly evident in the cardiovascular system. The relationship between stress and enhanced myocardial sensitivity has been investigated in the atrial strip preparation. Both ACTH 1–24 and ACTH 1–39 potentiate the action of norepinephrine (NE)[81–83] but not through the cyclic AMP second messenger system, although ACTH 1–39 binds specifically to atrial tissue.[83] ACTH 1–24 also potentiates NE-induced contractile responses in aortic strips from spontaneously hypertensive rats: NE-induced contractions are normally weaker in these hypertensive rats and the resulting response to ACTH is greater than the response of the normotensive aortic strips.[84]

Interaction of the melanocortins with the serotonergic system of the brain during ontogeny was discussed on page 77. Together, these observations lend credence to the probability that many of the actions of the melanocortins may be via neurotransmitters as well as through interactions with other growth factors.

## CLINICAL IMPLICATIONS

As the melanocortins clearly have beneficial actions on nerve growth and regeneration, it is to be expected that they will be of most value in clinical conditions involving neural degradation and nerve trauma. Cisplatin-induced neuropathy in rats is lessened by prior Org 2766 treatment and clinical studies on cisplatin-treated women with ovarian cancer are underway.[85,86] Studies on patients likely to develop diabetic neuropathy are also being considered: in all these cases, preventive therapy is essential as there is no evidence that the melanocortins can reverse existing degeneration. For this reason, cases of nerve trauma that can be immediately treated with the melanocortins are most likely to benefit from peptide therapy.

## CONCLUSIONS

We conclude that the melanocortins have specific organizational and maturational effects upon peripheral and central neurons. The potency of these effects is time-dependent and dosage-dependent: they are also limited by the boundaries of physiological homeostasis. The response to the melanocortins varies according to the state of plasticity of the tissue substrate, the presence or absence of neurotransmitters, modifying hormones, and other growth factors. Working through the continuously changing internal environment, the melanocortins are able to fine-tune the responses of a growing tissue. This permits the correct chronological response to the synchronous changes occurring in the target cells.

Consequently, there is no simple answer to the question posed earlier in this paper. Depending on the particular tissue substrate, its stage of development or its metabolic state, melanocortins may be highly specific in their growth-promoting actions, may depend upon the presence or absence of other hormones, growth factors, or neurotransmitters, or may be completely redundant in that their presence or absence does not seem to affect a particular growth process at that particular time. Is this a fail-safe mechanism designed to maintain vital developmental and regenerative growth processes within a circumscribed physiological range? We tend to believe so.

## REFERENCES

1. CIVELLI, O., N. BIRNBERG & E. HERBERT. 1982. Detection and quantitation of pro-opiomelanocortin mRNA in pituitary and brain tissues from different species. J. Biol. Chem. **257:** 6783–6787.

2. ROBERTS, J. L. & E. HERBERT. 1977. Characterization of a common precursor to corticotrophin and beta-lipotrophin: cell-free synthesis of the precursor and identification of corticotrophin peptides in the molecule. Proc. Natl. Acad. Sci. USA **74:** 4826–4830.
3. NAKANISHI, S., A. INOUE, T. KITA, M. NAKAMURA, A. C. CHANG, S. N. COHEN & S. NUMA. 1979. Nucleotide sequence of cloned cDNA for bovine corticotropin-β-lipotropin precursor. Nature **278:** 423–427.
4. BECKWITH, B. E. & A. J. KASTIN. 1987. Central actions of melanocyte-stimulating hormone (MSH). *In* Peptide Hormones: Effects and Mechanisms of Action. A. Negro-Villar & P. M. Conn, Eds. CRC Press. Boca Raton, FL.
5. BIJLSMA, W. A., F. G. I. JENNEKENS, P. SCHOTMAN & W. H. GISPEN. 1981. Corticotropin (ACTH) like peptides stimulate peripheral nerve regeneration. *In* Functional Recovery from Brain Damage. M. W. van Hof & H. Mohn, Eds. 411–416. Elsevier. North Holland, Amsterdam.
6. BIJLSMA, W. A., F. G. I. JENNEKENS, W. H. GISPEN & D. DE WIED. 1983. The enhanced recovery of sensorimotor function in rats is related to the melanotropic moiety of ACTH/MSH neuropeptides. Eur. J. Pharmacol. **92:** 231–236.
7. STRAND, F. L., L. A. ZUCCARELLI, B. KIRSCHENBAUM & R. E. FRISCHER. 1988. Sprouting pattern and B-50 phosphorylation in regenerating sciatic nerve respond to ACTH peptides. *In* Post-Lesion Neural Plasticity. H. Flohr, Ed. Springer-Verlag. New York, NY.
8. GREVEN, H. M. & D. DE WIED. 1973. The influence of peptides derived from corticotrophin (ACTH) on performance: Structure activity studies. Prog. Brain Res. **39:** 429–441.
9. VERHOEF, J., M. PALKOVITS & A. WITTER. 1977. Distribution of a behaviorally highly potent ACTH 4–9 analog in rat brain after intraventricular administration. Brain Res. **126:** 89–104.
10. ACKER, G. R., J. BERRAN & F. L. STRAND. 1985. ACTH neuromodulation of the developing motor system and neonatal learning in the rat. Peptides 6(Suppl. 2): 41–49.
11. FRISCHER, R. E. & F. L. STRAND. 1988. ACTH peptides stimulate motor nerve sprouting in development. Exp. Neurol. **100:** 531–541.
12. FRISCHER, R. E. & F. L. STRAND. 1988. Neural effects of ACTH peptide treatment in the developing rat neuromuscular junction. Ann. N. Y. Acad. Sci. **529:** 126–127.
13. SAINT-COME, C. & F. L. STRAND. 1988. ACTH 4–9 analogue (Org 2766) improves qualitative and quantitative aspects of motor nerve regeneration. Peptides 8(Suppl. 1): 215–221.
14. DEKKER, A. J. A. M., M. M. PRINCEN, H. DE NIJS, L. G. J. DE LEEDE & C. L. E. BROEKKAMP. 1987. Acceleration of recovery from sciatic nerve damage by the ACTH(4–9) analog. Org 2766: Different routes of administration. Peptides **8:** 1057–1059.
15. VERHAAGEN, J., P. M. EDWARDS, F. G. I. JENNEKENS, P. SCHOTMAN & W. H. GISPEN. 1987. Early effect of an ACTH 4–9 analog (Org 2766) on regenerative sprouting demonstrated by the use of neurofilament-binding antibodies isolated from a serum raised by α-MSH immunization. Brain Res. **404:** 147–150.
16. VERHAAGEN, J., P. M. EDWARDS, F. G. I. JENNEKENS & W. H. GISPEN. 1987. Pharmacological aspects of the influence of melanocortins on the formation of regenerative peripheral nerve sprouts. Peptides **8:** 581–585.
17. SPORN, M. B. & A. B. ROBERTS. 1988. Peptide growth factors are multifunctional. Nature **332:** 217–219.
18. BARKER, J. L., M. IFSHIN & H. GAINER. 1975. Studies on bursting pacemaker potential activity in molluscan neurons. Effects of hormones. Brain Res. **84:** 501–513.
19. KRIVOY, W. A. & E. ZIMMERMAN. 1977. An effect of α-melanocyte stimulating hormone (α-MSH) on α-motoneurons of cat spinal cord. Eur. J. Pharmacol. **46:** 315–322.
20. DE WIED, D. & E. R. DE KLOET. 1987. Pro-opiomelanocortin (POMC) as homeostatic control system. *In* The Hypothalamic-Pituitary-Adrenal Axis Revisited. W. F. Ganong, M. F. Dallman & J. L. Roberts, Eds. Vol. 512: 328–335. New York Academy of Sciences, New York, NY.
21. STRAND, F. L., K. ROSE, J. A. KING, A. C. SEGARRA & L. A. ZUCCARELLI. 1989. ACTH modulation of nerve development and regeneration. Prog. Neurobiol. **33:** 45–85.
22. RICHTER-LANDSBERG, C., I. BRUNS & H. FLOHR. 1987. ACTH neuropeptides influence development and differentiation of embryonic rat cerebral cells in culture. Neurol. Res. Comm. **1:** 153–162.
23. AZMITIA, E. C. & E. R. DE KLOET. 1987. ACTH neuropeptide stimulation of serotonergic

neuronal modulation maturation in tissue culture: Modulation by hippocampal cells. Prog. Brain Res. **72:** 311–317.

24. DEMENEIX, B. & N. J. GRANT. 1988. Alpha-melanocyte stimulating hormone promotes neurite outgrowth in chromaffin cells. FEBS Lett. **226:** 337–342.

25. VAN DER NEUT, R., P. R. BAR, P. SODAAR & W. H. GISPEN. 1988. Trophic influence on alpha-MSH and ACTH 4–10 on neuronal growth in vitro. Peptides **9:** 1015–1020.

26. STRAND, F. L. & C. M. SMITH. 1986. LPH, ACTH, MSH and motor systems. *In* Neuropeptides and Behavior; CNS Effects of ACTH, MSH and Opioid Peptides. D. De Wied, W. H. Gispen & Tj. B. van Wimersma Greidanus, Eds. 245–272. Pergamon Press. New York, NY.

27. CRESCITELLI, L., K. L. KEIM & F. L. STRAND. 1983. The effects of MSH/ACTH peptides on fast axonal transport in rat sciatic nerve. Soc. Neurosci. Abs. **9:** 51.

28. CRESCITELLI, L. A. 1985. The effect of MSH/ACTH peptides on fast axonal transport in intact and regenerating sciatic nerves. Ph.D. thesis. New York University.

29. SKENE, J. H. P. & M. WILLARD. 1981. Changes in axonally transported proteins during axon regeneration in toad retinal ganglion cells. J. Cell Biol. **89:** 86–95.

30. ZWIERS, H., D. VELDHUIS, P. SCHOTMAN & W. H. GISPEN. 1976. ACTH, cyclic nucleotides and brain protein phosphorylation in vitro. Neurochem. Res. **1:** 669–677.

31. GISPEN, W. H., H. ZWIERS, V. M. WIEGANT, P. SCHOTMAN, & J. E. WILSON. 1979. The behaviorally active neuropeptide ACTH as neurohormone and neuromodulator: The role of cyclic nucleotides and membrane phosphoproteins. Adv. Exp. Med. Biol. **116:** 119–224.

32. SMITH, C. M. & F. L. STRAND. 1981. Neuromuscular response of the immature rat to ACTH/MSH 4–10. Peptides **2:** 197–206.

33. SAINT-COME, C., G. R. ACKER & F. L. STRAND. 1982. Peptide influences on the development and regeneration of motor performance. Peptides **3:** 439–449.

34. SAINT-COME, C., G. R. ACKER &F. L. STRAND. 1985. Development and regeneration of motor systems under the influence of ACTH peptides. Psychoneuroendocrinology **10:** 445–495.

35. ROSE, K. J., R. E. FRISCHER, J. A. KING & F. L. STRAND. 1988. Neonatal neuromuscular parameters vary in susceptibility to postnatal ACTH/MSH 4–10 administration. Peptides **9:** 151–156.

36. ROSE, K. & F. L. STRAND. 1988. Mammalian neuromuscular development accelerated with early but slowed with late gestational administration of ACTH peptides. Synapse **2:** 200–204.

37. PHOENIX, C. H., R. W. GOY, A. A. GERALL & W. C. YOUNG. 1959. Organizing action of prenatally administered testosterone propionate on the tissue mediating mating behavior in the female guinea pig. Endocrinology **65:** 369–382.

38. DAHLOF, L. G., E. HARD & K. LARSSON. 1977. Influence of maternal stress on offspring sexual behavior. Anim. Behav. **25:** 958–963.

39. GOTZ, F. & G. DORNER. 1980. Homosexual behavior in prenatally stressed male rats after castration and estrogen treatment in adulthood. Endocrinology **76:** 115–117.

40. HERRENKOHL, L. R. 1979. Prenatal stress reduces fertility and fecundity in female offspring. Science **206:** 1097–1098.

41. HERRENKOHL, L. R. 1986. Prenatal stress disrupts reproductive behavior and physiology in offspring. *In* Reproduction: A Behavioral and Neuroendocrine Perspective. B. R. Komisaruk, H. I. Siegel, M. F. Cheng & H. H. Feder, Eds. Vol. 474: 120–128. New York Academy of Sciences. New York, NY.

42. WARD, I. L. & O. B. WARD. 1985. Sexual behavior differentiation: Effects of prenatal manipulation in rats. *In* Handbook of Behavioral Neurobiology. N. Adler, D. Pfaff & R. W. Goy, Eds. 77–98. Plenum Press. New York, NY.

43. SEGARRA, A. & F. L. STRAND. 1989. Perinatal administration of nicotine alters subsequent sexual behavior and testosterone levels of male rats. Brain Res. **480:** 151–159.

44. RENNER, K. J. & V. N. LUINE. 1984. Determination of monoamines in brain nuclei by high performance liquid chromatography with electrochemical detection: Young vs. middle aged rats. Life Sci. **34:** 2193–2199.

45. RENNER, K. J., D. L. ALLEN & V. N. LUINE. 1986. Monoamine levels and turnover in brain: Relationship to priming actions of estrogen. Brain Res. Bull. **16:** 469–475.

46. McEWEN, B. S., I. LIEBERBURG, C. CHAPTAL & L. C. KREY. 1977. Aromatization: Important for sexual differentiation of the neonatal rat brain. Horm. Behav. **9:** 249–263.

47. McEwen, B. S. & D. W. Pfaff. 1985. Hormone effects on hypothalamic neurons: Analysing gene expression and neuromodulator action. TINS. March 1985. 105–110.
48. Raisman, G. & P. M. Field. 1973. Sexual dimorphism in the neuropil of the preoptic area of the rat and its dependence on neonatal androgen. Brain Res. **54:** 1–29.
49. Ward, I. L. 1972. Prenatal stress feminizes and demasculinizes the behavior of males. Science **175:** 82–84.
50. Rhees, R. W. & D. E. Fleming. 1981. Effects of malnutrition, maternal stress, or ACTH injections during pregnancy on sexual behavior of male offspring. Physiol. Behav. **27:** 879–882.
51. Ward, I. L. & J. Weisz. 1980. Maternal stress alters plasma testosterone in fetal males. Science **207:** 328–329.
52. Weisz, J. & I. L. Ward. 1980. Plasma testosterone and progesterone titers of pregnant rats, their male and female fetuses, and neonatal offspring. Endocrinology **106:** 306–316.
53. Krecek, J. 1973. Sex differences in salt taste: the effect of testosterone. Brain Res. **10:** 683–688.
54. Krecek, J., V. Novakova & K. Stibral. 1972. Sex differences in the taste preference for a salt solution in the rat. Physiol. Behav. **8:** 183–188.
55. Van der Helm-Hylkema, H. & D. De Wied. 1976. Effect of neonatally injected ACTH and ACTH analogues on eye opening of the rat. Life Sci. **18:** 1099–1104.
56. Malmnas, C. O. 1973. Monoaminergic influence on testosterone-activated copulatory behavior in the castrated male rat. Acta. Physiol. Scand. **395:** 1–128.
57. de Medinaceli, L., W. J. Freed & R. J. Wyatt. 1976. An index of the functional condition of rat sciatic nerve based on measurements made from walking tracks. Exp. Neurol. **77:** 634–643.
58. Strand, F. L. & T. T. Kung. 1980. ACTH accelerates recovery of neuromuscular function following crushing of peripheral nerve. Peptides **1:** 135–138.
59. Bijlsma, W. A., F. G. I. Jennekens, P. Schotman & W. H. Gispen. 1983. Stimulation by ACTH 4–10 of nerve fiber regeneration following sciatic nerve crush. Muscle & Nerve **6:** 102–110.
60. Verhaagen, J., P. M. Edwards, F. G. I. Jennekens, P. Schotman & W. H. Gispen. 1986. Melanocyte-stimulating hormone stimulates the outgrowth of myelinated nerve fibers after peripheral nerve crush. Exp. Neurol. **92:** 451–454.
61. Saint-Come, C. & F. L. Strand. 1985. ACTH 4–10 improves motor unit reorganization during peripheral nerve regeneration in the rat. Peptides 6(Suppl. 1): 77–83.
62. Strand, F. L., T. T. Kung & C. Saint-Come. 1981. Regenerative ability of spinal motor systems as influenced by ACTH/MSH peptides. *In* Functional Recovery from Brain Damage; Developments in Neuroscience. M. W. van Hof & G. Mohn, Eds. 369–409. Elsevier, North Holland, Amsterdam.
63. Flohr, H. & U. Luneburg. 1982. Effects of ACTH 4–10 on vestibular compensation. Brain Res. **248:** 169–173.
64. Luneberg, U. & H. Flohr. 1988. Effects of melanocortins on vestibular compensation. Prog. Brain Res. **76:** 421–429.
65. Isaacson, R. L. & A. Poplawsky. 1983. An ACTH 4–9 analog (Org 2766) speeds recovery from septal hyperemotionality in the rat. Behav. Neural. Biol. **39:** 52–59.
66. Isaacson, R. E. & A. Poplawsky. 1985. ACTH 4–10 produces a transient decrease in septal hyperemotionality. Behav. Neural Biol. **43:** 109–113.
67. Nyakis, C., H. D. Veldhuis & D. De Wied. 1985. Beneficial effect of chronic treatment with Org 2766 and α-MSH on impaired reversal learning of rats with bilateral lesions of their parafascicular area. Brain Res. Bull. **15:** 257–265.
68. Hershkowitz, M., D. Heron, D. Samuel & M. Shinitzky. 1982. The modulation of protein phosphorylation and receptor binding in synaptic membranes by changes in lipid fluidity: implications for aging. Prog. Brain Res. **56:** 419–434.
69. Tonnaer, J., M. Van Vugt & J. S. De Graaf. 1986. In vitro interaction of ACTH with rat brain muscarinic receptors. Peptides **7:** 425–429.
70. Rees, H. D., J. Verhoef, A. Witter, W. H. Gispen & D. De Wied. 1980. Autoradiographic studies with a behaviorally potent $^{3}$H-ACTH 4–9 analog in the brain after intraventricular injection in rats. Brain Res. Bull. **5:** 509–514.

71. DEKKER, A. J. A. M. & J. A. D. M. TONNAER. 1989. Binding of the neurotrophic peptide Org 2766 to rat spinal cord sections is affected by a sciatic nerve crush. Brain Res. **477:** 327–331.
72. FRISCHER, R. E., N. M. EL-KAWA & F. L. STRAND. 1985. ACTH peptides as organizers of neuronal patterns in development: Maturation of the rat neuromuscular junction as seen by scanning electron microscopy. Peptides **6**(Suppl. 2):13–18.
73. STRAND, F. L., A. CAYER, E. R. GONZALEZ & H. STOBOY. 1976. Peptide enhancement of neuromuscular function: Animal and clinical studies. Pharmacol. Biochem. Behav. **5:** 179–187.
74. KASTIN, A. J., R. D. OLSON, A. V. SCHALLY & D. H. COY. 1979. CNS effects of peripherally administered brain peptides. Life Sci. **25:** 401–414.
75. KASTIN, A. J., J. E. ZADINA, W. A. BANKS & M. V. GRAF. 1984. Misleading concepts in the field of brain peptides. Peptides **5**(Suppl. 1): 249–253.
76. VAN DER ZEE, C. E. E. M., J. H. BRAKKEE & W. H. GISPEN. 1988. α-MSH and Org.2766 in peripheral nerve regeneration: Different routes of delivery. Eur. J. Pharmacol. **147:** 351–357.
77. EDWARDS, P. M., R. R. F. KUITERS, G. J. BOER & W. H. GISPEN. 1986. Recovery from peripheral nerve transection is accelerated by local application of α-MSH by means of microporous Accurel® polypropylene tubes. J. Neurol. Sci. **74:** 171–176.
78. EDWARDS, P. M., C. E. E. M. VAN DER ZEE, J. VERHAAGEN, P. SCHOTMAN, F. G. I. JENNEKENS & W. H. GISPEN. 1984. Evidence that the neurotrophic actions of α-MSH may derive from its ability to mimic the actions of a peptide formed in degenerating nerve stumps. J. Neurol. Sci. **64:** 333–340.
79. VERHAAGEN, J., P. M. EDWARDS, F. G. I. JENNEKENS, P. SCHOTMAN & W. H. GISPEN. 1986. Melanocyte-stimulating hormone stimulates the outgrowth of myelinated nerve fibers after peripheral nerve crush. Exp. Neurol. **92:** 451–454.
80. GONZALEZ, E. R. & F. L. STRAND. 1981. Neurotropic action of ACTH/MSH 4–10 on neuromuscular function in hypophysectomized rats. Peptides **2**(Suppl. 1): 107–113.
81. KEIM, K., E. B. SIGG & F. L. STRAND. 1978. ACTH 1–24 influences contractility in rat atrial strip. Fed. Proc. **37:** 523.
82. KEIM, K. L. 1978. Effects of synthetic ACTH 1–24 and selected peptide fragments on rat heart. Ph.D. thesis. New York University.
83. ZEILER, R. H., F. L. STRAND & N. EL-SHERIF. 1982. Electrophysiological and contractile response of canine atrial tissues to adrenocorticotropin. Peptides **3:** 815–822.
84. VERGONA, R. A., F. L. STRAND & M. R. COHEN. 1985. ACTH 1–24 induced potentiation of norepinephrine contractile responses in aortic strips from spontaneously hypertensive (SH) and normotensive (WKY) rats. Peptides **6:** 581–584.
85. DE KONING, P., J. P. NEIJT, F. G. I. JENNEKENS & W. H. GISPEN. 1987. Org 2766 protects from cisplatin-induced neurotoxicity in rats. Exp. Neurol. **97:** 746–750.
86. VAN DER HOOP, R. G., P. DE KONING, E. BOVEN, J. P. NEIJT, F. G. I. JENNEKENS & W. H. GISPEN. 1988. Efficacy of the neuropeptide Org 2766 in the prevention and treatment of cisplatin-induced neurotoxicity in rats. Eur. J. Cancer Clin. Oncol. In press.

# Opioid Peptides and Perinatal Development: Is Beta-Endorphin a Natural Teratogen?

## Clinical Implications

CURT A. SANDMAN,[a] JENNIFER L. BARRON,
EDWARD M. DEMET, ALEKSANDRA CHICZ-DEMET,
STEPHEN J. ROTHENBERG,[b] AND FRANCISCO J. ZEA[b]

*Department of Psychiatry*
*University of California, Irvine Medical Center*
*State Developmental Research Institute*
*100 City Drive South*
*Orange, California 92668*
*and*
*[b]National Institute of Perinatology*
*Mexico City, Mexico*

Profound changes in brain organization can occur during critical periods of development[1] These critical periods generally correspond to epochs when the brain is undergoing critical transformations such as cell migration or receptor development. Since many of these events occur *in utero*, fetal changes in neurochemical state may have greater and longer lasting changes in brain organization than similar alterations in neonates or adults.

Although the fetus appears well-protected from many neurotoxic insults, it is vulnerable to the neurochemical responses of its mother. For instance, stressful or pleasurable experiences of the mother may have distinctive chemical signatures. As this signature circulates in a pregnant woman, providing information about the environment and giving instructions for action, it will interact with the placenta. The placenta may pass the signal through to the fetus or the signal may stimulate a receptor and initiate another series of signals. In either case, the fetal nervous system is bathed in the mother's chemical response to the environment. In this way, the environment contributes to the organization and disorganization of the brain during critical fetal periods. Because the endogenous opiate system proliferates in the second and third trimester of pregnancy,[2,3] it may make important contributions to brain development. The role of β-endorphin in early brain and behavioral organization will be examined and extended to possible consequences of opiate system disregulation.

### β-Endorphin and Perinatal Events

Over the course of gestation, β-endorphin levels increase in maternal plasma but decrease in amniotic fluid.[4-8] Genazzani *et al.*[9] reported the highest levels of amniotic

[a]Address for correspondence: Research 5A, Fairview Developmental Center, 2501 Harbor Blvd., Costa Mesa, CA 92626.

**TABLE 1.** Exclusion Criteria

| |
|---|
| Women |
|     1. Consumption of 1 or more alcoholic drinks/day |
|     2. Drug addiction or habitual use of any drug |
|     3. Under 15 or over 42 years of age |
|     4. Kidney disease, diabetes, or toxoplasmosis |
|     5. Psychosis |
| Infants |
|     1. Birthweight under 2000 grams |
|     2. APGAR at 5 minutes under 6 |
|     3. Gestation age under 36 weeks |
|     4. Serious birth defects |

β-endorphin in the first trimester (173 fmol/ml), decreasing to 75 fmol/ml in the second and to 14 fmol/ml in the third trimester. Maternal plasma values increase over the same time period. From the tenth week to term, plasma β-endorphin but not met-enkaphalin levels rise approximately 140%. These changes are not due to greater abundance of the prohormone, pro-opiomelanocortin (POMC), suggesting increased activity of enzymes.[10]

Maternal plasma levels of β-endorphin are significantly elevated during labor and increase to maximal levels at delivery.[11] Umbilical cord blood levels also are elevated at delivery, but to a lesser extent. Elevated endorphins in maternal plasma probably serve as an endogenous analgesic for the mother resulting from the pain of birth. Neonatal (cord) endorphins probably reflect fetal viability. For instance, Kofinas et al.[12] found that maternal β-endorphin was five-fold higher after vaginal compared with caesarean delivery. However, neonatal (cord) β-endorphin levels did not differ with the type of delivery but were higher than maternal levels in caesarean (i.e., complicated) deliveries. These findings suggest that maternal and neonatal sources for β-endorphin at birth are independently determined.

Endorphin levels also respond to perinatal complications, especially hypoxia.[6,13-17] Although maternal hypoxia (10% $O_2$ for 30 minutes) results in only small increases in plasma β-endorphin in pregnant sheep, circulating β-endorphin dramatically increases in the fetus (from 125 to 503 pg/ml).[18,19] Cord arterial samples are slightly higher than cord venous samples in complicated pregnancies suggesting a primary fetal contribution.[14] Arterial pH (acidosis, a marker of fetal hypoxia) is highly correlated (r = −0.83) with β-endorphin level. β-endorphin is elevated in infants with features of distress (lowered and flattened fetal heart rate) regardless of means of delivery.[16] Interestingly, arteriovenous ratio in cord plasma is higher in normal pregnancies, suggesting a contribution from the placenta. However, in the fetal distress group, the primary contribution is from arteries. Thus, during distress, the fetal contribution to cord β-endorphin levels increases.[14,16]

β-endorphin also is elevated in amniotic fluid during fetal distress. Gautry et al.[13] reported a 2–20-fold increase of immunoassayable β-endorphin-like activity in cases of fetal distress. β-endorphin concentration in amniotic fluid increases two-fold during the third trimester in women with premature labor and intrauterine growth retardation.[6]

*Comparison of Two Markers of Hypoxia*

The present study compares β-endorphin and another marker of perinatal hypoxia (hypoxanthine) in healthy mother/infant pairs. Hypoxanthine is elevated in hypoxic infants due to catabolism of ATP and generation of free radical neurotoxins. Only pregnant women and infants not at risk were selected (see TABLE 1). Complete histories from mothers were collected and the first blood samples drawn at twelve weeks of pregnancy. Women were followed every eight weeks up to 36 weeks of pregnancy and then weekly until delivery. Details of the assay have been reported elsewhere.[20]

Correlations among umbilical cord and maternal plasma β-endorphin and hypoxanthine are presented in TABLE 2. None of the correlations is statistically significant, ranging from $-0.04$ to $+0.24$ with sample sizes from $N = 40$ to $N = 49$. These data suggest several conclusions. First, it appears that maternal and cord β-endorphin are unrelated to maternal and cord hypoxanthine. Since both are used as markers of perinatal distress, they measure different phenomena. Second, consistent with the literature reviewed above, maternal and cord β-endorphin are not related ($r = 0.12$). Third, maternal and cord hypoxanthine are not significantly related. To our knowledge, this has not been examined previously.

**TABLE 2.** Correlations among Maternal and Umbilical Cord β-Endorphin and Hypoxanthine

|  | Cord β-Endorphin | Maternal Hypoxanthine | Cord Hypoxanthine |
|---|---|---|---|
| Maternal β-endorphin | 0.12(N = 43) | 0.10(N = 49) | −0.04(N = 41) |
| Cord β-endorphin |  | −0.10(N = 43) | 0.12(N = 43) |
| Maternal hypoxanthine |  |  | 0.24(N = 40) |

## Modeling the Markers

To understand these findings multivariate models were constructed for each marker. Women ($N = 32$) with vaginal delivery had higher concentrations of β-endorphin than women ($N = 21$) with caesarean (164.7 to 112.5 μg/ml). For cord concentrations, several variables were statistically related to β-endorphin. Of special interest was the highly significant relationship between β-endorphin and number of previous stillbirths and the marginal relationship with number of children dying before age one year. The variables predicting elevated hypoxanthine differ from those predicting β-endorphin. It is interesting that psychiatric factors (*i.e.*, anxiety, history of psychiatric illness) are related to elevated hypoxanthine, especially in mothers.

## Maternal Blood Pressure and β-Endorphin

In our sample, maternal blood pressure was measured in 25–30 (different numbers for the separate markers) normotensive women within one hour of delivery and correlated with β-endorphin and hypoxanthine. As presented in TABLE 3, systolic pressure was positively related to maternal β-endorphin but negatively to cord concentration. The difference between systolic and diastolic pressure was positively correlated with maternal levels of β-endorphin and hypoxanthine but negatively correlated with cord β-endorphin levels.

**TABLE 3.** Correlations among β-Endorphin, Hypoxanthine, and Maternal Blood Pressure

| | Maternal | | Infant | |
|---|---|---|---|---|
| | β-E | HYPO | β-E | HYPO |
| Systolic | 0.38* | 0.19 | −0.35 | 0.01 |
| Diastolic | 0.09 | −0.19 | −0.02 | −0.25 |
| Systolic-diastolic | 0.35* | 0.44* | −0.39* | 0.30 |

*$p < 0.05$.

### Summary of Perinatal Factors

β-endorphin increases in maternal plasma during pregnancy. Both maternal and fetal (cord) levels of β-endorphin increase in response to the stress of hypoxia. However, under "normal" circumstances there is a clear dissociation between maternal and fetal levels. Maternal levels relate to pain and cord levels to fetal viability. The source of endorphins in fetal plasma (umbilical vessels) is uncertain. The absence of an association between cord and maternal levels would argue against direct contributions by the mother, at least in risk-free birth. Two possibilities, the fetal pituitary,[21,22] and the placenta itself[23-25] remain to be tested.

The dissociation between two biochemical markers of perinatal hypoxia, β-endorphin and hypoxanthine, in both maternal and cord samples is surprising. Multivariate modeling described heuristic profiles unique for β-endorphin and hypoxanthine. Psychiatric variables predict both maternal and cord hypoxanthine levels. Maternal β-endorphin relates primarily to the stress of delivery. Cord opiates also correlate with stress of delivery, but most interestingly, with maternal history of fetal viability. The relationship of cord β-endorphin to fetal viability is a new and important possibility and supports a model[26] describing elevations of β-endorphin as an endogenous signal to abort the fetus.

Hypertension during pregnancy is a model system for examining the relationship between β-endorphin and hypoxia (and stress). Maternal hypertension can expose the fetus to extended periods of hypoxia by reducing respiratory reserve of the placenta[27-31] and has been reported as a risk factor in neurological complications, especially mental retardation.[32]

The relationship of maternal and cord β-endorphin to the difference in systolic and diastolic blood pressure is a promising new lead. Since the mothers were healthy and had blood pressure within normal limits, these findings suggest that β-endorphin may be remarkably sensitive to even subtle changes in the oxygen-carrying capacity of blood in pregnant women. The significance of the positive correlation of blood pressure with maternal β-endorphin and negative correlation with the cord sample may be a function of the risk-free sample. This possibility awaits further study in high-risk mother/infant pairs.

### β-Endorphin, Perinatal Hypoxia, and Autism

β-endorphin appears to be a marker of hypoxia, the most serious environmental complication of birth. Prenatal hypoxic-ischemic brain injury is believed to be the major cause of cerebral palsy[33-35] and of the common diagnosis in mental retardation of "unknown perinatal complication".[36-38] The studies of Windle[39-42] provide remarkable evidence that only seven minutes of oxygen deprivation produces permanent structural damage to the brain of primates. Developmental delay is almost always associated with asphyxiation. Permanent decrements in learning and memory often, but not always[43-44] are associated with milder oxygen deprivation in human patients even though evidence of structural damage may be absent.

A series of studies[36–38,45] in our laboratory provides linkage among hypoxia, β-endorphin, and developmentally delayed patients. An extremely high incidence of "paradoxical" excitement to sedative-hypnotic medication is observed in patients with autistic behavior (stereotypy and self-injurious behavior, SIB).[36] These autistic patients can be separated with 93%+ accuracy from similar patients who respond normally simply with a history of perinatal hypoxia.

*Two Questions*

Two questions evolve from these observations. First, are there long term changes in β-endorphin levels in patients exposed to perinatal hypoxia and presumably exposed to elevated opiates at a critical period? Second, if there is a long term sensitivity or tolerance to opiates, can the behavior be treated with opiates or opiate blockers? Following the lead of our earlier studies we have examined these questions in autistic-like patients with SIB.

1. *Is β-endorphin elevated in autistic patients?*

The endogenous opiate system is proposed as a possible biological substrate of autistic[46–48] and, specifically, self-injurious behavior.[20,45,49–54] However, reports of physiological measures of endogenous opiates are inconsistent. "Humoral" endorphin, a unique endogenous opiate, is decreased in plasma of neuroleptically treated autistic patients compared to normal controls.[55] β-endorphin levels in cerebrospinal fluid (CSF) does not differentiate autistic from normal children.[53] However, autistic children with SIB have significantly higher CSF β-endorphin levels than non-SIB patients. Sandman's[20] report that patients with SIB and/or stereotypy have higher levels of β-endorphin than hospitalized control patients contributes to the confusion (TABLE 4). The following results are an extension of the preliminary data and compare normal control subjects, patient controls, and autistic patients without SIB or stereotypy.

Plasma concentration of β-endorphin for both morning and evening samples are significantly lower for patient controls than normal controls (see FIG. 1). Cortisol concentrations are not different for the groups at either sampling period. Similar results are obtained when normal controls are compared with all patients exhibiting stereotypy or SIB. Both morning and evening plasma β-endorphin levels are lower in the the patient groups. Plasma cortisol concentration is not different among the groups. However, compared with the patient controls, concentration of plasma β-endorphin is elevated in the SIB and stereotypy patients (FIG. 2). The most severe patients have the highest β-endorphin levels. Cortisol concentration is not different even in these groups.

The correlation between β-endorphin and cortisol is significant and positive in the normal controls. Roughly a 25% covariation exists between β-endorphin and cortisol. This relationship is not significant in the patient controls or any of the other patient groups (FIG. 3).

TABLE 4. Endorphin, SIB, and Autism

| Name | Year | Number of Patients | Results |
|------|------|--------------------|---------|
| Wiezman *et al.*[55] (plasma) | 1984 | 12 | autism lower |
| Gillberg *et al.*[53] (CSF) | 1985 | 20+ | SIB higher |
| Sandman[20] (plasma) | 1988 | 20+ | SIB higher (patients) |
|  |  |  | SIB lower (norms) |

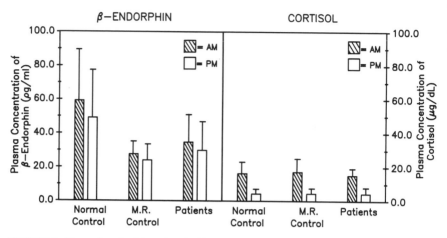

**FIGURE 1.** Plasma β-endorphin and cortisol levels in normal controls (N = 17), mentally retarded (MR) control patients (N = 13), and autistic-like patients (N = 40). The bars reflect one standard deviation.

A tentative "yes" is suggested to the question "Is β-endorphin elevated in autism?" β-endorphin is elevated in plasma and CSF[53] of subgroups of autistic patients, especially those with SIB. Since cortisol levels are not different among the groups, elevation of β-endorphin in SIB and stereotypy cannot be explained by general pituitary-adrenal dysfunction or increased stress levels. This finding is suggestive of either unique opiate receptor sensitivity in SIB and stereotypy, or a dissociation between two POMC products. Although cortisol is not a direct POMC fragment, its release is stimulated by the POMC fragment, ACTH. A dissociation of β-endorphin and ACTH can result from specific

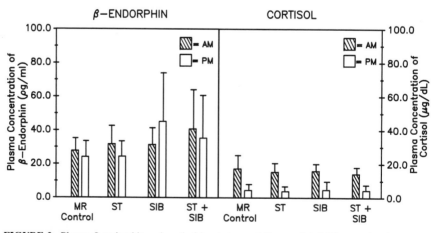

**FIGURE 2.** Plasma β-endorphin and cortisol levels in mentally retarded (MR) control patients (N = 13), patients with stereotypy (ST, N = 17), patients with self-injury (SIB, N = 9), and patients with ST and SIB (N = 14). Bars reflect one standard deviation.

enzyme activity either to cleave the peptides from POMC or to degrade the active fragment after its release.

These results may resolve the apparent contradiction illustrated in TABLE 4. Wiezman *et al.*[55] reported that autistic patients had lower plasma concentrations of humoral endorphin than healthy controls. Gillberg *et al.*[53] found that autistic patients with SIB had higher levels of β-endorphin than patient controls. The current study suggests that both studies are correct and the choice of comparison groups accounts for the differences between them.

Support is provided for the two central opiate hypotheses of SIB. One hypothesis is that SIB reflects an insensitivity to pain and perhaps a general sensory depression.[20,36–38,45,48,50,54,56] The strongest evidence in support of this hypothesis is the attenuation of SIB with opiate blockers (see below). The observations that opiate blockers reverse congenital insensitivity to pain[57,58] and hypothalamic dysfunction coexisting with elevated pain threshold[59] are consistent with an extensive animal literature demonstrating the hyperalgesic influence of naloxone.[60,61] However, it is plausible that naloxone attenuates SIB by blocking opiate-mediated euphorogenic effects. In this context, the purpose of SIB is pain-induced release of opiates. An opiate "high" might be stimulated by SIB (pain releases β-endorphin). In this analysis SIB is an addiction, since it is maintained to supply the "fix" for tolerant, down-regulated opiate receptors. This possibility is supported by findings that repeated β-endorphin administration results in tolerance,[62,63] physical dependence,[64] and euphoric-like effects.[65]

*2. Can autistic patients with SIB be treated with opiate blockers?*

The strongest evidence linking the opiate system to autism is attenuation of SIB by blocking the opiate receptor. There are six studies of naloxone and four studies of naltrexone in the literature describing the effects on autistic and/or SIB (see TABLE 5). In most cases the salutary effects are dose dependent. We examined dosage effects on a range of behaviors in four patients exhibiting SIB.

Fixed doses (0, 25, 50, or 100 mg) of naltrexone are given at 0800 two days/week (Monday and Wednesday) in a double blind design. All of the patients have a long history of SIB, perinatal complications, and ineffective interventions. The patients are evaluated daily for frequency and severity of SIB, duration of stereotypy, and level of activity.

Naltrexone significantly attenuated SIB in all of the patients (FIG. 4). The effect is dose dependent in three patients; the 100-mg dose produced the largest decrease in SIB. However RM (the smallest patient, thus receiving the largest mg/kg dose), responded favorably to 25 and 50 mg but not 100 mg. There is no consistent effect of naltrexone on stereotypy, activity, daily behavior, or general measures of functioning.

The reduction in SIB with naltrexone treatment is consistent with previous naloxone studies[45,50–52] and nearly identical with the dose-dependent reduction in SIB by naltrexone.[66] Parallel analysis of other behaviors indicated that naltrexone was specific for SIB. The most self-abusive patient was most sensitive to naltrexone. MC has extremely high rates of SIB during placebo periods, but his SIB is eliminated for one week (during observation) when given 100 mg. In addition, only MC showed positive changes after naltrexone in stereotypy, activity, and measures of daily behavior. This observation is consistent with Herman's *et al.*[66] observations.

The suggestion that patients with severe SIB have greater sensitivity to opiate blockers may favor the subsensitive (addiction) hypothesis. However, the effects of naltrexone and naloxone are not restricted to the opiate receptor (see REF. 71), and the fate of the opiate receptor may be complicated by perinatal factors.[20,72] Nevertheless, opiate blockers appear to be very powerful tools for examination of SIB. Although there is evidence of a dose-response effect, very small doses can control the behavior. The effectiveness of small doses may favor a supersensitive opiate receptor in this syndrome. Supersensitive opiate receptors are most compatible with the sensory modulation (*i.e.*, pain) hypothesis.

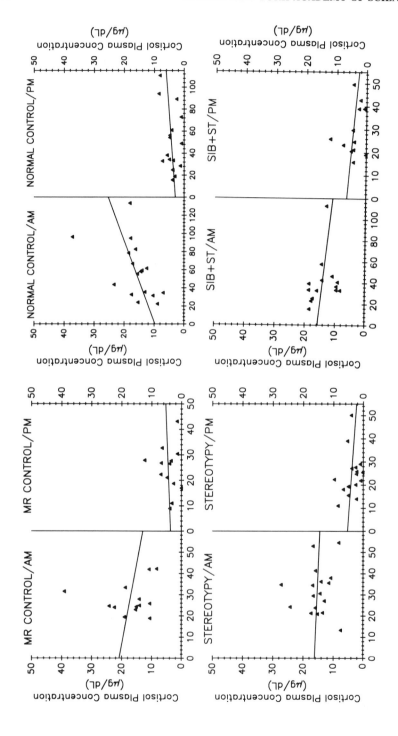

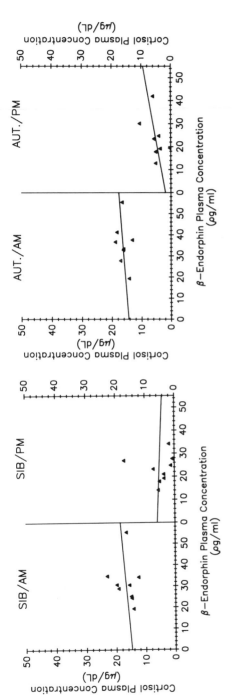

**FIGURE 3.** Scatter plots of correlations between β-endorphin and cortisol in morning and evening. Only values for normal controls are significant.

**TABLE 5.** Studies with Naloxone and Naltrexone

| Name | Year | Number of Patients | Results |
|------|------|--------------------|---------|
| Naloxone | | | |
| Davidson et al.[50] | 1983 | 1 | positive |
| Richardson and Zaleski[51] | 1983 | 1 | positive |
| Sandman et al.[45] | 1983 | 2 | positive |
| Sandyk[52] | 1985 | 1 | positive |
| Sandman et al.[49] | 1987 | 1 | positive |
| Beckwith et al.[88] | 1986 | 2 | negative |
| Bernstein et al.[68] | 1987 | 1 | positive |
| Naltrexone | | | |
| Syzmanski et al.[69] | 1987 | 2 | negative |
| Herman et al.[66] | 1987 | 3 | positive |
| Campbell et al.[67] | 1988 | 7 | positive (5) |
| Sandman[20] | 1988 | 4 | positive |
| Leboyer et al.[70] | 1988 | 2 | positive |

Since opiate blockers lower sensory threshold,[49,73] it is plausible that naltrexone attenuates SIB because it lowers the threshold for pain.

*Summary of β-endorphin and Developmental Delay*

β-endorphin is elevated in autistic patients with SIB. Opiate receptor blockade in these patients attenuates this otherwise untreatable behavior. Thus, there is sufficient evidence to warrant the conclusion that the opiate system is implicated in severe neurodevelopmental disorders. If these behaviors have roots in perinatal complications and early exposure of the nervous system to elevated β-endorphin, early treatment of the opiate system is suggested. Such treatments are effective in adults and may be even more dramatic when applied to the developing nervous system. Early identification of perinatal difficulties may provide treatment opportunities during critical periods.

## CONCLUSION

The major points are:

1. β-Endorphin increases in maternal plasma during pregnancy and peaks at delivery.
2. β-Endorphin increases in amniotic fluid and cord blood with perinatal complications, especially hypoxia.
3. Fetuses exposed to elevated β-endorphin have delayed patterns of behavior and changes in neural organization.
4. SIB in conjunction with paradoxical responding to sedative-hypnotics is significantly related to perinatal complications, especially hypoxia.
5. Patients with SIB may have elevated levels of β-endorphin in plasma and CSF.
6. SIB can be significantly attenuated with opiate blockers.

### Extending the Conclusions

The studies conducted in our laboratory and those reviewed are intended to address the larger question, ''Is β-endorphin a final common pathway for the effects of hypoxia (and stress) on the developing nervous system?'' As suggested above, maternal hypertension can be a model system for exploring this hypothesis. Hypoxia results from severe hypertension (preclampsia and eclampsia) by reducing the respiratory reserve of the placenta. We presented preliminary evidence in this report that maternal blood pressure even in normotensive women is significantly related to maternal and cord plasma β-endorphin. If this system is a valid model for exploring the relationships proposed, it may be extended even further.

For instance, the incidence of concurrent (stress-related) hypertension with pregnancy is at least 20% of problem pregnancies due to hypertension.[29] Since elegant descriptions characterize the relationship between stress and physiological maladaption such as hypertension,[74,75] the model is extended (FIG. 5) to suggest that stress contributes to pregnancy outcome. In our model, the solid lines are relationships based upon research findings and the dotted lines are inferred or indirect relationships. The evidence supports three major conclusions. First, β-endorphin serves as a final common pathway for the effects of hypoxia on the fetus. Second, maternal hypertension, working through the endorphinergic system influences neural and behavioral outcome. Third, stress, independent of hypertension, influences pregnancy outcome.

Positing an endorphinergic mechanism for the effects of stress on the fetus and on infant outcome explains interesting findings in the literature. For instance, several studies have reported that the experience of stress by pregnant women predicts obstetric complications. Increases in stress (fear, dependency, etc.) correlate with decreased APGARs and delivery complications.[76] Women with more life change events (a quantifiable index of stress), elevated anxiety,[77-79] and unfavorable psychosocial conditions[80] are at risk for abnormal pregnancies. Negative attitude[81] and fear[82] about having children result in higher incidents of perinatal death, congenital anomaly, and lowered APGARs. Furthermore, taken singly, these factors are not predictive of complications.[80] In a study of 114 women, Andreoli *et al.*[79] found that uncontrolled life change events during the second trimester (though third was not fairly assessed) were significantly greater in complicated pregnancies.

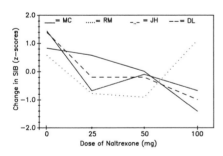

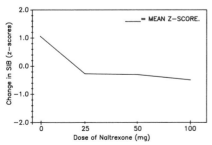

FIGURE 4. Normalized scores for change in SIB when challenged with naltrexone for four patients (*top panel*) and for averages (*bottom panel*).

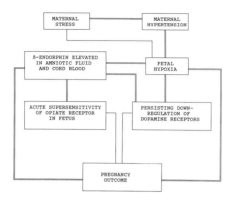

**FIGURE 5.** Proposed model for endorphenergic influence of maternal hypertension on pregnancy outcome. *Double lines* are connections firmly established and *single lines* are inferred relationships.

A further extension suggests that psychological factors such as life-related stress, either perceived or expected, influence fetal development (FIG. 6). The effects of stress are not constant and some women are more susceptible than others. The vulnerability buffer (social support, etc.) can protect the woman from the effects of stress. If this buffer is weak, maladaptive responses (*e.g.*, overproduction of peptides, hypertension, etc.) are stimulated. The placenta is a barrier for many teratogenic agents, but it may actively participate in the passage of β-endorphin to the fetus. The stress signal from the mother (*i.e.*, increased β-endorphin) may be detected by receptors on the placenta for a cascade of events including the synthesis and release of β-endorphin into the fetal environment, resulting in perinatal complications. Evolutionarily, this system may exist to protect the fetus from surviving in a hostile environment and is an abortion process triggered by environmental events. However, because of advances in medicine, the fetus survives and suffers neurological, cognitive, and behavioral deficits.

The model suggests new areas for intervention and opens the question of whether perinatal β-endorphin levels merely "mark" distress or whether β-endorphin actually is the cause of neurological difficulties. If β-endorphin is *the* major common pathway for stress-hypoxia-linked perinatal complications, blocking this system may have positive effects on outcome even in the presence of hypoxic conditions. The dramatic study of Chernick and Craig[83] suggests that endogenous opiates are *the* cause of neurological complications related to hypoxia. Pregnant rabbits were either pretreated with naloxone or placebo and then asphyxiated. The pups were delivered by caesarean section. Pups borne to naloxone pretreated mothers were viable but the placebo-pretreated pups were not. An equally compelling clinical study by Goodlin[84] suggested that fetal distress could be reversed by maternal injections of naloxone. Naloxone given to eight women when fetuses displayed intrapartum flat fetal heart rate (an index of hypoxia) produced normal beat-to-beat variability within twenty minutes. These findings add further support for the critical role of β-endorphin in mediating the effects of hypoxia and perhaps stress during fetal development. Thus, the model not only describes possible etiological links between stress and pregnancy outcome but also intervention "windows" for mitigating the effects of endorphin-related outcome.

Finally, a neuronal model is presented (FIG. 7). Fetal exposure to β-endorphin results in supersensitive opiate[85,86] and subsensitive dopamine[87] postsynaptic receptors. The persisting quality of this phenomenon, especially with the dopamine system, reflects the absence of receptor plasticity. This implies that the nervous system is permanently limited in its range of responses to stimulation. Because behavioral and pharmacological rigidity often characterize the profile of survivors of perinatal complications, the hypothesis of receptor rigidity is appealing. Several possible mechanisms contributing to this effect are suggested in the model, including altered synthesis of POMC, delayed degradation of β-endorphin either intracellularly or in the synaptic cleft, and presynaptic disinhibition of dopamine by endorphin. As oversimplified by the model, the opiate system may affect the brain and behavior both as a primary transmitter and as a modulator of other transmitters such as dopamine. This analysis coupled with the growing literature relating dopamine with β-endorphin (see REFS. 20,26 for reviews) suggests that developmental disorders

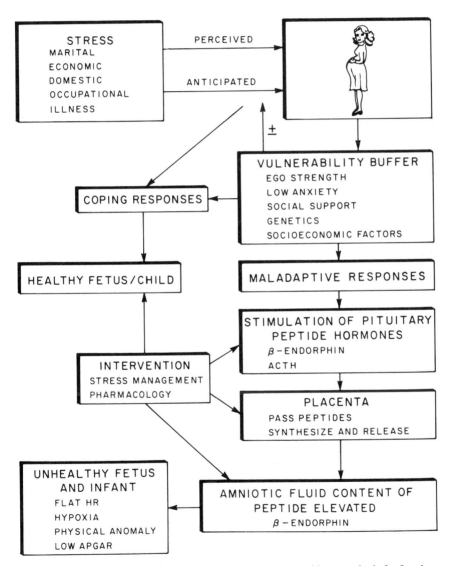

**FIGURE 6.** Biopsychological model of stress on pregnant women with a central role for β-endorphin.

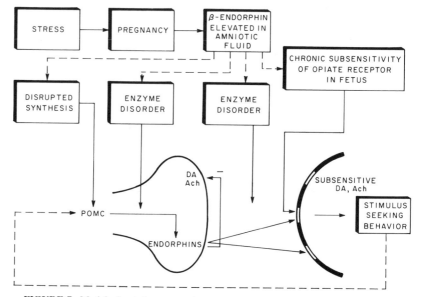

**FIGURE 7.** Model of putative neuronal events associated with stressful pregnancy.

ascribed to dopamine disregulation may have their roots, with varied expression, in hypoxic episodes. In summary, an endogenous teratogen, β-endorphin may be a final common pathway for the effects on the fetus of hypoxia and other stress-related complications of pregnancy.

## REFERENCES

1. PHOENIX, C. H., R. W. GOY, A. A. GERALL & W. D. YOUNG. 1959. Organizing action of prenatally administered testosterone propionate on the tissue mediating mating behavior in the female guinea pig. Endocrinology **65:** 369–382.
2. KENT, J. L., C. B. PERT & M. HERKENHAM. 1982. Ontogeny of opiate receptors in rat forebrain: Visualization by in vitro autoradiography. Dev. Brain Res. **2:** 487–504.
3. ALLESSI, N. E., H. KHACHATURIAN, S. WATSON & H. AKIL. 1983. Postnatal ontogeny of acetylated and non-acetylated β-endorphin in rat pituitary. Life Sci. **33:** 57–60.
4. BROWNING, A. J. F., W. R. BUTT, S. S. LYNCH & R. A. SHAKESPEAR. 1983. Maternal plasma concentrations of beta-lipotrophin, beta-endorphin, and gamma-lipotrophin throughout pregnancy. Br. J. Obstet. Gynaecol. **90:** 1147–1151.
5. WILKES, M. M., R. D. STEWART, J. F. BRUNI, M. D. QUIGLEY, S. S. C. YEN, N. LING & M. CHRETIEN. 1980. A specific homologous radioimmunoassay for human β-endorphin: Direct measurement in biological fluids. J. Clin. Endocrinol. Metab. **50:** 309–315.
6. DIVERS, W. S., R. D. STEWART, M. M. WOLKES & S. S. C. YEN. 1982. Amniotic fluid, β-endorphin and α-melanocyte-stimulating hormones immunoreactivity in normal and complicated pregnancies. Am. J. Obstet. Gynecol. **144:** 539–546.
7. EVANS, M. I., A. M. FISHER, A. G. ROBICHAUX, R. S. STATON, D. ROBARD, J. W. LARSEN & A. B. MUKHERJEE. 1985. Plasma and red blood cell β-endorphin immunoreactivity in normal and complicated pregnancies. Am. J. Obstet. Gynecol. **151:** 433–437.
8. NEWNHAM, J. P., S. TOMLIN, S. J. RATTERS, G. L. BOURNE & L. H. REES. 1983. Endogenous opioid peptides in pregnancy. Br. J. Obstet. Gynaecol. **90:** 535–538.
9. GENNAZZANI, A. R., F. PETRAGLIA, D. PARRINI, A. NASI, G. ARGIONI & F. FACCHINETTI.

1984. Lack of correlation between amniotic fluid and maternal plasma contents of beta endorphin, beta lipotropin and adrenocorticotropin hormone in normal and pathologic pregnancies. Am. J. Obstet. Gynecol. **148:** 198–203.

10.  LIS, M. , J. JULESZ, V. M. SENICAS, E. HAMILTON, T. PERRY, K. HERMANN & D. HEINRICH. 1983. N-terminal peptide of pro-opiomelanocortin in human amniotic fluid. Am. J. Obstet. Gynecol. **146**(5): 575–579.

11.  CSONTOS, K., M. RUST, V. HOLLT, W. MAHR, W. KROMER & H. J. TESCHEMACHER. 1979. Elevated plasma β-endorphin levels in pregnant women and their neonates. Life Sci. **25:** 835.

12.  KOFINAS, G. D., A. D. KOFINAS & F. M. TAVAKOLI. 1985. Maternal and fetal β-endorphin release in response to the stress of labor and delivery. Am. J. Obstet. Gynecol. **152**(1):56–59.

13.  GAUTRAY, J. P., A. JOLIET, J. P. VIELH & R. GUILLEMIN. 1977. Presence of immunoassayable β-endorphin in human amniotic fluid: Elevation in cases of fetal distress. Am. J. Obstet. Gynecol. **123:** 211–212.

14.  WARDLAW, S. L., R. I. STARK, L. BOCI & A. G. FRANTZ. 1979. Plasma β-endorphin and β-lipotropin in the human fetus at delivery: Correlation with arterial pH and pO2. J. Clin. Endocrinol. Metab. **79:** 888–891.

15.  GOLAND, R. S., S. L. WARDLAW, R. I. STARK & A. G. FRANTZ. 1981. Human plasma β-endorphin during pregnancy, labor, and delivery. J. Clin. Endocrinol. Metab. **52:** 74–78.

16.  SHAABAN, M. M., T. T. HONG, D. I. HOFFMAN, R. A. LOBO & U. GOEBELSMANN. 1982. Beta-endorphin and beta-lipotropin concentrations in umbilical cord blood. Am. J. Obstet. Gynecol. **144:** 560–568.

17.  DAVIDSON, S., I. GIL-AD, H. ROGOVIN, Z. LARON & S. H. REISNER. 1987 Cardiorespiratory depression and plasma β-endorphin levels in low-birthweight infants during the first day of life. Am. J. Diseases Child. **141:** 145–148.

18.  WARDLAW, S. L., R. I. STARK, S. DANIEL & A. G. FRANTZ. 1981. Effects of hypoxia on β-lipotropin release in fetal, newborn and maternal sheep. Endocrinology **108:** 1710–1715.

19.  STARK, R. I., S. L. WARDLAW, S. S. DANIEL, M. K. HUSAIN, U. M. SANOKA, L. S. JAMES & R. L. VANDE WIELE. 1982. Vasopressin secretion induced by hypoxia in sheep: Developmental changes and relationship to β-endorphin release. Am. J. Obstet. Gynecol. **143:** 204–215.

20.  SANDMAN, C. A. 1988. β-endorphin disregulation in autistic and self-injurious behavior: A neurodevelopmental hypothesis. Synapse **2:** 193–199.

21.  FACHINETTI, F., F. BAGNOLI, R. BRACCI & A. R. GENAZZANI. 1982. Plasma opioids in the first hours of life. Pediatr. Res. **16:** 95–99.

22.  BRUBAKER, P. L., A. C. BAIRD, H. P. BENNET, C. A. BROWNE & S. SOLOMON. 1982. Corticotropic peptides in the human fetal pituitary. Endocrinology **111:** 115–1154.

23.  NAKAI, Y., K. NAKAO, S. OKI & H. IMURA. 1978. Presence of immunoreactive β-lipotropin and β-endorphin in human placenta. Life Sci. **23:** 2013.

24.  FRAIOLI, F. & A. R. GENAZZANI. 1980. Human placental β-endorphin. Gynecol. Obstet. Invest. **11:** 37–42.

25.  ODAGIRI, E., B. J. SHERELL, C. D. MOUNT, W. E. NICHOLSON & D. N. ORTH. 1979. Human placental immunoreactive corticotropin, beta-lipotropin, and beta-endorphin: Evidence for a common precursor. Proc. Natl. Acad. Sci. USA **76:** 2027–2031.

26.  SANDMAN, C. A. & A. J. KASTIN. Neuropeptide modulation of development and behavior: Implications for Psychopathology. *In* Application of Basic Neuroscience to Child Psychiatry. S. Deutsch, A. Weizman & R. Weisman, Eds. Plenum Press. New York, NY. In press.

27.  ZUSPAN, F. P. 1981. *In* Toxemia of Pregnancy in Gynecology and Obstetrics. F. Sciara, Ed. Vol. 2: 44, 1–20. Harper and Ross. New York, NY.

28.  DAVIDSON, J. M. & M. D. LINDHEIMAR. 1981. *In* Hypertension in Pregnancy. F. Sciarra, Ed. Vol. 1: 1–28. Harper and Ross. New York, NY.

29.  WELT, S. I. & M. D. CRENSHAW. 1978. Concurrent hypertension and pregnancy. Clin. Obstet. Gynecol. **21:** 619–648.

30.  DUNLOP, T. C. H. 1966. Chronic hypertension and perinatal. Proc. R. Soc. Med. **59:** 838.

31.  ALVAREZ, R. A. 1973. Hypertensive disorders in pregnancy. Clin. Obstet. Gynecol. **16:** 47–71.

32.  SALOMEN, J. J. & O. P. HERMONEN 1984. Mental retardation and mother's hypertension during pregnancy. J. Ment. Defic. Res. **28:** 53–56.

33. CROTHERS, B. S. & R. S. PAINE. 1959. *The Natural History of Cerebral Palsy*. Harvard University Press, Cambridge, MA.
34. HILL, A. & J. J. VOLPE. 1981. Seizures, hypoxic-ischemic brain injury and intraventricular hemmorhage in the newborn. Ann. Neurol. **10**: 109–121.
35. JOHNSTON, M. V. 1983. Neurotransmitter alteration in a model of prenatal hypoxic-ischemic brain injury. Ann. Neurol. 511–518.
36. BARRON, J. L. & C. A. SANDMAN. 1983. Relationship of sedative-hypnotic response to self-injurious behavior and stereotypy in mentally retarded clients. Am J. Ment. Defic. **2**: 177–186.
37. BARRON, J. L. & C. A. SANDMAN. 1984. Self-injurious behavior and stereotypy in an institutionalized mentally retarded population. Appl. Res. Ment. Retard. **5**: 81–93.
38. BARRON, J. L. & C. A. SANDMAN. 1985. Paradoxical excitement to sedative-hypnotics in mentally retarded clients. Am. J. Ment. Defic. **2**: 124–129.
39. WINDLE, W. F. 1966. An experimental approach to prevention or reduction of the brain damage of birth asphyxia. Dev. Med. Child Neurol. **8**: 129–140.
40. WINDLE, W. F. 1967. Brain damage at birth. J. Am. Med. Assoc. **206**: 1967–1972.
41. DAWES, G. S., E. HIBBARD & W. F. WINDLE. 1964. The effect of alkali and glucose infusion on permanent brain damage in rhesus monkeys asphyxiated at birth. J. Pediatr. **65**: 801–806.
42. SECHZER, J. A., M. D. FARO, J. N. BARKER, D. BARSEY, S. GUTIERREZ & W. F. WINDLE. 1971. Developmental behaviors: Delayed appearance in monkeys asphyxiated at birth. Science **171**: 1173–1175.
43. BROMAN, S. H. 1979. Perinatal anoxia and cognitive development in early childhood. *In* Infants Born at Risk. T. Field, A. M. Sostek, S. Goldberg, Eds. 25. Spectrum Books. New York, NY.
44. LOW, J. A., R. S. GALBREATH, D. W. MUIR, H. L. KELLEN, E. A. PATER & E. J. KARCHMAN. 1984. Factors associated with motor and cognitive deficits in children after intrapartum fetal hypoxia. Am. J. Obstet. Gynecol. **148**: 533–539.
45. SANDMAN, C. A., P. DATTA, J. L. BARRON, F. HOEHLER, C. WILLIAMS & J. SWANSON. 1983. Naloxone attenuates self-abusive behavior in developmentally disabled clients. Appl. Res. Ment. Retard. **4**: 5–11.
46. PANKSEPP, J. 1979. A neurochemical theory of autism. Trends Neurosci. **2**: 174–177.
47. PANKSEPP, J., R. CONNER, P. K. FORISTER, P. BISHOP & J. P. SCOTT. 1983. Opioid effects on social behavior of kennel dogs. Appl. Anim. Psychol. **10**: 63–74.
48. DEUTSCH, S. I. 1986. Rationale for the administration of opiate antagonists in treating infantile autism. Am. J. Ment. Defic. **90**: 631–635.
49. SANDMAN, C. A., J. L. BARRON, F. M. CRINELLA & J. F. DONNELLY. 1987. Influence of naloxone on brain and behavior of a self-injurious woman. Biol. Psychiatr. **22**: 899–906.
50. DAVIDSON, P. W., B. M. KLEENE, M. CARROLL & R. J. ROCKOWITZ. 1983. Effects of naloxone on self-injurious behavior: A case study. Appl. Res. Ment. Retard. **4**: 1–4.
51. RICHARDSON, J. S. & W. A. ZALESKI. 1983. Naloxone and self-mutilation. Biol. Psychiatr. **18**: 99–101.
52. SANDYK, R. 1985. Naloxone abolished self-injuring in a mentally retarded child. Ann. Neurol. **17**: 520.
53. GILLBERG, C., L. TERENIUS & G. LONNERHOIM. 1985. Endorphin activity in childhood psychosis. Arch. Gen. Psychiatr. **42**: 780–783.
54. FARBER, J. M. 1987. Psychopharmacology of self-injurious behavior in the mentally retarded. J. Am. Acad. Adol. Psychiat. **26**:296–302.
55. WEIZMAN, R., A. WEIZMAN, S. TYANO, B. A. SZEKELY & Y. SARNE. 1984. Humoral-endorphin blood levels in autistic, schizophrenic and healthy subjects. Psychopharmacology **82**: 368–370.
56. CATALDO, M. F. & J. HARRIS. 1982. The biological basis for self-injury in the mentally retarded. Anal. Intervention Dev. Disabil. **2**: 21–39.
57. DEHEN, H., J. C. WILLER, F. BOUREAU & J. CAMBIER. 1977. Congenital insensitivity to pain, and endogenous morphine-like substances. Lancet **2**: 293–294.
58. PIRODSKY, D. M., J. L. GIBBS, R. A. HESSE, M. C. HSIEH, R. B. KRAUSE & W. H. RODRIGUEZ. 1985. Use of dexamethasone suppression test to detect depressive disorders of mentally retarded individuals. Am. J. Ment. Defic. **92**: 245–252.

59. DUNGER, D. B., J. V. LEONARD, O. H. WOLFF & M. A. PREECE. 1980. Effect of naloxone in a previously undescribed hypothalamic syndrome. Lancet 1277–1281.
60. SANDMAN, C. A., R. F. McGIVERN, C. BERKA, J. M. WALKER, D. H. COY & A. J. KASTIN. 1979. Neonatal administration of β-endorphin produces "chronic" insensitivity to thermal stimulus. Life Sci. **25:** 1755–1760.
61. GREVERT, P. & A. GOLDSTEIN. 1977. Effect of naloxone experimentally induced ischemic pain and on mood in human subjects. Proc. Natl. Acad. Sci. USA **74:** 1291–1294.
62. LAL, H. 1975. Narcotic dependence, narcotic action, and dopamine receptors. Life Sci. **17:** 483–496.
63. MADDEN, J. IV, H. AKIL, R. L. PATRICK & J. D. BARCHAS. 1977. Stress-induced parallel changes in central opioid levels and pain responsiveness in the rat. Nature **265:** 358–360.
64. WEI, E. & H. LOH. 1976. Physical dependence of opiate-like peptides. Science **193:** 1242–1243.
65. BELLUZZI, J. D. & L. STEIN. 1977. Enkephalin may mediate euphoria and drive-reduction reward. Nature **266:** 556–558.
66. HERMAN, B. H., M. K. HAMMOCK, A. ARTHUR-SMITH, J. EGAN, I. CHATOOR, A. WERNER & N. ZELNIK. 1987. Naltrexone decreases self-injurious behavior. Ann. Neurol. **22:** 550–552.
67. CAMPBELL, M., P. ADAMS, A. M. SMALL, L. M. TESCH & E. L. CURRENS. 1988. Naltrexone in infantile autism. Psychopharmacol. Bull. **24:** 135–139.
68. BERNSTEIN, G. A., J. R. HUGHES, J. R. MITCHELL & T. THOMPSON. 1987. Effects of narcotic antagonists on self-injurious behavior: A sample case study. J. Am. Acad. Child Adolesc. Psychiatr. **26:** 886–889.
69. SZYMANSKI, L., J. KEDESDY, S. SULKES, A. CUTLER & P. STEVENS-OUR. 1987. Naltrexone in treatment of self injurious behavior: A clinical study. Res. Dev. Disabil. **8:** 179–190.
70. LEBOYER, M., M. P. BOUVARD & M. DUGAS. 1988. Effects of naltrexone on infantile autism. Lancet 715.
71. FEIGENBAUM, J. & J. YANAI. 1985. The role of dopaminergic mechanisms in mediating the central behavioral effects of morphine in rodents. Neuropsychobiology **11:** 98–105.
72. SAHLEY, T. L. & J. PANKSEPP. 1987. Brain opioids and autism: An updated analysis of possible linkages. J. Autism Dev. Disord. 201–216.
73. ARNSTEN, A. F. T., D. S. SEGAL, H. B. NEVILLE, S. A. HILLYARD, D. S. JANOWSKY, L. L. JUDD & F. S. BLOOM. 1983. Naloxone augments electrophysiological signs of selective attention in man. Nature **304:** 725–727.
74. AXELROD, J. & T. D. REISINE. 1984. Stress hormones: Their interaction and regulation. Science **224:** 452–459.
75. SELYE, H. 1956. The Stress of Life. McGraw-Hill. New York, NY.
76. ERICKSON, M. T. 1976. The relationship between variables and specific complications of pregnancy, labor, and delivery. J. Psychosom. Res. **20:** 207–210.
77. GORSUCH, R. L. & M. K. KEY. 1974. Abnormalities of pregnancies as a function of anxiety and life stress. Psychosom. Med. **36:** 352–362.
78. BROWN, W. A., T. MANNING & J. GRODIN. 1972. The relationship of antenatal and perinatal psychological variables to the use of drugs in labor. Psychosom. Med. **34:** 119–127.
79. ANDREOLI, C., G. MAGNI & R. RIZZARDO. 1984. Stressful life events, anxiety and obstetric complications. *In* Endorphins, Neuroregulators and Behavior in Human Reproduction. P. Pancheri, L. Zichella & P. Falsachi, Eds. 297–304. Excerpta Medica. Amsterdam.
80. NUCKOLLS, K. B., J. CASSEL & B. H. KAPLAN. 1972. Psychosocial assets, life crisis, and the prognosis of pregnancy. Am. J. Epidemiol. **95**(5): 431–441.
81. LUAKARAN, V. H. & B. J. VAN DE BERG. 1980. The relationship of maternal attitude to pregnancy outcomes and obstetric complications. Am. J. Obstet. Gynecol. **136:** 374–379.
82. LEDERMAN, E., R. P. LEDERMAN, B. A. WORK & D. S. McCANN. 1981. Maternal psychobiological and physiological correlates of fetal-newborn health status. Am. J. Obstet. Gynecol. **139:** 956–958.
83. CHERNICK, V. & R. J. CRAIG. 1982. Nalaxone reverses neonatal depression caused by fetal asphyxia. Science **216:** 1252–1253.
84. GOODLIN, R. C. 1981. Naloxone and its possible relationship to fetal endorphin levels and fetal distress. Am. J. Obstet. Gynecol. **139:** 16–19.
85. ZADINA, J. E., A. J. KASTIN, D. H. COY & B. A. ADINOFF. 1985. Developmental, behavioral,

and opiate receptor changes after prenatal or postnatal β-endorphin, CRF, or Tyr-MIF-1. Psychoneuroendocrinology **10:** 367–383.

86.  ZADINA, J. E. & A. J. KASTIN. 1986. Neonatal peptides affect developing rats: β-Endorphin alters nociception and opiate receptors, corticotropin-releasing factor alters corticosterone. Dev. Brain Res. **29:** 21–29.

87.  SANDMAN, C. A. & N. YESSIAN. 1986. Persisting subsensitivity of the striatal dopamine system after fetal exposure to β-endorphin. Life Sci. **39:** 1755–1763.

88.  BECKWITH, B. E., D. I. COUK & K. SCHUMACHER. 1986. Failure of naloxone to reduce self-injurious behavior in two developmentally disabled females. Appl. Res. Ment. Retard. **7:** 183–188.

# Function of Opioids Early in Embryogenesis

ANTONIA VERNADAKIS,[a] NIKOS SAKELLARIDIS,[b]
TAKIS GELADOPOULOS,[c] AND DIMITRA MANGOURA

*Departments of Psychiatry and Pharmacology*
*University of Colorado School of Medicine*
*Denver, Colorado 80262*

## INTRODUCTION

The cellular and molecular events involved in early embryogenesis and neurogenesis have received considerable attention during the last decade. We and others have demonstrated that brain growth is regulated by endogenous substances such as hormones, neurohumoral and neurotransmitter substances, and other soluble factors provided by the intrinsic environment.[1–3] Recently, the emphasis has been centered on the role of neuropeptides and more specifically opioid peptides, such as endorphins and enkephalins, in early brain growth. We have proposed that these peptides are involved in early embryonic cellular processes based on the observations, which will be discussed below, that these substances are present in the intrinsic milieu during early embryonic development and also that opiate receptors appear early in embryogenesis.

In this paper we shall focus on *in vivo* and *in vitro* studies of the ontogenesis of opiate receptors and early opioidergic neuronal expression and discuss the role that opioids may play in neuronal proliferation, migration and phenotypic expression.

### Ontogenesis of Opioid Receptors

Numerous pharmacological studies have demonstrated that the effects of opiates *in vitro* and *in vivo* reflect their interaction with specific neuronal receptors (see refs. in REF. 4). Therefore, the ontological development of opiate receptors is relevant to our understanding of the role of opiates in growth. Early studies of the ontogenesis of opiate receptors are those reported by Pert *et al.*,[5] Clendeninn *et al.*,[6] and Coyle and Pert.[7] We initiated our studies in 1982 with the chick embryo as an experimental animal.[4] Using etorphine as an opiate receptor ligand, we detected stereospecific $^3$H-etorphine binding activity in chick embryos as early as 4 days of incubation in both brain and body tissue (FIG. 1). These ubiquitous opiate binding sites early in embryogenesis are high affinity and respond to ion and GTP regulation in a manner similar to adult brain tissue.

Stereospecific $^3$H-etorphine binding activity in body tissue was not unexpected. Or-

---

[a]Address for correspondence: Dr. Antonia Vernadakis, Departments of Psychiatry and Pharmacology, University of Colorado, School of Medicine, C263, 4200 East Ninth Ave., Denver, CO 80262.

[b]Dr. Nikos Sakellaridis's present address is: Department of Pharmacology, University of Indiana School of Medicine, Northwest Center for Medical Education, 3400 Broadway, Gary, IN 46408.

[c]Mr. Takis Geladopoulos's present address is: National Hellenic Research Foundation, Athens, Greece.

ganogenesis occurs at 4 days of incubation,[8] including the formation of the peripheral nervous system, gut, and adrenals, tissues that contain neuronal elements and are reported to possess opiate receptors in the adult.[9-11] It was unusual, however, that we found the same amount of binding activity per mg of protein in brain and body tissue. We considered two possible explanations: (1) the peripheral neuronal elements have many more binding sites for ³H-etorphine than brain neuronal elements, and (2) all cells, neurons and nonneuronal cells, possess a small number of ³H-etorphine binding sites.

The plateau in amount of binding activity between day 4 and 7 of incubation on both body and brain tissue (FIG. 1), a time when a great deal of cell proliferation is taking place, suggests that synthesis of sites is occurring in parallel with cell proliferation. As embryonic development proceeds, the nonneuronal cells may no longer need the function associated with the early opiate binding sites, and synthesis of binding sites stops. Cell proliferation and synthesis of opiate binding sites are no longer in concert, and, consequently, the binding sites are diluted out in the nonneuronal cells. As neuroblasts differentiate into specific neurons, the opiate binding sites may shift to a function necessary for neurons, *i.e.*, neurotransmitter regulation.

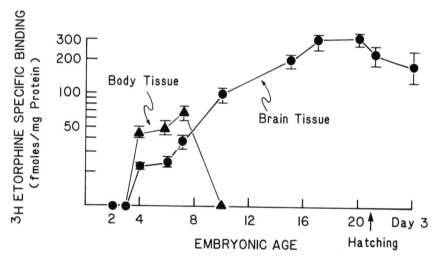

**FIGURE 1.** Changes in stereospecific binding of ³H-etorphine with days of incubation in the developing chick brain. ³H-etorphine concentration: 2.4 nM. (From Gibson and Vernadakis.[4] Reprinted by permission from *Developmental Brain Research*.)

In contrast to the nonneuronal cells, the neurons maintain or accelerate synthesis of opiate binding sites in parallel with proliferation and neuronal process formation. Thus ³H-etorphine binding activity would not be detected in nonneuronal tissue and would be increased in neuronal tissue at later stages of embryonic development. The greatest increase (approximately 5 ×) observed in ³H-etorphine binding activity is in the brain between day 7 and day 15 of incubation, the period that corresponds in the chick to active neuronal proliferation and differentiation and the beginning of synaptogenesis (see refs. in REFS. 12, 13).

In an attempt to further understand the role of early appearance of opiate receptors during neuroembryogenesis, we used more selective opiate receptor agonists, ³H-dihydromorphine for μ and ³H-(D-Ala²-D-Leu⁵)-enkephalin for δ receptors, and examined the

**TABLE 1.** Specific Binding Properties of $^3$H-DHM to Chick Brain during Embryonic Development[a]

| | $^3$H-Dihydromorphine | | | | | |
|---|---|---|---|---|---|---|
| | (A) | | | (B) | | |
| Embryonic Age (Days) | Kd (nM) | Bmax fmol/mg Protein | r | Kd (nM) | Bmax fmol/mg Protein | r |
| 5 | H = 0.10 | H = 5.1 | 0.940 | H = 0.34 | H = 1.9 | 0.976 |
| | L = 1.91 | L = 10.5 | 0.980 | L = 14.90 | L = 21.8 | 0.972 |
| 6 | H = 0.23 | H = 9.8 | 0.914 | H = 0.25 | H = 2.2 | 0.974 |
| | L = 4.62 | L = 34.6 | 0.950 | L = 5.73 | L = 10.2 | 0.997 |
| 15 | H = 0.37 | H = 13.3 | 0.964 | [b]H = 0.1 | H = 2.7 | 0.983 |
| | L = 3.38 | L = 32.9 | 0.860 | [b]L = 4.7 | L = 29.6 | 0.995 |
| 18 | 1.70 | 30.3 | 0.975 | | | |
| 20 | 0.91 | 33.6 | 0.982 | | | |

[a]Crude membranes were prepared from whole brains of 5- or 6-day-old chick embryos and from cerebral hemispheres of 15- to 20-day-old chick embryos. Specific binding of $^3$H-dihydromorphine was assessed in the presence of $5 \times 10^{-7}$ M levorphanol alone (A) and both $5 \times 10^{-7}$ M levorphanol and $1 \times 10^{-6}$ M (D-Ala$^2$, D-Leu$^5$) enkephalin (B). Binding affinities (H = high and L = low) and capacities represent the mean of fitting 2–3 experiments utilizing the Microdecision computer for Scatchard analysis.

[b]Specific binding of $^3$H-DHM with levorphanol for nonspecific binding was performed in the presence of $1 \times 10^{-6}$ M DSLET.

developmental binding patterns in the chick embryonic brain from 5 to 20 days of incubation.[14] Both μ and δ opiate receptors were present during early embryogenesis and as early as day 5 (TABLES 1, 2). Analysis of binding sites revealed high and low affinity μ sites during early embryogenesis on days 5,6, and 15 (TABLE 1) but only one δ site (TABLE 2). By 18 days of embryonic age, only one μ site remained. In contrast, only one δ binding site was detected throughout embryonic age; δ binding sites were high during early embryogenesis, reaching a lower level by 18 days.

**TABLE 2.** Specific Binding Properties of $^3$H-DADLE to Chick Brain during Embryonic Development[a]

| | $^3$H-(D-Ala$^2$,D-Leu$^5$)Enkephalin | | | | | |
|---|---|---|---|---|---|---|
| | (A) | | | (B) | | |
| Embryonic Age (Days) | Kd (nM) | Bmax fmol/mg Protein | r | Kd (nM) | Bmax fmol/mg Protein | r |
| 5 | | | | 1.73 | 15.5 | 0.880 |
| 6 | 5.04 | 35.1 | 0.959 | 4.52 | 32.84 | 0.947 |
| 15 | | | | 3.10 | 63 | 0.941 |
| 18 | | | | 2.58 | 44.79 | 0.968 |
| 20 | | | | 2.07 | 56.55 | 0.977 |

[a]Crude membranes were prepared from whole brains of 5- or 6-day-old chick embryos and from cerebral hemispheres of 15- to 20-day-old chick embryos. Specific binding for $^3$H-(D-Ala$^2$, D-Leu$^5$)enkephalin was assessed in the presence of $1 \times 10^{-6}$ M (D-Ala$^2$,D-Leu$^5$)enkephalin in (A) and in the presence of (D-Ser-Gly-Phe-Leu-Thr)enkephalin (B). Binding affinities and capacities represent the mean of fitting 2–3 experiments utilizing the Microdecision computer for Scatchard analysis. (From Geladopoulos *et al.*[14] Reprinted by permission from *Neurochemical Research*.)

The presence of a dual binding site pattern for the μ receptor in early embryogenesis is implicated to have a functional significance in the pluripotential role of the endogenous opioids in early development. We have put forward the hypothesis that the low affinity μ binding sites reflect binding sites on neuroblasts at a transitional stage of differentiation and that the high affinity μ binding sites are expressed by differentiated neurons. Moreover, these low affinity binding sites may be involved in the process of early neuronal differentiation. Furthermore, we speculate that these same neuronal sites may also bind $^3$H-DADLE. Evidence that some neurons have both μ and δ receptors has been reported.[15,16] In other words, some neuroblasts still at an early differentiation stage do not discriminate among opioid ligands. These receptor sites could be designated as "undifferentiated sites." Supportive evidence to this proposal are the findings from a subsequent study using $^3$H-(D-Ala$^2$, mePhe$^4$, Gly-ol$^5$)-enkephalin (DAGO), as a more specific μ receptor ligand, where we found one binding site (high affinity) throughout chick embryonic development (TABLE 3). Thus, we suggest that high affinity sites, whether detected using $^3$H-DAGO or $^3$H-DHM, are expressed by differentiated neurons.

It is of importance to note that binding sites using $^3$H-DADLE as ligand were detected as early as 5 days of embryonic age (TABLE 2), a period of active neuronal differentiation. In the rat, δ sites are not detected at birth in contrast to μ and k sites. However, between 7 and 14 days, δ sites increase almost twofold.[17] The period between 7 and 14 days in the rat is characterized by active neuronal maturation and synaptogenesis.[12,13] Whether δ receptors are involved in synaptogenesis remains to be elucidated.

TABLE 3. Changes in the Binding of $^3$H-DAGO to Chick Brain during Embryonic Development[a]

| Embryonic Age (Days) | Bmax fmoles/mg Protein | Kd (nM) | r |
|---|---|---|---|
| E3 | 11–5 | 0.35 | 0.874 |
| E6 | 40 | 0.64 | 0.985 |
| E15 | 87 | 0.81 | 0.933 |
| E20 | 91 | 2.55 | 0.927 |

[a]Crude membranes were prepared from whole brain of 3- and 6-day-old chick embryos, and cerebral hemispheres of 15- and 20-day-old chick embryos. Specific binding of $^3$H-(D-Ala$^2$-Mephe$^4$-Glyol$^5$)-enkephalin was assessed in the presence of $5 \times 10^{-7}$ M levorphanol and 0.05 mg/ml bacitracin. Scatchard curves were drawn by linear regression using a Microcdecision computer. (From Geladopoulos et al.[14] Reprinted by permission from *Neurochemical Research*.)

## Appearance of Endogenous Opioids during Early Embryogenesis

The presence of opiate receptors during early embryogenesis and neuroembryogenesis has been interpreted to signify the early appearance of endogenous opioids. Comprehensive reviews on endogenous opioids have been published.[18–23] In the rat brain Met- and Leu-ENK levels both increase 11-fold by 7 days postnatally; enkephalinase, the enzyme cleaving the Gly-Phe bond of ENKs more or less parallels the time-course of ENK levels and receptors.[24] In another study, Leu-ENK-like immunoreactivity is reported to be detectable in the rat hippocampus 12–14 days postnatally, after the peak period of last cell division for a given hippocampal region.[25] Both Met- and Leu-ENK have been detected in the chick embryonic retina at 11 days of incubation.[26] Human fetal and maternal endogenous opioid levels (primarily β-endorphin) increase during the course of normal pregnancy.[27–32] Dynorphin-(A)-like immunoreactivity in the hippocampal formation of the Sprague-Dawley rat is first detectable on postnatal day 6.[33]

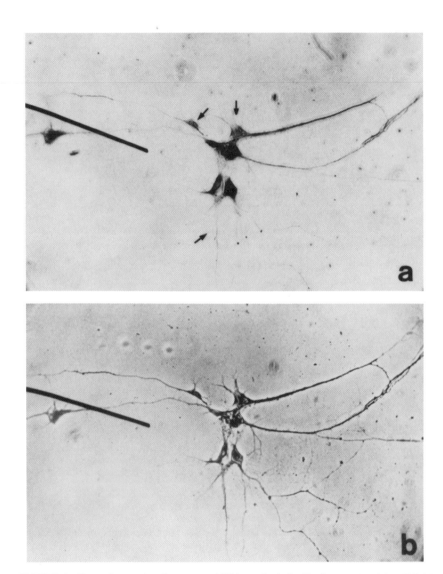

**FIGURE 2.** Photomicrographs of neurons exhibiting enkephalin-like immunoreactivity (Enk-LI) (Peroxidase-anti peroxidase—PAP—method). Neuronal cultures were derived from 6-day-old chick embryo cerebral hemispheres and grown in chemically defined medium. At day 7 in culture, cells on coverslips were fixed with 4% paraformaldehyde and 1% glutaraldehyde and processed for immunocytochemistry using the peroxidase-antiperoxidase method of Sternberger *et al.*[62] Primary antibody was Met-enkephalin (rabbit origin, AMERSHAM) at 1/3,000 in PBS. **(a)** Light microscopy, lens 40×. *Arrows* indicate nonstained neuronal somata and processes. **(b)** Phase contrast 2, lens 40×; both stained and nonstained neurons.

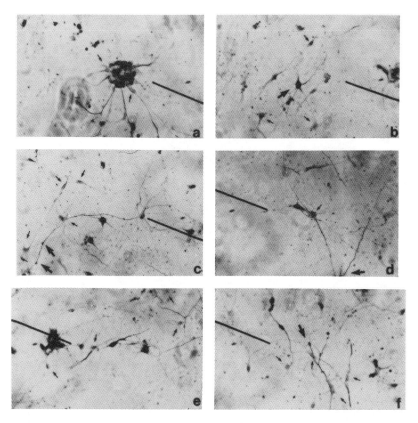

**FIGURE 3.** Cultures as in FIGURE 1. **(a)** Neuronal aggregate exhibiting Enk-LI on neuronal somata. *Light arrows* indicate some of the nonstained neurons (a–f); **(b)** *heavy arrow* indicates neuron positive for enkephalin, with Enk-LI being polarized on the right side of neuron; **(c,d,e)** *heavy arrows* indicate Enk-LI on varicosities of processes; **(f)** *heavy arrow* indicates growth cone exhibiting Enk-LI.

## Opioidergic Neuronal Expression during Embryogenesis

Localization of opioids in neuronal populations during neuroembryogenesis would support the view that these peptides may be involved in early neuronal differentiation. Early studies by Haynes and Zakurian[34,35] have shown the presence of leucine enkephalin-containing neurons in organotypic cultures derived from embryonic rat lumbar spinal cord (14–17 days gestation) using indirect immunofluorescence. Zagon et al.[36] have reported a study showing Met-ENK and Leu-ENK immunoreactivity being concentrated in the cerebellar external germinal layer, a matrix of proliferative cells of 10-day-old rats, whereas no staining was detected in differentiated neural cells in the cerebellum of 5-day-old rats. Recently, Surmeier et al.[37] have also reported Leu-ENK immunoreactivity in neurons in primary monolayer cultures of rat striatum; the proportion of Leu-ENK immunoreactive neurons grew gradually over the culturing period, increasing from about one-fifth of the neurons initially to one-half after 3–4 weeks *in vitro*. Fukuda et al.[38] have detected Leu-ENK immunoreactive neurons in retinal cultures derived from 7-day-old chick embryos.

In a preliminary study using neuronal-enriched cultures derived from 6-day-old chick embryonic brain, whose neurotransmitter expression have been fully characterized,[39-42] we detected enkephalin-like immunoreactivity in several neurons (FIGS. 2–4). The presence of opioidergic neurons would imply that opioid substances are secreted in the

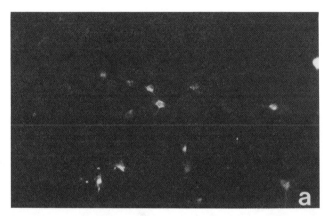

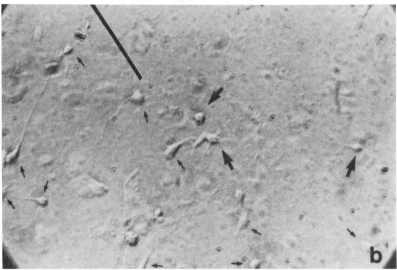

**FIGURE 4.** Photomicrographs of neurons exhibiting Enk-LI (immunofluorescence). Neuronal cultures were derived from 6-day-old chick embryo cerebral hemispheres and grown in chemically defined medium. **(a)** At day 3 in culture, cells on coverslips were stained with enkephalin antibody and IgG conjugated with fluorescein; **(b)** phase contrast photomicrograph of exactly the same field as in (a). *Heavy arrows* indicate neurons exhibiting Enk-LI shown on (a). *Light arrows* indicate nonstained neurons (print of (b) is magnified 2×).

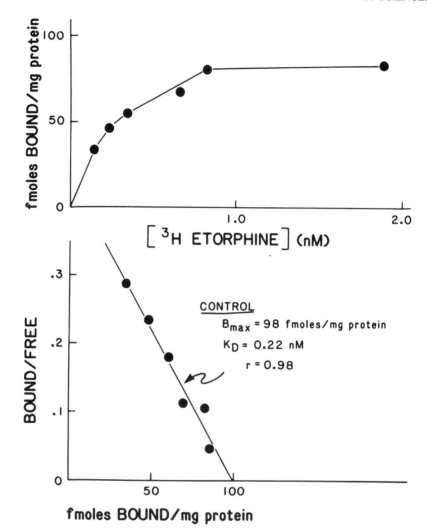

**FIGURE 5.** Stereospecific [³H]etorphine binding in neuronal-enriched cell cultures dissociated from 6.5-day-old chick embryo whole brain and plated on polylysine-coated dishes: 9 days in culture. *Upper half:* saturation curve. *Lower half:* Scatchard analysis. (From Gibson and Vernadakis.[43] Reprinted by permission from *Neurochemical Research.*)

neuronal microenvironment and could perhaps influence the maturation of other neurons expressing opiate receptors. In addition, in another study, we reported that ³H-etorphine specific binding sites in neuronal-enriched cultures derived from 7-day-old chick embryonic brain[43] (FIG. 5). The possibility that opioids and neurotransmitters coexist is very likely. Convincing evidence has been reported that opioids and neurotransmitter substances coexist in several neuronal populations: enkephalin and serotonin-like substance;[44] opioid peptides cotransmitters in noradrenergic sympathetic nerves;[45] coexistence of neuropeptides.[46]

## Neuromodulatory Role of Opioids during Neuroembryogenesis

The early appearance of opiate receptors and presence of opioid peptides has become the impetus for several groups of investigators to examine the role of opioids in neuroembryogenesis.

We have been studying the relationship between opioids and cholinergic neurons using as a model neuronal-enriched cultures derived from a 6-day-old chick embryonic brain. We have tested the effects of morphine and methadone on cholinergic neuronal differentiation using the activity of choline acetyltransferase (ChAT) the synthesizing enzyme of acetylcholine (Ach) as a marker.[47] We found that cholinergic neurons, detected immunocytochemically, are present as early as 3 days in culture, a time period in which we also detect ChAT activity measured biochemically.[41] Marked morphological alterations were observed in cultures treated with $10^{-5}$ or $10^{-6}$ M morphine sulfate: a striking increase in the number of flat cells, presumably glia, between the neuronal aggregates and drastically reduced neurite arborization. Several speculations can be offered at present for these findings. The fact that flat cells are very few in control cultures, but abundant in the opiate-treated cultures is interpreted to mean that morphine either directly influenced proliferation of flat cells, or that some neuron-produced factors in the morphine-treated cultures influenced proliferation of flat cells. In an earlier study,[48] we found that methadone, $10^{-5}$ M, markedly increases the activity of cyclic nucleotide phosphohydrolase, a marker of oligodendrocytes,[49] in neuronal-glial mixed cultures derived from 8-day-old chick embryo cerebral hemispheres. Since oligodendrocytes respond to neuronal inputs,[12] we interpret this increase in glial activity to be neuron-mediated as a response to morphine. On the other hand, the possibility that morphine directly influences glia cell proliferation is not unlikely. Hansson and Ronnback[50] and Ronnback and Hansson[51] have

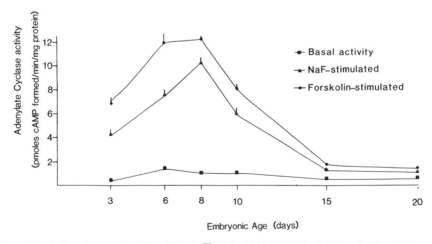

**FIGURE 6.** Developmental profile of basal (■), 10 mM NaF-stimulated (▲), and 100 μM forskolin-stimulated (●) adenylate cyclase activity in chick embryo vs embryonic age. Adenylate cyclase activity was assayed in a whole-embryo preparation at embryonic age day 3 and whole-brain preparations from then on. Activity is plotted vs days of embryonic age. Points represent means ± SEM of three or four experiments, each of at least four samples. (From Sakellaridis and Vernadakis.[59] Reprinted by permission from the National Academy of Sciences.)

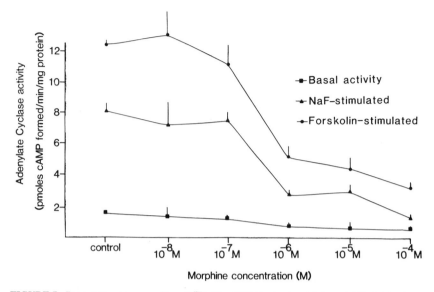

**FIGURE 7.** Dose-response curve of basal (■), 10 mM NaF-stimulated (▲), and 100 μM forskolin-stimulated (●) adenylate cyclase activity from a 6-day-old chick embryo whole brain to morphine. The tissue had been preincubated with morphine for 90 min. Points represent means ± SEM of three or four experiments, each of at least four samples. (From Sakellaridis and Vernadakis.[59] Reprinted by permission from the National Academy of Sciences.)

reported that in astroglia-enriched cultures derived from newborn rats, morphine treatment $10^{-7}$ M to $10^{-5}$ M, resulted in an increased $^3$H-valine incorporation into protein. In view of the role of glial cells in maintenance of neuronal homeostasis,[12] the consequences of this "reactive gliosis," as it appears in our cultures, on neuronal function are still to be evaluated. Although it appears paradoxical that glial cells may have interfered with neuronal differentiation, in view of the contrary evidence (see refs. in REF. 12), it is not surprising that an imbalance of one or more factors will disturb neuronal homeostasis and thus have negative consequences. In support of this possibility, we also found in the same cultures a decreased choline acetyltransferase activity after either morphine or methadone treatment.[47] Thus, an increase in glial proliferation, and consequently an augmentation of glial factors secreted in the microenvironment, appears to have a negative effect on cholinergic neuronal growth. We suggest that morphine exposure of cultures consisting of differentiating neuroblasts results in down regulation of opioid receptors and consequently interfers with neuron-neuron interactions; recently, evidence of enkephalinergic-cholinergic interaction has been reported.[52]

A series of studies has been published by Zagon and McLaughlin[53-55] providing evidence that endogenous opioids influence neuronal proliferation. For example, they have found that after naloxone administration, during early postnatal development, there is an increase in cerebellar growth. Thus the view is that the endogenous opioid-opioid receptor interaction modulates neuronal growth. Our findings of a decrease in cholinergic neuronal expression in cultures treated with morphine provide further evidence of a neuromodulatory role of opioids.

The molecular mechanisms involved in the neuromodulation of opioids during early neuroembryogenesis have not been actively pursued. In view of the established relationship of adenylate cyclase and opiates,[56-58] we initiated a study to investigate this inter-relationship during chick embryonic development.[59] First, the developmental profile of basal, NaF- and forskolin-stimulated adenylate cyclase was established (FIG. 6). The highest activities were observed from day 6 to day 8. Morphine at doses $10^{-6}$ M to $10^{-4}$ M inhibits NaF- and forskolin-stimulated adenylate cyclase activity but only at days 6 and 8 (FIG. 7). Moreover, this inhibition is not reversed by the opiate antagonist naloxone, $10^{-6}$ M, and in fact naloxone appears to act as the agonist and inhibits both NaF- and forskolin-stimulated adenylate cyclase (FIG. 8). These findings imply that the inhibitory effect of morphine is not mediated through the conventional opiate receptor-adenylate system. Furthermore, they support our view that the role of opioids during early development is different from their role in the mature organism where they are intimately related to neurotransmitter systems. It is of importance to note that these unconventional effects of opioids are exerted during a specific embryonic period, 6 to 8 days, characterized by active neuronal differentiation and migration. There is abundant evidence that cyclic AMP is involved in cell differentiation.[60] An interaction, therefore, of opioid substances and adenylate cyclase would be of paramount importance in the regulation of neuronal differentiation during neuroembryogenesis.

## CONCLUSIONS

It has been established that both opiate receptors and endogenous opioids are present early in embryogenesis. Their role in early neuronal processes continues to be speculative.

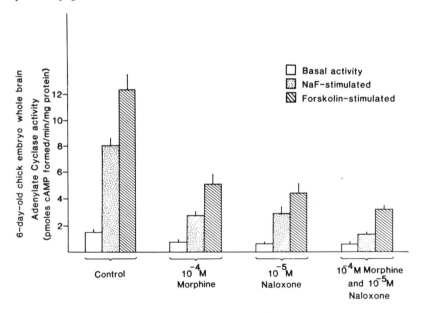

**FIGURE 8.** Response of basal (□), 10 mM NaF-stimulated (▨) and 100 μM forskolin-stimulated (▨) adenylate cyclase from a 6-day-old chick embryo whole brain to 100 μM morphine, 10 μM naloxone, and the combination of 100 μM morphine/10 μM naloxone. The drugs were preincubated with the tissue for 90 min. Bars represent means ± SEM of three to four experiments, each of at least four samples. (From Sakellaridis and Vernadakis.[59] Reprinted by permission from the National Academy of Sciences.)

The evidence thus far strongly supports the view that endogenous opioids have a pluripotential function ranging from influencing early neuronal growth and differentiation to affecting neuron-glia interactions. They thus modulate the neuronal microenvironment and finally assume their role in neurotransmission processes. It is our belief that elucidating the cellular and molecular mechanisms of opioids early in embryogenesis may be fundamental to our understanding the complex manifestations of fetal exposure to exogenous opiates, ranging from newborn addiction to developmental disabilities.

## REFERENCES

1. BOTTENSTEIN, J. E. & G. SATO, Eds. 1985. Cell Culture in Neuroscience. Plenum Press. New York, NY.
2. PEREZ POLO, J. R., J. DE VELLIS & B. HABER, Eds. 1983. Growth and Trophic Factors. Alan R. Liss, Inc. New York, NY.
3. VERNADAKIS, A., N. SAKELLARIDIS, D. MANGOURA & C. ESTIN. 1988. Factors influencing glia growth in culture: Nutrients and cell-secreted factors. In Nutrition, Growth and Cancer. G. P. Tryfiates and K. N. Prasad, Eds. 57–59. Alan R. Liss, Inc. New York, NY.
4. GIBSON, D. A. & A. VERNADAKIS. 1982. $^3$H-etorphine binding activity in early chick embryos: Brain and body tissue. Dev. Brain Res. **4:** 23–29.
5. PERT, C. B., D. SPOSHIAN & S. H. SNYDER. 1974. Phylogenetic distribution of opiate receptor binding. Brain Res. **75:** 356–361.
6. CLENDENINN, N. J., M. PETRAITIS & E. J. SIMON. 1976. Ontological development of opiate receptors in rodent brain. Brain Res. **118:** 157–160.
7. COYLE, J. T. & C. B. PERT. 1976. Ontogenetic development of $^3$H-naloxone binding in rat brain. Neuropharmacology **15:** 555–560.
8. PATTEN, D. M. 1952. Early Embryology of the Chick. 159–170. Blakeston. New York, NY.
9. CHANG, K. J. & P. CUATRECASAS. 1979. Multiple opiate receptors. Enkephalins and morphins binding to receptors of different specificity. J. Biol. Chem. **254:** 2610–2618.
10. KELLY, P. D., A. C. LANE, M. F. J. RANCE & F. R. TRAYNOR. 1980. Opiate receptors in rat spinal cord. In Proc. Behav. Pharmacol. Soc., 9–11 April 1980, 153 pp.
11. KAMAKURA, K., F. KARUM, A. GUIDOTTI & E. COSTA. 1970. Modulation of nicotinic receptors by opiate receptor agonists in cultured adrenal chromatin cells. Nature (London) **23:** 489–492.
12. VERNADAKIS, A. 1988. Neuron-glia interrelations. Int. Rev. Neurobiol. **30:** 149–224.
13. VERNADAKIS, A. 1988. Synaptogenesis: Morphological, biochemical and electrophysiological correlates. In Handbook of Human Biological Development. Vol. 1. Neural, Sensory, Motor and Integrative Development. E. Meisami & P. S. Timiras, Eds. 75–93. CRC Press. Boca Raton, FL.
14. GELADOPOULOS, T., N. SAKELLARIDIS & A. VERNADAKIS. 1987. Differential maturation of μ and δ receptors in the chick embryonic brain. Neurochem. Res. **12:** 279–288.
15. WILLIAMS, J. T. & W. ZIEGLGÄNSBERGER. 1981. Neurons in the frontal cortex of the rat carry multiple opiate receptors. Brain Res. **226:** 304–308.
16. EGAN, T. M. & R. A. NORTH, 1981. Both μ and δ receptors exist on the same neuron. Science **214:** 923–924.
17. PETRILLO, P., A. TAVANI, D. VEROTTA, L. E. ROBSON & H. W. KOSTERLITZ. 1987. Differential postnatal development of μ-, δ- and κ- opioid binding sites in rat brain. Dev. Brain Res. **31:** 53–58.
18. AKIL, H., S. J. WATSON, E. YOUNG, M. E. LEWIS, H. KHACHATURIAN & J. M. WALKER. 1984. Endogenous opioids: Biology and function. Annu. Rev. Neurosci. **7:** 223–255.
19. CIVELLI, O., C. MACHINDA, J. BUNSOW, P. ALBERT, E. HANNEMAN, J. SALON, J. BIDLACK & D. GRANDY. 1987. The next frontier in the molecular biology of the opioid system. Mol. Neurobiol. **1:** 373–391.
20. OLSON, G. A., R. D. OLSON, A. J. KASTIN & D. H. COY. 1982. Endogenous opiates: 1981. Peptides **3:** 1039–1072.
21. OLSON, G. A., R. D. OLSON & A. J. KASTIN. 1984. Endogenous opiates: 1983. Peptides **5:** 975–992.

22. OLSON, G. A., R. D. OLSON & A. J. KASTIN. 1986. Endogenous opiates: 1985. Peptides 7: 907–933.

23. ZAGON, I. S., P. J. MCLAUGHLIN, D. J. WEAVER & E. ZAGON. 1982. Opiates, endorphins and the developing organism: A comprehensive bibliography. Neurosci. Biobehav. Rev. 6: 439–479.

24. ZAGON, I. S., P. J. MCLAUGHLIN & E. ZAGON. 1984. Opiates, endorphins and the developing organism: A comprehensive bibliography, 1982–1983. Neurosci. Biobehav. Rev. 8: 387–403.

25. PATEY, G., S. DE LA BLUME, C. GROS & J.-C. SCHWARTZ. 1980. Ontogenesis of enkephalinergic systems in rat brain: Post-natal changes in enkephalin levels, receptors and degrading enzyme activities. Life Sci. 27: 245–252.

26. GALL, C., N. BRACHA, K.-J. CHANG & H. J. KARTEN. 1984. Ontogeny of enkephalin-like immunoreactivity in the rat hippocampus. Neuroscience 11: 359–380.

27. HUMBERT, J., P. PRADELLES, C. GROS & F. DRAY. 1979. Enkephalin-like products in embryonic chicken retina. Neurosci. Lett. 12: 259–263.

28. GAMTRAY, J., A. JOLIVET, J. VIELH & R. GUILLEMIN. 1977. Presence of immunoassayable beta-endorphin in human amniotic fluid: Elevation in cases of fetal distress. Am. J. Obstet. Gynecol. 129: 211–212.

29. MOSS, I. R., H. CONNER, W. F. H. YEE, P. IORIO & E. M. SCARPELLI. 1982. Human $\beta$-endorphin-like immunoreactivity in the perinatal neonatal period. J. Pediatr. 101: 443–446.

30. NEWNHAM, J. P., S. TOMLIN, S. J. RATTER, G. L. BROUNE & L. H. REES. 1983. Endogenous opioid peptides in pregnancy. Br. J. Obstet. Gynaecol. 90: 535–538.

31. PANERAI, A. E., A. MARTINI, A. M. DI GUILIO, F. FRAISLI, C. VEGNI, G. PARDI, A. MARINI & P. MONTEGAZZA. 1983. Plasma beta-endorphin, beta-lipotropin, and met-enkephalin concentration during pregnancy in normal and drug-addicted women and their newborns. J. Clin. Endocrinol. Metab. 57: 537–543.

32. WARDLAW, S. L., R. I. STARK, L. BANS & A. G. FRANTZ. 1979. Plasma $\beta$-endorphin and $\beta$-lipotropin in the human fetus at delivery: Correlation with arterial pH and $Po_2$. J. Clin. Endocrinol. Metab. 79: 888–891.

33. GALL, C. 1984. Ontogeny of dynorphin-like immunoreactivity in the hippocampal formation of the rat. Brain Res. 307: 327–331.

34. HAYNES, L. W. & S. ZAKARIAN. 1979. Morphological differentiation of enkephalin-containing neurons in tissue culture. J. Physiol. (London) 295: 34P.

35. HAYNES, L. W. & S. ZAKARIAN. 1981. Microanatomy of enkephalin-containing neurones in the developing rat spinal cord in vitro. Neuroscience 6: 1899–1916.

36. ZAGON, I. S., R. E. RHODES & P. J. MCLAUGHLIN. 1985. Distribution of enkephalin immunoreactivity in germinative cells of developing rat cerebellum. Science 227: 1049–1051.

37. SURMEIER, D. J., H. KITA & S. T. KITAI. 1988. The expression of $\gamma$-aminobutyric acid and leu-enkephalin immunoreactivity in primary monolayer cultures of rat striatum. Dev. Brain Res. 42: 265–282.

38. FUKUDA, M., H. H. PEH & D. G. PURO. 1987. Avian retinal cells express enkephalin-like immunoreactivity in culture. Dev. Brain Res. 31: 147–150.

39. VERNADAKIS, A., N. SAKELLARIDIS & D. MANGOURA. 1986. Growth patterns of primary cultures dissociated from 3-day-old chick embryos: Morphological and biochemical comparisons. J. Neurosci. Res. 16: 397–407.

40. MANGOURA, D., N. SAKELLARIDIS & A. VERNADAKIS. 1988a. Factors influencing neuronal growth in primary cultures derived from 3-day-old chick embryos. Int. J. Dev. Neurosci. 6: 89–102.

41. MANGOURA, D., N. SAKELLARIDIS & A. VERNADAKIS. 1988b. Cholinergic neurons in cultures derived from three-, six- or eight-day-old chick embryos. A biochemical and immunocytochemical study. Dev. Brain Res. 40: 37–46.

42. MANGOURA, D. & A. VERNADAKIS. 1988. Gabaergic neurons in cultures derived from three-, six-, or eight-day-old chick embryos: A biochemical and immunocytochemical study. Dev. Brain Res. 40: 25–35.

43. GIBSON, D. A. & A. VERNADAKIS. 1983. Effects of N-LAAM on $^3$H-etorphine binding in neuronal-enriched cell cultures. Neurochem. Res. 8: 1197–1202.

44. KANAGAWA, Y., T. MATSUYAMA, A. WANAKA, S. YONEDA, K. KIMURA, T. KAMADA, H. W. M. STEINBUSCH & M. TOHYAMA. 1986. Co-existence of enkephalin- and serotonin-like substances in single small intensely fluorescent cells of the guinea pig superior cervical ganglion. Brain Res. **379:** 377–379.

45. WILSON, S. P., R. Z. KLEIN, K.-J. CHANG, M. S. CASPARIS, D. H. VIREROS & W.-H. YANG. 1980. Are opioid peptides co-transmitters in noradrenergic vesicles of sympathetic nerves? Nature **288:** 707–709.

46. PAPADOPOULOS, G. C., J. G. PARNAVELAS & M. E. CAVANAGH. 1987. Extensive co-existence of neuropeptides in the rat visual cortex. Brain Res. **420:** 95–99.

47. SAKELLARIDIS, N., D. MANGOURA & A. VERNADAKIS. 1986. Effects of opiates on the growth of neuron-enriched cultures from chick embryonic brain. Int. J. Dev. Neurosci. **4:** 293–302.

48. VERNADAKIS, A., C. ESTIN, D. A. GIBSON & S. AMOTT. 1982. Effects of methadone on ornithine decarboxylase and cyclic nucleotide phosphohydrolase in neuronal and glial cell cultures. J. Neurosci. Res. **7:** 111–117.

49. PODUSLO, S. & W. T. NORTON. 1972. Isolation and some chemical properties of oligoden-droglia from calf brain. J. Neurochem. **19:** 727–736.

50. HANSSON, E. & L. RONNBACK. 1985. Amino acid incorporation during morphine intoxication. II. Electrophoretic separation of extracellular proteins from cerebral hemisphere slices and astroglia-enriched primary cultures. J. Neurosci. Res. **14:** 479–490.

51. RONNBACK, L. & E. HANSSON. 1985. Amino acid incorporation during morphine intoxication. I: Dose and time effects of morphine on protein synthesis in specific regions of the rat brain and in astroglia-enriched primary cultures. J. Neurosci. Res. **14:** 461–477.

52. CHANG, H. T., G. R. PENNY & S. T. KITAI. 1987. Enkephalinergic-cholinergic interaction in the rat globus pallidus: A pre-embedding double labeling immunocytochemistry study. Brain Res. **426:** 197–203.

53. ZAGON, I. S. & P. J. MCLAUGHLIN. 1986a. Opioid antagonist-induced modulation of cerebral and hippocampal development: Histological and morphometric studies. Dev. Brain Res. **28:** 233–246.

54. ZAGON, I. S. & P. J. MCLAUGHLIN. 1986. Opioid antagonist (naltrexone) modulation of cerebellar development: Histological and morphometric studies. J. Neurosci. **6:** 1424–1432.

55. ZAGON, I. S. & P. J. MCLAUGHLIN. 1987. Endogenous opioid systems regulate cell prolif-eration in the developing rat brain. Brain Res. **412:** 68–72.

56. SHARMA, S. K., M. NIRENBERG & W. A. KLEE. 1975a. Dual regulation of adenylate cyclase accounts for narcotic dependence and tolerance. Proc. Natl. Acad. Sci. USA **72:** 3092–3096.

57. SHARMA, S. K., M. NIRENBERG & W. A. KLEE. 1975b. Morphine receptors as regulators of adenylate cyclase activity. Proc. Natl. Acad. Sci. USA **72:** 590–594.

58. COOPER, D. M. F., C. LONDOS, D. L. GILL & M. RODBELL. 1982. Opiate-receptor mediated inhibition of adenylate cyclase in rat striatal plasma membrane. J. Neurochem. **38:** 1164–1167.

59. SAKELLARIDIS, N. & A. VERNADAKIS. 1986. An unconventional response of adenylate cyclase to morphine and naloxone in the chicken during early development. Proc. Natl. Acad. Sci. USA **83:** 2738–2742.

60. PRASAD, K. 1975. Differentiation of neuroblastoma cells. Biol. Rev. **50:** 129–165.

61. STERNBERGER, L. A., P. H. HARDY, JR., J. J. CUCULIS & H. G. MEGER. 1970. The unlabelled antibody-enzyme method of immunocytochemistry. Preparation and properties of soluble antigen-antibody complex (horse-radish peroxidase-anti-horseradish peroxidase) and its use in the identification of spirochetes. J. Histochem. Cytochem. **18:** 315–333.

# Opioid Peptides and Aging

JOHN E. MORLEY,[a] JAMES F. FLOOD, AND

ANDREW J. SILVER

*Geriatric Research, Education and Clinical Center*
*Sepulveda Veterans Administration Medical Center*
*Sepulveda, California 91343*
*and*
*Department of Medicine*
*University of California at Los Angeles School of Medicine*
*Los Angeles, California 90024*

## INTRODUCTION

The population of the United States is aging to such an extent that by the year 2030 one in five Americans will be over the age of 65. With advancing age, there are a number of behavioral changes that occur with greater frequency. These include an increasing prevalence of cognitive disturbances, anorexia, hypodipsia, and decreased sexual function. In addition, there are major changes in immune function with advancing age. Opioid peptides have been implicated in the regulation of all these functions[1] and there is evidence that alterations in opioid peptide secretion and/or receptor activity with aging may play a role in these behavioral alterations.

Diabetes mellitus has been considered a model of premature aging, particularly in tissues with poor replicative ability, such as the central nervous system.[2] In addition, both diabetes mellitus and hyperglycemia occur with increasing frequency in older individuals.[3] There is cumulative evidence that glucose *per se* can alter the response to opioid peptides.[4] Behavioral alterations occur in older patients with diabetes mellitus and these appear to be related to alterations in opioid function. This paper discusses the evidence correlating age-related changes in opioid peptide secretion with age related changes in behavior functions of the immune system, and a diabetes mellitus model of aging.

### Effects of Aging on Opioids and Their Receptors

With advancing age, there is evidence that there is a decrease in both opioid peptide and opioid receptor levels in the brain of rodents. Methionine- and leucine-enkephalin, as well as beta-endorphin and arg[6]phe[7] met-enkephalin, have all been found to be present in reduced concentrations of the hypothalamus of old compared to young rats.[5-7] In addition, a study of discrete nuclei found that beta-endorphin was reduced in all the major nuclei of the hypothalamus with the exception of the median eminence.[8] A decrease in a number of receptor sites and an increase in the affinity for dihydromorphine binding have been shown in mature and old rats.[9,10] Also, there was an increase in affinity of kappa opioid receptor sites, with no change in receptor density.[10] Delta receptor binding, uti-

[a]Direct correspondence to: John E. Morley, M.D., VAMC, GRECC (11E), 16111 Plummer Street, Sepulveda, CA 91343.

lizing $^3$H-(D-Ser$^2$-Leu$^5$) enkephanilyl-Thr, was not different between mature and old mice.

Changes of beta-endorphin with aging have also been examined in humans. No age-related differences in circulating beta-endorphin response to exercise[11] or to a cold pressor test[12] could be detected. In older persons, however, there is a blunting of the circadian rhythm of beta-endorphin secretion seen in younger persons.[13] Cerebrospinal fluid levels of beta-endorphin are reduced in older individuals compared with younger ones.[14]

## Opioids, Feeding, and Aging

It is now well recognized that reduced food intake is associated with advancing age.[15] While there are a number of pathological causes of the anorexia of aging, it is clear that there is also a physiological decrement in the desire to eat in older animals and humans.[16] Numerous studies have supported a physiological role of endogenous opioids in the modulation of food intake.[17,18] Most studies support the viewpoint that the major opioid involved in the genesis of the feeding drive is the endogenous ligand of the kappa opiate receptor, dynorphin.[19] Opioids appear to predominantly modulate the intake of highly palatable fatty foods.[20]

Gosnell et al.[21] examined the role of the opioid feeding system in the anorexia of aging in Fisher-344 rats aged 2, 12, 22, and 28 months. The general opiate antagonist, naloxone, reduced food intake in 2- and 12-month-old rats at 0.1 and 10 mg/kg doses. Only the highest dose (10 mg/kg) was effective at reducing food intake in the 22- and 28-month-old animals. Similarly, the mixed opiate agonist/antagonist, butorphanol tartrate, was more effective at increasing food intake in the 2- and 12-month-old rats than in the 22-month-old rats. Kavaliers and Hirst[22] found a similar poor response to opiate agonists and antagonists in old mice.

The regulation of food intake depends on a delicate balance of a number of neurotransmitters and hormones.[18] Studies on a number of centrally active, putative neurotransmitters, i.e., neuropeptide Y,[23] corticotropin releasing factor,[24] and norepinephrine (unpublished observations), have suggested that there is minimal or no change in responsiveness to these neurotransmitters with advancing age. This suggests a relative specificity for the role of endogenous opioids in the pathogenesis of the anorexia of aging.

Cholecystokinin (CCK) is a gastrointestinal hormone that appears to play a role in the termination of a meal.[25] Recently, Silver et al.[26] demonstrated that older mice showed an excessive satiety response to exogenously administered CCK-8. Previous studies suggested that CCK may act as a physiological antagonist to endogenous opioids.[27] Thus, it seems reasonable to postulate that the biochemical basis of the anorexia of aging is an excessive satiety effect of CCK, in combination with a decrease in the opioid feeding drive.

## Opioids, Drinking, and Aging

A classic study by Phillips et al.[28] demonstrated that older humans fail to perceive thirst in response to overnight water deprivation. This results in a failure of older individuals to drink adequate amounts of fluid and places them continuously at risk for developing dehydration. The development of dehydration in some elderly subjects has been related to decreases in circulating angiotensin II levels, secondary to the presence of decreased angiotensin converting-enzyme levels.[29]

The endogenous opioid system is believed to induce fluid intake, possibly through the activation of mu receptors.[17] The ability of naloxone to decrease fluid in old mice (26 months) is attenuated, compared to the effects of naloxone in adult mice (8 months).[30] We have extended these studies to humans. Two groups of humans, aged 28 to 36 and 70 to 74 years of age, were studied.[31] We confirmed the previously reported decrease in fluid intake seen in older subjects compared to younger subjects after a period of fluid deprivation. In addition, young humans had their fluid intake decreased by 100 μg/kg of nalaxone, while this dose was ineffective at reducing fluid intake in older subjects.

These studies suggest that lack of an opioid drinking drive may play a role in the susceptibility to develop dehydration that is often seen in older individuals.

### Opioids and Memory

Morphine and beta-endorphin produce retrograde amnesia when administered shortly after training.[32-35] The effects of the opioid peptides are time-dependent and blocked by the concomitant administration of naloxone.[36,37] In addition, a number of studies have suggested that administration of the opioid antagonist, naloxone, increases retention of recently learned tasks in rats.[38-40]

Flood et al.[41] demonstrated that naloxone produced an inverted U-shaped dose response improvement of memory retention when administered to undertrained mice after learning an aversive task. When administered to overtrained mice, naloxone produced a monotonic decrease in retention as the dose increased. Nalmefene (6-desoxy-6-methylene-naltrexone) was equally effective at enhancing retention at a 500-fold lower dose. The effect of naloxone was stereospecific; and it was 1,000-fold more potent when administered intracerebroventricularly, suggesting that the opioid effects on memory are produced within the central nervous system. Naloxone had no effects on acquisition but did improve recall. Naloxone showed anti-amnestic properties against the protein-synthesis inhibitor, anisomycin, and against the acetylcholine receptor blocker, scopolamine. Administration of the mu-specific opioid receptor blocker, beta-funaltrexamine (B-FNA) 72 hours before training did not alter acquisition but did enhance retention. When the mu receptors were blocked with B-FNA, naloxone could no longer enhance retention. B-FNA had no effect on the memory-enhancing properties of arecholine, fluoxetine, or clonidine. Thus, B-FNA specifically prevented naloxone from enhancing memory, suggesting that the amnestic effects of opioids are mediated by the mu receptor.

Studies in humans have yielded contrasting results on the effects of opioid antagonists on memory function. Opioid antagonists either improved,[42] impaired,[43-45] or had no effect on memory function[46-49] in human subjects. These opposing results could be due to failure to take into account the inverted U-shaped dose response of the memory-enhancing properties of naloxone. Unlike the situation with ingestive behaviors, the amnestic effect of opioids appears to be present into old age. Naloxone reversed the mild memory defect present in old mice.[50]

Like naloxone, peripherally administered CCK enhanced memory.[51] The effects of CCK were vagally dependent and appear to account for the ability of feeding to enhance memory. Again, these findings would be compatible with CCK acting as a physiological antagonist of endogenous opioids.

Measurements of beta-endorphin levels in the cerebrospinal fluid of patients with dementia of the Alzheimer's type have yielded conflicting results. One study showed progressive decreases in beta-endorphin with worsening dementia.[52] Raskind et al.[53] reported no change in CSF beta-endorphin levels in Alzheimer's disease. However, careful perusal of their data suggests a small decrease in beta-endorphin was present. In view of the decrease reported in memory-enhancing neurotransmitters, such as acetylcholine and somatostatin, a failure of beta-endorphin levels to be reduced may result in an increased amnestic effect of beta-endorphin in Alzehimer's disease.

To summarize, beta-endorphin is a potent amnestic agent. The opioid effects on memory are not attenuated with advancing age. Excessive opioid tone may play a role in the pathophysiology of Alzheimer's disease.

### Opioids and Sexual Dysfunction

Over the age of 50 years, one in three males visiting a physician is impotent.[54] Approximately 10% of these patients have secondary hypogonadism, *i.e.*, low testosterone levels and inappropriately normal luteinizing hormone (LH) levels. Our early studies suggested that in humans, LH was under tonic opioid inhibition.[55] We, therefore, postulated that the secondary hypogonadism seen in some impotent patients could be due to excessive opioid tone. In a preliminary study, we examined the effects of opiate antagonism with nalmefene on the hypothalmic-pituitary-testicular axis in men with secondary hypogonadism. Significant increases in both LH and testosterone occurred after administration of nalmefene, suggesting that excessive inhibitory opioid tone may play a role in the secondary hypogonadism associated with aging.

### Beta-Endorphin, Immune System, and Aging

It is now clear that a number of peptides modulate immune function.[56] The best studied of these peptide-immune system interactions are those produced by beta-endorphin. The effects of opioids on the immune system include enhanced chemotaxis, increased histamine release, modulation of PHA-stimulated proliferation, and enhanced natural killer (NK) cell activity.[57] With advancing age, some, but not all, elements of the immune system decline, *i.e.*, immunosenescence occurs.[58]

Norman *et al.*[59] examined the effects of beta-endorphin on the spleen cell response to conconavalin A. In 2- to 4-month-old mice, beta-endorphin enhanced conconavalin A mitogenesis. This appeared to be a non-opiate effect, as it was not blocked by naloxone. In contrast, beta-endorphin was ineffective at stimulating conconavalin A mitogenesis in 24-month-old mice.

In humans, beta-endorphin is a potent stimulator of NK cells.[60] This effect appears to involve opioid receptors, although Des-Tyr-endorphins can produce the same effects.[61] In a large series of healthy elderly volunteers (mean age 73; range 65 to 89), we found that NK activity and the percentage of the lymphocyte markers, Leu-11a and Leu-19, were significantly increased compared to values found in young subjects. Beta-endorphin stimulation of NK activity was seen in 43% of old and 21% of young subjects.[62]

We also found that exercise increased NK activity in both young and old females.[63] The older females responded as well as the younger ones. We showed that the enhanced NK activity produced by exercise could be attenuated by naloxone infusion, suggesting that the acute increase in NK activity is mediated by endogenous opioid release.[64]

Sharp *et al.*[65] found that beta-endorphin and dynorphin stimulated superoxide radical production. These effects were observed at concentrations as low as $10^{-12}$ M. The response was inhibited by naloxone. Simpkins *et al.*[66] found that both D- and L-naloxone inhibited fMLF-stimulated superoxide release from human neutrophils. This suggested that superoxide production stimulated by endogenous opioids is not specific to any of the classic opioid receptors. These findings may have major significance for aging, as it has been suggested that many aging changes occur secondary to free radical damage.

In summary, with aging some opioid effects on the immune system are attenuated while others are not altered. Opioid generation of free radicals during stressful episodes may accelerate the aging process.

### Opioids, Diabetes Mellitus, and Aging

A number of studies have suggested an intimate relationship between glucose and opiates. Claude Bernard showed that morphine injections produced hyperglycemia. Abnormal fasting and two-hour postprandial glucose levels are present in 10 to 20% of patients on chronic methadone maintenance.[67] Following a mixed meal, we found an elevated glucose area under the curve in four of nine methadone maintenance subjects (Willenbring and Morley: unpublished observations). This was associated with an impaired insulin response. Glucose utilization following intravenous glucose administration was markedly impaired in 15 heroin addicts,[68] and heroin addicts have elevated glycosylated $HbA_1$ levels.[69] One theory of aging suggests it is secondary to glycosylation of tissues.[70] The above studies suggest that opioids may accelerate tissue glycosylation. Bryant *et al.*[71] showed that hypercholesterolemia produced by stressful stimuli was secondary to endogenous opioid release, and other studies found a decreased HDL in opiate addicts.[72] These changes would accelerate atherosclerosis development.

In 1956, Davis *et al.*[73] reported that glucose could potentiate the analgesic effect of morphine in the tail-flick test. Subsequently, Simon *et al.*[74] reported that diabetes mellitus decreased the potency of morphine-induced analgesia. In other studies, the effects of opioid antagonism on food intake were altered in diabetic animals and this effect could be modulated by exposure to a novel environment.[75,76] In morphine-addicted animals, opiate withdrawal is attenuated in animals with diabetes mellitus.

Humans with diabetes mellitus complain of pain more often than other patients with chronic diseases.[77] In our studies, we infused glucose into normal volunteers and found that this increased the sensitivity to pain.[78] Diabetic patients had a lower pain tolerance than did age-matched controls.

Patients with diabetes mellitus have impaired cognitive function compared to patients with other chronic diseases.[79,80] A similar impairment of retention is seen in mice with streptozotocin-induced diabetes mellitus.[81] This impairment of memory retention can be reversed by the administration of insulin and naloxone.

The mechanism by which glucose alters opiate responsiveness appears to involve a direct effect on the opiate receptor. Brase *et al.*[82] showed that glucose decreased receptor affinity for [³H]-naloxone and [³H]-dihydromorphine without a change in the number of binding sites. Morley *et al.*[83] found that glucose decreased the affinity for, but increased the number of, binding sites in the brain.

Overall, it appears that hyperglycemia, which is commonly present with advancing age,[84] modulates the effects of endogenous opioids through a direct interaction with the opioid receptor. In addition, there is some evidence that opioid release may, itself, produce hyperglycemia which would then feed back to modulate the effects of opioids.

## CONCLUSION

There is clear evidence that alterations in opioid function are associated with some of the behavioral changes seen with aging. With aging, there is a decreased opioid peptide content in the central nervous system and a decrease in mu opioid receptor numbers. Both the anorexia and hypodipsia associated with aging appear to involve the decrease in opioid regulation of ingestive behaviors. Beta-endorphin is a potent amnestic agent. There is some evidence that the secondary hypogonadism that occurs commonly in older males is due partly to excessive opioid tone. Beta-endorphin enhancement of NK activity is not altered by aging. Stress-induced beta-endorphin release may play a role in the pathogenesis of aging secondary to free radical generation.

Diabetes mellitus has been postulated to produce premature aging. Opiate addiction is associated with hyperglycemia and centrally administered beta-endorphin produces hyperglycemia. Hyperglycemia can modulate a number of opiate effects. A comparison of the effects of aging and diabetes mellitus on opioid-mediated behaviors is shown in TABLE 1.

**TABLE 1.** Comparison of the Effects of Aging and Diabetes Mellitus on Opioid-Mediated Behaviors[a]

| Behavior | Aging | Diabetes Mellitus |
|---|---|---|
| Food intake | ↓ opioid-mediated | ↑ or ↓ opioid-mediated (dependent on environment) |
| Water intake | ↓ opioid-mediated | ↓ opioid-mediated |
| Memory retention | ↓ but no change in opioid effects | ↓ reversed by naloxone |
| Impotence | ↑ (? ↓ testosterone due to excessive opioid tone) | ↑ |
| Menopause | ↓ estrogen leads to loss of naloxone ↑ in LH | ? |
| Immune function | β-endorphin ↑ NK activity and free radical formation | ? |
| Pain | Enhanced effect of morphine (? related to clearance). | ↓ effect of morphine |
| | Variable responses to pain. | hyperalgesia |

[a] ↓ = decreased; ↑ = increased.

## REFERENCES

1.　MORLEY, J. E. 1983. Neuroendocrine effects of endogenous opioid peptides in human subjects: A review. Psychoneuroendocrinology **8:** 361–379.
2.　MOORADIAN, A. D. 1988. Tissue specificity of premature aging in diabetes mellitus: the role of cellular replicative capacity. J. Am. Geriatr. Soc. **36:** 831–839.
3.　MORLEY, J. E., A. D. MOORADIAN, M. J. ROSENTHAL & F. E. KAISER. 1987. Diabetes mellitus in elderly patients: Is it different? Am. J. Med. **83:** 533–544.
4.　BRASE, D. A. & W. L. DEWEY. 1988. *In:* Nutritional Modulation of Neural Function. J. E. Morley, B. Sterman & J. H. Walsh, Eds. 263–268. Academic Press. San Diego, CA.
5.　GAMBERT, S. R., T. L. GARTHWAITE, C. M. PONTZER & T. C. HAGEN. 1980. Age-related changes in central nervous system beta-endorphin and ACTH. Neuroendocrinology **31:** 252–255.
6.　MISSALE, C., S. GOVONI, L. CROCE, A. BONO, P. F. SPANO & M. TRABUCCHI. 1983. Changes of β-endorphin and met-enkephalin in the hypothalamus-pituitary axis induced by aging. J. Neurochem. **40:** 20–24.
7.　TANG, F., J. TANG, J. CHOU & E. COSTA. 1984. Age-related and diurnal changes in met$^5$-enk-Arg$^6$-phe$^7$ and met$^5$-enkephalin contents of pituitary and rat brain structures. Life Sci. **35:** 1005–1014.

8.  DUPONT, A., P. SAVARD, Y. MERAND, F. LABRIE & J. R. BOISSIER. 1981. Age-related changes in central nervous system enkephalins and substance P. Life Sci. **29:** 2317–2322.

9.  MESSING, R. B., B. J. VASQUEZ, V. R. SPIEHLER, J. L. MARTINEZ, R. A. JENSEN, H. RIGTER & J. MCGAUGH. 1980. ³H-dihydromorphine binding in the brain regions of young and aged rats. Life Sci. **26:** 921–927.

10. UENO, E., D. D. LIU, I. K. HO & B. HOSKINS. 1988. Opiate receptor characteristics in brains from young, mature, and aged mice. Neurobiol. Aging **9:** 279–283.

11. HATFIELD, B. D., A. H. GOLDFARB, G. A. SFORZO & M. A. FLYNN. 1987. Serum-beta-endorphin and affective responses to graded exercise in young and elderly men. J. Gerontol. **42:** 429–431.

12. CASALE, G., M. PECORINI, G. CUZZONI & P. DENICOLA. 1985. Beta-endorphin and old pressure test in the aged. Gerontology **31:** 101–105.

13. ROLAND, E., R. FRANCESCHINI, A. MARABINI, V. MESSINA, A. CATALDI, M. SALVERNINI & T. BARRECA. 1987. Twenty-four-hour beta-endorphin secretory pattern in the elderly. Acta Endocrinol. **115:** 441–448.

14. FACCHINETTI, F., F. PETRAGLIA, G. NAPPI, E. MARTIGNONI, G. ANTONI, D. PASSINI & A. R. GENAZZANI. 1983. Different patterns of central and peripheral beta EP, beta LPH and ACTH throughtout life. Peptides **4:** 469–475.

15. MORLEY, J. E. 1986. Nutritional status of the elderly. Am. J. Med. **81:** 679–695.

16. MORLEY, J. E. & A. J. SILVER. 1988. Anorexia in the elderly. Neurobiol. Aging **9:** 9–16.

17. MORLEY, J. E., A. S. LEVINE, G. K. YIM & M. T. LOWY. 1983. Opioid modulation of appetite. Neurosci. Biobehav. Rev. **7:** 281–305.

18. MORLEY, J. E. 1987. Neuropeptide regulation of appetite and weight. Endocrinol. Rev. **8:** 256–287.

19. MORLEY, J. E. & A. S. LEVINE. 1983. Involvement of dynorphin and the kappa opioid receptor in feeding. Peptides **4:** 797–800.

20. ROMSOS, D. R., B. A. GOSNELL, J. E. MORLEY & A. S. LEVINE. 1987. Effects of kappa opiate agonists, cholecystokinin and bombesin on intake of diets varying in carbohydrate to fat ratio in rats. J. Nutrition **177:** 976–985.

21. GOSNELL, B. A., A. S. LEVINE & J. E. MORLEY. 1983. The effects of aging on opioid modulation of feeding in rats. Life Sci. **32:** 2793–2799.

22. KAVALIERS, M. & M. HIRST. 1985. The influence of opiate agonists on day-night feeding rhythms in young and old mice. Brain Res. **326:** 160–167.

23. MORLEY, J. E., E. N. HERNANDEZ & J. F. FLOOD. 1987. Neuropeptide Y increases food intake in mice. Am. J. Physiol. **253:** R516–R522.

24. ROSENTHAL, M. J. & J. E. MORLEY. 1989. CRF and age-related differences in behavior of mice. Neurobiol. Aging **10:** 167–171.

25. MORLEY, J. E. 1982. The ascent of cholecystokinin (CCK): From gut to brain. Life Sci. **30:** 479–493.

26. SILVER, A. J., J. F. FLOOD & J. E. MORLEY. 1988. Effect of gastrointestinal peptides on ingestion in young and old mice. Peptides **9:** 221–226.

27. FARIS, P. L., B. R. KOMISARUK, L. R. WATKINS & D. J. MAYER. 1983. Evidence for the neuropeptide cholecystokinin as an antagonist of opiate-analgesia. Science **219:** 310–312.

28. PHILLIPS, P. A., B. J. ROLLS, J. G. G. LEDINGHAM *ET AL.* 1984. Reduced thirst after water deprivation in healthy elderly men. N. Engl. J. Med. **311:** 753–759.

29. YAMAMOTO, T., H. HARADA, J. FUKUYAMA, T. HYASHI & I. MORI. 1988. Impaired arginine-vasopressin secretion associated with hypoangiotensinemia in hypernatremic dehydrated elderly patients. J. Am. Med. Assoc. **259:** 1039–1042.

30. SILVER, A. J., J. F. FLOOD & J. E. MORLEY. 1988. Effect of aging on fluid ingestion in mice. Gerontologist **28:** 137A.

31. SILVER, A. J. & J. E. MORLEY. 1989. Role of the opioid system in hypodipsia of aging. Clin. Res. **37:** 90A.

32. IZQUIERDO, I. 1979. Effect of naloxone and morphine on various forms of memory in the rat: possible role of endogenous opiate mechanisms in memory consolidation. Psychopharmacology **66:** 199–203.

33. KOVACS, G. L., B. BOHUS & D. DEWIED. 1980. Retention of passive avoidance behavior in

rats following γ-endorphin administration: effects of postlearning treatments. Neurosci. Lett. **19:** 197–201.

34. MARTINEZ, J. L., JR., & H. RIGETER. 1980. Endorphins alter acquisition and consolidation of inhibitory avoidance response in rats. Neurosci. Lett. **19:** 197–201.

35. IZQUIERDO, I. & R. D. DIAS. 1981. Effect of ACTH, epinephrine, B-endorphin, naloxone and of the combination of naloxone and B-endorphin with ACTH or epinephrine on memory consolidation. Psychoneuroendocrinology **8:** 81–87.

36. GALLAGHER, M., P. R. RAPP & R. J. FANELLI. 1985. Opiate antagonist facilitation of time-dependent memory processes: dependence upon intact norepinephrine function. Brain Res. **347:** 284–290.

37. MESSING, R. B., R. A. JENSEN, J. L. MARTINEZ, JR., V. R. SPIEHLER, B. J. VASQUEZ, B. SOUMIREU-MOURAT, K. C. LIANG & J. L. MCGAUGH. 1979. Naloxone enhancement of memory. Behav. Neural. Biol. **27:** 266–275.

38. FANELLI, R. J., R. A. ROSENBERG & M. Gallagher. 1985. Role of noradenergic function in the opiate antagonist facilitation of spatial memory. Behav. Neurosci. **99:** 751–755.

39. FULGINITTI, S. & L. M. CANCELA. 1983. Effect of naloxone and amphetamine on acquisition and memory consolidation of active avoidance responses in rats. Psychopharmacology **79:** 45–48.

40. TURNBULL, B. A., D. L. HILL, L. H. MILLER, J. MCELROY & R. S. FELDMAN. 1983. Effect of high doses of naloxone on shuttle avoidance acquisition in rats. Pharmacol. Biochem. Behav. **19:** 423–426.

41. FLOOD, J. F., A. C. CHERKIN & J. E. MORLEY. 1987. Antagonism of endogenous opioids modulates memory processing. Brain Res. **422:** 218–234.

42. REISBERG, B., S. H. FERRIS, R. ANAND, P. MIR, V. GEIBEL, M. S. DELEON & E. ROBERTS. 1983. Effects of naloxone on senile dementia: a double-blind study. N. Engl. J. Med. **108:** 721–722.

43. COHEN, M. R., R. M. COHEN, D. PICKAR, H. WEINGARTNER & D. MURPHY. 1983. High-dose naloxone infusions in normals. Arch. Gen. Psychiatr. **40:** 613–619.

44. COHEN, R. M., M. R. COHEN, H. WEINGARTNER, D. PICKAR & D. MURPHY. 1983. High-dose naloxone affects task performance in normal subjects. Psychiatr. Res. **8:** 127–136.

45. MORLEY, J. E., H. G. BARANETSKY, T. D. WINGERT, H. E. CARLSON, J. M. HERSHMAN, S. MELMED, S. R. LEVIN, K. JAMISON, R. WEITZMAN, J. CHANG & A. A. VANER. 1980. Endocrine effects of naloxone-induced opiate receptor blockade. J. Clin. Endocrinol. Metab. **50:** 251–257.

46. FILES, S. E. & T. SILVERSTONE. 1981. Naloxone changes self-ratings performance in normal subjects. Psychopharmacology **74:** 353–354.

47. HATSUKAMI, D. K., J. E. MITCHELL, J. E. MORLEY, S. F. MORGAN & A. S. LEVINE. 1986. Effect of naltrexone on mood and cognitive functioning among overweight men. Biol. Psychiatr. **21:** 291–300.

48. JUDD, J. L., D. S. JANOWSKY, D. S. SEGAL & L. HUEY. 1980. Naloxone-induced behavioral and physiological effects in normal and manic subjects. Arch. Gen. Psychiatr. **37:** 583–586.

49. VOLAVKA, J., R. DOMBUSH, A. MALLYA & D. CHO. 1977. Naloxone fails to affect short-term memory in man. Psychiatr. Res. **1:** 89–92.

50. FLOOD, J. F. & J. E. MORLEY. 1989. Pharmacological enhancement of long-term memory retention of old mice. J. Gerontol. In press.

51. FLOOD, J. F., G. E. SMITH & J. E. MORLEY. 1987. Modulation of memory processing by cholecystokinin: dependence on the vagus nerve. Science **236:** 832–834.

52. KAIYA, H., K. TANAKA, K. TAKEUCHI, K. MONTA, S. ADACHI, H. SHIRAKAWA, H. UEKI & M. NAMBA. 1983. Decreased level of β-endorphin-like immunoreactivity in cerebrospinal fluid of patients with senile dementia of Alzheimer's type. Life Sci. **33:** 1039–1043.

53. RASKIND, M. A., E. R. PESKIND, T. M. LAMPE, S. C. RESSE, G. J. TABORSKY & D. DORSA. 1986. Cerebrospinal fluid vasopressin, oxytocin, somatostatin and β-endorphin in Alzheimer's disease. Arch. Gen. Psychiatr. **43:** 382–388.

54. SLAG, M. F., J. E. MORLEY, M. K. ELSON, D. L. TRENCE, C. J. NELSON, A. E. NELSON, W. B. KINLAW, H. S. BEYER, F. Q. NUTTALL & R. B. SHAFER. 1983. Impotence in medical clinic outpatients. J. Am. Med. Assoc. **249:** 1736–1740.

55. MORLEY, J. E., N. G. BARANETSKY, T. D. WINGERT, H. E. CARLSON, J. M. HERSHMAN, S.

MELMED, S. R. LEVIN, K. R. JAMISON, R. WEITZMAN, R. J. CHANG & A. A. VARNER. 1980. Endocrine effects of naloxone-induced opiate receptor blockade. J. Clin. Endocrinol. Metab. **50:** 251–257.

56. MORLEY, J. E., N. E. KAY, G. F. SOLOMON & N. P. PLOTNIKOFF. 1987. Neuropeptides: conductors of the immune orchestra. Life Sci. **41:** 527–544.

57. MORLEY, J. E., N. KAY & G. F. SOLOMON. 1989. Opioid peptides, stress and immune function. In: Neuropeptides and Stress. Y. Tache, J. E. Morley & M. R. Brown, Eds. 222–234. Springer-Verlag.

58. SOLOMON, G. F., M. A. FIATARONE, D. BENTON, J. E. MORLEY, E. BLOOM & T. MAKINODAN. 1988. Psychoimmunologic and endorphin function in the aged. Ann. N.Y. Acad. Sci. **521:** 43–58.

59. NORMAN, D. C., J. E. MORLEY & M.-P. CHANG. 1988. Aging decreases beta-endorphin enhancement of T-cell mitogenesis in mice. Mech. Age Develop. **44:** 185–191.

60. KAY, N., J. ALLEN & J. E. MORLEY. 1984. Endorphins stimulate normal human peripheral blood lymphocyte natural killer activity. Life Sci. **35:** 53–59.

61. KAY, N., J. E. MORLEY & J. M. VAN REE. 1987. Enhancement of human lymphocyte natural killing function by non-opioid fragments of beta-endorphin. Life Sci. **40:** 1083–1087.

62. SOLOMON, G. F., M. A. FIATARONE, D. BENTON, J. E. MORLEY, E. BLOOM & T. MAKINODAN. 1988. Psychoimmunologic and endorphin function in the aged. Ann. N.Y. Acad. Sci. **521:** 43–58.

63. FIATARONE, M. A., J. E. MORLEY, E. T. BLOOM, D. BENTON, G. F. SOLOMON & T. MAKINODAN. 1989. The effect of exercise on natural killer cell activity in young and old subjects. J. Gerontol. **44:** M37–46.

64. FIATARONE, M. A., J. E. MORLEY, E. T. BLOOM, D. BENTON, T. MAKINODAN & G. F. SOLOMON. 1988. Endogenous opioids and the exercise-induced augmentation of natural killer cell activity. J. Lab. Clin. Med. **112:** 544–552.

65. SHARP, B. M., W. F. KEANE & H. J. SUH. 1985. Opioid peptides rapidly stimulate superoxide production by human polymorphonuclear leukocytes and macrophages. Endocrinology **117:** 793–795.

66. SIMPKINS, C. O., N. IVES & E. TATE. 1985. Naloxone inhibits superoxide release from human neutrophils. Life Sci. **37:** 1381–1386.

67. KREEK, M. J. 1973. Medical safety and side effects of methadone in tolerant individuals. J. Am. Med. Assoc. **223:** 665–668.

68. PASSARIELLO, N., D. GIUGLIANO, A. QUATRARO *ET AL.* 1983. Glucose tolerance and hormonal responses in heroine addicts. Metabolism **32:** 1163–1165.

69. GIUGLIANO, D., A. CENELLO, A. QUATRARO & F. D'ONOFRIO. 1985. Endogenous opiates, heroin addiction and non-insulin-dependent diabetes. Lancet **2:** 769–770.

70. BROWNLEE, M., A. CERAMI & H. VLASSARA. 1988. Advanced glycosylation end products in tissue and the biochemical basis of diabetic complications. N. Engl. J. Med. **318:** 1315–1321.

71. BRYANT, H. U., J. A. STORY & G. K. W. YIM. 1988. Assessment of endogenous opioid mediation in stress-induced hypercholesterolemia in the rat. Psychosom. Med. **50:** 576–585.

72. MORLEY, J. E. 1988. Drug abuse and the diabetic patient. City Medicine **2**(3): 16–19.

73. DAVIS, W. M., T. S. MIYA & T. D. EDWARDS. 1956. The influence of glucose and insulin pretreatment upon morphine analgesia in the rat. J. Am. Pharmacol. Assoc. Sci. Ed. **45:** 60–62.

74. SIMON, G. S., J. BORZELLECCA & W. L. DEWEY. 1981. Narcotics and diabetes II. Streptozotocin-induced diabetes selectively alters the potency of certain narcotic analgesics. J. Pharmacol. Exp. Ther. **218:** 324–329.

75. LEVINE, A. S., J. E. MORLEY, D. M. BROWN & B. S. HANDWERGER. 1982. Extreme sensitivity of diabetic mice to naloxone-induced suppression of food intake. Physiol. Behav. **28:** 987–989.

76. LEVINE, A. S., J. E. MORLEY, J. KNEIP, M. GRACE & D. M. BROWN. 1985. Environment modulates naloxone's suppressive effect on feeding in diabetic and non-diabetic rats. Physiol. Behav. **34:** 391–393.

77. N. MAYNE 1965. Neuropathy in the diabetic and non-diabetic populations. Lancet **2:** 1313–1316.

78. MORLEY, G. K., A. D. MOORADIAN, A. S. LEVINE & J. E. MORLEY. 1984. Why is diabetic peripheral neuropathy painful? The effect of glucose on pain perception in humans. Am. J. Med. **77:** 79–83.

79. PERLMUTER, L. C., M. K. HAKAMI & C. HODGSON-HARRINGTON. 1984. Decreased cognitive function in aging non-insulin-dependent diabetic patients. Am. J. Med. **77:** 1043–1048.

80. MOORADIAN, A. D., K. PERRYMAN, L. J. FITTEN, G. D. KAVONIAN & J. E. MORLEY. 1988. Cortical function in elderly non-insulin dependent diabetic patients. Behavioral and electrophysiological studies. Arch. Int. Med. **148:** 2369–2373.

81. FLOOD, J. F., J. E. MORLEY & A. D. MORRADIAN. 1987. Learning and memory impairment in diabetic mice. Fed. Proc. **46:** 1279A.

82. BRASE, D. A., Y.-H. HAN & W. L. DEWEY. 1987. Effects of glucose and diabetes on binding of naloxone and dihydromorphine to opiate receptors in mouse brain. Diabetes **36:** 1173–1177.

83. MORLEY, J. E., A. S. LEVINE, S. A. HESS, D. B. BROWN & B. S. HANDWERGER. 1981. Evidence for *in vivo* and *in vitro* modulation of the opiate receptor by glucose. Soc. Neurosci. Abstr. **7:** 854.

84. ROSENTHAL, M. J., J. M. HARTNELL, J. E. MORLEY, A. D. MOORADIAN, M. FIATARONE, F. E. KAISER & D. OSTERWEIL. 1987. UCLA Geriatric Grand Rounds: Diabetes in the Elderly. J. Am. Geriatr. Soc. **35:** 435–447.

# Mechanism of Autonomic Dysreflexia

## Contributions of Catecholamine and Peptide Neurotransmitters[a]

N. ERIC NAFTCHI

*New York University Medical Center*
*Institute of Rehabilitation Medicine*
*400 East 34th Street*
*New York, New York 10016*

Quadriplegic (tetraplegic) subjects are often afflicted with "autonomic hyperreflexia" or "autonomic dysreflexia" (AD), a term describing several events which are generally manifested by cardiovascular symptoms. Autonomic dysreflexia occurs only in subjects with transverse lesions of the cervical and thoracic spinal cord above the level of the thoracic sixth vertebrae (T6), *i.e.*, in subjects with lesion above the sympathetic outflow from the spinal cord. The bulbospinal monoaminergic terminals contain norepinephrine (NE), epinephrine (alpha-2), and serotonin (5-HT). A transection of spinal cord in the rat causes a disappearance of NE and 5-HT from the distal stump and their accumulation above the lesion and in the brain stem. In contrast to biogenic amines, substance P (SP), which is proposed as the putative neurotransmitter of the ascending, nociceptive spinothalamic pathways, accumulates below the level of transection in the spinal cord. Epinephrine terminals and alpha-2 receptors appear to complete a recurrent inhibitory pathway to sympathetic preganglionic neurons (SPGNs) which is activated by rapid increases in the excitability of SPGNs. The receptors for monoamines (with the exception of NE) and enkephalins are negatively coupled (inhibitory) to adenylate cyclase. The terminals for these transmitters, SP, and other neuropeptides innervate the sympathetic preganglionic neurons in the intermediolateral cell columns of the spinal cord. AD is also due to dysfunctions of the above-mentioned catecholamines and several other neurotransmitters/ neuromodulators. The role of neurotransmitters and neuropeptides in SPGNs, baroreceptors, and cardiovascular dysfunction in tetraplegia are evaluated in the presentations in this section.

Autonomic hyperreflexia, characterized by paroxysmal hypertension, has been well documented ever since Head and Riddoch (1917) first described the symptoms in quadriplegia.[1] Patients with high level spinal cord injury, above the sympathetic outflow at the level of thoracic six dermatome (T6), very often develop spontaneous hypertensive crises due to any one of several noxious stimuli.[2] These stimuli originate in areas below the lesion and usually arise from an irritated urinary bladder because of cystitis or kidney stone formation, or from the rectum because of rectal impaction. Since the quadriplegic patients are usually hypotensive, the high pressures that develop during autonomic dysreflexia represent pressure changes of a magnitude that can cause cerebrovascular accident and the death of a subject.

Considerable evidence[3-7] has implicated norepinephrine-containing nerves in certain

[a]This work was supported by the Edmund A. Guggenheim Clinical Research Endowment and by the Social and Rehabilitation Service, United States Department of Health, Education, and Welfare.

forms of hypertension and suggested that elevated levels of plasma and urinary catecholamines and serum dopamine-beta-hydroxylase activity reflect increased activity of the
sympathetic nervous system. Furthermore, it has been inferred[7] that measurement of
serum dopamine-beta-hydroxylase activity may be of diagnostic value in differentiating
various types of hypertension.

Synthesis of norepinephrine is catalyzed by the enzyme dopamine-beta-hydroxylase
from the precursor 3,4-dihydroxyphenyl-ethylamine, dopamine. Dopamine-beta-hydroxylase has been found in the catecholamine-containing granules in the heart[8] and in the
synaptosomes of the brain[9] and the splenic nerves.[10] It is also present in cell bodies and
nerve terminals[11] and localized in chromaffin granules of the adrenal medulla.[12] The
enzyme is found in the serum of a variety of mammalian species.[13] Analysis of dopamine-
beta-hydroxylase has provided evidence for the simultaneous release of the neurotransmitter norepinephrine and dopamine-beta-hydroxylase from the sympathetic nerve endings by the process of exocytosis.[14-17] Kvetnasky and Mikulaj (1979) have shown that
immobilization stress produces an increased release of catecholamines in the rat.[18] Weinshilboum et al. (1971) have also demonstrated an enhancement of serum dopamine-
beta-hydroxylase activity under the same stress conditions.[19] Wooten and Cardon (1973)
have found an elevation in serum dopamine-beta-hydroxylase activity during cold pressor
test and exercise in man.[20]

We have previously reported a rise in the excretion of catecholamine metabolites in
chronic quadriplegic subjects.[21,22] These levels are further enhanced during spontaneous
hypertensive episodes.[23,24] Tyrosine hydroxylase activity is also elevated in the rat brain,
brainstem and adrenal glands after transection of the spinal cord.[22] Therefore, as an index
of sympathetic activity, we decided to examine changes in serum dopamine-beta-hydroxylase activity in quadriplegic subjects with cervical spinal cord injury. The present paper
describes an enhancement in serum dopamine-beta-hydroxylase activity and in excretion
of catecholamine metabolites in quadriplegic humans that correlate directly with arterial
blood pressure during spontaneous hypertensive episodes or during hypertension resulting
from distension of the urinary bladder.

## METHODS

Excretory cystometry is a procedure preformed routinely on quadriplegic subjects to
measure the vesicular pressure produced by a given volume of urine and thereby determine whether a urinary bladder is hypertonic, normotonic, or hypotonic and whether the
distension of the urinary bladder produces reflex contractions.

A group of nine quadriplegic subjects were self-compared during routine excretory
cystometry before and after expansion of the urinary bladder by water intake. (Informed
consent was obtained from all subjects with approval from the Human Studies Commit-
tee.) All the subjects had complete physiological transections at the cervical fifth to
seventh dermatomes (C5-7) during chronic phase (at least 6 months after onset of injury).
Subjects that showed signs and symptoms of renal or cardiovascular involvement were
eliminated from the study.

Intracystic pressure was measured using a cystometric apparatus attached to an intraurethral catheter or an intraurethral catheter attached to a mercury-in-rubber Whitney
gauge and a Honeywell recorder. Digital blood flow in the fourth finger and the great toe
were measured calorimetrically.[22] In four C5-7 subjects, blood flow in the thumb, the
hallux, and the calf was simultaneously monitored before, during, and after hypertensive
episodes by venous occlusion plethysmography with a Whitney mercury-in-rubber strain
gauge attached to a Honeywell recorder. Brachial blood pressure was determined by the

auscultatory technique, and digital blood pressure with a Gaertner capsule using the flush-throb method.[22] Mean arterial and digital blood pressures were measured by adding one-third the pulse pressure to the diastolic pressure, *i.e.,* 1/3 (systolic-diastolic) + diastolic. Effective mean digital blood pressure was derived from the mean digital blood pressure.[22] Digital vascular resistance was calculated from the ratio of the effective mean digital pressure and the digital blood flow.

Control blood samples were drawn after the subject had been recumbent for 30 minutes and his bladder had been emptied and was free from all autonomic symptoms. The test samples during routine cystometric studies were not obtained at constant time intervals, since the time required for the rise in intracystic pressure varies in different individuals and depends on the type of bladder. The time relationship between dopamine-beta-hydroxylase data reported in FIGURES 1–3 is clear. A comparison between FIGURES 1–3 shows the variations in time and in the nature of the response between different subjects.

Serum dopamine-beta-hydroxylase activity was analyzed before and during spontaneous hypertensive crises and when the subject's blood pressure was at resting control levels, *i.e.,* when the urinary bladder was empty and no adverse autonomic signs were present. Serum dopamine-beta-hydroxylase activity was determined by a modification[26] of the sensitive isotopic method of Molinoff *et al.*[11] This technique utilizes the conversion of phenylethanolamine. The latter is converted to [14]C-labelled N-methylphenylethanolamine by purified bovine adrenal phenylethanolamine-N-methyltransferase in the presence of the active methyl donor s-adenosyl-methionine methyl [14]C. Serum dopamine-beta-hydroxylase units are given in nmoles phenylethanolamine/ml serum hour-1. The standard error of the mean for a repetitive analysis of dopamine-beta-hydroxylase activity in a given blood sample was 1.8 nmoles/ml hour-1 (ten assays)

Control urine specimens were withdrawn directly from the urinary bag attached to a urethral catheter. The urinary bag was immediately emptied, and the urine that had collected in the bag during hypertensive episodes was used as the samples during crises. Since urine specimens were obtained from the subjects who were undergoing spontaneous crises, the control values could have been somewhat higher than they should have been, since a spontaneous crisis cannot be predicted before its occurrence. This possibility was also reflected in higher than usual control values of arterial blood pressures. The specimens were acidified with a few drops of concentrated HCl and the creatinine concentration was determined by the method of Jaffe.[27] Urinary metabolites of catecholamines, 4-hydroxy-3-methoxymandelic acid (vanilmandelic acid) and 4-hydroxy-3-methoxyphenyl acetic acid (homovanillic acid) were analyzed by bidimensional paper chromatography.[28] Urinary 4-hydroxy-3-methoxyphenylethylene glycol (HMPG) was analyzed by gas-liquid chromatography.[29] The urine samples were incubated overnight with 0.1–0.2 ml of glusulase, a mixture of aryl sulfatase and beta-glucuronidase, derived from the digestive juices of *Helix pomatia* (Endo Corporation) at pH 5.2 and 37°C to hydrolyze conjugated HMPG. The free HMPG was then extracted with ethyl acetate at pH 6. By a modification of the latter method, a derivative of the extracted HMPG was made by reacting it with trifluoracetic acid anhydride. After drying with nitrogen gas, the 4-hydroxy-3-methoxyphenylethylene glycol-trifluoroacetate derivative was brought into solution by the addition of redistilled ethyl acetate and chromatographed on a 3% OV-17 coiled steel column (6 ft × 4 mm, o.d.) at 125°C. Nitrogen was used as the carrier gas; the flow rate of the nitrogen was regulated at 60 ml/min, and an electron capture detector was used for the detection of the 4-hydroxy-3-methoxyphenylethylene glycol-trifluoroacetate derivative in a model 1400 varian gas chromatograph.

Urinary-free metanephrine (3-0-methylepinephrine) and normetanephrine (3-0-methylnorepinephrine) were also analyzed. A urine sample was subjected to acid hydrolysis for 20 minutes in a boiling water bath, adsorbed on Amberlite CG-50 at pH 6.0–6.5, and

TABLE 1. Serum Dopamine-Beta-Hyrdoxylase Activity and Urinary Catecholamine Metabolites before and during Hypertensive Crises in Spinal Cord Injury[a]

| Subject | Brachial Blood Pressure (mm Hg) | | VMA (µg/mg Creatinine) | | HVA (µg/mg Creatinine) | | HMPG (µg/mg Creatinine) | | DβH (nmoles Phenylethanolamine/ml Serum Hour$^{-1}$). | |
|---|---|---|---|---|---|---|---|---|---|---|
| | Before | During | Before | During | Before | During | Before | During | Before | During |
| 1 | 108/68 | 230/130 | 1.5 | 5 | 2 | 10 | 2 | 6 | 718 | 1652 |
| 2 | 144/102 | 210/126 | 3 | 7 | 6 | 16 | 4 | 8 | 1155 | 1916 |
| 3 | 128/80 | 176/122 | 3 | 5 | 4 | 7 | 2 | 3 | 594 | 646 |
| 4 | 136/98 | 172/110 | 2.5 | 5 | 6 | 12 | 3 | 5.5 | 1394 | 1617 |
| 5 | 112/78 | 150/90 | 2 | 2.5 | 2 | 5 | 2 | 4 | 307 | 484 |
| Mean ± SD | 126 ± 15 | 188 ± 32 | 2.2 ± 0.91 | 4.9 ± 1.6 | 4.0 ± 2.0 | 10 ± 4.3 | 2.6 ± 0.89 | 5.3 ± 1.9 | 833 ± 437 | 1263 ± 650 |
| | 85 ± 14 | 116 ± 16 | | | | | | | | |
| p | | $<0.001$ | | $<0.001$ | | $<0.001$ | | $<0.001$ | | $<0.05$ |

[a] VMA = vanilmandelic acid, HVA = homovanillic acid, HMPG = 4-hydroxy-3-methoxyphenylethylene glycol, DβH = dopamine-beta-hydroxylase.

TABLE 2. Correlation between Serum Dopamine-Beta-Hydroxylase Activity and Excretion of Normetanephrine in Five C5–7 Quadriplegic Subjects

| Subject | Metanephrine (µg/100 mg Creatine) | | Normetanephrine (µg/100 mg Creatine) | | Dopamine-Beta-Hydroxylase (nmoles Phenylethanol amine/ml Serum Hour$^{-1}$) | |
|---|---|---|---|---|---|---|
| | Before | During | Before | During | Before | During |
| 1 | 12.2 | 16.4 | 42.0 | 175 | 718 | 1652 |
| 2 | 13.0 | 12.1 | 24.7 | 110 | 307 | 484 |
| 3 | 9.1 | 14.0 | 75.1 | 230 | 1394 | 1617 |
| 4 | 13.7 | 12.3 | 43.5 | 91 | 410 | 1069 |
| 5 | 15.3 | 18.2 | 87.0 | 220 | 1155 | 1916 |
| Mean + SD | 12.7 ± 2.3 | 14.6 + 2.7 | 54.5 ± 27.7 | 165.2 ± 62.9 | 796.8 ± 469.2 | 1347.6 ± 572.7 |
| p | | <0.15 | | <0.001 | | <0.001 |

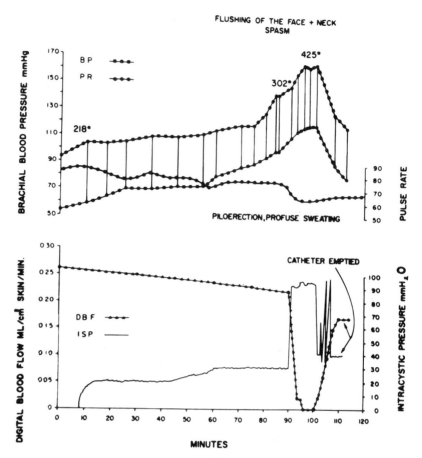

**FIGURE 1.** Water intake during excretory cystometry was used to test the urinary bladder function in this C7 quadriplegic subject. The brachial blood pressure was measured by the auscultatory technique and the blood flow in the fourth finger was determined calorimetrically. A cystometric apparatus attached to an indwelling catheter was used for measurement of intracystic pressure. B.P. = blood pressure, P.R. = pulse rate, D.B.F. = digital blood flow, and I.S.P. = intracystic pressure. An *asterisk* indicates the numbers that represents units of dopamine-beta-hydroxylase activity (nmoles phenylethanolamine formed/ml serum hour).

eluted with ammonium hydroxide. Separation of metanephrine and normetanephrine was achieved by the modification[30] of the Taniguchi and Armstrong technique.[31]

## RESULTS

Arterial pressure changes and changes in serum dopamine-beta-hydroxylase activity in nine quadriplegic subjects before and during hypertension precipitated by the excretory cystometry showed that the brachial blood pressure and dopamine-beta-hydroxylase activity were higher in all subjects examined. During spontaneous hypertensive crisis, autonomic hyperreflexia, serum dopamine-beta-hydroxylase activity and excretion of metabolites of dopamine, norepinephrine, and epinephrine were elevated in five C5–7 quadriplegic subjects (TABLE 1). In one C5–7 quadriplegic subject who developed hypertensive episodes on five separate occasions, there was an increase in serum dopamine-beta-hydroxylase activity and catecholamine metabolite excretion proportional to the severity of the crises. The increase in dopamine-beta-hydroxylase activity during spontaneous or induced hypertension correlated directly with the elevated levels of normetanephrine, a metabolite of norepinephrine, but not those of metanephrine, a metabolite of epinephrine (TABLE 2). The ratio of normetanephrine to metanephrine increased from 4.5 to 11.1 during hypertension.

FIGURE 1 illustrates the effect of gradual bladder filling and thereby stretching of the vesicular wall in one C7 quadriplegic subject; the filling was accompanied by a progressive rise in brachial blood pressure and serum dopamine-beta-hydroxylase activity. These changes were inversely proportional to pulse rate and blood flow in the fourth finger; blood flow dropped to unmeasurable amounts at the height of intracystic pressure. Similar results were obtained in one C6–7 quadriplegic subject (FIG. 2); the blood flow in the great toe significantly decreased from a control value of approximately 0.10 ml/cm 2 min-1 to 0.02 ml/cm 2 min-1 at the height of intracystic and brachial blood pressures. The high level of dopamine-beta-hydroxylase activity dropped to the control level or below the control level after the urinary bladder was emptied. In another C7 subject, the baseline level of serum dopamine-beta-hydroxylase was low and did not change appreciably at the

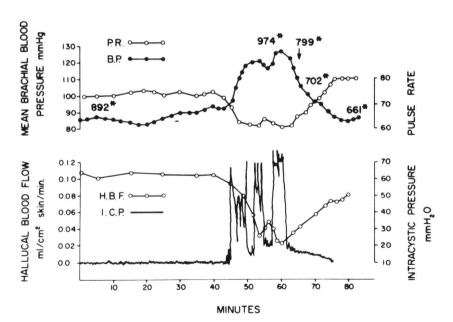

**FIGURE 2.** The blood flow in the great toe fell as did fourth finger blood flow in FIGURE 1 at the height of autonomic dysreflexia in this C6–7 quadriplegic subject. Serum dopamine-beta-hydroxylase activity enhanced 9% during the hypertension but dropped 18% (5 minutes) and 28% (8 minutes) after the bladder was emptied. I.C.P. = intracystic pressure, and H.B.F. = hallux blood flow (Other abbreviations and *asterisk* as in FIG. 1.)

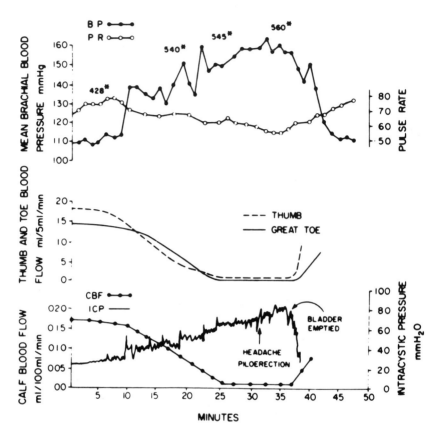

**FIGURE 3.** In this C5–6 quadriplegic subject, the blood flow in the thumb, the great toe, and the calf and the intracystic pressure were simultaneously monitored by a Whitney mercury-in-rubber strain gauge attached to a Honeywell recorder. The arterial blood pressure response followed the sudden spikes of intracystic pressures by 3–6 seconds. As the intravesicular pressure rose there was a simultaneous increase in arterial blood pressure and serum dopamine-beta-hydroxylase activity. First there was an increase and then a compensatory fall in the pulse rate as the peak pressures were sustained. At this time a concomitant and severe vasoconstriction in the upper and lower extremeties and the calf musculature occurred. This state of marked autonomic dysfunction was accompanied by flushing, profuse diaphoresis, piloerection, severe headache, and chest pain, which were relieved soon after the bladder was emptied. Abbreviations are the same as those in FIGURE 2, except that C.B.F. = calf blood flow.

height of dysreflexia or bladder emptying. By contrast, in the C5–7 quadriplegic subject (FIG. 2), whose baseline level of serum dopamine-beta-hydroxylase activity was high, there was a significant rise in dopamine-beta-hydroxylase activity at the height of the hypertension and autonomic dysfunction. After the urinary bladder was emptied, serum dopamine-beta-hydroxylase activity dropped below the baseline level. In another C5–6 subject whose baseline serum dopamine-beta-hydroxylase activity was 718 nmoles phe-nylethanolamine/ml serum hour-1, serum dopamine-beta-hydroxylase activity increased to 1652 nmoles/ml hour-1 during 25 minutes of sustained spontaneous hypertension. The arterial blood pressure had risen to 230/130 mm Hg at the height of the crisis. This 15-year-old subject experienced extreme headache, profuse flushing, and diaphoresis of the face and upper extremities. He was in a state of complete exhaustion, and, approximately 5 minutes after the remission of the crisis following the removal of a rectal impaction, his serum dopamine-beta-hydroxylase activity and arterial blood pressure had dropped to 137 nmoles/ml hour-1 and 84/54 mm Hg, respectively.

Similar to the findings in other subjects, in a C5–6 quadriplegic subject (FIG. 3), the gradual increase in intracystic pressure was accompanied by a proportional rise in arterial blood pressure and serum dopamine-beta-hydroxylase activity. There was a concomitant decrease in the pulse rate and the blood flow of the calf, the thumb, and the great toe. In three other C5–6 quadriplegic subjects, the distension of the urinary bladder by water intake was accompanied by the same autonomic and hemodynamic changes (FIG. 3). In all subjects the finger was more sensitive in response than were the hallux and the calf.

The changes in digital blood flow, digital blood pressure, and digital vascular resistance consequent to the expansion of the vesicular wall in a C5–6 quadriplegic subject are illustrated in FIGURE 4. In this subject the digital vascular resistance increased markedly at pressures greater than 105 mm Hg; when the effective mean digital blood pressure reached 115 mm Hg, the digital vascular resistance rose sharply and became almost asymptotic.

The increase in serum dopamine-beta-hydroxylase activity during hypertension in some subjects exceeded 150% of control values (TABLES 1 and 2).

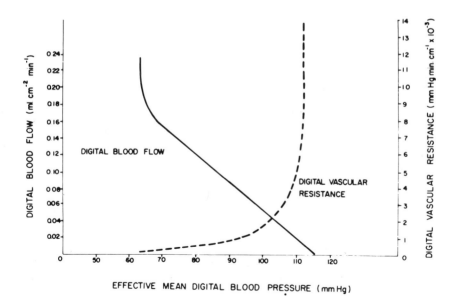

**FIGURE 4.** The relationship between digital blood flow and blood pressure in this C5–6 quadriplegic subject. The urinary bladder was distended by water intake. The increase in intravesicular pressure was accompanied by elevations in arterial and digital blood pressures and was commensurate with a precipitous fall in digital blood flow during hypertension. At mean digital pressure greater than 105 mm Hg, the digital vascular resistance increased rapidly and became asymptotic above 110 mm Hg.

## DISCUSSION

During the past 25 years a great deal of evidence has accumulated to implicate dysfunction in norepinephrine storage, release, and metabolism in certain forms of hypertension.[3-5] Engleman et al.,[6] DeQuattro and Chan,[32] and Louis et al.[33] have shown an increase in the concentrations of plasma catecholamines in essential hypertension. Geffen et al.[34] have shown that although circulating catecholamines are greatly increased in subjects with phaeochromocytoma, plasma dopamine-beta-hydroxylase is not significantly elevated. By contrast, they found a correlation between dopamine-beta-hydroxylase and plasma catecholamines in essential hypertension.[34] These findings agree with those of Weinshilboum et al.[19] who found that adrenalectomy in the rat does not alter the baseline levels of serum dopamine-beta-hydroxylase. Therefore, the activity of serum dopamine-beta-hydroxylase represents the amounts released from sympathetic nerve endings. These results[34] also agree with our finding of a direct correlation of arterial blood pressure with serum dopamine-beta-hydroxylase activity and concentrations of urinary normetanephrine but not with levels of urinary metanephrine. Normetanephrine is the immediate 3-0-methylated catabolite of norepinephrine, and metanephrine is the comparable metabolite of epinephrine synthesis mainly in the adrenal medulla. Since there was no appreciable change in metanephrine during hypertension (TABLE 2), the release of epinephrine from adrenal glands did not contribute to the hypertension in quadriplegia and, in the subjects examined in the present study, the hypertensive stress was not sympathoadrenal but rather it was purely sympathetic and due to norepinephrine release. A physiological corollary of these findings is the occurrence of bradycardia at the height of hypertension, an effect generally seen after norepinephrine infusion; the administration of epinephrine causes tachycardia.

During autonomic dysreflexia induced by infusion of saline into the urinary bladder, Garnier and Girtsch[35] have reported increased excretion of urinary concentration of epinephrine and vanilmandelic acid. Sizemore and Winternitz[36] found no change in catecholamine and vanilmandelic acid concentrations in 24-hour urine specimens from two quadriplegic subjects, although they succeeded in suppressing all adverse autonomic symptoms by treatment with the alpha-receptor blocker, phenoxybenzamine.

Our studies in quadriplegia clearly demonstrate that during spontaneous or induced hypertension there is a definite, direct correlation between serum dopamine-beta-hydroxylase activity, concentration of urinary normetanephrine, and levels of arterial blood pressure. These findings are consistent with the concept that there is a proportional release of the neurotransmitter norepinephrine together with dopamine-beta-hydroxylase from the sympathetic nervous system of man, possibly by the process of exocytosis. The process of exocytosis involves a fusion of the norepinephrine storage vesicle with the neuronal membrane. Nerve depolarization is followed by an opening of the cell membrane whereupon norepinephrine and all the soluble vesicular contents are extruded into the postjunctional cleft; one such vesicle-specific soluble protein is dopamine-beta-hydroxylase. This process has already been demonstrated in other mammalian species.[14-17] Since the concentration of urinary homovanilic acid, the major catabolite of dopamine, is sharply elevated during hypertensive episodes, the results suggest that dopamine, which serves as a substrate for the biosynthesis of norepinephrine, is also released concomitantly with norepinephrine and dopamine-beta-hydroxylase after hypertensive episodes (FIG. 2) and suggests that the half-life of circulating dopamine-beta-hydroxylase released during stress is shorter than that previously reported.[37]

In quadriplegia there were large individual variations in serum dopamine-beta-hydroxylase activity as previously described by Weinshilboum and Axelrod[19] and Freedman et al.[38] for normal subjects. The ease with which a hypertensive response is brought about in these subjects during routine test of their bladder function makes a self-controlled study of hypertension very facile and provides the unique advantage of studying changes in sympathetic activity and biochemical parameters under conditions that are not readily available in other models of hypertension.

An intense vasoconstriction in the upper and lower extremities of all nine subjects accompanied by a simultaneous decrease in the blood flow of the calf musculature was observed during the expansion of the urinary bladder. This generalized vasoconstriction below the level of the lesion correlated with elevated levels of arterial blood pressure, enhanced serum dopamine-beta-hydroxylase levels, and increased excretion of catecholamine metabolites, notably normetanephrine. Roussan et al.[39] showed that blood flow in the calf of one quadriplegic subject was decreased during autonomic hyperreflexia. They speculated that consequent to the expansion of the urinary bladder there was a gradual facilitation of the spinal cord which served as a primary cause for the reduced circulation in the calf musculature. They also suggested that the cause of or the increase in hypertension was the result of sudden shifts of large blood volumes from skeletal muscle circulation to the capacitance vessels. Our findings of marked vasoconstriction in the upper and lower extremities and the calf musculature indicate that the blood shift into the capacitance vessels at the height of hypertension must be of enormous magnitude; it may act as positive feedback causing compensatory vasodilation, profuse flushing, and diaphoresis in the head and neck and ultimately, chest pain and headache. Due to the lack of data on venous blood volume and compliance of these vessles, however, this line of reasoning remains speculative.

Dahlstrom and Fuxe,[40] using the histochemical fluorescence technique, demonstrated in the rat that soon after a transection of the spinal cord, norepinephrine and 5-hydroxytryptamine accumulate above the level of the lesion, not only in the descending fibers but also in certain norepinephrine and 5-hydroxytryptamine terminals of the sympathetic lateral column and the ventral horn. Furthermore, the increase in fluorescence intensity was accompanied by swollen varicosities. It has also been shown[22,40–42] that not only do norepinephrine and 5-hydroxytryptamine accumulate above, but they also disappear from the cord below the level of transection. Their disappearance suggests that one of these biogenic amines may be an inhibitory neurotransmitter within the spinal cord, since both norepinephrine and 5-hydroxytryptamine depress anterior horn cells and Renshaw cells.[43,44] Previous work has shown that GABA content of the spinal cord below the lesion increased significantly and presynaptic inhibition became maximally depressed.[45] Our results suggested that during the chronic phase of spinal cord injury there is a decrease in release of GABA, the interneuronal inhibitory neurotransmitter which mediates presynaptic inhibition.[46] The loss of the inhibitory neurotransmitter(s) after spinal cord injury may cause permanent facilitation of the cord below the level of the lesion. In subjects with injuries to the cervical spinal cord, this absence or curtailment of inhibition within the greater segment of the cord (thoracolumbar and sacral) coupled with the lack of control from higher centers could be the primary reason why noxious stimuli easily produce extreme autonomic responses. For example, stimuli arising from the mucosa and muscle coats of the stretched vesicular wall reach the spinal cord via presacral and pelvic nerves. Unimpeded by suprasegmental inhibitory influences or by an inhibitory neurotransmitter within the cord, these impulses travel rostrally by way of lateral spinothalamic tracts to the level of transection and reflexly stimulate the intact sympathetic chain. This process results in arteriolar vasoconstriction in the skin vessels and the splanchnic bed in direct proportion to the amount of norepinephrine released. The peak of the vasoconstriction below the level of the lesion coincides with the peak of intracystic pressure at which time the increased release of norepinephrine has caused the highest rise in arterial blood pressure and maximal peripheral resistance (FIG. 4).

*Inevitability of Autonomic Dysreflexia*

The hypertension is sensed by the baroreceptors in the carotid sinus and aortic arch which are strategically located to sense changes in arterial blood pressure. The stretch of arterial walls caused by elevations in arterial blood pressure generates afferent impulses from baroreceptors. The afferent impulses from the mechanoreceptors in the carotid sinuses and aortic arch,[47] are transmitted via the carotid sinus nerve and conducted chiefly through the glossopharyngneal, IXth, and vagal, Xth, cranial nerves.[48,49] These afferent pathways make their first synapse in the nucleus tractus solitarii (NTS) located in the medulla oblongata.[50-53] The efferent pathway is comprised of the cardiac vagus nerve, the sympathetic adrenergic nerves to the heart, and the capacitance and resistance vessels. Control of heart rate, particularly in human, appears to reside in aortic arch.[54] Efferent impulses from the cardiovascular center via the vagus cause bradycardia. The afferent discharges from the baroreceptors to the cardiovascular center cause vasodilation in the face and the neck pulsating temporal arteries, a histamine-like flush, profuse diaphoresis, and headache in contrast to the pallor, chest pain, extreme vasoconstriction, and pilo-erection below the level of transection. However, without the removal of the stimulus or the administration of ganglioplegic or sympatholytic drugs, these remaining regulatory mechanisms cannot appreciably lower the blood pressure. In spinal cord injury, because of chronic hypotension, the pressure threshold for carotid sinus is set at a lower arterial blood pressure level or a lower set point. Thus, the baroreceptors are reset at a lower arterial blood pressure and would tend to regulate and maintain the blood pressure at the hypotensive level.

The rate of impulse transmission in a Hering's nerve is different at variable pressures and has a sigmoid shape. The response is highest at or near the region of mean arterial blood pressure where the baroreceptors need to be most sensitive in order to keep the arterial blood pressure at the normal range. The baroreceptors are inherently more sensitive to a rising rather than a falling blood pressure; they are ineffective at a mean arterial blood pressure of less than 60 mm Hg and higher than and approximately 160 mm Hg. Further, in quadriplegia ineffectiveness of the baroreceptors is enhanced because they are reset at a low basal arterial blood pressure. During autonomic dysreflexia, therefore, at a certain level of arterial blood pressure, the baroreceptor ineffectiveness coupled with the lack of reflex vasodilation of peripheral organs below the lesion, make the pressure rise assymptotically (FIG. 4). Although the low pressure receptors in the walls of atria and pulmonary arteries cannot detect alterations of systemic arterial blood pressure, they can distinguish changes in low pressure areas in the circulatory system. They thus evoke reflexes which are additive with those of baroreceptors in controlling blood pressure homeostasis.

During an attack of autonomic dysreflexia, the increase in arterial blood pressure leads to a rise in the activity of mechanoreceptors in carotid sinus and aortic arch. The efferent impulses, in turn, increase the tonic inhibition of NTS in the medulla oblongata which leads to the enhanced vagal impulses to the heart, and reduced sympathetic outflow to the heart and blood vessels. The ensuing reflex, vasodilation of the systemic, vascular beds, brought about by the afferent impulses from the baroreceptors, in addition to brachycardia, would then tend to lower the total peripheral resistance. Despite marked bradycardia in high spinal cord injury (above T6), the arterial blood pressure does not abate but keeps rising during autonomic dysreflexia (FIG. 4).

Supersensitivity of alpha-adrenoceptors in the microvasculature is in part responsible for exaggerated response to noxious stimuli in quadriplegia.[55-57] The blockade of sympathetic outflow from the spinal cord at or above thoracic sixth vertebrae, T6, however, must be considered the most important factor which contributes to autonomic dysreflexia.

Despite central and peripheral adrenoceptor supersensitivity, paraplegic subjects with spinal cord lesions one or two vertebral levels below T6, do not experience autonomic dysreflexia. Hypertensive episodes are accompanied by a complete peripheral vasoconstriction in the toes, calves, fingers, and paradoxically in the splanchnic circulation without compensatory vasodilation. Similar to the occurrence after histamine administration,[58] there is a profuse flushing of the face which diffuses downward. This may be due to neurotransmitter and/or neuropeptide vasodilator(s) such as histamine, prostaglandin [PGE-2],[59] substance P, or vasoactive intestinal peptide (VIP) co-released into the local microcirculation.

Autonomic dysreflexia results from dysfunction of a number of neurotransmitters and neuropeptides. Descending monoaminergic pathways containing norepinephrine and 5-hydroxytryptamine are disrupted removing the inhibitory function of these transmitters.[25,40–42,55,60] Ascending neuronal pathways containing substance P are blocked, with a resultant buildup of this putative/neurotransmitter (modulator) below the level of transection.[61] A predominance of excitatory effects has been reported after iontophoretic application of substance P on brain and spinal cord neurons.[62–64] Although inhibitory effects of substance P are rarely observed, when they occur they consistently block the excitatory action of acetylcholine on Renshaw cells, thus preventing the inhibitory action of these interneurons.[65,66]

The concentrations of glycine (inhibitory) and aspartate (excitatory) also decline in the canine spinal cord post-transection.[23] The decrease in glycine correlates with the decrement in postsynaptic and recurrent inhibition observed by Herman et al.[66] and Veale et al.[67] in humans with various neurological lesions. Therefore, in addition to changes observed in GABA-ergic transmission, spinal cord lesions also affect other interneuronal neurotransmitters.

The major factors contributing to the inadequate regulation of arterial blood pressure in spinal cord injury are:

1. Baroreceptors' inherent insensitivity at high levels of arterial blood pressure aggravated by reseting, due to hypotension, at a low arterial blood pressure level.
2. Supersensitivity of the spinal alpha-adrenoceptors below the lesion because of chronic lack of the neurotransmitter norepinephrine.
3. Supersensitivity of peripheral microvascular adrenoceptors.
4. Accumulation of substance P below the lesion in the ascending substance Pergic pathways.
5. Impairment of GABA release from the GABAergic interneurons.
6. The level of myelopathy above sympathetic outflow from the spinal cord (T6).

Factors 1–5 contribute to and the last factor 6 helps maintain and exacerbate the high arterial blood pressure by allowing vasoconstriction rather than permitting a reflex vasodilation of systemic blood vessels including those subserving the splanchnic circulation.

## REFERENCES

1. HEAD, H. & J. RIDDOCH. 1976. Autonomic bladder, excessive sweating, and some other reflex conditions in gross injuries of the spinal cord. Brain **40:** 188–263.
2. GUTTMAN, L. & D. WHITTERIDGE. 1974. Effects of bladder distension on autonomic mechanisms after spinal cord injuries. Brain **70:** 361–405.
3. GITLOW, S. E., M. MENDLOWITZ, E. K. WILK, S. WILK, R. L. WOLF & N. E. NAFTCHI. 1964. Plasma clearance of D.L.-β-³H-norepinephrine in normal human subjects and patients with essential hypertension. J. Clin. Invest. **43:** 2009–2015.
4. DECHAMPLAIN, J., L. KARKOFF & J. AXELROD. 1969. Interrelationships of sodium intake, hypertension, and norepinephrine storage in the rat. Circ. Res. **24**(Suppl. 1): 75–92.

5. SPECTOR, S., J. TARVER & B. BERKOWITZ. 1972. Catecholamine biosynthesis and metabolism in vasculature of normotensive and hypertensive rats. *In* Spontaneous Hypertension; Its Pathogenesis and Complications. K. Okamoto, Ed. 41–45. Igaku Shoin, Ltd. Tokyo.

6. ENGELMAN, K., B. PORTNEY & A. SJOERDSMA. 1970. Plasma catecholamine concentrations in patients with hypertension. Circ. Res. **27** (Suppl. 1): 141–146.

7. SCHANBERG, S., R. STONE, N. KIRSHNER, J. GUNNELS & R. ROBINSON. 1974. Plasma dopamine-beta-hydroxylase: a possible aid in the study and evaluation of hypertension. Science **183**: 523–525.

8. POTTER, J. T. & J. AXELROD. 1963. Properties of norepinephrine storage particles in the rat heart. J. Pharmacol. Exp. Ther. **142**: 299–305.

9. COYLE, J. T. & J. AXELROD. 1974. Dopamine-beta-hydroxylase in the rat brain: development characteristics. J. Neurochem. **19**: 449–459.

10. STJARNE, L. & F. LISHAJKO. 1967. Localization of different steps in noradrenaline synthesis to different fractions of bovine splanchnic nerve homogenates. Biochem. Pharmacol. **16**: 1719–1798.

11. MOLINOFF, P. B., W. S. BRIMIJOIN, R. M. WEINSHIBOUM & J. AXELROD. 1970. Neurally mediated increases in dopamine-beta-hydroxylase activity. Proc. Natl. Acad. Sci. USA **66**: 453–458.

12. KIRSHNER, N. 1957. Pathway of noradrenaline formation from dopa. J. Biol. Chem. **226**: 821–825.

13. WEINSHILBOUM, R. M. & J. AXELROD. 1971. Serum dopamine-beta-hydroxylase activity. Circ. Res. **28**: 307–315.

14. WEINSHILBOUM, R. M., N. B. THOA, D. G. JOHNSON, I. J. KOPIN & J. AXELROD. 1971. Proportional release of norepinephrine and dopamine-beta-hydroxylase from sympathetic nerves. Science **174**: 1349–1351.

15. VIVEROS, O.H., L. ARQUEROS & N. KIRSHNER. 1968. Release of catecholamine and dopamine-beta-oxidase from adrenal medulla. Life Sci. **7**: 609–618.

16. GEWIRTZ, G. P. & I. J. KOPIN. 1970. Release of dopamine-B-hydroxylase with norepinephrine during cat splenic nerve stimulation. Nature (London) **227**: 406–407.

17. GEFFEN, L. B., B. G. LIVETT & R. A. RUSH. 1969. Immunohistochemical localization of protein components of catecholamine storage vesicles. J. Physiol. (London) **204**: 593–605.

18. KVETNANSKY, R. & L. MIKULAJ. 1970. Adrenal and urinary catecholamines in rats during adaptation to repeated immobilization stress. Endocrinology **87**: 738–743.

19. WEINSHILBOUM, R. N. M., R. KVETNANSKY, J. AXELROD & I. J. KOPIN. 1971. Elevation of serum dopamine-beta-hydroxylase activity with forced immobilization. Nature (New-Biol.) **230**: 287–288.

20. WOOTEN, G. F. & P. CARDON. 1973. Plasma dopamine-beta-hydroxylase activity: elevation in man during cold pressor test and exercise. Arch. Neurol. **28**: 103–106.

21. NAFTCHI, N. E., E. W. LOWMAN, H. RUSK & T. REICH. 1969. Urinary catecholamine metabolites in spinal cord injured human. Fed. Proc. **28**: 544.

22. NAFTCHI, N. E., E. W. LOWMAN, G. H. SELL & H. A. RUSK. 1972. Peripheral circulation and catecholamine metabolism. in paraplegia and quadriplegia Arch Phys. Med. Rehab. **53**: 357–362.

23. NAFTCHI, N. E., E. W. LOWMAN, H. SELL & H. RUSK. 1971. Hypertensive crises associated with increased urinary catecholamine catabolites in spinal man. Fed. Proc. **30**: 678.

24. SELL, G. H., N. E. NAFTCHI, E. W. LOWMAN & H. RUSK. 1972. Autonomic hyperreflexia and catecholamine metabolites in spinal cord injury. Arch. Phys. Med. Rehab. **53**: 415–418.

25. NAFTCHI, N. E., M. DEMENY, A. KERTESZ & E. W. LOWMAN 1972. CNS and adrenal tyrosine hydroxylase activity and norepinephrine, serotonin and histamine in the spinal cord after transection. (Abstr.) Fed. Proc. **31**: 3483.

26. WEINSHILBOUM. R. M. & J. AXELROD. 1971. Reduced plasma dopamine-beta-hydroxylase activity in familial dysautonomia, N. Engl. J. Med. **285**: 938–942.

27. JAFFE, M. 1886. Über den Niederschlag, welchen Pilerinsaure in normalen Harnerzeugt und über eine neue Reaction des Kreatinis. Z. Physiol. Chem. **10**: 391–400.

28. ARMSTRONG, M. D., K. N. F. SHAW & P. E. WALL. 1956. The phenolic acids. J. Biol. chem. **218**: 293–303.

29. WILK, E., S. E. GITLOW, D. D. CLARKE & D. H. PALEY. 1967. Determination of urinary

3-methoxy-4-hydroxyphenylethyleneglycol by gas-liquid chromatography and electron capture detections. Clin. Chem. Acta **16**: 403–408.

30. WILK, E., S. GITLOW & L. BERTANI. 1968. Modification of the Taniguchi method for the determination of normetanephrine and metanephrine. Clin. Chem. Acta **20**: 147–148.

31. TANIGUCHI, K., Y. KAKIMOTO & M. ARMSTRONG. 1964. Quantitative determination of metanephrine and normetanephrine in urine. J. Lab. Clin. Med. **64**: 469–484.

32. DEQUATTRO, V. & S. CHAN. 1972. Raised plasma catecholamines in some patients with primary hypertension. Lancet **1**:806–809.

33. LOUIS, W. J., A. E. DOYLE & S. ANAVEKAR. 1973. Plasma norepinephrine levels in essential hypertension. N. Engl. J. Med. **288**:599–601.

34. GEFFEN, L. B., R. A. RUSH, W. J. LOUIS & A. E. DOYLE. 1973. Plasma catecholamines and dopamine-beta-hydroxylase amounts in phaeochromocytoma. Clin. Sci. **44**: 421–424.

35. GARNIER, V. B. & R. GERTSCH. 1964. Autosome Hyperreflexia und Katecholaminausschel-dung beim Paraplegiker. Schweiz Med. Wochenschr. **94**: 124–130.

36. SIZEMORE, G. W. & W. W. WINTERNITZ. 1970. Autonomic hyperreflexia: suppression with alpha-adrenergic blocking agents. N. Engl. J. Med. **282**: 795.

37. RUSH, R. A. & L. B. GEFFEN. 1972. Radioimmunoassay and clearance of circulating dopamine-beta-hydroxylase. Circ. Res. **31**: 444–452.

38. FREEDMAN, L. S., T. OHUCHI, M. GOLDSTEIN, F. AXELROD, I. FISH & J. DANCIS. 1972. Changes in human serum dopmaine-beta-hydroxylase activity with age. Nature (London) **236**: 310–311.

39. ROUSSAN, M. S., A. S. ABRAMSON, H. I. LIPPMANN & G. DIORONZIO. 1966. Somatic and autonomic responses to bladder filling in patients with complete transverse myelopathy. Arch. Phys. Med. **47**: 450–456.

40. DAHLSTROM, A. & K. FUXE. 1965. Evidence for the existence of monoamine neurons in the central nervous system: II. Experimentally induced changes in the intraneuronal amine levels of bulbospinal neuron systems. Acta Physiol. Scand. (Suppl.) **64**: 1–85.

41. ANDEN, N. E., E. HAGGENDAL, T. MAGNUSSON & E. ROSENGREN. 1964. Time course of the disappearance of noradrenaline and 5-hydroxytryptamine in spinal cord after transection. Acta Physiol. Scand. **62**: 115–118.

42. MAGNUSSON, T. & E. ROENGREN. 1963. Catecholamines of the spinal cord normally and after transection. Experimentia **19**: 229–230.

43. PHILLIS, J. W., A. K. TEBECIS & D. H. YORK. 1968. Depression of spinal motoneurons by noradrenaline, 5-hydroxytryptamine and histamine. Eur. J. Pharmacol. **4**: 471–475.

44. WEIGHT, F. F. & G. C. SALMOIRAGHI. 1966. Adrenergic responses of Renshaw cells. J. Pharmacol. Exp. Ther. **154**: 391–396.

45. SMITH, J. E., P. V. HAII, R. L. CAMPELL, A. R. JONES & M. H. APRISON. 1976. Levels of aminobutyric acid in the dorsal grey lumbar spinal cord during the development of experimental spinal spasticity. Life Sci. **19**: 1525–1530.

46. NAFTCHI, N. E., W. SCHLOSSER & W. D. HORST. 1979. Correlation of changes in the GABA-ergic system with the development of spasticity in paraplegic cats. GABA-Biochemistry and CNS Function. 431–450. Plenum Publishing. New York, NY.

47. ABRAHAM, A. 1969. Microscopic innervation of the heart and blood vessels in vertebrates including man. 260–304. Pergamon Press. Oxford.

48. SATO, A, S. FIDONE & C. EYZAGUIRRE. 1968. Presence of chemoreceptor C-fibers in the carotid nerve of the cat. Brain Res. **11**: 459–463.

49. FIDONE, S. J. & A. SATO. 1969. Study of chemoreceptor and baroreceptor A and C fibers in the cat carotid nerve. J. Physiol. (London) **205**: 527–548.

50. PALKOVITS, M., E. MEZEY & L. ZABORSKY 1979. Neuroanatomical evidences for direct neural connections between the brain stem baroreceptor centers and the forebrain areas involved in the neural regulation of the blood pressure, *In* Nervous System and Hypertension. H. Schmidt, Ed. 18–30. Wiley-Flamerion. Paris.

51. CRILL, W. E. & D. J. REIS. 1968. Distribution of carotid sinus and depressor nerves in cat brainstem. Am. J. Physiol. **214**: 269–276.

52. BISCOE, T. J. & S. R. SAMPSON 1970. Field potentiates evoked in the brain system of the cat by stimulation of the carotid sinus, glossopharyngeal, aortic and superior larngeal nerves. J. Physiol. (London) **209**: 341–358.

53. VATNER, S. F. & E. BRAUNWALD. 1975. Cardiovascular control mechanisms in conscious state. N. Engl. J. Med. **293:** 970–976.
54. LONGHURST, J. C. 1982. Arterial baroreceptors in health and disease. Cardiovasc. Rev. Rep. **3:** 271–298.
55. NAFTCHI, N. E., G. F. WOOTEN, E. W. LOWMAN & J. AXELROD. 1974. Relationship between serum dopamine-beta-hydroxylase activity, catecholamine metabolism, and hemodynamic changes during paroxysmal hypertension in quadriplegia. Circ. Res. **35:** 850–861.
56. NAFTCHI, N. E., M. DEMENY & A. T. VIAU. 1981. Changes neurotransmitter receptors in the spinal cord after paraplegia. Trans. Am. Soc. Neurochem. **12:** 259.
57. NAFTCHI, N. E., K. T. RAGNARSSON, G. H. SELL & E. LOWMAN. 1975. Increased digital vascular reactivity to L-norepinephrine in quadriplegia. Am. Congr. Rehab. Med. **37:** 53.
58. NAFTCHI, N. E., M. MENDLOWITZ, S. RACOCEANU & E. W. LOWMAN. 1969. Catecholamine metabolism and digital circulation after histamine and its analogue. *In* Oxygen Transport to Tissue. 699–712. Plenum Publishing Corporation.
59. NAFTCHI, N. E., M. DEMENY, E. W. LOWMAN & J. TUCKMAN. 1978. Hypertensive crises in quadriplegic patients: changes in cardiac output, blood volume, serum dopamine-beta-hydroxylase activity and arterial prostaglandin PGE-2. Circulation **57:** 336–341.
60. CARLSSON, A., T. MAGNUSSON & E. ROSENGREN. 1963. 5-Hydroxytryptamine of the spinal cord normally and after transection. Experimentia (Basel) **19:** 359–360.
61. NAFTCHI, N. E. S. J. ABRAHAMS, H. ST. PAUL, E. W. LOWMAN & W. SCHLOSSER. 1978. Localization and changes of substance P in spinal cord of paraplegic cats. Brain Res. **153:** 507–513.
62. HENRY, J. L. 1976. Effects of substance P on functionally identified units in cat spinal cord. Brain Res. **114:** 439–452.
63. KRNJEVIC, K. & D. LEKIC. 1977. Substance P selectively blocks excitation of Renshaw cell by acetylcholine. Can. J. Physiol. Pharmacol. **53:** 923–932.
64. OTSUKA, M. & S. KONISHI. 1976. Substance P and excitatory transmitter of primary sensory neurons. Cold Spring Harbor Symp. Quant. Biol. **40:** 135–143.
65. HALL, P. V., J. E. SMITH, R. L. CAMPELL, D. L. FELTEN & M. H. APRISON. 1976. Neurochemical correlates of spasticity. Life Sci. **18:** 1467–1472.
66. HERMAN, R., W. FREEDMAN & S. MEEKS. 1973. Physiological aspects of hemiplegic paraplegic spasticity. New Dev. Electromyogr. Clin. Neurophysiol. **3:** 579–588.
67. VEALE, J. L., S. REES & R. F. MARK. 1973. Renshaw cell activity in normal and spastic man. New Dev. Electromyogr. Clin. Neurophysiol. **3:** 523–537.

# Distribution and Coexistence of Neuropeptides in Bulbospinal and Medullary Autonomic Pathways[a]

C.J. HELKE, K.B. THOR, AND C.A. SASEK

*Department of Pharmacology*
*Uniformed Services University of the Health Sciences*
*4301 Jones Bridge Road*
*Bethesda, Maryland 20814-4799*

Neuropeptide modulation of sympathetic control of cardiovascular activity may consist of both excitatory and inhibitory influences from neurons of the medullary midline raphe and parapyramidal region. Several putative neurotransmitter systems were identified in the midline medullary raphe (raphe pallidus, magnus obscurus) and in the parapyramidal region (located close to the ventral surface and lateral to the pyramidal tract) of the ventral medulla oblongata (FIG. 1). Many of the neurons contained serotonin (5HT) and thus are part of the midline B1 and B3 cell groups and their lateral extensions.[1–3] In addition, many of the neurons contained immunoreactivity (ir) for neuropeptides (TABLE 1).

Neurons of the midline raphe and the parapyramidal region project to the intermediolateral cell column (IML) of the thoracic spinal cord[16,19,20] and to the nucleus of the solitary tract (NTS).[8,20,21] The IML is the site of origin of sympathetic preganglionic neurons and the NTS is the site of termination of visceral afferent fibers including those from baroreceptors. Thus, a neuroanatomical substrate for effects on cardiovascular regulation by these medullary regions exists. In addition, activation of the midline raphe and the parapyramidal region affects mean arterial blood pressure.[22–24]

## Transmitter-Identified Projections

For some transmitter-identified (SP, TRH, 5HT, ENK) neurons, projections to the IML were demonstrated (FIG. 2).[2,16,19,25,26] Other transmitter-specific (*e.g.*, proctolin, somatostatin, cholecystokinin) projections from the midline raphe and the parapyramidal region to the spinal cord were demonstrated, but specific termination sites were not determined.[5,8,13] In addition, SP- and 5HT-ir neurons projected from the midline raphe and parapyramidal region to the NTS.[21,27] Other transmitter-specific projections from ventral medulla are relatively unexplored.

## SP- and TRH-ir Projections to the IML

Ventral medullary SP- and TRH-ir projections to the IML were investigated using multiple approaches. Projections were initially studied using electrolytic lesions of the ventral medulla and subsequent RIA of SP and TRH in microdissected IML.[28,29] Sub-

[a]This work was supported by National Institutes of Health Grants NS24876 and NS20991 to C.J.H. NRSA fellowship awards supported K.B.T. (NSO8084) and C.A.S. (HLO7565).

**149**

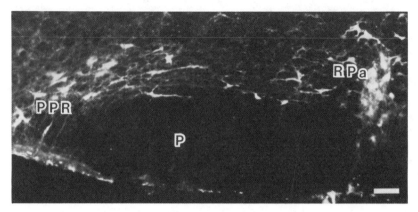

**FIGURE 1.** Montage of low power photomicrographs of substance P-ir neurons in the midline raphe pallidus and lateral to the pyramidal tract in the parapyramidal region of the medulla. Calibration bar = 100 μm. Abbreviations: P = pyramidal tract, PPR = parapyramidal region, RPa = raphe pallidus. (Adapted from Charlton and Helke.[16])

sequently, bulbospinal SP- and TRH-ir projections to the IML were more directly studied using the retrograde transport of rhodamine-labeled latex microspheres (rhodamine beads) from the T3 IML combined with immunohistochemistry.[16,19] IML-projecting neurons which contained SP- and TRH-ir were primarily found in the parapyramidal region, and in the midline medullary raphe pallidus and magnus.[16,19] There is also evidence for IML-projecting serotonergic neurons in the midline raphe and the parapyramidal region. The loss of anterograde transport from the ventral medulla to the IML subsequent to destruction of serotonergic neurons with a neurotoxin suggested a ventral medullary serotonergic projection to the IML.[2] Recently, we confirmed this finding and mapped the location of the cells in the midline medullary raphe and the parapyramidal region by using retrograde transport of rhodamine beads from the IML combined with 5HT immunocytochemistry. The IML-projecting 5HT-ir neurons were found in the same sites as the IML-projecting SP-ir and TRH-ir neurons.[26]

**TABLE 1.** Putative Peptide Neurotransmitters Present in Midline Raphe and Parapyramidal Neurons of the Ventral Medulla

| Neuropeptide | Reference |
| --- | --- |
| Beta-lipotropin | 4 |
| Cholecystokinin | 5 |
| Enkephalin (ENK) | 6–9 |
| Galanin | 10 |
| Human growth hormone | 11 |
| Neuropeptide K | 12 |
| Proctolin | 13 |
| Somatostatin | 7–8 |
| Substance P (SP) | 14–16 |
| Thyrotropin-releasing hormone (TRH) | 11,17–19 |

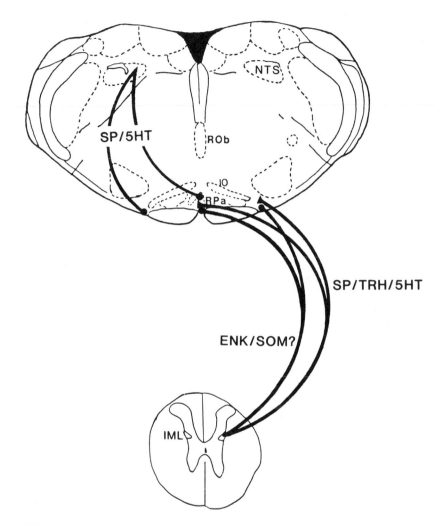

**FIGURE 2.** Schematic of rat medulla oblongata. *Left side* of the medulla shows the neuronal projections to the NTS which colocalize SP and 5HT (actual projection was demonstrated to more caudal regions of the NTS[24,27]). *Right side* of the medulla shows the neuronal projections to the IML which colocalize SP, TRH and 5HT, or which contain ENK (and perhaps SOM based on the demonstration of such a coexistence in spinal projections[8]). Abbreviations: ENK = enkephalin, 5HT = 5-hydroxytryptamine (serotonin), IO = inferior olive, NTS = nucleus of the solitary tract, ROb = raphe obscurus, RPa = raphe pallidus, SOM = somatostatin, TRH = thyrotropin-releasing hormone.

*ENK Projections to the IML*

Bulbospinal ENK-ir cells were previously demonstrated in the parapyramidal region and midline raphe pallidus.[7–9,30] In addition, ENK-ir terminals were detected in the

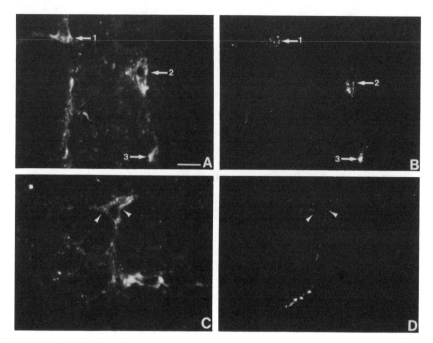

**FIGURE 3.** Paired photomicrographs of ventral medullary neurons which were ENK-ir (**A & C**) and projected to the thoracic IML. *Arrows* point to ENK-ir neurons (A & C) which also contained rhodamine beads (**B & D**) subsequent to retrograde transport from the T3 IML. Calibration bar = 12.5 μm (A) and 14 μm (C). (From Sasek and Helke.[25] Reprinted by permission from the authors.)

IML.[31,32] It was not known whether the ventral medullary or intraspinal neurons provided ENK-ir innervation of the IML. By combining retrograde transport of rhodamine beads and immunocytochemistry, we recently found that parapyramidal and midline raphe ENK-ir cells project to the IML[25] (FIG. 3).

*SP and 5HT Projections to the NTS*

Neurons of the midline raphe and the parapyramidal region were also shown to project to the medial NTS.[21] In addition, many of these projection neurons were SP- or 5HT-ir.[21] Thus, cells in the ventral medulla project to the NTS as well as to the IML, and cells that project to each region are neurochemically similar.

*Coexistence of Putative Neurotransmitters*

Given the multiplicity of putative transmitters in cells of the midline raphe and the parapyramidal region, it is not surprising that certain of the agents were colocalized in the same neuron. SP, TRH, ENK, and cholecystokinin were each found in ventral medullary serotonergic neurons.[4,5,17,26,27] SP and TRH, and ENK and somatostatin were also colocalized.[7,8,17] However, there appears to be some heterogeneity in combinations of colocalized neurotransmitters. For example, SP was frequently colocalized with 5HT and TRH but was infrequently colocalized with ENK.[7,17,25] Thus, there may be multiple populations of 5HT-ir cells (in addition to non-5HT neurons) which colocalize SP and/or TRH, or ENK.

*Transmitter Coexistence in Projections to the IML*

Our initial work on coexistence of SP or TRH with serotonin in bulbospinal IML projections employed the approaches of serotonin neurotoxin-induced lesions and RIA of microdissected IML.[28,29] The serotonin neurotoxin, 5,7-dihydroxytryptamine (5,7-DHT), depleted the serotonin content of the spinal cord, and reduced the TRH content of the IML by 45%. It did not significantly alter the SP content of the IML. However, the ventral horn content of both TRH and SP was reduced by 92% and 42%, respectively, in 5,7-DHT-treated rats.[29] Although indirect, these data suggested that whereas TRH coexisted with 5HT in IML projections, SP did not. The question of TRH coexistence with SP could not be addressed by this approach. More recently, coexistence in IML projections from the ventral medulla was studied with dual color immunohistochemistry combined with retrograde tracing (FIG. 4). Multiple antigens were viewed in individual IML-projecting cells (*i.e.*, containing rhodamine beads retrogradely transported from T3-4 IML) by dual color immunofluorescence. Using primary antibodies from different species and secondary antisera coupled with either FITC (green) or 7-amino-4-methyl-coumarin-3-acetic acid (AMCA, blue), two antigens could be seen in a single projection-specific neuron. In some studies, a third antigen was identified in a single neuron by comparing adjacent 4-μm sections.

Several coexistences were found in IML-projecting neurons, *i.e.*, SP and TRH; SP and 5HT; SP, TRH and 5HT.[26] These cells were found in the midline raphe and the

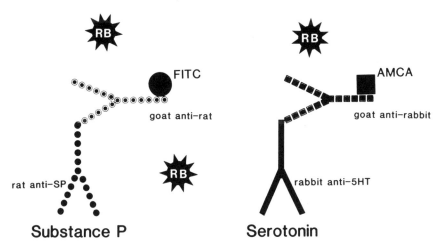

**FIGURE 4.** Schematic of procedure used for dual-color immunocytochemistry to visualize substance P- and serotonin-ir in projection-identified neurons of a single medullary tissue section. Abbreviations: AMCA = 7-amino-4-methyl-coumarin-3-acetic acid (Jackson Immunoresearch Labs, West Grove, PA), 5HT = serotonin, FITC = fluorescein isothiocyanate (Cappel, Downington, PA), RB = rhodamine beads (rhodamine-labeled latex microspheres) (Lumafluor, New City, NY), SP = substance P.

parapyramidal region. Of the ventral medullary IML-projecting cells, the majority of SP- or TRH-ir neurons contained both peptides; many were also serotonergic (FIG. 2). In addition, immunocytochemical studies of SP and TRH colocalization in terminals in the IML clearly showed their presence in both serotonergic and nonserotonergic terminals[33] (Sasek and Helke, unpublished). Thus, the SP RIA data of microdissected IML following serotonin neurotoxin lesions were misleading. The RIA studies showed that the content of SP did not significantly decline in the IML following destruction of serotonin nerve terminals.[28,29] We interpreted those data to suggest that SP was not present in seroto- nergic projections to the IML. However, the SP content of the IML arises from several sources besides ventral medullary neurons (some of which also contain 5HT, some of which do not). SP-ir is also present in terminals of intraspinal neurons[34] and in SP-ir cell bodies in the IML.[35] Thus, the SP-ir terminals and the cell bodies in the IML which remain after a 5,7-DHT lesion are likely to contribute to the SP content. Sprouting of remaining terminals may further maintain the SP content of the nucleus.[34] In contrast, the TRH content of the IML, and both the SP and TRH contents of the ventral horn which arise largely from medullary sources, were significantly reduced after serotonin neuro- toxin treatment.[28,29] Because of the similar localization of ENK cells with cells containing SP and/or 5HT, coexistence of ENK with SP or 5HT was of interest. However, ENK rarely coexisted with SP in IML-projecting neurons of the ventral medulla or in terminals in the IML[25] (FIG. 5). In addition, although ENK was occasionally colocalized with 5HT[6] (Sasek and Helke, unpublished), our preliminary studies suggest that the proportion of nonserotonergic ENK-ir cells was considerably higher (Sasek and Helke, unpublished). Thus, it appears that SP and ENK-ir projections to the IML from the ventral medulla are largely from separate groups of neurons (FIG. 2).

### Transmitter Coexistence in Projections to the NTS

In the medial NTS, another nucleus that receives projections from the ventral medulla, we demonstrated the coexistence of SP and 5HT in terminals.[36] The presence of both SP and 5HT neuronal projections to the NTS from the parapyramidal region and from the midline[21] prompted studies of the coexistence of SP and 5HT in these NTS projections. 5HT and SP-ir were visualized using dual color immunocytochemistry with AMCA- and FITC-conjugated secondary antibodies. NTS-projecting neurons were visualized in the ventral medulla by retrograde labeling with rhodamine beads following injection into the NTS. Extensive colocalization of 5HT and SP-ir was seen in NTS-projecting neurons located in the midline medullary raphe and the parapyramidal region[27] (FIGS. 2 and 6).

### Transmitter Coexistence in IML-Projecting RVL Neurons

Another group of ventral medullary neurons which project to the IML and the NTS are the more laterally located epinephrine-ir neurons of the C1 area of the rostral ventrolateral medulla (RVL).[37,38] The RVL neurons are functionally distinct from the medially located midline raphe and parapyramidal neurons.[23] We examined the RVL and focused on differences in the neurochemical content between IML-projecting neurons of the RVL and the medial groups. In retrograde transport and immunocytochemical studies, we found IML-projecting RVL cells which were ir for phenylethanolamine n-methyltransferase (PNMT) (presumably epinephrine-containing), for neuropeptide Y, and much less fre- quently for ENK and SP (Sasek and Helke, unpublished). Whereas PNMT and neuro- peptide Y were generally colocalized in IML-projecting neurons in the C1 area, neuro- peptide Y-ir neurons of the C1 area only rarely colocalized SP (Sasek and Helke, unpublished). In addition, although an early study[39] suggested extensive colocalization of SP and PNMT in spinal cord-projecting neurons of the ventral medulla, subsequent studies[40,41] did not substantiate this coexistence.

These data suggest that IML-projecting ventral medullary neurons can be subdivided based on both their relative anatomic location (*e.g.*, medially located SP/TRH/5HT cells

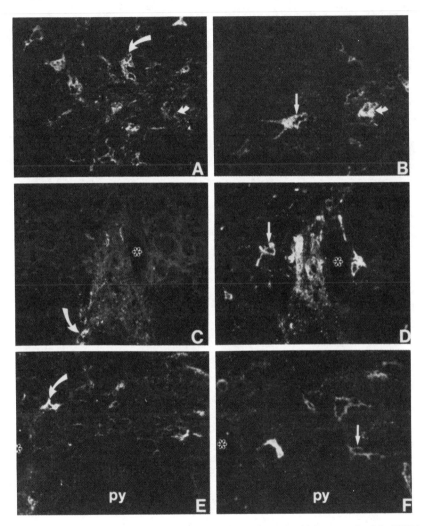

**FIGURE 5.** Paired photomicrographs of ventral medullary neurons which were stained for ENK-ir (**A, C, & E**) and SP-ir (**B, D, & F**). A & B, C & D, and E & F show the same field of view in single sections which were stained for both peptides. *Large curved arrows* in A, C, & E point to ENK-ir neurons that do not contain SP-ir. *Straight arrows* in B, D, & F point to the same neuron that contains both ENK- and SP-ir. *Asterisk* in C & D and E & F denotes the same blood vessels. Abbreviations: py = pyramidal tract. Calibration bar = 370 μm. All photomicrographs are of equal magnification. (From Sasek and Helke.[25] Reprinted by permission from the authors.)

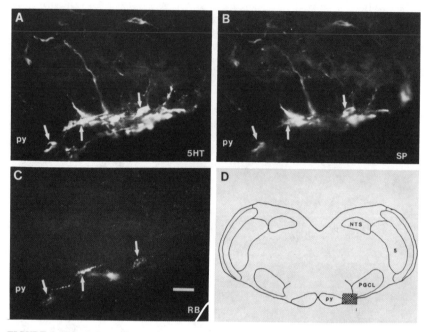

**FIGURE 6.** Paired photomicrographs of three (*arrows*) ventral medullary neurons which are labeled with rhodamine beads retrogradely transported from the NTS (**C**) and which colocalize 5HT-ir (**A**) and SP-ir (**B**). One neuron which contains only 5HT-ir (A) and rhodamine beads (C) is indicated by *arrowheads*. Field of view in A, B & C corresponds to the shaded area in panel **D**. Calibration bar = 40 μm. (From Thor and Helke.[27] Reprinted by permission from the authors.)

vs laterally located PNMT/neuropeptide Y cells), and within a region, by their putative neurotransmitters and patterns of coexistence (*e.g.*, ENK vs SP/TRH/5HT) (Fɪɢ. 2).

## CONCLUSION

Studies on the chemical neuroanatomy of the neurons of the parapyramidal region provide further evidence for the significance of the region in neural regulation of the cardiovascular systems. Neurons of the parapyramidal region project to two cardiovascular control sites, the IML and the NTS. In addition, the neurons contain various putative neurotransmitters (*e.g.*, SP, TRH, 5HT, ENK) that were shown to alter preganglionic neuronal activity in the IML[42–45] and cardiovascular function.[46–50]

When the numerous putative neurotransmitters and combinations of transmitters in IML- and NTS-projecting neurons are considered, it becomes apparent that the modulation of sympathetic activity by the midline raphe and the parapyramidal region may be quite complex. The relationship of neurochemically specific projections from the ventral medulla to the IML to functional heterogeneity seen in sympathetic outflow elicited from the same region[51] remains to be determined. However, given that the putative transmitters of at least one projection (SP/TRH/5HT) to the IML are excitatory whereas those of another projection to the IML (ENK and perhaps SOM) are inhibitory,[43,52,53] it is likely that sympathoexcitatory and sympathoinhibitory influences elicited from the midline raphe and the parapyramidal region result from activation of neurochemically distinct neurons. A very sophisticated level of modulation of sympathetic activity could also be provided for by colocalized putative neurotransmitters, frequency-dependent differential release of colocalized transmitters,[54] and difference in afferent and/or efferent connections of specific ventral medullary neurons. Considering the subtle differences found between the cardiovascular and regional hemodynamic effects of SP and TRH when each is administered intrathecally,[47,48] the possibility of intricate and selective modulatory influences becomes likely.

In summary, the midline raphe and the parapyramidal region of the ventral medulla are neurochemically complex groups of cells that project to cardiovascular-related central nervous system nuclei and that affect sympathetic activity to the cardiovascular system. The importance of this neurochemical complexity in either discrete regulation and/or refinement of sympathetic activity to specific vascular beds and/or the heart remains to be determined.

## REFERENCES

1. STEINBUSCH, H.W.M. 1981. Distribution of serotonin-immunoreactivity in the central nervous system of the rat. Cell bodies and terminals. Neuroscience **6:** 557–618.
2. LOEWY, A.D. & S. McKELLAR. 1981. Serotonergic projections from the ventral medulla to the intermediolateral cell column in the rat. Brain Res. **211:** 146–152.
3. SKAGERBERG, G. & A. BJORKLUND. 1985. Topographic principles in the spinal projections of serotonergic and non-serotonergic brainstem neurons in the rat. Neuroscience **15:** 445–480.
4. HUNT, S.P. & T.A. LOVICK. 1982. The distribution of serotonin, met-enkephalin and beta-lipotropin-like immunoreactivity in neuronal perikarya of the cat brain. Neurosci. Lett. **30:** 139–145.
5. MANTYH, P.W. & S.P. HUNT. 1984. Evidence for cholecystokinin-like immunoreactive neurons in the rat medulla oblongata which project to the spinal cord. Brain Res. **291:** 49–54.
6. LEGER, L., Y. CHARNAY, P. DUBOIS & M. JOUVET. 1986. Distribution of enkephalin-immunoreactive cell bodies in relation to serotonin-containing neurons in the raphe nuclei of the cat: Immunohistochemical evidence for coexistence of enkephalin and serotonin in certain cells. Brain Res. **362:** 63–73.
7. BOWKER, R.M. 1987. Evidence for the co-localization of somatostatin- and methionine-enkephalin-like immunoreactivities in raphe and gigantocellularis nuclei. Neurosci. Lett. **81:** 75–81.
8. MILLHORN, D.E., K. SEROOGY, T. HÖKFELT, L.C. SCHMUED, L. TERENIUS, A. BUCHAN & J.C. BROWN. 1987. Neurons of the ventral medulla oblongata that contain both somatostatin and enkephalin immunoreactivities project to nucleus tractus solitarius and spinal cord. Brain Res. **424:** 99–108.
9. Menetery, D. & A.I. BASBAUM. 1987. The distribution of substance P-, enkephalin- and dynorphin-immunoreactive neurons in the medulla of the rat and their contribution to bulbospinal pathways. Neuroscience **23:** 173–187.
10. SKOFITSCH, G. & D.M. JACOBOWITZ. 1985. Immunohistochemical mapping of galanin-like neurons in the rat central nervous system. Peptides **6:** 509–546.
11. LECHAN, R.M., M.E. MOLITCH & I. JACKSON. 1983. Distribution of immunoreactive human growth hormone-like material and thyrotropin-releasing hormone in the rat central nervous system: Evidence for their coexistence in the same neuron. Endocrinology **112:** 877–884.
12. VALENTINO, K.L., K. TATEMOTO, J. HUNTER & J.D. BARCHAS. 1986. Distribution of neuropeptide K-immunoreactivity in the rat central nervous system. Peptides **7:** 1043–1059
13. HOLETS, V., T. HÖKFELT, J. UDE, M. ECKERT, H. PENZLIN, A.A.J. VERHOFSTAD & T.J. VISSER. 1987. A comparative study of the immunohistochemical localization of a presumptive proctolin-like peptide, thyrotropin-releasing hormone and 5-hydroxytryptamine in the rat central nervous system. Brain Res. **408:** 141–153.
14. LJUNGDAHL, A., T. HÖKFELT & G. NILSSON. 1978. Distribution of substance P-like immu-

noreactivity in the central nervous system of the rat-I. Cell bodies and nerve terminals. Neuroscience **3**: 861–944.

15. MARSON, L. & A.D. LOEWY. 1985. Topographic organization of substance P and monoamine cells in the ventral medulla of the cat. J. Auton. Nerv. Syst. **14**: 271–285.

16. CHARLTON, C.G. & C.J. HELKE. 1987. Substance P-containing medullary projections to the intermediolateral cell column: Identification with retrogradely transported rhodamine-labeled latex microspheres and immunohistochemistry. Brain Res. **418**: 245–254.

17. JOHANSSON, O., T. HÖKFELT, B. PERNOW, S.L. JEFFOCATE, N. WHITE, H.W.M. STEINBUSCH, A.A.J. VERHOFSTAD, P.C. EMSON & E. SPINDEL. 1981. Immunohistochemical support for three putative transmitters in one neuron: Coexistence of 5-hydroxytryptamine, substance P- and thyrotropin-releasing hormone-like immunoreactivity in medullary neurons projecting to the spinal cord. Neuroscience **6**: 1857–1881.

18. BOWKER, R.M., K.N. WESTLUND, M.C. SULLIVAN, J.F. WELBER & J.D. COULTER. 1982. Transmitters of the raphe-spinal complex: Immunocytochemical studies. Peptides **3**: 291–298.

19. HIRSCH, M.D. & C.J. HELKE. 1988. Bulbospinal thyrotropin-releasing hormone projections to the intermediolateral cell column: A double fluorescence immunohistochemical-retrograde tracing study. Neuroscience **25**: 625–637.

20. LOEWY, A.D., J.H. WALLACH & S. McKELLAR. 1981. Efferent connections of the ventral medulla oblongata in the rat. Brain Res. Rev. **3**: 63–80.

21. THOR, K.B. & C.J. HELKE. 1987. Serotonin and substance P-containing projections to the nucleus tractus solitarii of the rat. J. Comp. Neurol. **265**: 275–293.

22. McCALL, R.B. 1984. Evidence for a serotonergically mediated sympathoexcitatory response to stimulation of medullary raphe nuclei. Brain Res. **311**: 131–139.

23. MINSON, J.B., J.P. CHALMERS, A.C. CAON & B. RENAUD. 1987. Separate areas of rat medulla oblongata with populations of serotonin- and adrenaline-containing neurons alter blood pressure after L-glutamate stimulation. J. Auton. Nerv. Syst. **19**: 39–50.

24. HASELTON, J.R., R.W. WINTERS, D.R. LISKOWSKY, C.L. HASELTON, P.M. McCABE & N. SCHNEIDERMAN. 1988. Cardiovascular responses elicited by electrical and chemical stimulation of the rostral medullary raphe of the rabbit. Brain Res. **453**: 167–175.

25. SASEK, C.A. & C.J. HELKE. 1989. Medullary enkephalin-immunoreactive neuronal projections to the intermediolateral cell column: Relationship to substance P-immunoreactive neurons. J. Comp. Neurol. **287**: 484–494.

26. SASEK, C.A., M. W. WESSENDORF & C.J. HELKE. 1989. Evidence for coexistence of thyrotropin-releasing-hormone-, substance P-, and serotonin-immunoreactivities in ventral medullary neurons that project to the intermediolateral cell column of the rat. Neuroscience. In press.

27. THOR, K.B. & C.J. HELKE. 1989. Serotonin and substance P colocalization in medullary projections to the nucleus tractus solitarius: Dual-color immunohistochemistry combined with retrograde tracing. J. Chem. Neuroanat. **2**: 139–148.

28. HELKE, C.J., J.J. NEIL, V.J. MASSARI & A.D. LOEWY. 1982. Substance P neurons project from the ventral medulla to the intermediolateral cell column and ventral horn in the rat. Brain Res. **243**: 147–152.

29. HELKE, C.J., S.C. SAYSON, J.R. KEELER & C.G. CHARLTON. 1986. Thyrotropin-releasing hormone neurons project from the ventral medulla to the intermediolateral cell column: Partial coexistence with serotonin. Brain Res. **381**: 1–7.

30. HÖKFELT, T., L. TERENIUS, H.G.J.M. KUYPERS & O. DANN. 1979. Evidence for enkephalin immunoreactive neurons in the medulla oblongata projecting to the spinal cord. Neurosci. Lett. **14**: 55–60.

31. HOLETS, V. & R. ELDE. 1982. The differential relationship of serotonergic and peptidergic fibers to sympathoadrenal neurons in the intermediolateral cell column of the rat: a combined retrograde axonal transport and immunofluorescence study. Neuroscience **7**: 1155–1174.

32. KRUKOFF, T.L. 1987. Peptidergic inputs to sympathetic preganglionic neurons. Can. J. Physiol. Pharmacol. **65**: 1619–1623.

33. APPEL, N.M., M.W. WESSENDORF & R. ELDE. 1986. Coexistence of serotonin- and substance P-like immunoreactivity in nerve fibers apposing identified sympathoadrenal preganglionic neurons in the intermediolateral cell column. Neurosci. Lett. **65**: 241–246.

34. DAVIS, B.M., J.E. KRAUSE, J.F. McKELVY & J.B. CABOT. 1984. Effects of spinal lesions on substance P levels in the rat sympathetic preganglionic cell column: Evidence for local spinal regulation. Neuroscience **13**: 1311–1316.

35. KRUKOFF, T.L., J. CIRIELLO & F.R. CALARESU. 1985. Segmental distribution of peptide-like immunoreactivity in cell bodies of the thoracolumbar sympathetic nucleus of the cat. J. Comp. Neurol. **240**: 90–102.

36. THOR, K.B., K.M. HILL, C. HARROD & C.J. HELKE. 1988. Immunohistochemical and biochemical analysis of serotonin and substance P colocalization in the nucleus tractus solitarii and associated afferent ganglia of the rat. Synapse **2**: 225–231.

37. ROSS, C.A., D.A. RUGGIERO, T.H. JOH, D.H. PARK & D.J. REIS. 1984. Rostral ventrolateral medulla: Selective projections to the thoracic autonomic cell column from the region containing C1 adrenaline neurons. J. Comp. Neurol. **228**: 168–185.

38. THOR, K.B. & C.J. HELKE. 1988. Catecholamine-synthesizing neuronal projections to the nucleus tractus solitarii in the rat. J. Comp. Neurol. **268**: 264–280.

39. LORENZ, R.G., C.B. SAPER, D.L. WONG, R.D. CIARENELLO & A.D. LOEWY. 1985. Colocalization of substance P and phenylethanolamine-N-methyltransferase- like immunoreactivity in neurons of ventrolateral medulla that project to the spinal cord: Potential role in control of vasomotor tone. Neurosci. Lett. **55**: 255–260.

40. PILOWSKY, P., J. MINSON, A. HODGSON, P. HOWE & J. CHALMERS. 1986. Does substance P coexist with adrenaline in neurones of the rostral ventrolateral medulla in the rat? Neurosci. Lett. **71**: 293–298.

41. MILNER, T.A., V.M. PICKEL, C. ABATE, T.H. JOH & D.J. REIS. 1988. Ultrastructural characterization of substance P-like immunoreactive neurons in the rostral ventrolateral medulla in relation to neurons containing catecholamine-synthesizing enzymes. J. Comp. Neurol. **270**: 427–445.

42. GILBEY, M.P., K. McKENNA & L.P. SCHRAMM. 1983. Effects of substance P on sympathetic preganglionic neurons. Neurosci. Lett. **41**: 157–159.

43. McCALL, R.B. 1983. Serotonergic excitation of sympathetic preganglionic neurons: a microiontophoretic study. Brain Res. **289**: 121–127.

44. MA, R.C. & N.J. DUN. 1986. Excitation of lateral horn neurons of the neonatal spinal cord by 5-hydroxytryptamine. Dev. Brain Res. **24**: 89–98.

45. DUN, N.J. & N. MO. 1988. In vitro effects of substance P on neonatal rat sympathetic preganglionic neurones. J. Physiol. **399**: 321–333.

46. KEELER, J.R., C.G. CHARLTON & C.J. HELKE. 1985. Cardiovascular effects of spinal cord substance P: studies with a stable receptor agonist. J. Pharmacol. Exp. Ther. **233**: 755–760.

47. HELKE, C.J., E.T. PHILLIPS & J.T. O'NEILL. 1987. Regional peripheral and CNS hemodynamic effects of intrathecal administration of a substance P receptor agonist. J. Auton, Nerv. Syst. **21**: 1–7.

48. HELKE, C.J. & E.T. PHILLIPS. 1988. Thyrotropin-releasing hormone receptor activation in the spinal cord increases blood pressure and sympathetic tone to the vasculature and adrenals. J. Pharmacol. Exp. Ther. **245**: 41–46.

49. LI, S.-J., X. ZHANG & A.J. INGENITO. 1988. Depressor and bradycardic effects induced by spinal subarachnoid injection of D-Ala$^2$-D-Leu$^5$-enkephalin in rats. Neuropeptides **12**: 81–88.

50. SOLOMON, R.E. & G.F. GEBHART. 1988. Mechanisms of effects of intrathecal serotonin on nociception and blood pressure. J. Pharmacol. Exp. Ther. **245**: 905–912.

51. McCALL, R.B. & M.E. CLEMENTS. 1988. Identification of serotonergic and sympathetic neurons in medullary raphe nuclei. Brain Res. In press.

52. FRANZ, D.N., B.D. HARE & K.L. McCLOSKEY. 1982. Spinal sympathetic neurons: Possible sites of opiate-withdrawal suppression by clonidine. Science **215**: 1643–1645.

53. BACKMAN, S.B. & J.L .HENRY. 1984. Effects of substance P and thyrotropin-releasing hormone on sympathetic neurons in the upper thoracic intermediolateral nucleus of the cat. Can. J. Physiol. Pharmacol. **62**: 248–251.

54. LUNDBERG, J.M. & T. HÖKFELT. 1983. Coexistence of peptides and classical neurotransmitters. Trends Neurosci. **6**: 325–332.

# Neuropeptide Regulation of Autonomic Outflow at the Sympathetic Preganglionic Neuron

## Anatomical and Neurochemical Specificity[a]

TERESA L. KRUKOFF

*Department of Anatomy and Cell Biology*
*Faculty of Medicine*
*University of Alberta*
*Edmonton, Canada T6G 2H7*

## INTRODUCTION

Early theories proposed that the entire sympathetic nervous system functioned as a single unit so that outflow increased or decreased as a whole. It has become clear, however, that there is selective regional control of sympathetic outflow to specific targets or organs. In this paper, I shall discuss some of the possibilities of how such control might be achieved at the level of the spinal cord and the role that neuropeptides may play in this function.

### Sympathetic Preganglionic Neurons

Sympathetic preganglionic neurons (SPN), cells of the spinal cord which provide sympathetic innervation to the periphery, are found within discrete nuclei of the spinal cord between cervical segment 8 (C8) and lumbar segment 4 (L4) in the cat.[1] The largest number of SPN in the thoraco-lumbar (T-L) cord is found in the intermediolateral cell column pars principalis (IMLp). These neurons are segregated into clumps or nests along the length of the T-L cord. A smaller number of SPN is found in the part of the inter-mediolateral cell column (IML) which extends into the white matter, the IML pars funicularis (IMLf). Transverse bands of SPN span the area between the IML and the central canal and make up the nucleus intercalatus. Small numbers of SPN are found in the region dorsal and dorsolateral to the central canal and make up the central autonomic area.[1–5]

### Viscerotopic Organization of SPN

The most straightforward way in which specificity of sympathetic output is achieved is through the viscerotopic organization of SPN. First and best known is the distribution of SPN in spinal cord segments which provide innervation to specific visceral organs. Therefore, sympathetic ganglia receive projections from SPN which are located *primarily*

[a]The author's work cited in this paper was supported by the Medical Research Council of Canada, the Canadian Heart Foundation, and the Alberta Heritage Foundation for Medical Research.

in the following segments: superior and middle cervical ganglia: T1 to T7;[6,7] stellate ganglion: T1 to T7;[4,8,9] greater splanchnic nerve: T2 to T10;[10] adrenal glands: T7 to T10;[11-14] inferior mesenteric ganglia and/or hypogastric nerve: T13 to L4.[6,15-18] Furthermore, stimulation of T1 and T2 ventral roots produces dilation of the pupils whereas stimulation of T3 and T4 roots produces piloerection of the face and neck and vasoconstriction of the ear.[19,20]

SPN may also be viscerotopically organized by region according to separate spinal autonomic nuclei. Paravertebral ganglia appear to receive the largest innervation from SPN in the IML,[3] whereas prevertebral ganglia receive innervation from relatively more SPN in the nucleus intercalatus and central autonomic area.[21] Of SPN projecting to the lumbar sympathetic trunk, those with vasocontrictor functions are located primarily in the IML and those with visceral destinations are generally located more medially.[16] Target-specificity of SPN is also suggested by the finding that, in areas where the populations overlap, SPN projecting to the cervical sympathetic trunk and to the adrenal medulla form two distinct populations within the IML.[14]

## Neurochemical Specificity at the Level of SPN

There can be little doubt that the neurochemistry of spinal cord structures confers an important level of complexity onto specificity of sympathetic outflow. Only the peptidergic nature of these structures will be discussed in this paper.

### Peptidergic Nerve Terminals and Fibres in Spinal Autonomic Nuclei

That spinal autonomic neurons receive catecholaminergic inputs from brain stem neurons has been known for more than two decades.[22] In addition, nerve terminal-like structures and fibres of the autonomic nuclei contain the following neuropeptides: substance P,[13,23,24] oxytocin and vasopressin (OXY, AVP),[13,23,25,26] enkephalin (ENK),[13,23,27] and somatostatin[13,14,23] (SS). Furthermore, terminal-like structures and fibers in the cat IMLp contain ENK, neuropeptide Y (NPY, FIG. 1), neurotensin, substance P, and neurophysin II along the entire length of the T-L cord, although quantities vary at different spinal levels.[23,28,29] SS and OXY, on the other hand, were found in segments C8-T10 and C8, T2-T7, T13, L2-L4, respectively.[23] Our findings suggest that SS and OXY function in pathways to discrete populations of SPN.[23] Finally, it has been shown that SPN projecting to the cervical sympathetic trunk receive afferents containing SS and OXY, whereas SPN projecting to the adrenal gland receive only SS-containing afferents.[14]

*Functions of Peptidergic Inputs onto SPN.* Most of our knowledge regarding possible functions of peptidergic inputs onto SPN comes from pharmacological studies. Iontophoretically applied substance P alters the firing frequency of SPN.[30,31] Intrathecal administration of OXY increases heart rate in rats, presumably by acting on SPN,[32] while intrathecal AVP increases arterial pressure and heart rate.[33] When applied directly onto SPN, OXY inhibits SPN firing and AVP inhibits about two-thirds of the cells tested and excites the remaining one-third in rat[34] whereas these neuropeptides elicit predominantly excitatory effects in cat SPN.[35]

*Neuropeptides in SPN*

SPN in the cat spinal cord contain at least six neuropeptides.[5,36] These peptidergic SPN can be divided into two groups (TABLE 1). In the first group, SPN containing ENK, neurotensin (FIG. 2), SS, and substance P are found in all autonomic nuclei along the entire length of the T-L cord.[5] In the second group, SPN containing corticotropin releasing factor (CRF) and vasoactive intestinal polypeptide (VIP) are found only in specific segments of the T-L cord, are present in much smaller numbers, and are found only in the IMLp and IMLf.[36]

Distribution of neuropeptides in SPN may offer clues to selective function of that group of SPN. Because of the wide distribution of SPN in group 1, they may be involved in more generalized functions of the autonomic nervous system such as providing innervation to blood vessels.[5] On the other hand, SPN in group 2 are much more selectively distributed, suggesting that SPN containing CRF and VIP may participate in peptide-specific pathways to peripheral organs. The coexistence of neuropeptides may confer another level of selectivity onto SPN: substance P is colocalized with ENK, neurotensin, and SS, and neurotensin coexists with SS, but ENK does not coexist with either neurotensin or SS.[37]

**TABLE 1.** Characteristics of Peptidergic Sympathetic Preganglionic Neurons of Cat Spinal Cord[a]

|  | Group 1 | Group 2 |
|---|---|---|
| Location | IMLp | IMLp |
|  | IMLf | IMLf |
|  | IC |  |
|  | CA |  |
| Numbers | large | small |
| Distribution | entire T-L | limited |
|  | cord |  |

[a]Group 1: cells contain ENK, neurotensin, SS, and substance P; Group 2: cells contain CRF and VIP. Abbreviations as in text.

*Function of Neuropeptides in SPN.* Acetylcholine (ACh) is the "classical" transmitter of SPN released in sympathetic ganglia; a single preganglionic impulse of threshold intensity evokes an excitatory postsynaptic current in the ganglionic neuron.[38] Other events occur in these structures, however, that cannot be explained by cholinergic transmission alone. For example, release of norepinephrine from principal neurons of the superior cervical ganglion after preganglionic stimulation[39] is regulated in part by ACh and in part by noncholinergic transmittter.[40] In addition, activation of tyrosine hydroxylase in rat superior cervical ganglion appears to be regulated, in part, by neuropeptides such as VIP.[41]

$3',5'$-cyclic guanosine monophosphate (cGMP) may be a second messenger molecule involved in synaptic transmission in sympathetic ganglia.[42,43] There appear to be at least two different routes to elevation of cGMP levels in ganglionic neurons: one may utilize a cholinergic mechanism[42,44,45] while the other is as yet undefined[46,47]. These results suggest that another neurotransmitter is released upon depolarization of the cholinergic nerve terminals[44] and neuropeptides are emerging as prime candidates for this function.[48-50] Our own demonstrations of neuropeptides in SPN (see above) suggest that these cells are the source of at least some of these neuropeptides. Coexistence of VIP, substance P, and ENK in cholinergic preganglionic nerve terminals of the avian ciliary ganglion[51] supports this possibility.

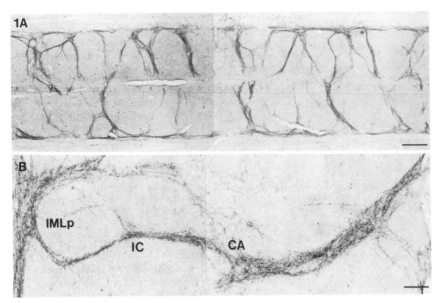

FIGURE 1. Photomicrographs of sections from cat thoracic cord demonstrating neuropeptide Y-immunoreactive structures in autonomic areas. (A) Horizontal section from segment $T_6$ demonstrating ladder-like appearance of immunoreactive structures. Rostral is to the *left*. (B) higher magnification of horizontal section from $T_6$ demonstrating immunoreactivity in the intermediolateral cell column pars principalis (IMLp), nucleus intercalatus (IC), and central autonomic area (CA). Note that some fibers appear to cross over the midline (*center*) to reach the IC of the opposite side. Rostral is to the *top*. Bars = 300 μm in A and 80 μm in B. (From Krukoff.[29] Reprinted by permission from *Brain Research*.)

What are the possible functions of preganglionic neuropeptides in ganglionic transmission? ENK released from preganglionic fibers or applied to the superior cervical ganglion decreases release of ACh and substance P (the latter presumably from sensory

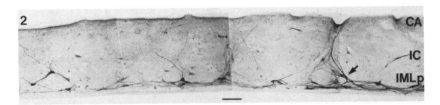

FIGURE. 2. Photomicrographic montage of horizontal section from segment $T_5$ of cat demonstrating immunoreactivity for neurotensin in cell bodies within the IMLp, IC, and CA. Note that many processes connect cell bodies in different clusters of neurons and that processes from cell bodies often extend into the IC and CA (*arrow*). The central canal is to the *top* and rostral is to the *left*. Bar = 160 μm. (From Krukoff et al.[5] Reprinted by permission from the *Journal of Comparative Neurology*.)

fibers)[52-54] and decreases excitability of ganglionic cells.[55,56] Substance P excites the cells of autonomic ganglia;[57-59] the slow noncholinergic depolarization in the inferior mesenteric ganglion may be due to the release of substance P.[60,61] AVP and OXY both cause a presynaptic reduction in ACh release and a concomitant postsynaptic membrane depolarization when applied in micromolar concentrations to the bath of superior cervical ganglion cells *in vitro*;[62] the physiological significance of these findings is, however, unknown as AVP and OXY have not been demonstrated in SPN.

The vasodepressor effect of intravenous SS is thought to be due to a selective depression of sympathetic outflow to the blood vessels via a presynaptic inhibitory effect on adrenergic neurons.[63] The role of neurotensin, substance P, and VIP in cardioacceleration has been studied by applying these peptides to the stellate ganglion of anesthetized cats.[64] Only neurotensin produced a response: cardioacceleration occurred over a prolonged time-course and was likely mediated by catecholamines released by principal ganglion neurons.

## CONCLUSIONS

The emergence of neuropeptides as an important group of putative neurotransmitters has revolutionized the concept of communication in the central nervous system. The autonomic nervous system is no exception, and the localization and possible roles of neuropeptides in afferents to and within SPN discussed in this paper demonstrate that we have only begun to understand how regional control of sympathetic outflow might be achieved.

## REFERENCES

1. HENRY, J. L. & F. R. CALARESU. 1972. Topography and numerical distribution of neurons of the thoraco-lumbar intermediolateral nucleus in the cat. J. Comp. Neurol. **144:** 205–214.
2. PETRAS, J. M. & J. F. CUMMINGS. 1972. Autonomic neurons in the spinal cord of the rhesus monkey: a correlation of the findings of cytoarchitectonics and sympathectomy with fiber degeneration following dorsal rhizotomy. J. Comp. Neurol. **146:** 189–218.
3. CHUNG, J. M., K. CHUNG & R. D. WURSTER. 1975. Sympathetic preganglionic neurons of the cat spinal cord: horseradish peroxidase study. Brain Res. **91:** 126–131.
4. OLDFIELD, B. J. & E. M. MCLACHLAN. 1981. An analysis of the sympathetic preganglionic neurons projecting from the upper thoracic spinal roots of the cat. J. Comp. Neurol. **196:** 329–345.
5. KRUKOFF, T. L., J. CIRIELLO & F. R. CALARESU. 1985a. Segmental distribution of peptide-like immunoreactivity in cell bodies of the thoracolumbar sympathetic nuclei of the cat. J. Comp. Neurol. **240:** 90–102.
6. DALSGAARD, C.-J. & L.-G. ELFVIN. 1979. Spinal origin of preganglionic fibers projecting onto the superior cervical ganglion and inferior mesenteric ganglion of the guinea pig, as demonstrated by the horseradish peroxidase technique. Brain Res. **172:** 139–143.
7. RUBIN, E. & D. PURVES. 1980. Segmental organization of sympathetic preganglionic neurons in the mammalian spinal cord. J. Comp. Neurol. **192:** 163–174.
8. CHUNG, K., J. M. CHUNG, F. W. LAVELLE & R. D. WURSTER. 1979. Sympathetic neurons in the cat spinal cord projecting to the stellate ganglion. J. Comp. Neurol. **185:** 23–30.
9. PARDINI, B. J. & R. D. WURSTER. 1984. Identification of the sympathetic preganglionic pathway to the cat stellate ganglion. J. Auton. Nerv. System. **11:** 13–25.
10. TORIGOE, Y., R. D. CERNUCAN, J. A. S. NISHIMOTO & R. H. I. BLANDS. 1985. Sympathetic preganglionic efferent and afferent neurons mediated by the greater splanchnic nerve in rabbit. Exp. Neurol. **87:** 334–348.

11.  ELLISON, J. P. & G. M. CLARK. 1975. Retrograde axonal transport of horseradish peroxidase
     in peripheral autonomic nerves. J. Comp. Neurol. **161:** 103–114.
12.  HAASE, P., A. CONTESTABILE & B. A. FLUMERFELT. 1982. Preganglionic innervation of the
     adrenal gland of the rat using horseradish peroxidase. Exp. Neurol. **78:** 217–221.
13.  HOLETS, V. & R. ELDE. 1982. The differential distribution and relationship of serotoninergic
     and peptidergic fibres to sympathoadrenal neurons in the intermediolateral cell column of the
     rat: a combined retrograde axonal transport and immunofluorescence study. Neuroscience **7:**
     1155–1174.
14.  APPEL, N. M. & R. P. ELDE. 1988. The intermediolateral cell column of the thoracic spinal
     cord is comprised of target-specific subnuclei: evidence from retrograde transport studies and
     immunohistochemistry. J. Neurosci. **8:** 1767–1775.
15.  HANCOCK, M. B. & C. A. PEVETO. 1979. A preganglionic autonomic nucleus in the dorsal
     gray commissure of the lumbar spinal cord of the rat. J. Comp. Neurol. **183:** 65–72.
16.  JÄNIG, W. E. M. MCLACHLAN. 1987. Organization of lumbar spinal outflow to distal colon
     and pelvic organs. Physiol. Rev. **67:** 1332–1404.
17.  NADELHAFT, I. & K. E. MCKENNA. 1987. Sexual dimorphism in sympathetic preganglionic
     neurons of the rat hypogastric nerve. J. Comp. Neurol. **256:** 308–315.
18.  NEUHUBER, W. 1982. The central projections of visceral primary afferent neurons of the
     inferior mesenteric plexus and hypogastric nerve and the location of the related sensory and
     preganglionic sympathetic cell bodies in the rat. Anat. Embryol. **164:** 413–425.
19.  LICHTMAN, J. W., D. PURVES & J. W. YIP. 1979. On the purpose of selective innervation of
     guinea-pig superior cervical ganglion cells. J. Physiol. **292:** 69–84.
20.  NJA, A. & D. PURVES. 1977. Specific innervation of guinea-pig superior cervical ganglion
     cells by preganglionic fibres arising from different levels of the spinal cord. J. Physiol. **264:**
     565–583.
21.  PETRAS, J. M. & A. I. FADEN. 1978. The origin of sympathetic preganglionic neurons in the
     dog. Brain Res. **144:** 353–357.
22.  DAHLSTRÖM, C.-J. & K. FUXE. 1965. Evidence for the existence of monoamine neurons in the
     central nervous system—II. Experimentally induced changes in the intraneuronal amine levels
     of bulbospinal neuron systems. Acta Physiol. Scand. **64** (Suppl. 247): 5–36.
23.  KRUKOFF, T. L., J. CIRIELLO & F. R. CALARESU. 1985b. Segmental distribution of peptide-
     and 5HT-like immunoreactivity in nerve terminals and fibers of the thoracolumbar sympa-
     thetic nuclei of the cat. J. Comp. Neurol. **240:** 103–116.
24.  OLDFIELD, B. J., A. SHEPPARD & G. NILAVER. 1985. A study of the substance P innervation
     of the intermediate zone of the thoracolumbar spinal cord. J. Comp. Neurol. **236:** 127–140.
25.  SWANSON, L. W. & S. MCKELLAR. 1979. The distribution of oxytocin- and neurophysin-
     stained fibers in the spinal cord of the rat and monkey. J. Comp. Neurol. **188:** 87–106.
26.  JENKINS, J. S., V. T. Y. ANG, J. HAWTHORN, M. N. ROSSOR & L. L. IVERSON. 1984.
     Vasopressin, oxytocin and neurophysins in the human brain and spinal cord. Brain Res.
     **291:** 111–117.
27.  ROMAGNANO, M. A., J. BRAIMAN, M. LOOMIS & R. W. HAMILL. 1987. Enkephalin fibers in
     autonomic nuclear regions: intraspinal vs. supraspinal origin. J. Comp. Neurol. **266:** 319–
     331.
28.  KRUKOFF, T. L. 1986a. Peptidergic inputs to sympathetic preganglionic neurons. Can. J.
     Physiol. Pharmacol. **65:** 1619–1623.
29.  KRUKOFF, T. L. 1987a. Neuropeptide Y-like immunoreactivity in cat spinal cord with special
     reference to autonomic areas. Brain Res. **415:** 300–308.
30.  GILBEY, M. P., K. E. MCKENNA & L. P. SCHRAMM. 1983. Effects of substance P on sym-
     pathetic preganglionic neurons. Neurosci. Lett. **41:** 157–159.
31.  BACKMAN, S. B. & J. L. HENRY. 1984a. Effects of substance P and thyrotropin-releasing
     hormone on sympathetic preganglionic neurones in the upper thoracic intermediolateral nu-
     cleus of the cat. Can. J. Physiol. Pharmacol. **62:** 248–251.
32.  YASHPAL, K., S. GAUTHIER & J. L. HENRY. 1987. Oxytocin administered intrathecally pref-
     erentially increases heart rat rather than arterial pressure in the rat. J. Auton. Nerv. System.
     **20:** 167–178.
33.  RIPHAGEN, C. L. & Q. J. PITTMAN. 1985. Cardiovascular responses to intrathecal adminis-
     tration of arginine vasopressin in rats. Regul. Peptides **10:** 293–298.

34. GILBEY, M. P., J. H. COOTE, S. FLEETWOOD-WALKER & D. F. PETERSON. 1982. The influence of the paraventriculo-spinal pathway, and oxytocin and vasopressin on sympathetic preganglionic neurones. Brain Res. **251**: 283–290.
35. BACKMAN, S. B. & .J. L. HENRY. 1984b. Effects of oxytocin and vasopressin on thoracic sympathetic preganglionic neurones in the cat. Brain Res. Bull. **13**: 679–684.
36. KRUKOFF, T. L. 1986b. Segmental distribution of corticotropin-releasing factor-like and vasoactive intestinal peptide-like immunoreactivities in presumptive sympathetic preganglionic neurons of the cat. Brain Res. **382**: 153–157.
37. KRUKOFF, T. L. 1987b. Coexistence of neuropeptides in sympathetic preganglionic neurons of the cat. Peptides **8**: 109–112.
38. SKOK, V.I. 1987. Nicotinic acetylcholine receptors in the neurones of autonomic ganglia. J. Auton. Nerv. System. **21**: 91–99.
39. NORBERG, K.-A. & F. SJÖQVIST. 1966. New possibilities for adrenergic modulation of ganglionic transmission. Pharmacol. Rev. **18**: 743–751.
40. IP, N. Y., R. L. PERLMAN & R. E. ZIGMOND. 1983. Acute transsynaptic regulation of tyrosine 3-mono-oxygenase in the rat superior cervical ganglion: evidence for both cholinergic and non-cholinergic mechanisms. Proc. Natl. Acad. Sci. USA **80**: 2081–2085.
41. IP, N. Y., C. BALDWIN & R. E. ZIGMOND 1985. Regulation of the concentration of adenosine $3',5'$-cyclic monophosphate and the activity of tyrosine hydroxylase in the rat superior cervical ganglion by three neuropeptides of the secretin family. J. Neurosci. **5**: 1947–1954.
42. KEBABIAN, J. W., A. L. STEINER & P. GREENGARD. 1975. Muscarinic cholinergic regulation of cyclic guanosine $3',5'$-monophosphate in autonomic ganglia: possible role in synaptic transmission. J. Pharmacol. Exp. Ther. **193**: 474–488.
43. WEIGHT, F. F., G. PETZOLD & P. GREENGARD. 1974. Guanosine $3',5'$-monophosphate in sympathetic ganglia: increase associated with synaptic transmission. Science **186**: 942–944.
44. DE VENTE, J., J. GARSSEN, F. J. H. TILDERS, H. W. M. STEINBUSCH & J. SCHIPPER. 1987. Single cell quantitative immunocytochemistry of cyclic GMP in the superior cervical ganglion of the rat. Brain Res. **411**: 120–128.
45. WAMSLEY, J. K., J. R. WEST, A. C. BLACK & T. H. WILLIAMS. 1979. Muscarinic cholinergic and preganglionic physiological stimulation increases cGMP levels in guinea pig superior cervical ganglia. J. Neurochem. **32**: 1032–1035.
46. BRIGGS, C. A., G. J. WHITING, M. A. ARIANO & D. A. McAFEE. 1982. Cyclic nucleotide metabolism in the sympathetic ganglion. Cell. Mol. Neurobiol. **2**: 129–141.
47. QUENZER, L. F., B. A. PATTERSON & R. L. VOLLE. 1980. $K^+$-induced accumulation of guanosine $3',5'$-monophosphate in sympathetic ganglia. J. Neurochem. **34**: 1782–1784.
48. BONE, E. A. & R. H. MITCHELL. 1985. Accumulation of inositol phosphates in sympathetic ganglia. Effects of depolarization and of amine and peptide neurotransmitters. Biochem. J. **227**: 236–269.
49. BONE, E. A., P. FRETTEN, S. PALMER, C. J. KIRK & R. H. MITCHELL. 1984. Rapid accumulation of inositol phosphates in isolated rat superior cervical sympathetic ganglia exposed to $V_1$-vasopressin and muscarinic cholinergic stimuli. Biochem. J. **221**: 803–811.
50. KAWATANI, M., M. RUTIGLIANO & W. C. DE GROAT. 1985. Depolarization and muscarinic excitation induced in a sympathetic ganglion by vasoactive intestinal polypeptide. Science **229**: 879–881.
51. REINER, A. 1987. A VIP-like peptide co-occurs with substance P and enkephalin in cholinergic preganglionic terminals of the avian ciliary ganglion. Neurosci. Lett. **78**: 22–28.
52. JIANG, J. G., M. A. SIMMONS & N. J. DUN. 1982. Enkephalinergic modulation of noncholinergic transmission in mammalian prevertebral ganglia. Brain Res. **235**: 185–191.
53. KONISHI, S., A. TSUNOO & M. OTSUKA. 1979. Enkephalins presynaptically inhibit cholinergic transmission in sympathetic ganglia. Nature **282**: 515–516.
54. ARAUJO, D. M. & B. COLLIER. 1987. Effects of endogenous opioid peptides on acetylcholine release from the cat superior cervical ganglion: selective effect of a heptapeptide. J. Neurosci. **7**: 1698–1704.
55. MACHOVA, J. & Z. KVALTINOVA. 1983. The actions of [leu$^5$]enkephalin and morphine in cat sympathetic ganglion. Eur. J. Pharmacol. **87**: 277–282.
56. PROSDOCIMI, M., M. FINESSO & A. GORIO. 1986. Enkephalin modulation of neural transmis-

sion in the cat stellate ganglion: pharmacological actions of exogenous opiates. J. Auton. Nerv. System. **17:** 217–230.

57. HEYM, C., M. REINECKE, E. WEIHE & W. G. FORSSMAN. 1984. Dopamine-hydroxylase, neurotensin, substance P, vasoactive intestinal polypeptide and enkephalin immunohisto-chemistry of paravertebral and prevertebral ganglia in the cat. Cell Tiss. Res. **235:** 411–418.

58. MATTHEWS, M. R. & A. C. CUELLO. 1982. Substance P immunoreactive peripheral branches of sensory neurons innervate guinea-pig sympathetic neurons. Proc. Natl. Acad. Sci. USA **79:** 1668–1672.

59. SIMMONS, M. A. 1985. The complexity and diversity of synaptic transmission in the prever-tebral sympathetic ganglia. Progr. Neurobiol. **24:** 43–93.

60. DUN, N. I. & A. G. KARCZMAR. 1979. Actions of substance P on sympathetic neurons. Neuropharmacology **18:** 215–218.

61. NEILD, T. O. 1978. Slowly-developing depolarization of neurones in the guinea-pig inferior mesenteric ganglion following repetitive stimulation of the preganglionic nerves. Brain Res. **140:** 231–239.

62. KIRALY, M., M. MAILLARD, J. J. DREIFUSS & M. DOLIVO. 1985. Neurohypophyseal peptides depress cholinergic transmission in a mammalian sympathetic ganglion. Neurosci. Lett. **62:** 89–95.

63. RIOUX, F., R. KEROUAC & S. ST-PIERRE. 1981. Somatostatin: interaction with the sympathetic nervous system in guinea pigs. Neuropeptides **1:** 319–327.

64. BACHOO, M. & C. POLOSA. 1988. Cardioacceleration produced by close intra-arterial injection of neurotensin into the stellate ganglion of the cat. Can. J. Physiol. Pharmacol. **66:** 408–412.

# Dysfunctions of Regulatory Neurotransmitters and Neuropeptides following Spinal Cord Injury[a]

N. ERIC NAFTCHI

*Laboratory of Biochemical Pharmacology*
*New York University Medical Center*
*Rusk Institute of Rehabilitation Medicine*
*400 East 34th Street*
*New York, New York 10016*

A transection of the spinal cord severs the nerve fiber tracts which communicate with different discrete centers in the brain. Spinal cord injury in mammals including human leads to perturbation of the "milieu interieur," the integrity of which is insured by the normal functioning of the central and autonomic nervous system as well as the endocrine glands. Transection results in a complete disruption of ascending and descending pathways including the neurotransmitter and neuropeptide-containing projections from ventral medullary neurons to intermediolateral cell columns (IML). The neurons in the ventral medulla oblongata are involved in neural regulation of cardiovascular function.

In 1965, using the histochemical fluorescence technique, Dahlstrom and Fuxe demonstrated in the rat that soon after lesion of the spinal cord norepinephrine and 5-hydroxytryptamine accumulate above the level of transection and disappear caudal to the lesion.[1] Further, they showed that the monoaminergic terminals belong to bulbospinal pathways with the cell bodies located in the medulla oblongata. After spinal cord transection the blockade of ascending substance P pathways renders the spinal cord-injured mammal devoid of tactile, thermal, and nociceptive sensation below the lesion level. In contrast, the interruption of bulbospinal monoaminergic pathways leading to the loss of noradrenergic and serotonergic descending fibers is associated with a loss of locomotor function. This paper will deal with some of the important descending monoaminergic and ascending peptidergic (substance P) pathways and the dysfunctions brought about by spinal cord injury.

## Substance P

Substance P was extracted in 1931 from equine brain and intestine by Von Euler and Gaddum.[2] It was found to possess a vasodilative effect and to stimulate smooth muscle. It was not until 1970, however, when Chang and Leeman[3] isolated a sialogogic peptide from bovine hypothalamus, which was purified, characterized as substance P, and later synthesized that it was found to be an undecapeptide.[4] Subsequently, antibodies to substance P were prepared and using radioimmunoassay, it was found that substance P had an uneven distribution in the central nervous system (CNS).[5] Its highest concentrations occurred in the substantia nigra, hypothalamus, pineal gland, and the dorsal gray matter

[a]This work was supported by the Edmund A. Guggenheim Research Endowment and the Murry and Leonie Guggenheim Foundation.

of the spinal cord.[6] These results have been confirmed by immunofluorescence and immunoperoxidase methods in a variety of animals: human, cat, rat, and monkey.[7-10] In the substantia gelatinosa, the immunoreactivity seems to occur within unmyelinated fibers, which are classically known to carry thermal and pain stimuli. This finding suggests that substance P is the first chemical signal of exteroceptive perception in the spinal cord.[9] Physiological evidence indicates that substance P can produce slow, long-lasting excitation in spinal neurons when it is applied iontophoretically. These neurons include motoneurons, Renshaw cells, and dorsal horn interneurons in the substantia gelantinosa and Rexed's lamina V.[11,12] The data support the view that substance P may be a transmitter or modulator that is involved in the perception of pain.

The presence of substance P (SP) in sympathetic ganglia was demonstrated by Pernow.[13] Substance P was also demonstrated to be present in nerve fibers of the prevertebral ganglia. Although no SP immunoreactive ganglion cell bodies could be observed,[14,15] Kessler et al. found SP-like immunoreactivity within the principal ganglion cells of neonatal sympathetic superior cervical ganglia. Substance P is also present in various parts of the peripheral nervous system including the vagal nerve[16,17] and in the intrinsic neurons of the intestine.[15,18] SP-containing axons of the prevertebral ganglia were thought to be peripheral processes of primary sensory neurons with cell bodies located in dorsal root ganglia.[7,19] Matthew and Cuello[20] have shown, however, that some nerve fibers containing substance P persist in the inferior mesenteric ganglion of the guinea-pig after transection of the splanchnic nerve; administration of capsaicin caused a complete loss of substance P-like immunoreactivity.

### Substance P, Enkephalins, and Opiate Receptors

Perception of pain in the CNS is first integrated in the spinal cord, in the narrow band of gray matter at the apex of the dorsal horns that is known as the substantia gelantinosa. Primary afferent neurons terminate in the substantia gelantinosa and interact with many small interneurons found in this region. High concentrations of the peptides substance P, leucine-enkephalin, and methionine-enkephalin have been found in the substantia gelantinosa (Rexed's lamina II and III) and in Rexed's lamina I.[21-23,6,24,7,25,26] In addition, a dense population of opiate receptors has been demonstrated in the substantia gelantinosa.[27] Thus, these three neuropeptides have been implicated in the mediation of pain and analgesia.

In 1973, binding of radioactive opiates, including morphine, to brain synaptosomal membranes was independently reported by three groups.[28-30] The binding could be blocked stereospecifically by the opiate antagonists naloxone and naltrexone. It was postulated, therefore, that opiates must bind to selective sites, or receptors, that are located on the surface of nerve cells in the CNS before they can produce their characteristic pharmacological responses; analgesia, euphoria, sleep, relaxation. The antagonists would then bind to these specific sites first and, thereby, prevent opiate (agonist) binding.[31]

Accordingly, opiate receptors have been reported in various regions of the brain, in especially high amounts in the limbic system (except the hippocampus), in the spinal cord (especially the dorsal gray matter), and in the intestine.[31,32] In addition, opiate receptor binding sites have been demonstrated by radiobinding assay and by autoradiography in brain and spinal cord.[27,28,33]

The presence of the opiate receptors in the CNS led to the belief that a biological ligand(s) for opiate receptors might exist in the CNS and might be a naturally occurring endogenous morphine-like substance(s). Several studies reported that electrical stimulation of certain parts of the brain could cause analgesia, which was prevented by injections of naloxone.[34-36] These studies suggested a release of an endogenous opiate-like substance. In a search for a substance with morphine-like effects on smooth muscle that could be blocked by naloxone, Hughes and Kosterlitz[37,38] screened pig brain extracts. After extensive purification, two such morphine-like substances were characterized as pentapeptides and were called "enkephalins." These compounds were also isolated by Simantov and Snyder[39] from calf brain. One of the enkephalins was found to have the amino acid sequence (Tyr-Gly-Gly-Phe-Met) and was called methionine-enkephalin. The other had the amino acid sequence (Tyr-Gly-Gly-Phe-Leu) and was named leucine-enkephalin. Beta-endorphin, a fragment of beta-lipoprotein, which is a pituitary peptide, also has a very strong opiate-like effect.[66] A very potent endogenous opioid peptide, dinorphin was also discovered.[67,68] There are now approximately fifteen known neuropeptides with opioid-like activity. The name endorphins was proposed by Simon[70] to denote endogenous morphine-like substances.

Endorphins and leu- and met-enkephalins are thought to be neurotransmitters or neuromodulators which are probably involved in pain pathways as well as pathways involving higher mental processes. These peptides have been demonstrated in rat CNS.[24,7,17,40,39,65] In the brain, fluorescence was confined to neurons, as opposed to glia, and was found most intensively in nerve endings where it would be expected to be concentrated if the peptides were acting as neurotransmitters.

In our laboratory, we have investigated the changes in substance P and leu-enkephalin in spinal cord transected rats, cats, and monkeys, using a sensitive and specific peroxidase-anti-peroxidase immunocytochemical method.[21-23] At varying intervals of time after transection, the distribution and changes of substance P and leu-enkephalin were studied in the spinal cord, both above and below the lesion.

In order to assess further the roles of the opiate receptors, substance P, and the enkephalins in spinal pain pathways, we studied the effects of chronic morphine treatment *in vivo*. Stereospecific opiate receptor binding is reduced in the substantia gelantinosa after dorsal rhizotomy.[41] Conceivably the opiate receptors are associated presynaptically with substance P-containing primary afferent fibers in the substantia gelantinosa. There is further evidence that opiate receptor sites interact with the enkephalins in this region.[41]

### Substance P Localization after Chordotomy

We have been exploring the neural circuits between these substances to elucidate the interaction between these peptides and their involvement in pre- and postsynaptic and interneuronal events. Examination of tissue from normal and sham-operated cats and rats (FIGS. 1a and 1b) displayed peroxide-positive staining that appeared as a band of nerve terminals in the dorsal horn at the junction between the white and gray matters, the substantia gelatinosa that corresponds to laminae II and III of Rexed.[42] Substance P-specific staining was also found in Rexed's lamina I.

There was a sharp increase in the amount of substance P below the lesion two and five days after transection of the spinal cord of the rats and cats, respectively. Substance P had outlined both dorsal horns and bridged the two together. Above the lesion, in the region of the substantia gelatinosa, the number of punctate bodies was fewer, and the intensity of staining around the dorsal horn was less than that in sections that were obtained from below the lesion. This pattern was repeated in sections from chronic cats that were sacrificed one to 12 weeks following transection. Substance P-specific, immunoreactive staining in sections that were cut from above the lesion (FIGS. 2a and 3a), was little compared with the great amount of staining found in sections that were cut from below the lesion (FIGS. 2b and 3b). In addition, punctate bodies, long fibers and varicosities were present in sections that were taken from below the lesion (FIG. 2c). A network of fibers located centrally within each dorsal horn (Rexed laminae IV and V) from the rats and cats that were sacrificed three and 12 weeks, respectively, after transection were found to be immunoreactive for substance P (FIGS. 3b and 3c). Some staining was often seen in the ventral horn in the form of small, dense punctate bodies that were scattered randomly throughout the horn (FIG. 4a). It was difficult to assess whether the amount of staining in the ventral horn changed with time either above or below the lesion. In chronically lesioned monkeys (six months or longer after spinal cord transection), staining was more prominent in ventral horn and central canal region compared with cats and rats (FIG. 4b). With a modified PAP method that amplifies immunological staining, especially in sparsely innervated regions,[10] ventral horn staining became more prominent in the rat around the motoneurons and other ventral horn cells and along the ventrolateral fringe of the ventral horn (FIG. 4c). Additionally, with this modified technique, punctate bodies and subependymal processes could sometimes be seen in the central canal region (FIG. 4d). In normal rat tissue, laminae IV and V appeared stained at times, but only when the double bridge amplification method was employed (FIG. 4e).

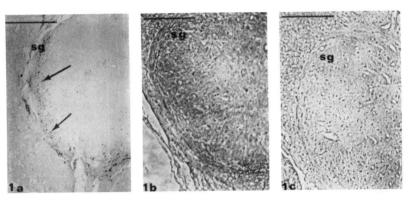

FIGURE 1. (a) Section from T 11–12 region of the spinal cord of a sham-operated cat. *Arrows* point to immunoreactive substance P (SP) specific bodies in dorsal horn (area of substantia gelantinosa). × 200. (b) Phase contrast micrograph of the same dorsal horn region seen in (a). The section was incubated for SP immunoreactivity. Note the presence of a dark ring in the substantia gelantinosa region, indicating the area of immunoreactivity. × 200. (c) Phase contrast micrograph of the same dorsal horn region seen in (a). The section was incubated with normal rabbit serum. Compared with (b), the absence of any SP-specific staining is evident. × 200.

Substitution of normal serum for immune serum as a control showed no staining in the gray matter of the spinal cord with the exception of red blood cells, which contain endogenous peroxidase (FIG. 3c). In some specimens, immunoreactive staining did appear in the white matter, which could be attributed, to some degree, to nonspecific affinity of the rabbit serum for the membranes in the regions where the myelin had leached out, since the same type of light-brown background staining appeared in control sections where normal rabbit serum was substituted for the specific antiserum. There were, however, some small, immunoreactive, substance P-specific, dark, punctate bodies present in the myelinated axons of the white matter in the ventrolateral and dorsolateral parts of the spinal cord. This may suggest a rostral axonal flow of substance P within myelinated fibers possibly belonging to lateral spinothalamic tracts or to shorter tracts concerned with

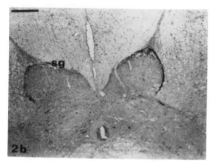

FIGURE 2. (a) Field showing dorsal horns above the lesion from a cat transected 5 weeks before perfusion. Substantia gelantinosa shows slight staining. × 125. (b) Tissue from the same cat as seen in (a) sectioned below the lesion. Note the intense reaction product delineating both dorsal horns. × 100. (c) The detail of the substantia gelantinosa seen in (b). *Arrows* point to darkly stained SP-immunoreactive punctate bodies and an intense band of bead-like varicosities delineating the entire substantia gelantinosa. × 250.

segmental transmission. In monkey tissue additional white matter was bilaterally stained in a uniform, symmetrical pattern that was extended to the ventrolateral white region (FIG. 4f).

## Effect of Morphine on Substance P Immunoreactivity

Immunocytochemical examination of rats that were treated chronically (10 days) with morphine sulfate revealed a nonuniform increase in substance P in certain regions of the spinal cord, compared with tissue from saline-treated rats (FIG. 5). Substance P was increased in the substantia gelantinosa, Rexed's laminae I, IV, and V and the ventral horn around the medial and lateral groups of motoneurons and traveling along the ventral roots.

Substance P, however, did not increase within processes that were found around the central canal.

## Leucine-Enkephalin after Chordotomy

Spinal cord sections from sham-operated cats that were taken from the T5 region, displayed a pattern of immunoreactive bodies in the substantia gelantinosa (FIG. 6a) and in a fairly dense region lateral and dorsal to the central canal (FIG. 6c). There was also a substantial scattering of immunoreactive bodies throughout the entire ventral horn (FIG. 7a). In the substantia gelantinosa of the cat spinal cord, specific leu-enkephalin immunoreactivity in the sections from below the level of the lesion was never as great as that found in comparable tissue sections reacted for substance P. In contrast to substance P, there was no apparent difference in the amount or distribution of staining with time after spinal cord transection, nor was there any difference in immunoreactivity above or below the level of the lesion (FIG. 6b).

Leucine-enkephalin immunoreactivity stained varicosities were often seen extending for short distances into the dorsal white matter (FIG. 6b). In the ventral horn, long fibrous elements were present that seemed to extend to the ventral horn cells after stretching a distance within the grey matter (FIG. 7a). Some long bead-like fibrillar processes were also seen extending a long distance from the grey to the white matter (FIG. 7b). In some instances immunoreactive fibers appeared to run for some distance along the ventral root fibers into the white matter (FIG. 7c). A great deal of immunoreactivity was visualized both dorsal and lateral to the central canal region, mostly in the form of varicosities (FIGS. 6c and 6d).

No specific immunoreactivity was present when normal serum was substituted for immunoserum or when leu-enkephalin antiserum was preincubated with the peptide leu-enkephalin.

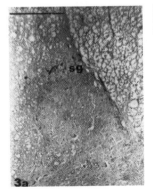

**FIGURE 3.** (a) Section from above the lesion of a cat transected 12 weeks before sacrifice. Note the sparse staining surrounding the dorsal horn in substantia gelantinosa. × 160. (b) Tissue from the same cat as in (a) sectioned below the lesion. The staining of the band of nerve terminals in the substantia gelantinosa is much more intense in this section than that in the section above the lesion. Note the appearance of the nerve plexus *(arrow)* near the center (Lamina V) of the dorsal horn. × 160. (c) A detail of the nerve plexus from (b). Immunoreactive substance P appears in bead-like, fibrillar varicosities, which may be nerve terminals originating from dorsal roots and entering the spinal cord. rbc = red blood cells present in small capillaries. × 960.

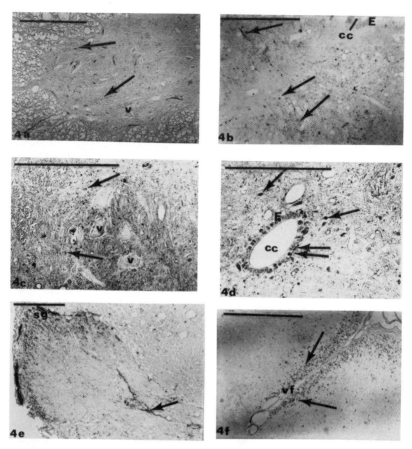

**FIGURE 4. (a)** Section of the ventral horn from below the lesion of a cat transected five weeks before sacrifice. Ventral horn cells (v) are present. *Arrows* point to immunopositive bodies that are scattered throughout. ×250. **(b)** Section of the area lateral and ventral to the central canal (cc) of a sham-operated monkey. *Arrows* point to a few of the large number of immunopositive bodies present. Endothelial cells (E) surround the cc. ×300. **(c)** Section of normal rat ventral horn to which the double bridge PAP method was applied. *Arrows* point to immunopositive punctate bodies. Ventral horn cells (v) are present. ×400. **(d)** Section of normal rat central canal area to which the double bridge PAP method was applied. A fiber (*double arrow*) that abuts on the ependymal cells (E) appears positively stained. Many stained punctate bodies are present (*arrows*). ×400. **(e)** Section from a normal rat dorsal horn area stained by the double bridge PAP method showing substance P localization in lamina V (*arrow*) as well as in the substantia gelantinosa. ×200. **(f)** Area showing the ventral fissure (vf) of the spinal cord of a four week transected monkey. Small bodies (*arrows*) that appear positively stained for substance P bilaterally, ring the fissure in the ventral white matter. ×300.

## DISCUSSION

The abundance of substance P immunoreactive nerve terminals in the substantia gelantinosa suggests that substance P is contained in the primary afferent fibers that penetrate the substantia gelantinosa and dorsolateral funiculus radially and terminate in the dorsal horn. These regions are classically associated with pain transmission. In addition, some SP-containing processes penetrate the intermediate gray regions and extend to the heavily innervated lamina V region and the ventral horn.

Otsuka and co-workers[43] ligated the dorsal roots of the cat and found that substance P concentration increased on the ganglion side of the ligature and decreased centrally. The findings suggested that substance P was synthesized in dorsal root ganglia and its presence in afferent fibers suggested a role in neurotransmission. Iontophoretic application of substance P to spinal neurons by Henry et al.[11,12] produced a strong but slow and

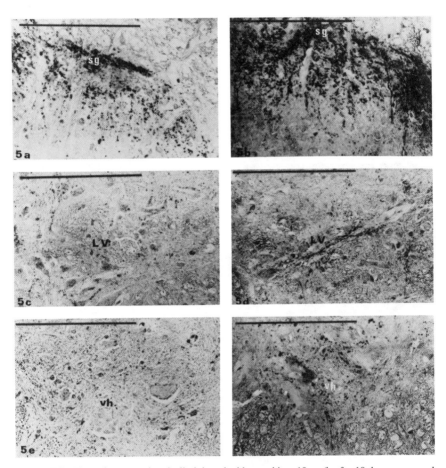

FIGURE 5. Tissue from rats chronically injected with morphine, 10 mg/kg for 10 days, compared with saline-injected controls. The double bridge PAP method was used. (a) A section of the SG region of the dorsal horn of a saline control; (b) a comparable section from a morphine-treated animal. (c) A section through lamina V (LV) of the dorsal horn of a saline control; (d) a comparable section from a morphine-treated animal. (e) A section of the ventral horn (vh) from a saline control; (f) A comparable section from a morphine-treated animal. At each of these levels (dorsal horn, lamina V, ventral horn) there is more immunoreactivity in the morphine-treated animal than in the saline control. × 500.

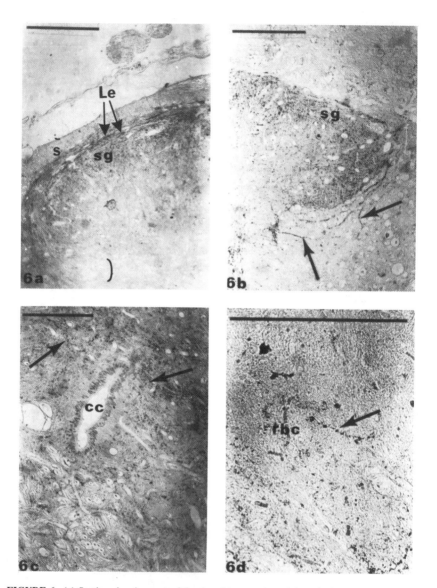

**FIGURE 6.** (a) Section showing part of the dorsal horn region of the spinal cord at T 11-12 of a sham-operated cat. Immunoreactive leucine-enkephalin (Le)-spefific bodies outline the substantia gelantinosa. ×200. (b) Section showing the substantia gelantinosa from below the lesion of a rat transected two weeks before sacrifice. The amount of immunoreactive Le-specific bodies is comparable to (a). Immunoreactivity is also present in fibers (*arrows*) extending into the white matter. ×200. (c) Region around the central canal area of a sham-operated cat. Many immunoreactive bodies (*arrows*) are seen in the region. ×200. (d) Region lateral to the central canal in a sham-operated cat. Le-positive punctate bodies as well as a beaded fiber (*arrow*) are seen. Red blood cells in a small vessel are present.

prolonged excitatory action on nearly half the neurons that were tested in the lumbar spinal cord of the cat. It is noteworthy that all units that were excited by substance P were also excited by noxious thermal stimulation of the skin. The highest number of units that were excited by substance P was found in lamina VI and the lowest in lamina IV. In two cases, treatment with substance P led to a response to noxious heat by units that had previously been unresponsive to thermal stimulation. Therefore, Henry suggested that substance P-containing fibers in peripheral afferent nerves are unmyelinated and that in the skin these fibers terminate in free nerve endings that are usually associated with pain transmission.[7,17,25]

Using immunohistochemical techniques for localization of substance P, we found extensive staining of the nerve plexus in lamina V below the lesion (FIGS. 3b and 3c)

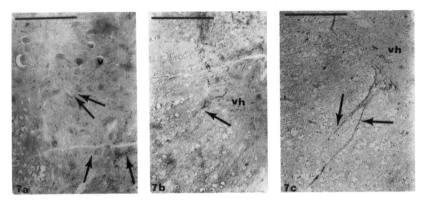

FIGURE 7. (a) Field from the ventral horn of a sham-operated cat. Ventral horn cells are present. Le-positive (*arrows*) noted at one point (*double arrow*) seem to impinge on one of the ventral horn cells. × 250. (b) Field showing Le-immunopositive bodies at the edge of the ventral horn in a sham-operated cat. *Arrow* points to a stained branching fiber extending into the white matter. × 250. (c) Long-distance Le-immunopositive fibers (*arrows*), extending well into the white matter, appearing to travel along with the ventral root fibers that exit from the ventral horn in this section taken from a sham-operated cat. × 250.

showing the presence of a network of varicosities in the nerve endings in the area classically known to be concerned with noxious transmission. Lamina V networks were never observed in the sections above the lesion. These results demonstrate accumulation of substance P below the lesion and suggest its rostral direction by axoplasmic flow in the spinal cord.

The slow course of substance P action observed by Henry et al.[12] was incompatible with a role as the main excitatory transmitter of primary afferent terminals, but its strong excitatory action might have functional significance as sensitizer or modulator over a long period. Pickel et al.,[44] using immunocytochemical techniques, reported that within axon terminals substance P appeared to be associated with one type of organelle, a large, round vesicle 60–80 nm in diameter. In addition, the same axon terminal, small unlabeled vesicles were also present. It is generally accepted that such small vesicles serve as storage sites for most neurotransmitters. This finding further supports the suggestion that substance P may act as a modulator rather than the neurotransmitter initiating synaptic events.

In the isolated frog spinal cord preparation, Konishi and Otsuka[45] showed that substance P was about 200 times more active, on a molar basis, than L-glutamate in depolarizing spinal motoneurons. The depolarizing action persisted after synaptic transmission was blocked by $Ca^{++}$-deficient Ringer's solution or by tetrodotoxin. Therefore, they concluded that substance P exerted a transsynaptic action on motoneurons and was probably a candidate for the excitatory transmitter of primary sensory neurons. In our work, immunoreactive substance P endings could often be seen in close association with motoneurons. The data concur with those of other investigators, suggesting a pathway for substance P starting from the dorsal root ganglion via primary afferent fibers toward their terminals in the dorsal horn of the spinal cord. It further extends the work by demonstrating that substance P accumulates in the dorsolateral part of the dorsal horn below the level of the lesion, indicating an upward flow of this peptide in the spinal cord in contrast to the downward movement, from the brainstem, of monoamine transmitters by axoplasmic flow.[46-48] Although our data indicate an anterograde direction of substance P in the spinal cord, they do not elucidate whether it arises in the collaterals of primary afferent fibers or in second order fibers.

The release of enkephalins from preganglionic fibers or their application to superior cervical ganglia results in a decrease in acetylcholine and substance P and concomitant reduction of ganglionic neuronal excitability.[49,50] Autonomic ganglia are excited by substance P to produce a slow depolarization, characteristic of substance P excitation,[11,12] in the inferior mesenteric ganglia.[50,51] Ventral medullary neurons of the midline raphe and the parapyramidal region, project to the intermediolateral cell column (IML, origin of preganglionic sympathetic neurons of the thoracic spinal cord and to the nucleus tractus solitarii, where visceral and baroreceptor afferents terminate.[52] Stimulation of parapyramidal region and medullary raphe nuclei elicits cardiovascular and sympathoexcitatory response.[53,54] These medullary regions thereby take part in neural regulation of and exert influence on cardiovascular function.

Substance P coexists with thyrotropin-releasing hormone (TRH) and serotonin (5-HT) in IML-projecting neurons. These ventral medullary neurons which project to IML are subdivided on the basis of their specificity of distribution and pattern of coexistence.[55-60] It has been shown that activation of spinal cord substance P or TRH receptors causes sympatho-excitatory and pressor effects.[61,62] The coexistence of multiple neurotransmitters and neuropeptides may regulate sympathetic activity in a manner that is comparable to their relative distribution and abundance; the overall effect of co-released neuropeptides or a neuropeptide and a neurotransmitter will differ from that of a single neuropeptide in maintaining homeostasis.

Dysfunction of several neurotransmitters and neuropeptides is responsible for a number of untoward clinical symptoms observed after spinal cord injury such as spinal spasticity, bone demineralization, and autonomic dysreflexia. Descending monoaminergic pathways containing norepinephrine and 5-HT are severed, removing the inhibitory function of these transmitters.[47,48] Further, the IML-projecting ventral medullary neurons containing enkephalins, substance P, TRH, and other neuropeptides are disrupted. Ascending neuronal pathways containing substance P are blocked with the resultant buildup of this putative neurotransmitter (modulator) below the level of transection.[47,48] A predominance of excitatory effects has been reported after iontophoretic application of substance P on brain and spinal cord neurons.[11,43] Inhibitory effects of substance P consistently blocked the excitatory action of acetylcholine on Renshaw cells, thus preserving the inhibitory action of these interneurons.

Previous studies by Franz and co-workers[63,64] have shown that clonidine, an alpha-2 adrenoceptor agonist, depresses transmission through sympathetic preganglionic neurons in the spinal cord, at least in part by reducing neuronal levels of cyclic AMP. Treatment of neonatal mice (second day of life) with capsaicin caused a selective loss of a large population of sensory, afferent C-fibers but did not affect the number or affinity of alpha-2 adrenoceptors.[69] These findings indicate that the location of alpha-2 adrenoceptors in the spinal cord is postsynaptic to the primary sensory neurons. Stimulation of alpha-2 adrenoceptors by their agonists, therefore, would inhibit the transmission of the nociceptive stimuli, since pain sensitivity to capsaicin was reduced by clonidine.[69] As mentioned previously, the bulbospinal monoaminergic terminals contain norepinephrine, epinephrine (alpha-2), and serotonin. The receptors for these monoamines (with the exception of norepinephrine and enkephalins) are negatively coupled (inhibitory) to adenylate cyclase. The terminals of these neurotransmitters/neuropeptides innervate the sympathetic preganglionic neurons (SPGNs) in the intermediolateral cell columns of the spinal cord. The work of Franz et al.[63,64] suggests that alpha-2, opiate, and 5-HT receptors are coupled negatively to adenylate cyclase, thereby preventing synthesis of cyclic AMP and reducing the excitability of sympathetic preganglionic fibers. In addition to the inhibitory influences of serotonin and epinephrine on adenylate cyclase, the epinephrine terminals and alpha-2 receptors also appear to complete a recurrent inhibitory pathway to sympathetic preganglionic neurons. This inhibitory pathway is activated by rapid increases in SPGNs' activity.[63,64] The loss of these inhibitory influences after spinal cord injury including the changes in substance P, enkephalins, monoamines, and GABA, etc. in the spinal cord is responsible for many dysfunctions observed in paraplegic humans.

## REFERENCES

1. DAHLSTROM, A. & K. FUXE. 1965. Evidence for the existence of monoamine neurons in the CNS: II Experimentally induced changes in the intraneuronal amine levels of bulbospinal neuron system. Acta Physiol. Scand. **64** (Suppl.): 245.
2. VON EULER, U. S. & J. H. G GADDUM. 1931. An unidentified depressor substance in certain tissue extracts. J. Physiol. **72**: 74–87.
3. CHANG, M. M. & S. E. LEEMAN. 1970. Isolation of a sialogogic peptide from bovine hypothalamic tissue and its characterization as substance P. J. Biol. Chem. **245**: 4787–4790.
4. CHANG, M. M., S. E. LEEMAN & H. D. NIALL. 1971. Amino acid sequence of substance P. Nature New Biol. **232**: 86–87.
5. POWELL, D., S. LEEMAN, G. W. TREGEAR, H. D. NIALL & J. T. POTTS. 1973. Radioimmunoassay for substance P. Nature New Biol. **241**: 252–254.
6. BROWNSTEIN, M. J., E. A. MROZ, J. S. KIZER, M. PALKOVITZ & S. E. LEEMAN. 1976. Regional distribution of substance P in the brain of the rat. Brain Res. **116**: 229–305.
7. HÖKFELT, T., J. O. KELLERTH, G. NILLSON & B. PERNOW. 1975. Substance P: localization in the central nervous system and some primary sensory neurons. Science **190**: 889–890.
8. NAFTCHI, N. E., S. J. ABRAHAMS, H. ST. PAUL, E. W. LOWMAN & W. SCHLOSSER. 1978. Localization and changes of substance P in spinal cord of paraplegic cats. Brain Res. **153**: 507–513.
9. CUELLO, A. C., J. M. POLAK & A. G. E. PEARSE. 1976. Substance P: a naturally occurring transmitter in human spinal cord. Lancet, 1054–1056.
10. VACCA, L. L., S. J. ABRAHAMS & N. E. NAFTCHI. 1980. A modified peroxidase antiperoxidase procedure for improved localization of tissue antigens: localization of substance P in rat spinal cord. J. Histochem. Cytochem. **28**: 297–307.
11. HENRY, J. L. 1976. Effects of substance on functionally identified units in cat spinal cord. Brain Res. **114**: 439–451.
12. HENRY, J. L., K. KRNJEVIC & M. E. MORRIS. 1975. Substance P and spinal neurones. Can. J. Physiol. Pharmacol. **53**: 423–432.
13. PERNOW, B. 1953. Studies on substance P; purification, occurrence, and biological actions. Acta Physiol. Scand. **29** (Suppl. 105): 1–9.
14. BAKER, S. C., A. C. CUELLO & M. MATTHEWS. 1980. Substance P-containing synapses via sympathetic ganglia and their possible origin as collaterals from sensory nerve fibers. J. Physiol. Lond. **308**: 76–77.

15. COSTA, M., A. C. CUELLO, J. B. FURNESS & F. FRANCO. 1980. Distribution of enteric neuron showing immunoreactivity for substance P in the guinea-pig ileum. Neuroscience 5: 323–331.
16. DALSGAARD, C. J., T. HOKFELT, L. G. ELFVIN, L. SKIRBOLL & O. EMSON. 1982. Substance P-containing primary sensory neurons projecting to the inferior mesenteric ganglion: evidence from combined retrograde tracing and immunohistochemistry. Neuroscience 7: 647–654.
17. HOKFELT, T., J. O. KELLERETH, G. NILSSON & B. PERNOW. 1975. Experimental immuno-histochemical studies on the localization and distribution of substance P in cat primary sensory neurons. Brain Res. 100: 235–252.
18. JESSEN, K. R., M. J. SAFFREY, S. VAN NOORDEN, S. R. BLOOM, J. M. POLAK & G. BURN-STOCK. 1980. Immunohistochemical studies of the enteric nervous system in tissue culture and in situ localization of vasoactive intestinal polypeptide (VIP), substance P and enkephalin-immunoreactive nerves in the guinea-pig gut. Neuroscience 5: 1717–1735.
19. ELFVIN, L. E. & C. J. DALSGAAARD. Retrograde axonal transport of horseradish peroxidase in afferent fibers of the inferior mesenteric ganglion of the guinea-pig. Identification of cells by origin in dorsal root ganglia. Brain Res. 126: 149–153.
20. MATTHEWS, M. R. & A. C. CUELLO. 1982. Substance P-immunoreactive peripheral branches of sensory neurons innervate guinea-pig sympathetic neurones. Proc. Natl. Acad. Sci. USA 79: 1668–1672.
21. NAFTCHI, N. E. 1985. Alterations of neuroendocrine functions in spinal cord injury. Peptides 6: 83–94.
22. NAFTCHI, N. E., S. J. ABRAHAMS, H. M. ST. PAUL, E. W. LOWMAN & W. SCHLOSSER. 1978. Localization and changes of substance P in spinal cord of paraplegic cats. Brain Res. 153: 507–513.
23. NAFTCHI, N. E., S. J. ABRAHAMS, H. M. ST. PAUL & L. L. VACCA. 1981. Substance P and leucine-enkephalin changes after chordotomy and morphine treatment. Peptides 2 (Suppl. 1): 61–70.
24. ELDE, R., T. HOKFELT, O. JOHANSSON & L. TERENIUS. 1976. Immunohistochemical studies using antibodies to leucine-enkephalin; initial observations on the nervous system of the rat. Neuroscience 1: 349–351.
25. HOKFELT, T., J. O. KELLERTH, G. NILLSON & B. PREERENOW. 1975. Experimental immu-nohistochemical studies on the localization and distribution of substance P in cat primary sensory neurons. Brain Res. 100: 235–252.
26. KANAZAWA, I. & I. JESSEL. 1976. Post mortem changes and regional distribution of substance P in the rat and mouse nervous system: Brain Res. 117: 362–367.
27. ATWEH, S. F. & M. J. HUHAR. 1977. Autoradiographic localization of opiate receptors in rat brain 1. Spinal cord and lower medulla. Brain Res. 124: 53–67.
28. PERT, C.B. & S. H. SNYDER. 1973. Opiate receptor: demonstration in nervous tissue. Science 179: 1011–1014.
29. SIMON, E. J., J. M. HILLER & I. EDELMAN. 1973. Stereospecific binding of the potent nar-cotic analgesic 3H-etorphine to rat brain homogenate. Proc. Natl. Acad. Sci. USA 70: 1947–1949.
30. TERENIUS, L. 1973. Stereospecific interaction between narcotic analgesics and a synaptic plasma membrane fraction of rat cerebral cortex. Acta Pharmacol. Toxicol. 32: 317–320.
31. SIMON, E. J. 1976. The opiate receptors. Neurochem. Res. 1: 3–28.
32. KUHAR, M. J., C. B. PERT & S. H. SNYDER. 1976. Opiate receptor autoradiographic local-ization in rat brain. Proc. Natl. Acad. Sci. USA 73: 3729–3722.
33. HILLER, J. M., J. PEARSON & E. J. SIMON. 1973. Distribution of stereospecific binding of the potent narcotic analgesic etorphine in the human brain; predominance of the limbic system. Res. Commun. Chem. Pathol. Pharmacol. 6: 1052–1062.
34. LIEBESKIND, J. C., D. J. MAYER & H. AKIL. 1974. Central mechanisms of pain inhibition: studies of analgesia from focal brain stimulation. In Advances in Neurology. J. J. Bonica, Ed. Vol. 4: 261–268. International Symposium on Pain. Raven Press. New York, NY.
35. MAYER, D. J. & R. HAYES. 1975. Stimulation-produced analgesia: development of tolerance and cross-tolerance to morphine. Science 188: 941–943.
36. MAYER, D. J. & J. C. LIEBESKIND. 1974. Pain reduction by focal electrical stimulation of the brain: an anatomical and behavioral analysis. Brain Res. 68: 73–93.

37. HUGHES, J. 1975. Isolation of an endogenous compound from the brain with properties similar to morphine. Brain Res. **88:** 295–308.
38. HUGHES, J., T. SMITH, H. W. KOSTERLITZ, L. A. FOTHERGILL, B. MORGAN & H. R. MORRIS. 1975. Identification of two related pentapeptides from the brain with potent opiate agonist activity. Nature **258:** 577–579.
39. SIMANTOV, R. & S. H. SNYDER. 1976. Morphine-like peptides in mammalian brain; isolation, structure, elucidation and interaction with the opiate receptor. Proc. Natl. Acad. Sci. USA **73:** 2515–2519.
40. HOKFELT, T., A. LJUNGDAHL, L. TERENIUS, R. ELDE & G. NILLSON. 1977. Immunohisto-chemical analysis of peptide pathways possibly related to pain and analgesia: enkephalin and substance P. Proc. Natl. Acad. Sci. USA **74:** 3081–3085.
41. LAMOTTE, C., C. B. PERT & S. H. SNYDER. 1976. Opiate receptor binding in primate spinal cord: distribution and changes after dorsal root section. Brain Res. **112:** 407–412.
42. REXED, B. 1954. A cytoarchitectonic atlas of the spinal cord in the cat. J. Comp. Neurol. **100:** 297–379.
43. OTSUKA, M., S. KONISHI & T. TAKAHASHI. 1975. Hypothalamic substance P as a candidate for transmitter of primary afferent neurons Fed. Proc. **34:** 1922–1928.
44. PICKEL, V. M., D. J. RESI & S. E. LEEMAN. 1977. Ultrastructural localization of substance P in neurons of rat spinal cord. Brain Res. **122:** 534–540.
45. KONISHI, S. & M. OTSUKA. 1974. The effects of substance P and other peptides on spinal neurons of the frog. Brain Res. **65:** 397–410.
46. DAHLSTROM, A. 1971. Axoplasmic transport. Philos. Trans. R. Soc. Lond. B. Biol. Sci. **261:** 325–358.
47. NAFTCHI, N. E., A. K. KIRSCHNER, M. DEMENY & A. VIAU. 1982. Changes in the CNS biogenic amines and tyrosine hydroxylase activity after spinal cord transection in the rat. *In* Spinal Cord Injury. N. E. Naftchi, Ed. 67–80. Spectrum Publications, Inc.
48. NAFTCHI, N. E., R. LEHRER & J. A. SLEIS. 1988. Effects of an alpha-2 adrenergic receptor agonist in spinal rats. *In* Neural Development and Regeneration. A. Gorio *et al.* Eds. 667–669. Springer-Verlag. Berlin and Heidelberg.
49. ARAUJO, D. M. & B. COLLIER. 1987. Effects of endogenous opioid peptides on acetylcholine release from the cat superior cervical ganglion: selective effect of a heptapeptide. J. Neurosci. **7:** 1698–1704.
50. HEYM, C., M. REINECKE, E. WEIHE & W. G. FORSSMAN. 1984. Dopamine-hydroxylase, neurotensin, substance P, vasoactive intestinal polypeptide and enkephalin immunohisto-chemistry of paravertebral and prevertebral ganglia in the cat. Cell Tissue Res. **235:** 411–418.
51. SIMMONS, M. A. 1985. The complexity and diversity of synpatic transmission in the prever-tebral sympathetic ganglia. Prog. Neurobiol. **24:** 43–93.
52. KRUKOFF, T. L. 1986b. Coexistence of neuropeptides in sympathetic preganglionic neurons of the cat. Peptides **81:** 109–112.
53. MCCALL, R. B. 1984. Evidence for a serotonergically mediated sympathoexcitatory response to stimulation of medullary raphe nuclei. Brain Res. **311:** 131–139.
54. HASELTON, J. R., R. W. WINTERS, D. R. LISKOWSKY, C. L. HASELTON, P. M. MCCABE & N. SCHNEIDERMAN. 1988. Cardiovascular responses elicited by electrical and chemical stim-ulation of the rostral medullary raphe of the rabbit. Brain Res. **453:** 167–175.
55. SASEK, C. A., M. GALEAZZA, M. WESSENDORF & C. J. HELKE. 1988. Coexistence of neu-rochemicals in ventral medullary cells that project to the intermediolateral cell column of the rat. Soc. Neurosci. Abst. **14:** 191.
56. THOR, K. B. & C. J. HELKE. 1989. Serotonin and substance P colocalization in medullary projections to the nucleus tractus solitarius: dual color immunohistochemistry combined with retrograde tracing. J. Chem. Neuroanat. In press.
57. HELKE, C. J., S. C. SAYSON, J. R. KEELER & C. G. CHARLTON. 1986. Thyrotrophin-releasing hormone neurons project from the ventral medulla to the intermediolateral cell column: partial coexistence with serotonin. Brain Res. **381:** 1–7.
58. KRUKOFF, T. L., J. CIRIELLO & F. R. CALARESU. 1985b. Segmental distribution of peptide and 5-HT-like immunoreactivity in nerve terminals and fibers of the thoracolumbar sympathetic nuclei of the cat. J. Comp. Neurol. **240:** 103–116.

59. KRUKOFF, T. L. 1987. Neuropeptide Y-like immunoreactivity in cat spinal cord with special reference to autonomic areas. Brain Res. **415:** 300–308.

60. KRUKOFF, T. L. 1986a. Segmental distribution of corticotrophin-releasing factor-like and vasoactive intestinal peptide-like immunoreactivities in presumptive sympathetic pregangli-onic neurons of the cat. Brain Res. **382:**153–157.

61. HELKE, C. J., E. T. PHILLIPS & J. T. O'NEILL. 1987. Regional peripheral and CNS hemo-dynamic effects of intrathecal administration of a substance P receptor agonist. J. Auton. Nerv. Syst. **21:** 1–7.

62. HELKE, C. J. & E. T. PHILIPS. 1988. Thyrotropin-releasing hormone receptor activation in the spinal cord increases blood pressure and sympathetic tone to the vasculature and adrenals. J. Pharmacol. Exp. Ther. **245:** 41–46.

63. FRANZ, D. N., B. D. HARE & K. L. McCLOSKEY. 1982. Spinal sympathetic neurons: possible sites of opiate-withdrawal suppression by clonidine. Science **215:** 1643–1645.

64. FRANZ, D. N., S. C. STEFFENSEN, L. C. MINER & C. SANGDEE. 1987. Neurotransmitter regulation of excitability in sympathetic preganglionic neurons through interactions with adenylate cyclase. *In* Organization of the Autonomic Nervous System: Central and Peripheral Mechanisms. 121–130. Alan R. Liss, Inc. New York, NY.

65. NAFTCHI, N. E., H. MAKER, E. LAPIN, J. SLEIS, A. LAJTHA & S. LEEMAN. 1988. Acute reduction of brain substance P induced by nicotine. Neurochem. Res. **13:** 305–309.

66. COX, B. M., F. GOLDSTEIN & C. H. LI. 1976. Opioid activity of a peptide beta-lipoprotein-(61-91) derived from beta-lipoprotein. Proc. Natl. Acad. Sci. USA **73:** 1821–1823.

67. GOLDSTEIN, A. S. TACHIBANA, L. I. LOWNEY, M. HUNKAPILLER & L. HOOD. 1979. Dynor-phin (1-13) an extraordinarily potent opioid peptide. Proc. Natl. Acad. Sci. USA **76:** 6666–6670.

68. GOLDSTEIN, A., W. FISCHLI, L. I. LOWNEY, M. HUNKAPILLAR & L. HOOD. 1981. Porcine pituitary dynorphin: complete amino acid sequence of a biologically active heptadecapeptide. Proc. Natl. Acad. Sci. USA **78:** 7219–7223.

69. WIKBERG, J. E. S. & M. HAJOS. 1987. Spinal cord alpha-2 adrenoceptors may be located postsynaptically with respect to primary sensory neurons: destruction of primary C-afferents with neonatal capsaicin does not affect the number of [3H] clonidine binding sites in mice. Neurosci. Lett. **76:** 63–68.

70. SIMON, E. J. 1988. Recent studies on opioid receptors. cellular and molecular basis of synaptic transmission. *In* Progress in Opioid Research. John W. Holaday *et al.*, Eds. NIDA Research Monograph 75. 525–539. NIDA. Rockville, MD.

# Is Corticotropin-Releasing Factor a Mediator of Stress Responses?[a]

ADRIAN J. DUNN AND CRAIG W. BERRIDGE

*Department of Pharmacology and Therapeutics*
*Louisiana State University Medical Center*
*P.O. Box 33932*
*Shreveport, Louisiana 71130-3932*

## INTRODUCTION

Corticotropin-releasing factor (CRF) was isolated and characterized by Vale *et al.*[1] as a 41-amino acid peptide. It is generally believed to be the major active principle that elicits the secretion of adrenocorticotropin hormone (ACTH) from the pituitary.[2,3] CRF is synthesized in neurons of the paraventricular nucleus (PVN) of the hypothalamus. These neurons project to the median eminence region, where terminals secrete CRF directly into the blood. Transported in the portal blood vessels to the anterior pituitary, CRF stimulates the release of ACTH into the general circulation, which subsequently elicits the secretion of glucocorticoids from the adrenal cortex. This cascade constitutes activation of the hypothalamic-pituitary-adrenal (HPA) axis, which is considered to be characteristic, and perhaps diagnostic, of stress.[4-6]

In addition to the localization of CRF within the PVN, CRF-like immunoreactivity has been identified in many extrahypothalamic regions of the brain.[7,8] A similar distribution is found for bioactive CRF.[9] The highest concentrations of extrahypothalamic immuno-reactive CRF are found in neocortex, areas of the limbic system, and regions involved in the regulation of the autonomic nervous system. High-affinity binding sites for CRF have been observed with a similar regional distribution, using both quantitative autoradio-graphic and biochemical techniques.[10,11] A neurotransmitter function for CRF is suggested because CRF-like immunoreactivity is reported to be released from samples of fresh brain tissue by $K^+$ in a $Ca^{2+}$-dependent manner.[12] Moreover, responses to ionto-phoretic application of CRF vary with the region; inhibition of cell firing has been recorded in the thalamus and lateral septum, whereas excitation occurred in the cortex and hypothalamus.[13] Thus cerebral CRF may have a neurotransmitter function in brain, in addition to its ability to activate the HPA axis. The release of extrahypothalamic CRF may be related to stressful situations, because regionally specific changes in the cerebral concentrations of CRF occur following both acute and chronic stressful treatments.[14] Moreover, in one brief report there was an increase in the cerebrospinal fluid (CSF) concentration of CRF in stressed rats.[15]

There are many reports of neurochemical, physiological, endocrine, and behavioral responses following administration of CRF to animals. Many of these responses resemble those observed during stress. These findings prompted the suggestion that CRF may coordinate a whole body response in stress.[16,17] In support of this hypothesis, a number of reports indicate that CRF-antagonists can attenuate or reverse stress-induced changes in physiological, behavioral, and endocrine function. This paper will review these findings,

[a]This research was supported by grants from the National Institutes of Health (MH25486 and NS27283) and a predoctoral fellowship from the National Institute of Mental Health to CWB.

including the relevant studies from our own work. TABLE 1 contains a summary of the reported effects of CRF administration.

## Neuroendocrine Effects of Administered CRF

CRF is instrumental in activating the HPA axis.[1] Because the anterior pituitary is outside the blood-brain barrier, this effect is exerted by peripherally administered CRF. However, intracerebroventricularly (ICV) administered CRF also activates the HPA axis, as indicated by increases of plasma ACTH and glucocorticoids.[18–23] It is not clear whether this occurs because of leakage of the ICV-injected CRF to the periphery (CRF administered by this route is generally less potent than peripheral administration), or

**TABLE 1.** Effects of CRF Administration That Resemble Those Observed in Stress

Endocrine
    Initiates the hypothalamic-pituitary-adrenal response[1]
    Decreases GH (GRH) secretion[20,26]
    Decreases LH (GnRH) secretion[20,25]
Physiological
    Increases sympathetic nervous system and splanchnic nerve activity[28–31]
    Decreases gastric acid secretion, decreases gastric emptying and small intestinal transit[32–36]
    Increases large bowel transit and fecal excretion[35,36]
Electrophysiological
    Activates the EEG; induces seizures at higher doses[37]
    Increases the firing rate of noradrenergic locus coeruleus neurons[38]
Neurochemical
    Increases the activity of cerebral noradrenergic and dopaminergic neurons[23,41]
Behavioral
    Decreases feeding[44,46]
    Decreases sexual behavior in males and females[47,48]
    Increases grooming[22,42–45]
    Increases locomotor activity[45] (high doses may decrease it in a novel environment)
    Decreases responding in a conflict test[42,49]
    Complex effects on avoidance behavior[22,52]
    Increases acoustic startle response[50]
    Decreases exploratory behavior in the multicompartment chamber[53,54]
    Decreases social interaction[55]
    Enhances footshock-induced fighting[70]
    Enhances footshock-induced freezing[51]

because of a direct action within the central nervous system. According to Ono *et al.*,[24] there may be a positive ultrashort feedback loop for CRF, such that intracerebral CRF stimulates its own release. If this is the case, ICV-administered CRF would stimulate the release of endogenous CRF. ICV CRF administration also inhibits the secretion of luteinizing hormone (LH)[20,25] and growth hormone (GH),[20,26] but not thyroid-stimulating hormone[20] or prolactin.[27]

## Other Physiologic Effects of Administered CRF

ICV CRF activates sympathetic and adrenomedullary output, increasing the circulating concentrations of norepinephrine (NE) and epinephrine (Epi) in both rats and dogs.[28,29] Mean arterial pressure, heart rate, and oxygen consumption are also elevated, along with the circulating concentrations of glucose and glucagon.[30] Presumably these changes occur because of the sympathetic activation. This presumption is supported by the observation that the sympathetic ganglionic blocker, chlorisondamine, prevents these effects of CRF.[29] Consistent with this, ICV CRF also increases the electrophysiological activity of the splanchnic nerve.[31] The effects are presumed to be central, because peripheral administration of CRF decreases blood pressure. Moreover, peripheral administration of antibody to CRF which blocks the effect of ICV CRF on plasma ACTH, fails to prevent the elevations of NE and Epi.[30]

CRF also has profound effects on the gastrointestinal system. ICV CRF decreases gastric acid secretion in rats[32] and dogs.[33] Vagotomy blocked this effect of CRF in rats,[32] but not in dogs, in which the effects were blocked by chlorisondamine.[33,34] In rats, ICV CRF also decreased gastric emptying and decreased small intestinal transit, while increasing large intestine transit and fecal excretion.[35,36] Each of these gastrointestinal responses is characteristic of stress.

## Electrophysiological Effects of Administered CRF

ICV CRF produced a dose-dependent activation of the electroencephalogram with signs of both EEG and behavioral arousal predominating at low doses (10–100 ng) and epileptiform activity and seizures observed at higher doses (1–20 μg).[37] ICV CRF also increased the firing of locus coeruleus (LC) neurons in anesthetized and awake rats.[38] Similar effects were observed following local injection of CRF on to LC neurons.[39] In the latter study, CRF was found to increase the basal firing rate, without affecting that due to noxious stimuli.

## Neurochemical Effects of Administered CRF

We found that CRF administered either ICV or subcutaneously to mice increased the concentrations of 3-methoxy-4-hydroxyphenylglycol (MHPG) and 2,5-dihydroxyphenyl-acetic acid (DOPAC) in various brain regions.[23] MHPG:NE and DOPAC:DA ratios were also increased, suggesting that the CRF activated both DA and NE systems throughout the brain. This result contrasted with an earlier study by van Loon et al.[40] which may have been flawed becase α-methyl-p-tyrosine was used to determine the catecholamine "turnover." Recently, Butler et al.[41] have confirmed a CRF-related activation of noradrenergic systems in rats. ICV or local locus coeruleus application of low doses of CRF increased 3,4-dihydroxyphenylethyleneglycol (DHPG) production.

## Behavioral Effects of Administered CRF

CRF administration elicits a wide spectrum of behavioral changes. In most cases only intracerebral application of CRF has been tested. In those cases where peripheral administration has been examined, effects were rarely observed, and, when they were observed, the doses of CRF effective in eliciting significant responses were lower with ICV than with systemic injections.

Grooming is increased by ICV CRF in rats,[22,42–45] but apparently not in mice[43] or rhesus monkeys.[18] Feeding but not drinking is reduced in rats.[44,46] ICV CRF reduces sexual behavior in both male and female rats.[47,48] Kalin et al.[18] reported depression-like effects of ICV CRF in rhesus monkeys.

In rats, ICV CRF produced a dose-dependent activation of locomotor behavior in a familiar environment.[45] In a novel open field, it decreased locomotion and rears and increased freezing, although locomotion was increased at the lowest dose (10 ng). These results were interpreted to reflect an increase in the aversive nature of the novel environment.[45] They were not observed with peripheral injections of CRF. CRF decreased approaches to food in a novel open field.[42] This effect was opposite to that seen following administration of benzodiazepines, suggesting that CRF enhances the anxiogenic nature of the novel environment. In the Geller-Seifter conflict test, CRF decreased punished responding, whereas benzodiazepines increased this response.[49] ICV CRF also potentiated the acoustic startle response[50] and shock-induced freezing.[51] The former effect was antagonized by benzodiazepines.[50] CRF has complex effects on avoidance behavior.[22,52]

We found that ICV CRF (5–100 ng) reduced the mean duration of contacts mice made with novel stimuli in a multicompartment chamber.[53] This change in a measure of exploratory behavior occurred in the absence of changes of locomotor activity, rears, or grooming. It also resembled very closely the effects of restraining the mice for 30–40 min before the test.[53] Similar observations were made in rats.[54] CRF ICV (100 or 300 ng) decreased social interaction in rats, an effect that was reversed by chlordiazepoxide, suggestive of an anxiogenic effect for CRF.[55]

### The Role of the HPA Axis in the Responses to Administered CRF

In every case where it has been tested, these effects of CRF appear to be independent of the pituitary-adrenal axis. Hypophysectomized animals showed a grooming response to ICV CRF,[44] increased locomotor activity,[56] and decreased exploratory behavior.[57] Moreover, the sympathetic nervous system activation caused by ICV CRF was present in hypophysectomized and adrenalectomized rats.[58] The decreased gastric acid secretion and inhibited gastric emptying responses to ICV CRF were likewise not affected by hypophysectomy.[32,36] The locomotor activating effects of ICV CRF were not prevented by dexamethasone treatment, which suppresses CRF-induced ACTH release from the pituitary.[59,60] Dexamethasone did not alter the CRF-induced decreases in responding in the conflict test,[59] nor did it alter the ICV CRF-induced increases in grooming[43,60] or decreases in feeding.[60]

### Experimental Results with CRF Antagonists

The stress-like effects of CRF discussed above suggest that CRF may be an endogenous mediator of stress responses. But what if the CRF administration were stressful, such that it merely activated the endogenous stress systems? Stronger evidence for CRF as a mediator of stress-related responses would be the demonstration that CRF antagonists could reverse those changes. Fortunately, Rivier et al.[61] have synthesized peptide antagonist, $\alpha$-helical CRF$_{9-41}$ (ahCRF). This antagonist binds to pituitary membranes with an affinity significantly lower than that of CRF itself, and rather large quantities of it are necessary to antagonize CRF's actions. Nevertheless, it appears to be relatively specific. A summary of the reports of the use of ahCRF is contained in TABLE 2.

Rivier et al.[62] initially demonstrated that immunoneutralization of endogenous CRF by systemic administration of CRF antibody could prevent the ether stress-induced secretion of ACTH. Subsequently, Rivier et al.[61] reported similar results with ahCRF (1 mg IV). Nakane et al.[63] found that immunoneutralization of CRF could reverse or attenuate the increases in plasma ACTH due to stress induced by ether inhalation, cold water swims, immobilization, or trauma due to bone fracture. Subsequently, it was shown that ahCRF (100 μg ICV) could reverse the electric shock-induced decreases in GH[64] and LH secretion in male rats.[65] ICV antibody to CRF similarly blocked the ether exposure-induced reduction in growth hormone secretion.[27]

Brown et al.[66] found that ICV ahCRF did not alter basal plasma concentrations of NE or Epi, but could reverse the ether-induced increase in plasma Epi, but not that of NE.[67] This suggests an effect selective for the adrenal medullary system. Williams et al.[35] showed that ICV ahCRF (50 μg IV or ICV) prevented the restraint-related increases of large intestinal transit time and fecal secretion. Similar results were obtained by Lenz et al.[68] Stephens et al.[69] showed that intracisternal ahCRF (10 or 50 μg) reversed the surgery-related inhibition of gastric acid secretion.

CRF antagonists have also been effective in reversing stress-related changes in behavior. In all cases central application of the antagonists appears to be necessary. Krahn et al.[46] first demonstrated that ICV ahCRF (50 or 100 μg) attenuated the shock-induced decrease in feeding. We found that ICV ahCRF (20 or 50 μg) reversed the effect of restraint on exploratory behavior in mice.[69] ICV ahCRF (5 or 25 μg) blocked footshock-induced fighting,[71] and 25 μg prevented footshock-induced freezing behavior in rats.[72]

The above results provide compelling evidence that endogenous CRF mediates at least some of the behavioral and physiological changes that occur in stress. Because intrace-

**TABLE 2.** Effects of $\alpha$-Helical CRF$_{9-41}$ in Stressed Animals

| |
|---|
| Prevents ether-induced release of ACTH from the pituitary[61] |
| Prevents the ether-induced increase in plasma epinephrine, but not norepinephrine[67] |
| Prevents the footshock-induced decrease in GH secretion[64] |
| Prevents the footshock-induced decrease in LH secretion[65] |
| Prevents the restraint-induced increase in large intestinal transit and fecal excretion[35,68] |
| Prevents the surgery-induced decrease in gastric acid secretion[69] |
| Attenuates the restraint-induced decrease in eating[46] |
| Prevents the restraint-induced decrease in exploratory behavior[70] |
| Prevents stress-induced fighting[71] |
| Prevents footshock-induced freezing behavior[72] |

rebral application of the antagonists is necessary (except when blockade of the pituitary-adrenal axis is required), the site(s) of action appear to be within the brain, probably in a periventricular location. Nevertheless, we do not know the sites of action for any of these effects. It is to be noted that the ultrashort positive feedback loop postulated by Ono et al.[24] would result in activation of endogenous cerebral CRF systems following ICV application of CRF, so that CRF-containing terminals throughout the brain may be activated indirectly. In one study, Brown[73] attempted to localize the sympathetic activating effects of CRF within the brain by injecting CRF into a large number of different brain locations, but found that many different sites appeared to be equally effective. Using the ventricular blocking technique, Tazi et al.[74] provided evidence that the behavioral activating effects of CRF were exerted on forebrain sites. Moreover, we have preliminary evidence that the effect of ICV CRF on exploratory behavior is exerted via a third ventricle, rather than a fourth ventricle, site.[54] But, neither set of experiments would reveal the final site of action of the CRF which could be anywhere in the brain.

The evidence reviewed above suggests that intracerebral administration of CRF can mimic many of the well characterized endocrine, physiological, neurochemical, and behavioral responses in stress. Experiments with CRF antagonists administered to stressed animals indicate that several of the stress-related changes can be attenuated or reversed, suggesting that endogenous CRF may indeed mediate certain stress responses. The hypothesis that release of endogenous CRF from brain sites may be both necessary and sufficient for a stress response is thus a viable one, and one on which future studies may be based. Interestingly, this concept tends to support the widely criticized proposal of Selye[4] that there is a nonspecific physiological response in stress.

## REFERENCES

1. VALE, W., J. SPIESS, C. RIVIER & J. RIVIER. 1981. Characterization of a 41-residue ovine hypothalamic peptide that stimulates secretion of corticotropin and β-endorphin. Science 231: 1394–1397.
2. ANTONI, F. A. 1986. Hypothalamic control of adrenocorticotropin secretion: advances since the discovery of 41-residue corticotropin-releasing factor. Endocrine Rev. 7: 351–378.
3. RIVIER, C. & P. M. PLOTSKY. 1986. Mediation by corticotropin releasing factor (CRF) of adenohypophysial hormone secretion. Ann. Rev. Physiol. 48: 475–494.
4. SELYE, H. 1950. The Physiology and Pathology of Exposure to Stress. Acta Med. Publ. Montreal.
5. MASON, J. W. 1968. A review of psychoendocrine research on the pituitary-adrenocortical system. Psychosom. Med. 30: 576–607.
6. DUNN, A. J. & N. R. KRAMARCY. 1984. Neurochemical responses in stress: relationships between the hypothalamic-pituitary-adrenal and catecholamine systems. In Handbook of Psychopharmacology. L. L. Iversen, S. D. Iversen & S. H. Snyder, Eds. Vol. 18: 455–515. Plenum Press. New York, NY.
7. MERCHENTHALER, I. 1984. Corticotropin releasing factor (CRF)-like immunoreactivity in the rat central nervous system. Extrahypothalamic distribution. Peptides 5 (Suppl. 1): 53–69.
8. SAWCHENKO, P. E. & L. W. SWANSON. 1985. Localization, colocalization, and plasticity of corticotropin-releasing factor immunoreactivity in rat brain. Fed. Proc. 44: 221–227.
9. NAKANE, T., T. AUDHYA, C. S. HOLLANDER, D. H. SCHLESINGER, P. KARDOS, C. BROWN & J. PASSARELLI. 1986. Corticotrophin-releasing factor in extrahypothalamic brain of the mouse: demonstration by immunoassay and immunoneutralization of bioassayable activity. J. Endocrinol. 111: 143–149.
10. WYNN, P. C., R. L. HAUGER, M. C., HOLMES, M. A. MILLAN, K. J. CATT & G. AGUILERA. 1984. Brain and pituitary receptors for corticotropin releasing factor: localization and differential regulation after adrenalectomy. Peptides 5: 1077–1084.
11. DE SOUZA, E. B., T. INSEL, M. PERRIN, J. RIVIER, W. VALE & M. KUHAR. 1985. Corticotropin-releasing factor receptors are widely distributed within the rat central nervous system: an autoradiographic study. J. Neurosci. 5: 3189–3203.
12. SMITH, M. A., T. A. SLOTKIN, D. L. KNIGHT & C. B. NEMEROFF. 1986. Release of corticotropin-releasing factor from rat brain regions in vitro. Endocrinology 118: 1997–2001.
13. EBERLY, L. B., C. A. DUDLEY & R. L. MOSS. 1983. Iontophoretic mapping of corticotropin-releasing factor (CRF) sensitive neurons in the rat forebrain. Peptides 4: 837–841.
14. CHAPPELL, P. B., M. A. SMITH, C. D. KILTS, G. BISSETTE, J. RITCHIE, C. ANDERSON & C. B. NEMEROFF. 1986. Alterations in corticotropin-releasing factor-like immunoreactivity in discrete rat brain regions after acute and chronic stress. J. Neurosci. 6: 2908–2914.
15. BRITTON, K. T., M. LYON, W. VAL & G. F. KOOB. 1984. Stress-induced secretion of corticotropin-releasing factor immunoreactivity in rat cerebrospinal fluid. Soc. Neurosci. Abstr. 10: 95.
16. GOLD, P. W. & G. CHROUSOS. 1985. Clinical studies with corticotropin-releasing factor: implications for the diagnosis and pathophysiology of depression, Cushing's disease, and adrenal insufficiency. Psychoneuroendocrinology 10: 401–419.
17. KOOB, G. F. & F. E. BLOOM. 1985. Corticotropin-releasing factor and behavior. Fed. Proc. 44: 259–263.
18. KALIN, N. H., S. E. SHELTON, G. W. KRAEMER & W. T. McKINNEY. 1983. Corticotropin-releasing factor administered intraventricularly to rhesus monkeys. Peptides 4: 217–220.
19. INSEL, T. R., J. A. ALOI, D. GOLDSTEIN, J. H. WOOD & D. C. JIMERSON. 1984. Plasma

cortisol and catecholamine responses to intracerebroventricular administration of CRF to rhesus monkeys. Life Sci. **34:** 1873–1878.

20. ONO, N., M. D. LUMPKIN, W. K. SAMSON, J. K. McDONALD & S. M. McCANN. 1984. Intrahypothalamic action of corticotrophin-releasing factor (CRF) to inhibit growth hormone and LH release in the rat. Life Sci. **35:** 1117–1123.

21. ROCK, J. P., E. H. OLDENFIELD, H. M. SCHULTE, P. W. GOLD, P. L. KORNBLITH, L. LORIAUX & G. P. CHROUSOS. 1984. Corticotropin releasing factor administered into the ventricular CSF stimulates the pituitary-adrenal axis. Brain Res. **323:** 365–368.

22. VELDHUIS, H. D. & D. DE WIED. 1984. Differential behavioral actions of corticotropin-releasing factor (CRF). Pharmacol. Biochem. Behav. **21:** 707–713.

23. DUNN, A. J. & C. W. BERRIDGE. 1987. Corticotropin-releasing factor administration elicits a stress-like activation of cerebral catecholaminergic systems. Pharmacol. Biochem. Behav. **27:** 685–691.

24. ONO, N., J. C. BEDRAN DE CASTRO & S. M. McCANN. 1985. Ultrashort-loop positive feedback of corticotropin (ACTH)-releasing factor to enhance ACTH release in stress. Proc. Natl. Acad. Sci. USA **82:** 3528–3531.

25. RIVIER, C. & W. VALE. 1984. Influence of corticotropin-releasing factor on reproductive functions in the rat. Endocrinology **114:** 914–921.

26. RIVIER, C. & W. VALE. 1984. Corticotropin-releasing factor (CRF) acts centrally to inhibit growth hormone secretion in the rat. Endocrinology **114:** 2409–2411.

27. ONO, N., W. K. SAMSON, J. K. McDONALD, M. D. LUMPKIN, J. C. BEDRAN DE CASTRO & S. M. McCANN. 1985b. Effects of intravenous and intraventricular injections of antisera directed against corticotropin-releasing factor on the secretion of anterior pituitary hormones. Proc. Natl. Acad. Sci. USA **82:** 7787–7790.

28. BROWN, M. R., L. A. FISHER, J. RIVIER, J. SPIESS, C. RIVIER & W. VALE. 1982. Corticotropin-releasing factor: effects on the sympathetic nervous system and oxygen consumption. Life Sci. **30:** 207–210.

29. BROWN, M. R. & L. A. FISHER. 1983. Central nervous system effects of corticotropin releasing factor in the dog. Brain Res. **280:** 75–79.

30. BROWN, M. R. & L. A. FISHER. 1985. Corticotropin-releasing factor: effects on the autonomic nervous system and visceral function. Fed. Proc. **44:** 243–248.

31. KUROSAWA, M., A. SATO, R. S. SWENSON & Y. TAKAHASHI. 1986. Sympatho-adrenal medullary functions in response to intracerebroventricularly injected corticotropin-releasing factor in anesthetized rats. Brain Res. **367:** 250–257.

32. TACHE, Y., Y. GOTO, M. GUNION, W. VALE, J. RIVIER & M. BROWN. 1983. Inhibition of gastric acid secretion in rats by intracerebral injection of corticotropin-releasing factor. Science **222:** 935–937.

33. LENZ, H. J., S. E. HESTER & M. R. BROWN. 1985. Corticotropin-releasing factor. Mechanisms to inhibit gastric acid secretion in conscious dogs. J. Clin. Invest. **75:** 889–895.

34. LENZ, H. J., A. RAEDLER, H. GRETEN & M. R. BROWN. 1987. CRF inititates biological actions within the brain that are observed in response to stress. Am. J. Physiol. **252:** R34–39.

35. WILLIAMS, C. L., J. M. PETERSON, R. G. VILLAR & T. F. BURKS. 1987. Corticotropin-releasing factor directly mediates colonic responses to stress. Amer. J. Physiol. **253:** G582–G586.

36. LENZ, H. J., M. BURLAGE, A. RAEDLER & H. GRETEN. 1988. Central nervous system effects of corticotropin-releasing factor on gastrointestinal transit in the rat. Gastroenterology **94:** 598–602.

37. EHLERS, C. L., S. J. HENRIKSEN, M. WANG, J. RIVIER, W. VALE & F. E. BLOOM. 1983. Corticotropin-releasing factor produces increases in brain excitability and convulsive seizures in rats. Brain Res. **278:** 332–336.

38. VALENTINO, R. J., S. L. FOOTE & G. ASTON-JONES. 1983. Corticotropin-releasing factor activates noradrenergic neurons of the locus coeruleus. Brain Res. **270:** 363–367.

39. VALENTINO, R. J. & S. L. FOOTE. 1988. Corticotropin-releasing hormone increases tonic but not sensory-evoked activity of noradrenergic locus coeruleus neurons in unanesthetized rats. J. Neurosci. **8:** 1016–1025.

40. VAN LOON, G. R., A. SHUM & D. HO. 1982. Lack of effect of corticotropin releasing factor

on hypothalamic dopamine and serotonin synthesis turnover rates in rats. Peptides **3:** 799–803.

41. BUTLER, P. D., J. M. WEISS, J. C. STOUT, C. D. KILTS, L. L. COOK & C. B. NEMEROFF. 1988. Corticotropin-releasing factor produces anxiogenic and behavioral activating effects following microinfusion into the locus coeruleus. Soc. Neurosci. Abstr. **14:** 288.

42. BRITTON, D. R., G. F. KOOB, J. RIVIER & W. VALE. 1982. Intraventricular corticotropin-releasing factor enhances behavioral effects of novelty. Life Sci. **31:** 363–367.

43. DUNN, A. J., C. W. BERRIDGE, Y. I. LAI & T. L. YACHABACH. 1987. CRF-induced excessive grooming behavior in rats and mice. Peptides **8:** 841–844.

44. MORLEY, J. E. & A. S. LEVINE. 1982. Corticotrophin releasing factor, grooming and ingestive behavior. Life Sci. **31:** 1459–1464.

45. SUTTON, R. E., G. F. KOOB, M. LE MOAL, J. RIVIER & W. VALE. 1982. Corticotropin releasing factor produces behavioral activation in rats. Nature **297:** 331–333.

46. KRAHN, D. D., B. A. GOSNELL, M. GRACE & A. S. LEVINE. 1986. CRF antagonist partially reverses CRF- and stress-induced effects on feeding. Brain Res. Bull. **17:** 285–289.

47. SIRINATHSINGHJI, D. J. S. 1985. Modulation of lordosis behavior in the female rat by corticotropin releasing factor, β-endorphin and gonadotropin releasing hormone in the mesencephalic central gray. Brain Res. **336:** 45–55.

48. SIRINATHSINGHJI, D. J. S. 1987. Inhibitory influence of coricotropin releasing factor on components of sexual behavior in the male rat. Brain Res. **407:** 185–190.

49. BRITTON, K. T., J. MORGAN, J. RIVIER, W. VALE & G. F. KOOB. 1985. Chlordiazepoxide attenuates response suppression induced by corticotropin-releasing factor in the conflict test. Psychopharmacology **86:** 170–174.

50. SWERDLOW, N. R., M. A. GEYER, W. W. VALE & G. F. KOOB. 1986. Corticotropin-releasing factor potentiates acoustic startle in rats: blockade by chlordiazepoxide. Psychopharmacology **88:** 147–152.

51. SHERMAN, J. E. & N. H. KALIN. 1988. ICV-CRH alters stress-induced freezing behavior without affecting pain sensitivity. Pharmacol. Biochem. Behav. **30:** 801–807.

52. SAHGAL, A., C. WRIGHT, J. A. EDWARDSON & A. B. KEITH. 1983. Corticotropin releasing factor is more potent than some corticotropin-related peptides in affecting passive avoidance behavior in rats. Neurosci. Lett. **36:** 81–86.

53. BERRIDGE, C. W. & A. J. DUNN. 1986. Corticotropin-releasing factor elicits naloxone-sensitive stress-like alterations in exploratory behavior in mice. Regul. Peptides **16:** 83–93.

54. BERRIDGE, C. W., F. SPADARO & A. J. DUNN. Corticotropin-releasing factor acts via a third ventricle site to reduce exploratory behavior in rats. Submitted for publication.

55. DUNN, A. J. & S. E. FILE. 1987. Corticotropin-releasing factor has an anxiogenic action in the social interaction test. Horm. Behav. **21:** 193–202.

56. EAVES, M., K. THATCHER-BRITTON, J. RIVIER, W. VALE & G. F. KOOB. 1985. Effects of corticotropin releasing factor on locomotor activity in hypophysectomized rats. Peptides **6:** 923–926.

57. BERRIDGE, C. W. & A. J. DUNN. 1989. CRF and restraint-stress decrease exploratory behavior in hypophysectomized mice. Pharmacol. Biochem. Behav. **34.** In press.

58. FISHER, L. A., G. JESSEN & M. R. BROWN. 1983. Corticotropin-releasing factor (CRF): mechanism to elevate mean arterial pressure and heart rate. Regul. Peptides **5:** 153–161.

59. BRITTON, K. T., G. LEE, R. DANA, S. C. RISCH & G. F. KOOB. 1986. Activating and 'anxiogenic' effects of corticotropin releasing factor are not inhibited by blockade of the pituitary-adrenal system with dexamethasone. Life Sci. **39:** 1281–1286.

60. BRITTON, D. R., M. VARELA, A. GARCIA & M. ROSENTHAL. 1986. Dexamethasone suppresses pituitary-adrenal but not behavioral effects of centrally administered CRF. Life Sci. **38:** 211–216.

61. RIVIER, J., C. RIVIER & W. VALE. 1984. Synthetic competitive antagonists of corticotropin-releasing factor: effects on ACTH secretion in the rat. Science **224:** 889–891.

62. RIVIER, C., J. RIVIER & W. VALE. 1982. Inhibition of adrenocorticotropic hormone secretion in the rat by immunoneutralization of corticotropin-releasing factor. Science **218:** 377–379.

63. NAKANE, T., T. AUDHYA, N. KANIE & C. S. HOLLANDER. 1985. Evidence for a role of endogenous corticotropin-releasing factor in cold, ether, immobilization, and traumatic stress. Proc. Natl. Acad. Sci. USA **82:** 1247–1251.

64. RIVIER, C. & W. VALE. 1985. Involvement of corticotropin-releasing factor and somatostatin in stress-induced inhibition of growth hormone secretion in the rat. Endocrinology **117:** 2478–2482.
65. RIVIER, C., J. RIVIER & W. VALE. 1986. Stress-induced inhibition of reproductive functions: role of endogenous corticotropin-releasing factor. Science **231:** 607–609.
66. BROWN, M. R., T. S. GRAY & L. A. FISHER. 1986. Corticotropin-releasing factor receptor antagonist: effects on the autonomic nervous system and cardiovascular function. Regul. Peptides. **16:** 321–329.
67. BROWN, M. R., L. A. FISHER, V. WEBB, W. W. VALE & J. E. RIVIER. 1985. Corticotropin-releasing factor: a physiologic regulator of adrenal epinephrine secretion. Brain Res. **328:** 355–357.
68. LENZ, H. J., G. DRUGE, M. BURLAGE, A. RAEDLER, H. GRETEN, W. W. VALE & J. E. RIVIER. 1988. Stress-induced gastrointestinal secretory and motor responses in rats are mediated by endogenous corticotropin-releasing factor. Gastroenterology **94:** A256.
69. STEPHENS, R. L., H. YANG, J. RIVIER & Y. TACHE. 1988. Intracisternal injection of CRF antagonist blocks surgical stress-induced inhibition of gastric secretion in the rat. Peptides **9:** 1067–1070.
70. BERRIDGE, C. W. & A. J. DUNN. 1987. A corticotropin-releasing factor antagonist reverses the stress-induced changes of exploratory behavior in mice. Horm. Behav. **21:** 393–401.
71. TAZI, A., R. DANTZER, M. LE MOAL, J. RIVIER, W. VALE & G. F. KOOB. 1987. Corticotropin-releasing factor antagonist blocks stress-induced fighting in rats. Regul. Peptides **18:** 37–42.
72. KALIN, N. H., J. E. SHERMAN & L. K. TAKAHASHI. 1988. Antagonism of endogenous CRH systems attenuates stress-induced freezing behavior in rats. Brain Res. **457:** 130–135.
73. BROWN, M. 1986. Corticotropin releasing factor: central nervous system sites of action. Brain Res. **399:** 10–14.
74. TAXI, A., N. R. SWERDLOW, M. LE MOAL, J. RIVIER, W. VALE & G. F. KOOB. 1987. Behavioral activation by CRF: evidence for the involvement of the ventral forebrain. Life Sci. **41:** 41–49.

# Striatonigral Prodynorphin: A Model System for Understanding Opioid Peptide Function

LISA A. THOMPSON, RAE R. MATSUMOTO,
ANDREA G. HOHMANN, AND J. MICHAEL WALKER

*Schrier Research Laboratory*
*Department of Psychology*
*Brown University*
*Providence, Rhode Island 02912*

Nearly fifteen years following the identification of the enkephalins, many questions remain about the functional role of the opioid peptides. Indeed, this is a complex issue since there are at least two dozen distinct opioid peptides and at least three types of opiate receptors.[1] Further, little is known about the actions of nonopiate peptides that are derived from the opioid peptide precursors, and some opioid peptides exert nonopiate effects.[2,3] Perhaps the greatest impediment to understanding opioid peptide function is their anatomical distribution; opioid peptides derived from the proopiomelanocortin (POMC), proenkephalin, and prodynorphin precursors overlap extensively.[4-6] As a consequence, understanding the actions of a specific family of peptides within most brain circuits has been very difficult. For example, if beta-endorphin is microinjected into the periaqueductal gray (PAG) and produces analgesia, the effect may occur because of interactions with receptors postsynaptic to enkephalinergic neurons, rather than with receptors postsynaptic to beta-endorphin-containing neurons. Thus, although the behavioral effects of opiates are well understood, it has been troublesome to elucidate the function of particular endogenous peptide families in specific areas of the brain. We describe below how the striatonigral prodynorphin pathway is an exception to this generalization and therefore, may be a model system for understanding opioid peptide function.

## Characteristics of the Striatonigral Prodynorphin System

Both the receptor binding profile and the relative isolation of prodynorphin peptides in the substantia nigra pars reticulata (SNR) provide a basis for understanding the function of these substances. The receptor binding profile of prodynorphin peptides allows investigation of this system with minimal influence from other opioid families. Prodynorphin gives rise to several opioid peptide products (including dynorphin, rimorphin, and the neoendorphins) that are distinguishable from peptides derived from the other opioid precursors in their selectivity for the commonly accepted opiate receptor subtypes, mu, kappa, and delta.[7-9] POMC and proenkephalin peptides bind principally to delta and mu receptors.[10] In contrast, prodynorphin peptides, while exhibiting significant mu binding, are generally the only natural opioids with a high affinity for kappa receptors.[8,11] This receptor binding profile permits the investigation of prodynorphin not only through the use of its peptide products, but also through the use of stable peptide analogs such as DAFPHEDYN[12] and some synthetic compounds that bind selectively to the kappa opiate receptor, such as U50,488[13] and U69,593.[14] Because it appears that kappa receptors are closely linked to prodynorphinergic neurons, the use of selective kappa ligands may provide a tool for selective activation of neuronal elements that normally respond to the secretory products of prodynorphin neurons.

Since prodynorphinergic neurons project heavily to the SNR and this area generally lacks inputs from proenkephalin and POMC, pharmacological studies of prodynorphin are much more interpretable in the SNR than in other regions of the brain. Prodynorphin-containing neurons comprise part of the major efferent projection from the caudate nucleus to the SNR,[15-17] and this is perhaps the only area of the brain in which prodynorphin is isolated from other opioid peptide systems. Prodynorphin products constitute nearly all of the opioid peptide immunoreactivity in the SNR.[4,15,18] Although some enkephalin immunoreactivity has been found in the dopamine-rich substantia nigra pars compacta (SNC), only scattered immunoreactivity has been found in the SNR.[5,19] Further, kappa receptors have been localized in the SNR but are undetectable in the SNC of the rat.[20] Thus, in contrast to the above example of beta-endorphin effects in the PAG, pharmacological effects of prodynorphin-derived peptides and kappa opiates in the SNR should reflect the natural functions of the striatonigral prodynorphin pathway.

The substantia nigra (SN) offers other advantages for the study of prodynorphin because its projections, neurochemistry, and role in movement are well understood. From this body of literature emerges the pertinent fact that besides prodynorphin, some striatonigral neurons secrete gamma aminobutyric acid (GABA) and tachykinins (substance P and substance K); these neurotransmitters appear to be colocalized with prodynorphin in some neurons.[21-24] Thus, it is important to consider the action of prodynorphin peptides as they interact with other transmitters in the SN.

At least three cell types of the SN can be identified based on their electrophysiological characteristics. Dopamine (DA) neurons are readily identified by their firing rate and pattern and their unusually long action potentials. These neurons comprise the major efferent projection of the SNC and terminate in the striatum, completing a striato-nigro-striatal loop.[25,26] Dendritic processes of these cells extend into the SNR and may be influenced by substances released there. A pars reticulata-DA interneuron is a second cell type that has been identified in the SNR. These interneurons are located in the dorsal aspect of the SNR and exhibit an inhibitory influence on the firing of SNC DA neurons.[27,28] SNR output neurons are the third cell type and form the second major efferent pathway of the SN. These cells exert significant influences on movement through terminations in many motor areas: the ventromedial nucleus of the thalamus, the superior colliculus, the striatum, the cuneiform nucleus, the pedunculopontine nucleus, and the medullary and pontine reticular formation.[29-31]

Both the SNC and the SNR exert important influences on movement but they act through different, although overlapping pathways. Either electrical or chemical activation of the dopaminergic nigrostriatal pathway evokes movement: bilateral activation results in general locomotor activation and stereotyped behavior, whereas unilateral activation produces circling towards the side contralateral to the stimulation.[32] This rotational model has been a useful experimental system for understanding the neurochemical substrates of movement in the SN. Motor activation may also be elicited by decreasing activity in the SNR.[33,34] SNR output neurons contain GABA and have a fast, regular firing rate suggesting a tonic inhibitory influence on their associated targets.[35,36] This synaptic/neurochemical arrangement is such that a decrease in the firing of SNR output cells releases other motor structures from a state of tonic inhibition.[37] This gating-action, described in more detail below, apparently gives the SNR considerable control over whether or not certain types of movements occur. Thus, inhibition of efferent neurons of the SNR leads to motor activation, whereas inhibition of dopaminergic neurons in the SNC leads to motor inhibition.

The presence of prodynorphin terminals and kappa receptors in the substantia nigra suggest a possible natural action of prodynorphin peptides in the striatonigral system.

Considering the well established role of this circuitry in the modulation of motor output, it is not surprising that prodynorphin peptides appear to influence this processing. In the following sections we describe experiments conducted by ourselves and others that lead to the conclusions that: (1) prodynorphin peptides exert dual opposing influences in the SN: an inhibitory influence on locomotion through actions on dopamine neurons in the SNC and a locomotor activating effect through actions on nondopaminergic neurons in the SNR, and (2) prodynorphin peptides in the SNR may regulate motor responses to sensory input, such as orienting responses. These experiments further suggest that kappa opiate systems may have an opposite function to the mu opiate system: prodynorphin peptides may enhance reactions to sensory stimuli through actions in the SN, while mu compounds suppress responses to painful stimuli in analgesia systems. If so, this would add to an increasingly long list of systems in which mu and kappa opioids exert opposite effects.[38-49]

### Kappa Opiate Effects on the SNC

Electrophysiological investigations suggest that kappa opioids exert inhibitory effects on movement through cellular inhibition of DA neurons in the SNC. Systemic injections of U50,488 elicit a dose-related decrease in the firing rate of SNC DA cells[49] (FIG. 1). However, neither dynorphin nor kappa opiates alter the spontaneous firing of SNC DA cells when applied locally by iontophoresis or pressure ejection; thus the observed effects of U50,488 must occur *indirectly*.[50-52] This is not surprising, since iontophoretic applications of mu and delta opiates also fail to alter the firing of DA neurons in the SNC.[53,54]

An inhibitory influence of striatonigral prodynorphin products on SNC DA activity is consistent with the results of biochemical analyses of this system. Systemic injections of U50,488 and bremazocine produce a dose-dependent decrease in striatal DA release detectable with *in vivo* microdialysis.[48] Similar decreases in DA release in the presence of U50,488 have been reported in striatal slices *in vitro*.[55] Likewise, intranigral injection of dynorphin$_{1-17}$ decreases DA release in the striatum.[56,57]

Behavioral data are also consistent with the hypothesis that striatonigral prodynorphin exerts motor inhibition through SNC DA neurons. However, these studies have revealed a significant motor-activating property of prodynorphin products through the nondopaminergic SNR. Unilateral microinjections of dynorphin$_{1-17}$, dynorphin$_{1-13}$, dynorphin$_{1-8}$, rimorphin, as well as U50,488 into the SNR produce dose-related contralateral rotation, a result that is indicative of locomotor activation on the injected side[43,44,56,58-61] (FIG. 2). The motor-activating effects of these compounds do not depend on the nigrostriatal DA system, however. Circling evoked by unilateral nigral microinjection of the kappa opiates rimorphin and U50,488 not only persists despite depletion of nigral DA with 6-hydroxydopamine (6-OHDA) lesions, it is in fact greatly *enhanced* by this manipulation[43,61] (FIG. 2). This finding suggests that kappa opiates induce circling by actions on neuronal substrates outside the DA system. It appears that in unlesioned animals this motor activation is curbed by kappa opiate inhibition of the SNC DA system, hence the enhancement following lesions of SNC DA neurons. Thus, the behavioral data are in agreement with other lines of investigation in suggesting motor inhibition through kappa opiate actions in the SNC. Moreover, it appears that important motor-activating effects of kappa compounds occur through actions outside the dopaminergic system.

In contrast to kappa opiate-induced circling, the rotational behavior produced by mu and delta opiates is greatly attenuated when SNC DA is depleted with 6-OHDA lesions.[43] These results suggest that the locomotor activation produced by these compounds is due to a stimulatory effect on the SNC DA pathway. This is supported by biochemical and electrophysiological evidence of increased activity in nigrostriatal DA cells following systemic administration of mu opiates.[48,49,54] Thus, prodynorphin-derived peptides and kappa opiates exert effects that are the functional opposite of mu and delta opiates in the SNC (FIG. 1).

The details of the synaptic mechanism for kappa effects in the SNC are lacking presently. To our knowledge, no direct effect of an opiate at the SNC DA somata has ever been reported (although effects on terminals may occur). Consequently, either presynaptic mechanisms or interneurons must mediate the kappa effects described above. A presynaptic action of kappa opiates is plausible, since some opiate receptors in the SN are localized on the terminals of striatonigral fibers.[62,63] Further, since kappa opiates may exert their effects by decreasing calcium conductance, a presynaptic modulation of neurotransmitter release could be one mechanism of kappa opiate action.[64-66] For example, prodynorphin peptides from striatonigral neurons may inhibit the release of substance P or substance K, two excitatory transmitters derived from protachykinin and found in striatonigral neurons.[23,56,67,68] While direct evidence for such a process is lacking, a kappa opiate action at presynaptic receptors could inhibit release of these excitatory tachykinins, thereby causing cellular inhibition.

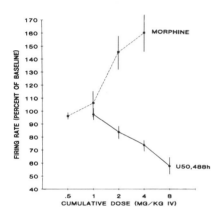

**FIGURE 1.** Kappa-selective opiates decrease the firing rate of substantia nigra pars compacta dopamine neurons, an effect opposite to that of mu-selective opiates. The graph shows the dose-response relationship for the effects of intravenous administration of the kappa opiate U50,488 and the mu opiate morphine on the firing rate of dopamine cells in the substantia nigra pars compacta of the rat. Computer-derived average firing rates ($\pm$ SE) are plotted against the dose for both drugs. (From Walker *et al.*[49] Reprinted by permission from the *European Journal of Pharmacology*.)

Alternatively, local release of prodynorphin peptides in the striatum could modulate dopaminergic activity through actions in the striatum. Kappa opiates can affect nigrostriatal DA firing through striatal actions, since intracaudate administration of U50,488 decreases the spontaneous firing rate of SNC DA neurons.[49] Further, opiate receptors are present on striatal DA terminals[62] and DA release is inhibited by kappa agonists in both striatal slice and synaptosomal preparations, which lack intact cell bodies.[55] Thus, modulatory actions of prodynorphin peptides may occur directly on DA terminals or indirectly to alter the firing of DA neurons.

## Kappa Opiate Effects in the SNR

The inhibitory effects of kappa-selective opiates on the SNC result in the reduction of motor behavior when the dopaminergic pathway is intact. Kappa agonists in the SN appear to have dual opposing influences on movement, however, since they may *activate* motor behavior as well. As noted above, kappa opiates and certain prodynorphin-derived peptides elicit contraversive circling in 6-OHDA-lesioned rats.[43,61] Since the DA cells in the SNC are absent in these animals, these effects presumably result from kappa actions in the SNR. This dopamine-independent circling behavior produced by kappa opiates resembles the direct effects of GABA agonists such as muscimol in the SNR.[33,34,69] These results thus suggest that kappa opiates activate movement through SNR output pathways.

Electrophysiological investigations have revealed that the action of kappa-selective opiates in the SNR is predominantly inhibitory, a finding consistent with increased movement. Pressure ejection of dynorphin$_{1-9}$ produces a long lasting, naloxone-reversible

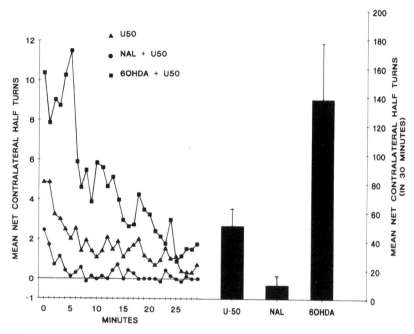

**FIGURE 2.** Effect of the opiate receptor antagonist naloxone (NAL) and 6-hydroxydopamine (6-OHDA) lesions on circling induced by the kappa opiate U50,488. Intranigral infusion of 10 nmol U50,488 on otherwise untreated animals produced significant circling. When naloxone HCL (10 mg/kg s.c.) was administered 10 min before microinjection of 10 nmol U50,488, significant antagonism of this effect was observed. 6-OHDA lesions of the medial forebrain bundle, however, increased the number of net contralateral half turns produced by 10 nmol U50,488. *Left panel,* time course of U50,488 under various conditions. *Right panel,* total net contralateral half turns (mean ± SE) during the 30 min after infusion of 10 nmol U50,488 in the substantia nigra pars reticulata. (From Matsumoto *et al.*[43] Reprinted by permission from the *Journal of Pharmacology and Experimental Therapeutics.*)

decrease in the spontaneous activity of SNR neurons.[50] Based on antidromic activation, this population apparently includes nigrotectal and nigrothalamic neurons.[70] Inhibitory effects of dynorphin$_{1-8}$ have also been reported, although this peptide is effective on fewer SNR cells and produces nonopiate effects.[51] In addition, both intravenous and iontophoretically applied U50,488 decrease spontaneous activity in SNR cells[49,52,71] (FIG. 3). It is thus likely that the inhibition of SNR output neurons may account for the

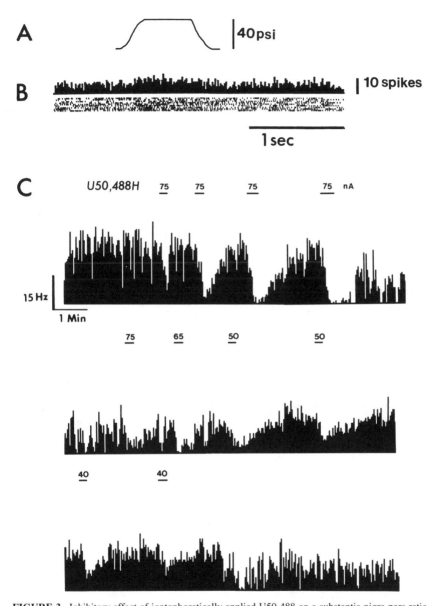

**FIGURE 3.** Inhibitory effect of iontophoretically applied U50,488 on a substantia nigra pars reticulata (SNR) neuron that showed excitation in response to a mechanical pressure stimulus. **(A)** Pressure over time (40 psi for 1 sec) applied by a computer-controlled air cylinder connected to a solid state pressure transducer used to deliver mechanical stimulus to the hindpaw contralateral to the cell under observation. This stimulus is aligned with the panel below to show time of onset. **(B)** Peristimulus histogram and raster plot for a SNR cell that showed excitation in response to the pressure stimulus. **(C)** Continuous ratemeter record shows the dose-dependent inhibitory effect of iontophoretically applied U50,488 on the pressure-sensitive SNR cell presented in panel B. The kappa agonist U50,488 is most efficacious in inhibiting this type of SNR neuron, which exhibits increased firing in response to mechanical pressure.

contraversive circling observed after intranigral injections of prodynorphin peptides and U50,488.

An increase in motor output following the inhibition of SNR neurons is consistent with the hypothesized gating action of these cells. Efferents from the SNR comprise a major output pathway of the basal ganglia. Indeed, it is through these projections that the SN may exert its greatest influence on the central nervous system. The most extensive projections from this area reach the ventromedial nucleus of the thalamus, the superior colliculus, the striatum, the pedunculopontine tegmental nucleus, and the medullary and pontine reticular formation, although a number of other structures are also targets.[31] Through this pathway, the SNR is directly linked to motor cortex via the thalamus and to the spinal cord through the tectospinal and reticulospinal tracts.[31] The SNR apparently controls its targets through a tonic inhibitory GABAergic influence.[72] It is clear from electrophysiological investigations that the fast, regular firing of these cells exerts profound inhibition of the projection sites of this pathway. Conversely, a decrease in the firing of SNR neurons releases targets from inhibition and permits movement.[35,36,73]

Although iontophoretic studies indicate a nigral site of action for the inhibitory effects of kappa-selective opiates, again a pre- versus postsynaptic effect can not be distinguished. Kappa opiate effects on SNR neurons may be the result of a direct inhibition of firing in those cells.[50-52,71] An alternative explanation, however, is that the decrease in spontaneous firing observed in SNR neurons may arise from a decrease in the release of an excitatory neurotransmitter from the presynaptic terminal, as we suggested for the SNC.

The influence of prodynorphin peptides in the SNR may not be limited to inhibition. Robertson et al.[51] reported some excitatory effects of dynorphin$_{1-8}$ on SNR cells. In fact, excitatory and inhibitory actions were equal in number. This excitatory effect may be the result of an interaction between GABA and dynorphin in the SNR since GABA-inhibition is markedly attenuated in a large percentage of SNR neurons when GABA and dynorphin$_{1-8}$ are applied simultaneously.[51] A reduction in the inhibitory actions of GABA could account for an excitatory effect of dynorphin on SNR cells via an indirect mechanism. The attenuation of GABA by dynorphin is not reversible with opiate antagonists and may also be produced with the nonopioid peptide dynorphin$_{2-17}$. Indeed, nonopiate actions of dynorphin are not uncommon and may reflect the actions of a rapidly formed metabolite.[2,3] Thus in the SNR, nonopiate effects of prodynorphin products must be considered.

### The Role of Prodynorphin Peptides in Sensory-Motor Processing

Considering the well established function of the substantia nigra in the control of movement, it is not surprising that striatonigral prodynorphin peptides modulate motor output. What is surprising, however, is the finding that these peptides have opposing effects on movement in the SN. The electrophysiological and behavioral data discussed here suggest that prodynorphin peptides and other kappa-selective opiates indirectly decrease movement via the SNC and directly increase movement via the SNR (FIG. 4).

Beyond their effects on locomotion, prodynorphin peptides in the SNR may play a role in gating activity in the tectum and thalamus. It is well established that inhibition of the SNR produces increased activity in thalamic and tectal neurons. A temporary decrease in SNR activity, induced either through microinjection of GABA directly into the SNR or through chemical stimulation of the striatum, produces a simultaneous increase in the activity of cells of the superior colliculus and the ventromedial thalamus.[35,36] Via these connections, the SNR gates movements through tectospinal and thalamocortical cells.[35,36,73] In particular, these connections implicate the SNR in the control of movements of the head and eyes. Indeed, nigrotectal cells make direct contact with tectospinal neurons that terminate on spinal motor neurons that control neck muscles.[74,75] Because SNR cells secrete an inhibitory transmitter (GABA), a *decrease* in nigral activity should facilitate coordinated movements of the head and eyes (e.g., orienting movements).[35,73] In keeping with this notion, saccadic eye movements to visual targets are associated with decreased firing in SNR neurons that project to the superior colliculus.[37] Likewise, the motor activation induced by intranigral administration of prodynorphin-derived peptides and kappa opiates is consistent with the cellular inhibition in the SNR observed with these compounds.[43,44,56,58–61]

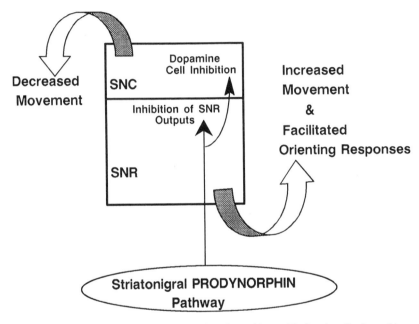

**FIGURE 4.** Schematic diagram of striatonigral prodynorphin peptide function. Prodynorphin peptides and kappa opiates indirectly decrease spontaneous activity of substantia nigra pars compacta (SNC) dopamine neurons, resulting in decreased movement. Kappa opioids decrease spontaneous activity in the substantia nigra pars reticulata (SNR) as well; this effect, however, results in increased movement. In particular, the inhibitory influence of kappa opioids in the SNR may facilitate coordinated eye and head movements in orienting responses.

Although direct evidence is lacking, prodynorphin peptides in the SNR may function in part to modulate head and eye movements to sensory stimuli, as in orienting responses. Based on the available electrophysiological data, it appears that the striatonigral prodynorphin projection inhibits SNR output neurons, releasing tectal and thalamic premotor neurons. Consistent with this view are observations that an increase in the activity of striatal cells, which is clearly related to decreased activity in the SNR, is associated with saccadic eye movements.[35,76] Increased activity in the striatal efferents would presumably increase release of prodynorphin peptides, in addition to GABA, which would then inhibit the inhibitory SNR outputs and release tectospinal neurons.

Further evidence suggesting a role of prodynorphin peptides in the modulation of orienting responses stems from the finding that the kappa opiate U50,488 is most efficacious in inhibiting a subpopulation of SNR neurons that increase their spontaneous firing rate in response to a mechanical pressure stimulus applied to the contralateral hindpaw[52,71] (FIG. 3). These SNR cells are inhibited more often by intravenous or iontophoretically applied U50,488 than are other SNR neurons. Certainly, examples of sensory responses of SN neurons exist.[77,78] The idea, however, that SNR neurons that are responsive to sensory stimuli may be differentially sensitive to kappa-selective opiates suggests that prodynorphin peptides may function as modulators of motor responses to sensory stimuli, such as orienting responses.

It is interesting to speculate that we have come full circle in these investigations. When one thinks of opiates, the modulation of responses to painful stimuli comes directly to mind. In particular, one might think of the gating action of opiates on sensory stimuli, such as the modulation of nociceptive transmission by opiates in the substantia gelatinosa of the spinal cord. In our studies of prodynorphin effects in the substantia nigra, we seem to have returned to this theme, because prodynorphin peptides seem to exert their most important action on cells that perform a very similar function: the gating of reactions to sensory stimuli.

## REFERENCES

1. AKIL, H., S. J. WATSON, E. YOUNG, M. E. LEWIS, H. KHACHATURIAN & J. M. WALKER. 1984. Endogenous opioids: Biology and function. Ann. Rev. Neurosci. **7:** 223–255.
2. WALKER, J. M., H. C. MOISES, D. H. COY, G. BALDRIGHI & H. AKIL. 1982. Nonopiate effects of dynorphin and des-tyr-dynorphin. Science **218:** 1136–1138.
3. YOUNG, E. A., J. M. WALKER, R. HOUGHTEN & H. AKIL. 1987. The degradation of dynorphin A in brain tissue *in vivo* and *in vitro*. Peptides **8:** 701–707.
4. KHACHATURIAN, H., S. J. WATSON, M. E. LEWIS, D. COY, A GOLDSTEIN & H. AKIL. 1982. Dynorphin immunocytochemistry in the rat central nervous system. Peptides **3:** 941–954.
5. KHACHATURIAN, H., M. E. LEWIS & S. J. WATSON. 1983. Enkephalin systems in diencephalon and brainstem of the rat. J. Comp. Neurol. **220:** 310–320.
6. WATSON, S. J. & J. D. BARCHAS. 1979. Anatomy of the endogenous opioid peptides and related substances: The enkephalins, beta-endorphin, and ACTH. *In* The 11th Miles International Symposium: Mechanisms of Pain and Analgesic Compounds. R. F. Beers & E. G. Bassett, Eds. 227–237. Raven Press. New York, NY.
7. KAKIDANI, H., Y. FURUTANI, H. TAKAHASHI, M. NODA, Y. MORIMOTO, T. HIROSE, M. ASAI, S. INAYAMA, S. NAKANISHI & S. NUMA. 1982. Cloning and sequence analysis of cDNA for porcine B-neo-endorphin/dynorphin precursor. Nature **298:** 245–249.
8. CHAVKIN, C., I. F. JAMES & A. GOLDSTEIN. 1982. Dynorphin is a specific endogenous ligand of the kappa opioid receptor. Science **215:** 413–415.
9. YOUNG, E., J. M. WALKER, M. E. LEWIS, R. A. HOUGHTON, J. H. WOODS & H. AKIL. 1986. [³H]Dynorphin A binding and kappa selectivity of prodynorphin peptides in rat, guinea-pig and monkey brain. Eur. J. Pharmacol. **121:** 355–365.
10. LORD, J. A. H., A. A. WATERFIELD, J. HUGHES & H. KOSTERLITZ. 1977. Endogenous opioid peptides: Multiple agonists and receptors. Nature **267:** 495–499.
11. HUIDOBRO-TORO, J. P., K. YOSHIMURA, N. M. LEE, H. H. LOH & E. WAY. 1981. Dynorphin interaction at the kappa opiate site. Eur. J. Pharmacol. **72:** 265–266.
12. WALKER, J. M., D. H. COY, E. A. YOUNG, G. BALDRIGHI, S. F. SIEGEL, W. D. BOWEN & H. AKIL. 1987. [D-Ala²,(F₅)Phe⁴]-Dynorphin₁₋₁₃-NH₂ (DAFPHEDYN): A potent analog of dynorphin 1–13. 1987. Peptides **8:** 811–817.
13. VON VOIGTLANDER, P. F., R. A. LAHTI & J. H. LUDENS. 1983. U-50,488: A selective and structurally novel non-mu (kappa) opioid agonist. J. Pharmacol. Exp. Ther. **224:** 7–12.
14. LAHTI, R. A., M. M. MICKELSON, J. M. MCCALL & P. F. VON VOIGTLANDER. 1985. [³H]U-69593 a highly selective ligand for the opioid kappa receptor. Eur. J. Pharmacol. **109:** 281–284.

15. VINCENT, S. R., T. HOKFELT, I. CHRISTENSSON & L. TERENIUS. 1982. Dynorphin-immuno-reactive neurons in the central nervous system of the rat. Neurosci. Lett. **33;** 185–190.
16. VINCENT, S., T. HOKFELT, I. CHRISTENSSON & L. TERENIUS. 1982. Immunohistochemical evidence for a dynorphin immunoreactive striato-nigral pathway. Eur. J. Pharmacol. **85:** 251–252.
17. FALLON, J. H., F. M. LESLIE & R. I. CONE. 1985. Dynorphin-containing pathways in the substantia nigra and ventral tegmentum: A double labeling study using combined immuno-fluorescence and retrograde tracing. Neuropeptides 5(4–6): 457–460.
18. WEBER, E., K. A. ROTH & J. D. BARCHAS. 1982. Immunohistochemical distribution of alpha-neoendorphin/dynorphin neuronal systems in the rat. Proc. Natl. Acad. Sci. USA **79:** 3062–3066.
19. JOHNSON, R. P., M. SAR & W. E. STUMPF. 1980. A topographic localization of enkephalin on the dopamine neurons of the rat substantia nigra and ventral tegmental area demonstrated by combined histofluorescence-immunocytochemistry. Brain Res. **194:** 566–571.
20. MANSOUR, A., H. KHACHATURIAN, M. E. LEWIS, H. AKIL & S. WATSON. 1987. Autoradio-graphic differentiation of mu, delta, and kappa opioid receptors in the rat forebrain and midbrain. J. Neurosci. **7:** 2445–2464.
21. GRAYBIEL, A. M. & C. W. RAGSDALE. 1983. Biochemical anatomy of the striatum. *In* Chemical Neuroanatomy. P. C. Emson, Ed. 427–504. Raven Press. New York, NY.
22. NAGASHIMA, A., Y. TAKANO, H. MASUI & H. KAMIYA. 1987. Evidence that neurokinin A (substance K) neurons project from the striatum to the substantia nigra in rats. Neurosci. Lett. **77:** 103–108.
23. LINDEFORS, N., E. BRODIN & U. UNGERSTEDT. 1986. Neurokinin A and substance P in striato-nigral neurons in rat brain. Neuropeptides **8:** 127–132.
24. ANDERSON, K. D. & A. REINER. 1988. Extensive co-occurrence of substance P and dynorphin in striatal projection neurons in rats. Soc. Neurosci. Abstr. **14:** 76.
25. GUYENET, P. G. & G. K. AGHAJANIAN. 1978. Antidromic identification of dopaminergic and other output neurons of the rat substantia nigra. Brain Res. **150:** 69–84.
26. GRACE, A. A. & B. S. BUNNEY. 1980. Nigral dopamine neurons: Intracellular recording and identification with L-dopa injection and histofluorescence. Science 210: 654–656.
27. GRACE, A. A. & B. S. BUNNEY. 1979. Paradoxical excitation of nigral dopaminergic cells: Indirect mediation through reticulata inhibitory neurons. Eur. J. Pharmacol. **59:** 211–218.
28. GRACE, A. A., D. W. HOMMER & B. S. BUNNEY. 1980. Peripheral and striatal influences on nigral dopamine cells: Mediation by reticulata neurons. Brain Res. Bull. 5 (Suppl. 2): 105–109.
29. DENIAU, J. M., C. HAMMOND, A. RISZK & J. FEGER. 1978. Electrophysiological properties of identified output neurons of the rat substantia nigra (pars compacta and pars reticulata): Evidences for the existence of branched neurons. Exp. Brain Res. **32:** 409–422.
30. BECKSTEAD, R. M., V. B. DOMESICK & W. J. H. NAUTA. 1979. Efferent connections of the substantia nigra and ventral tegmental area in the rat. Brain Res. **175:** 191–217.
31. FALLON, J. H. & S. E. LOUGHLIN. 1985. Substantia nigra. *In* The Rat Nervous System. G. Paxinos, Ed. Vol. **1:** 353–374. Academic Press Australia. North Ryde, N. S. W.
32. UNGERSTEDT, U. 1971. Postsynaptic supersensitivity after 6-hydroxydopamine induced degen-eration of the nigrostriatal dopamine system. Acta Physiol. Scand. [Suppl.] **347:** 69–73.
33. ARNT, J. & J. SCHEEL-KRUGER. 1979. GABAergic and glycinergic mechanisms within the substantia nigra: Pharmacological specificity of dopamine-independent contralateral turning behavior and interactions with other neurotransmitters. Psychopharmacology **62:** 267–277.
34. OLIANAS, M. C., G. M. DEMONTIS, G. MULAS & A. TAGLIAMONTE. 1978. The striatal dopaminergic function is mediated by the inhibition of a nigral, non-dopaminergic neuronal system via a strio-nigral GABAergic pathway. Eur. J. Pharmacol. **49:** 233–241.
35. CHEVALIER, G., S. VACHER, J. M. DENIAU & M. DESBAN. 1985. Disinhibition as a basic process in the expression of striatal functions. I. The striato-nigral influence on tecto-spinal/tecto-diencephalic neurons. Brain Res. **334:** 215–226.
36. DENIAU, J. M. & G. CHEVALIER. 1985. Disinhibition as a basic process in the expression of striatal functions. II. The striato-nigral influence on thalamocortical cells of the ventromedial thalamic nucleus. Brain Res. **334:** 227–233.
37. HIKOSAKA, O. & R. H. WURTZ. 1983. Visual and oculomotor functions of monkey substantia

nigra pars reticulata. IV. Relation of substantia nigra to superior colliculus. J. Neurophysiol. **53:** 292–308.

38. BRADLEY, P. B. & A. BROOKES. 1984. A microiontophoretic study of the actions of mu-, sigma-, and kappa-opiate receptor agonists in the rat brain. Br. J. Pharmacol. **83:** 763–772.
39. HUIDOBRO, F. 1978. Antidiuretic effect of morphine in the rat: Tolerance and physical dependence. Br. J. Pharmacol. **64:** 167.
40. IWAMOTO, E. T. 1981. Locomotor activity and antinociception after putative mu, kappa, and sigma opioid receptor agonists in the rat: Influence of dopaminergic agonists and antagonists. J. Pharmacol. Exp. Ther. **217:** 451–460.
41. IWAMOTO, E. T. & E. L. WAY. 1977. Circling behavior and stereotypy induced by intranigral opiate microinjections. J. Pharmacol. Exp. Ther. **203:** 347–359.
42. LEANDER, J. D. 1983. A kappa opioid effect: Increased urination in rat. J. Pharmacol. Exp. Ther. **224:** 89–94.
43. MATSUMOTO, R. R., K. H. BRINSFIELD, R. L. PATRICK & J. M. WALKER. 1988. Rotational behavior mediated by dopaminergic and nondopaminergic mechanisms after intranigral microinjection of specific mu, kappa, and delta opioid agonists. J. Pharmacol. Exp. Ther. **246:** 196–203.
44. MORELLI, M. & G. DICHIARA 1985. Non-dopaminergic mechanisms in the turning behavior evoked by intranigral opiates. Brain Res. **341:** 350–359.
45. MUCHA, R. F. & A. HERZ. 1986. Motivational properties of kappa and mu opioid receptor agonists studied with place and taste preference conditioning. Psychopharmacology **86:** 274–280.
46. SLIZGI, G. R. & J. H. LUDENS. 1982. Studies on the nature and mechanism of the diuretic activity of the opioid analgesic ethylketocyclazocine. J. Pharmacol. Exp. Ther. **220:** 585.
47. VON VOIGTLANDER, P. F., R. A. LAHTI & J. H. LUDENS. 1983. U50-488H: A selective and structurally novel non-mu (kappa) opioid agonist. J. Pharmacol. Exp. Ther. **224:** 7–12.
48. DI CHIARA, G. & A. IMPERATO. 1988. Opposite effects of mu and kappa opiate agonists on dopamine release in the nucleus accumbens and in the dorsal caudate of freely moving rats. J. Pharmacol. Exp. Ther. **244:** 1067–1080.
49. WALKER, J. M., L. A. THOMPSON, J. FRASCELLA & M. W. FRIEDERICH. 1987. Opposite effects of mu and kappa opiates on the firing rate of dopamine cells in the substantia nigra of the rat. Eur. J. Pharmacology **134:** 53–59.
50. LAVIN, A. & M. GARCIA-MUNOZ. 1985. Electrophysiological changes in substantia nigra after dynorphin administration. Brain Res. **369:** 298–302.
51. ROBERTSON, B. C., D. W. HOMMER & L. R. SKIRBOLL. 1987. Electrophysiological evidence for a non-opioid interaction between dynorphin and GABA in the substantia nigra of the rat. Neuroscience **23:** 483–490.
52. THOMPSON, L. A. & J. M. WALKER. 1988. Effects of iontophoretically applied U50,488h (a kappa opiate agonist) in the substantia nigra. Soc. Neurosci. Abstr. **14:** 1022.
53. COLLINGRIDGE, G. L. & J. DAVIES. 1982. Actions of substance P and opiates in the rat substantia nigra. Neuropharmacology **21:** 715–719.
54. HOMMER, D. W. & A. PERT. 1983. The actions of opiates in the rat substantia nigra: An electrophysiological analysis. Peptides **4:** 603–608.
55. WERLING, L. L., A. FRATTALI, P. S. PORTOGHESE, A. E. TAKEMORI & B. M. COX. 1988. Kappa receptor regulation of dopamine release from striatum and cortex of rats and guinea pigs. J. Pharmacol. Exp. Ther. **246:** 282–286.
56. HERRERA-MARSCHITZ, M., I. CHRISTENSSON-NYLANDER, T. SHARP, W. STAINES, M. REID, T. HOKFELT, L. TERENIUS & U. UNGERSTEDT. 1986. Striato-nigral dynorphin and substance P pathways in the rat. II. Functional analysis. Exp. Brain Res. **64:** 193–207.
57. REID, M., M. HERRERA-MARSCHITZ, T. HÖKFELT, L. TERENIUS & U. UNGERSTEDT. 1988. Differential modulation of striatal dopamine release by intranigral injection of gamma-aminobutyric acid (GABA), dynorphin A and substance P. Eur. J. Pharmacol. **147:** 411–420.
58. HERRERA-MARSCHITZ, M., T. HÖKFELT, U. UNGERSTEDT & L. TERENIUS. 1983. Functional studies with the opioid peptide dynorphin: Acute effects of injections into the substantia nigra reticulata of naive rats. Life Sci. **33:** 555–558.
59. HERRERA-MARSCHITZ, M., T. HÖKFELT, U. UNGERSTEDT, L. TERENIUS & M. GOLDSTEIN.

1984. Effect of intranigral injections of dynorphin, dynorphin fragments and alpha-neo-endorphin on rotational behavior in the rat. Eur. J. Pharmacol. **102:** 213–227.

60. FRIEDERICH, M. W., D. P. FRIEDERICH & J. M. WALKER. 1987. Effects of dynorphin(1-8) on movement: Non-opiate effects and structure-activity relationship. Peptides **8:** 837–840.

61. MATSUMOTO, R. R., A. M. LOHOF, R. L. PATRICK & J. M. WALKER. 1988. Dopamine-independent motor behavior following microinjection of rimorphin in the substantia nigra. Brain Res. **444:** 67–74.

62. LLORENS-CORTES, C., H. POLLARD & J. C. SCHWARTZ. 1979. Localization of opiate receptors in substantia nigra evidence by lesion studies. Neurosci. Lett. **12:** 165–170.

63. ABOU-KHALIL, B., A. B. YOUNG & J. B. PENNEY. 1984. Evidence for the presynaptic localization of opiate binding sites on striatal efferent fibers. Brain Res. **323:** 21–29.

64. WERZ, M. A. & R. L. MACDONALD. 1984. Dynorphin reduces calcium-dependent action potential duration by decreasing voltage-dependent calcium conductance. Neurosci. Lett. **46:** 185–190.

65. WERZ, M. A. & R. L. MACDONALD. 1985. Dynorphin and neoendorphin peptides decrease dorsal root ganglion neuron calcium-dependent action potential duration. J. Pharmacol. Exp. Ther. **234:** 49–56.

66. CHERUBINI, E. & R. A. NORTH. 1985. Mu and kappa opioids inhibit transmitter release by different mechanisms. Proc. Natl. Acad. Sci. USA **82:** 1860–1863.

67. NAWA, H., T. HIROSE, H. TAKASHIMA, S. INAYAMA & S. NAKANISHI. 1983. Nucleotide sequence of cloned cDNAs for two types of bovine brain substance P precursor. Nature **306:** 32–36.

68. INNIS, R. B., R. ANDRADE & G. K. AGHAJANIAN. 1985. Substance K excites dopaminergic and non-dopaminergic neurons in rat substantia nigra. Brain Res. **335:** 381–383.

69. KILPATRICK, N. C. & M. S. STARR. 1981. Involvement of dopamine in circling responses to muscimol depends on intranigral site of injection. Eur. J. Pharmacol. **69:** 407–419.

70. LAVIN, A. & M. GARCIA-MUNOZ. 1986. Effect of dynorphin on substantia nigra reticulata cells identified antidromically. Soc. Neurosci. Abstr. **12:** 650.

71. THOMPSON, L. A. & J. M. WALKER. Unpublished observations.

72. DICHIARA, G., M. L. PORCEDDU, M. MORELLI, M. L. MULAS & G. L. GESSA. 1979. Evidence for a GABAergic projection from the substantia nigra to the ventromedial thalamus and to the superior colliculus of the rat. Brain Res. **176:** 273–284.

73. CHEVALIER, G., S. VACHER & J. M. DENIAU. 1984. Inhibitory nigral influence on tectospinal neurons, a possible implication of basal ganglia in orienting behavior. Exp. Brain Res. **53:** 320–326.

74. MURRAY, E. A. & J. D. COULTER. 1982. Organization of tectospinal neurons in the cat and rat superior colliculus. Brain Res. **243:** 201–214.

75. WILLIAMS, M. N. & R. L. M. FAULL. 1988. The nigrotectal projection and tectospinal neurons in the rat. A light and electron microscopic study demonstrating a monosynaptic input to identified tectospinal neurons. Neuroscience **25:** 533–562.

76. HIKOSAKA, O. & M. SAKAMOTO. 1986. Cell activity in the monkey caudate nucleus preceding saccadic eye movements. Exp. Brain Res. **63:** 659–662.

77. CHIODO, L. A., S. M. ANTELMAN, A. R. CAGGIULA & C. G. LINBERRY. 1980. Sensory stimuli alter the discharge rate of dopamine (DA) neurons: Evidence for two functional types of DA cells in the substantia nigra. Brain Res. **189:** 544–549.

78. BARASI, S. 1979. Responses of substantia nigra neurones to noxious stimulation. Brain Res. **171:** 121–130.

# Contrasting Actions of Vasopressin and Beta-Endorphin on Rat Hippocampal Field Potentials[a]

TIM SMOCK, DAVID ALBECK, AND PATRICIA McMECHEN

*Center for Neurosciences*
*Department of Psychology*
*University of Colorado*
*Campus Box 345*
*Boulder, Colorado 80309*

## INTRODUCTION

Use of simple invertebrate nervous systems and the peripheral nervous system of vertebrates has provided evidence that peptides may act as neurotransmitters as well as neurohormones.[1,2] Similar evidence has been difficult to obtain in the vertebrate brain, however, because transmission between a single presynaptic and a single postsynaptic element is difficult to study in the brain and specific structural antagonists often are lacking for the candidate peptide transmitters.

Isolated brain preparations such as cortical, cerebellar, or hippocampal slices reduce the complications presented by polysynaptic interactions in the whole animal. However, this approach yields uncertainty regarding mechanism of action because of the complexity of local circuit interactions and inability to separate primary peptide effects from secondary consequences.

In this paper, we review evidence for two peptide transmitter types in the rat hippocampal slice preparation and describe the efforts to determine their mechanisms of action. In both cases the bulk of the evidence favors a common locus of primary action on inhibitory interneurons as well as separate primary and secondary actions on other cell types. Based on the analysis, we propose that arginine vasopressin and beta-endorphin are antagonistic neuromodulators of hippocampal pyramidal cell discharge. The fact that each of these modulators has action that can be blocked by a specific receptor antagonist presents the possibility that the antagonists may be used to block the action of endogenously released peptide as well as exogenously applied substance. With this approach in the intact animal, it may be possible to determine the role these hippocampal peptides play in the generation of behavior.

### Hippocampal Slice Preparation

Since the inception of brain slice technology over twenty years ago,[3] *in vitro* preparations have found favor with neuropharmacologists and neurophysiologists because they offer increased stability and experimental control over the composition of the extracellular

[a]Supported by grants from the Epilepsy Foundation of America, a grant from the University of Colorado Council on Research and Creative Work, and National Science Foundation Grant BNS 8520622.

medium.[4,5] In particular, slices of the mammalian hippocampus were appealing because this brain region has a simple trilaminar structure with well-defined synaptic circuitry.[6,7] FIGURE 1 illustrates the through-conducting excitatory pathway of the hippocampus. Excitatory input (triangular synapses) arrives from fibers in the perforant path (PP). These terminate on the dendrites of granule cells (GC) in the dentate gyrus, which in turn project excitatory synapses to pyramidal cells of the $CA_3$ region. Axons of these cells leave the hippocampus, and send collateral branches to another pyramidal cell region, $CA_1$. Excitation due to activity in these synapses is conveyed out of the hippocampus by $CA_1$ pyramidal cell axons in the alveus. Though the excitatory conductance pathway is relatively simple, additional nonpyramidal cell types participate in local circuit interactions.[8] These occur in all three regions of the hippocampus and give rise to feedforward and feedback integration. One such circuit is especially important for the understanding of

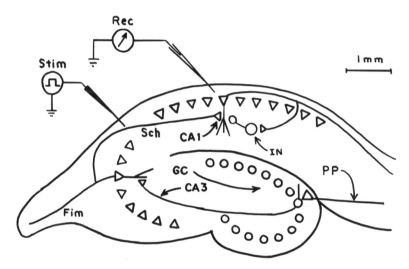

**FIGURE 1.** A cross section of the rat hippocampus, showing electrode positions. Stimulation for the test pulse is in the Schaffer's collaterals (Sch) in stratum radiatum. Recording electrode is in the $CA_1$ pyramidal cell somatic layer. Pyramidal cell axons give rise to collaterals that activate inhibitory interneurons (IN) which feed back to pyramidal cells. PP: perforant path, GC: granule cell layer, Fim: fimbria. *Triangle symbols* indicate excitatory contacts and *circular symbols* indicate inhibitory contacts. (Based on Schwartzkroin.[5])

peptide action and is shown in FIGURE 1. The $CA_1$ pyramidal cell axons, in addition to leaving the hippocampus, give rise to axon collaterals that make excitatory contacts on interneurons (IN) that provide inhibitory feedback to the pyramidal cell (circular synapse). The inhibitory interneurons are tonically active,[9] and their level of activity closely regulates the excitability of the pyramidal cells in $CA_1$.

In our experiments, transverse rat hippocampal slices (400 microns thick) are taken after freehand dissection of the hippocampus. These are incubated for an hour at the interface between a warm and humidified gas atmosphere (95% $O_2$/5% $CO_2$) and saline medium maintained at 35° (composition, in m$M$; NaCl 134, KCl 5, $NaH_2PO_4$ 1.25, $MgSO_4$ 2, $CaCl_2$ 2, $NaHCO_3$ 16, and glucose 10). A stimulating Pt wire electrode is placed in the $CA_3$ collaterals. Brief square-pulse stimulation of the collaterals (75 μsec duration) is adjusted to an intensity that evokes a submaximal response in $CA_1$ so as to be

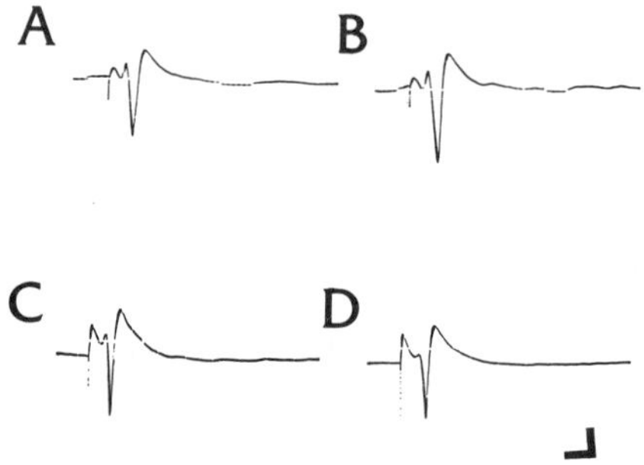

FIGURE 2. Beta-endorphin enhances population spike amplitude: Sample traces. (A) Before peptide application. (B) Response 10 min after beta-endorphin application (3 μM). (C) Before peptide application in presence of naloxone (1 μM). (D) Lack of response 10 min after beta-endorphin application (3 μM) in presence of naloxone. Stimuli of submaximal intensity are used, hence, epileptiform discharge is not apparent.[28] Synthetic peptides obtained from Peninsula Labs, San Carlos, CA. Bars = 1 mV, 5 msec.

able to observe both excitatory and inhibitory responses. The result in field potential recording is a positive wave representing a hybrid of excitatory and inhibitory synaptic activation and a superimposed negative wave representing the compound action potential in pyramidal cell somata and axons (FIGS. 2 and 3). Following this is the electrical consequence of collateral activation and interneuron discharge, which is superimposed on the falling phase of the waveform.

### Opioid Peptides

The hippocampus receives a projection of fibers containing enkephalin-like material and contains specific opiate receptors.[10,11] These receptors are likely to be predominantly of the *delta* type, though *mu* receptors are also present.[12]

In contrast to local circuit enkephalinergic systems, most brain beta-endorphin fibers arise from the arcuate nucleus in the hypothalamus and project to targets throughout the rest of the brain, including the hippocampus.[13,14] Since beta-endorphin shares sequence homology with met-enkephalin in the active region, there is overlapping binding specificity with opioid receptor types in the hippocampus. In addition, the precursor for beta-endorphin contains other biologically active peptide sequences related to melanotropin/adrenocorticotropic hormones[15] that may interact with beta-endorphin to produce an antagonistic action at the target tissue.[16,17]

### Mechanism of Opioid Peptide Action

Though the anatomical and biochemical evidence for opioid-mediated transmission in the hippocampus is strong, acquisition of physiological support has been hampered by confusion regarding the mechanism of opioid peptide action. In the intact animal, iontophoretically applied enkephalin increases the discharge rate of single units in extracellular recording.[18] This effect is naloxone-reversible, separating it from various nonspecific excitatory actions of opiates that are not reversed by this antagonist. The hippocampal excitation was surprising since the opiates and opioids generally inhibit cells elsewhere in the brain.[18] Furthermore, inhibition by presynaptic depression of excitatory transmitter release is the predominant mechanism of opiate action in the peripheral nervous system,[19,20] and biochemical studies of transmitter release show that presynaptic inhibition is the most likely mode of opiate analgesia in the spinal cord and brainstem.[21–23] Electrophysiological studies of opioid peptide action in both the peripheral and central nervous systems have revealed direct postsynaptic actions, but these are inhibitory not excitatory in nature.[24,25]

Therefore, a number of hippocampal slice studies were undertaken to understand the reason for the excitatory action of opiates in the hippocampus. When enkephalins or their metabolically stable derivatives are applied to the slice in field potential recording, the primary consequence is an increase in the size and number of evoked population spikes.[26,27] This effect is naloxone reversible. When intense stimuli are used, this increase can adopt the appearance of "epileptiform discharge."[28] The enhancement of the population spike amplitude can also be seen with beta-endorphin (FIG. 2). When micromolar concentrations of beta-endorphin are applied, this opioid peptide brings about an increase in this measure of pyramidal cell excitability (FIG. 2, A and B; n = 5) that is blocked by naloxone (FIG. 3, C and D, 1 $\mu M$; n = 3). In this case the epileptiform discharge is not seen with beta-endorphin application because test stimuli of low intensity were used.[28,29]

With intracellular recording, adjustments can be made to allow direct examination of inhibitory postsynaptic potentials as well as excitatory postsynaptic potentials, and when this is done opioids are seen to reduce the amplitude of evoked inhibition.[26] Furthermore, spontaneous inhibitory postsynaptic potentials also are attenuated by the peptides, and enkephalin analogs have no effect on the postsynaptic action of GABA, which is the transmitter likely to mediate the inhibitory postsynaptic potentials. The action of enkephalin and beta-endorphin in producing reduction in inhibitory potential amplitude is not associated with a change in the membrane potential or membrane resistance of the postsynaptic cell.[30] These results, taken in combination with evidence for presynaptic opiate mechanisms in other systems, have led these investigators to propose that the excitation produced by opioid peptides in the hippocampus also proceeds from presynaptic mechanisms, in this case disinhibition produced by presynaptic inhibition of GABA release from the tonically active inhibitory interneurons.[26,30]

Problems with this model arose with the observation that the enkephalin analogs also increased the size of the evoked intracellular excitatory postsynaptic potential,[27,28] again with no direct effect on postsynaptic membrane properties. This result presents the possibility that the excitatory action seen extracellularly might better be explained by increased presynaptic excitation rather than decreased presynaptic inhibition. In two studies, no effect on inhibitory mechanisms could be found.[27,31] Since synaptic potentials have hybrid inhibitory and excitatory nature and since feedforward inhibition exists in addition to recurrent, or feedback inhibition, it is difficult to identify an effect on one of these antagonistic potentials in distinction to an opposite effect on the other one on the basis of synaptic potential measurements alone.

The description of the electrophysiological properties of the nonpyramidal neurons

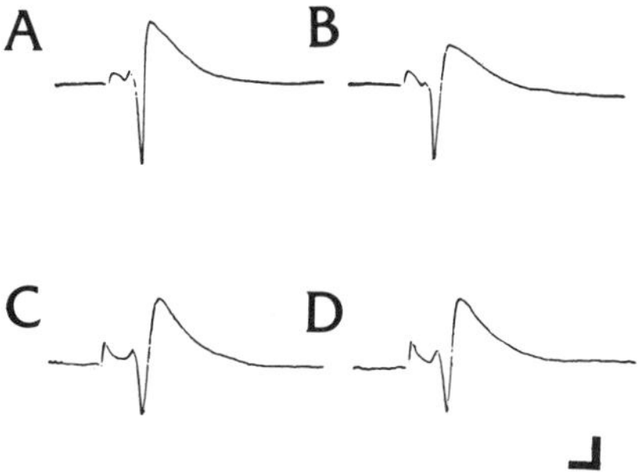

FIGURE 3. Vasopressin depresses population spike amplitude: Sample traces. (A) Before peptide application. (B) Response 10 min after arginine vasopressin application (1 $\mu M$). (C) Before peptide application in presence of specific $V_1$ pressor antagonist (1 $\mu M$).[51] (D) Lack of response 10 min after arginine vasopressin application in presence of antagonist. Stimuli of submaximal intensity are used to detect inhibitory effects. Synthetic peptides obtained from Peninsula Labs, San Carlos, CA. Bars = 0.5 mV, 5 msec.

likely to mediate local circuit inhibition in the hippocampus[8,9] presented an opportunity to address the issue of mechanism in another manner. An opioid-evoked depression in the activity of these neurons was proposed on the basis of experiments in the whole animal[32] and later reported on the basis of extracellular single unit recording from nonpyramidal cells in the slice.[33] This observation has been made on subsequent occasions[34] and probably constitutes the strongest evidence for the disinhibition model for opiate and opioid excitation in the hippocampus.

### Neurohypophyseal Peptides

In addition to the classic vasopressin and oxytocin projection from the hypothalamus to the neurohypophysis, there are fibers that arise from hypothalamic and extrahypothalamic nuclei and project to targets within the brain.[35] These nuclei, identified by either the presence of immunoreactive neurophysin or immunoreactive oxytocin- and vasopressin-like material in cell bodies, include the paraventricular, supraoptic and suprachiasmatic nuclei in the hypothalamus and the bed nucleus of the stria terminalis, the medial amygdaloid nucleus and the locus coeruleus elsewhere in the brain.[36] Some of these projections are sexually dimorphic, with stronger labeling in male rats that is reduced by castration and restored by testosterone treatment.[37]

The ventral hippocampus is one brain region that receives vasopressin containing fibers, and orthograde and retrograde tracing techniques have identified the source to be an ipsilateral, sexually dimorphic projection from the medial amygdaloid nucleus.[38] The discrete nature of this projection presents a promising avenue for investigation of central peptidergic transmission.

The brain vasopressin fibers make contact with neural targets as well as small blood vessels.[39,40] The peptide is released from brain tissue upon depolarization in the presence of calcium,[41] and specific receptors for vasopressin are found on both neural and microvascular membranes in the rat hippocampus.[42,43] Biochemical and antagonist data suggest that the brain receptor is predominantly of the $V_1$, or pressor type, but pharmacological results suggest that it may be a novel receptor with overlapping oxytocin specificity.[44]

### Mechanism of Neurohypophyseal Peptide Action

In contrast to opioid-induced enhancement of population spike amplitude (FIG. 2), vasopressin reduces the size of pyramidal cell action potentials in field potential recording.[29,45] As shown in FIGURE 3, A and B, bath applied vasopressin (1 $\mu M;$ n = 22) decreases the size of the population spike when test stimuli of moderate intensity are employed. This effect is not apparent in the presence of a structural $V_1$ pressor antagonist of vasopressin (FIG. 3, C and D, n = 9). FIGURE 4 is a direct comparison of beta-endorphin and vasopressin effects.

$CA_1$ pyramidal cells also can be activated antidromically by stimulating their axons in the alveus. Vasopressin-induced inhibition of population spikes can also be obtained in this circumstance, ruling out a depression in the excitability of stratum radiatum afferents as a mechanism for the inhibition.[29]

When vasopressin is applied to pyramidal cells in intracellular recording, an increase in evoked and spontaneous discharge frequency is reported.[46,47] As for opioid peptides, there is no change in membrane potential or resistance upon vasopressin application, suggesting that the source of the excitation is electrotonically remote from the electrode tip inside the cell.[46,47] In the case of opioid peptides this result together with consonant field potential data were used to argue for presynaptic mechanisms for the excitation (see above). However, this argument is not possible for vasopressin, since the intracellular and extracellular results are disparate, *i.e.*, there is an apparent depression of pyramidal cell excitability in field potentials and an increase in excitability with impaled neurons. Several possible explanations exist for this apparent conflict. Extracellular potentials are a reflection of transmembrane current. Therefore, an excitation can appear as an inhibition of population spike amplitude if there is substantial depolarization of the membrane in the excitable region that gives rise to the presumably somatic action potential, since extracellular current flow would be less in the depolarized state. Current shunting due to increased conductance in the excitable region of the soma could also reconcile the two results. Finally, excitation that produces discharge of such frequency as to produce refractoriness to a randomly presented stimulus might also lead to reduction of the population spike. The fact that none of these phenomena is seen after vasopressin application in intracellular recording[29,47] eliminates these possibilities as explanations for the disparity.

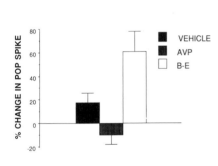

**FIGURE 4.** Action of vasopressin and beta-endorphin on population spike amplitude: Data summary. Change in population spike amplitude (mean ± SEM) is shown in each of three conditions. Acidic vehicle control (n = 15) has no effect on the spike, which increases during the course of the experiment. Arginine vasopressin (AVP, 1 μ$M$, n = 22) significantly depresses spike amplitude, while beta-endorphin (B-E, 3 μ$M$, n = 5) significantly increases spike amplitude (both $p$ <0.05 vs vehicle). Spike amplitude is measured as the length of the vertical line intersecting the maximum negative excursion and a tangent drawn between the two positive excursions of the field synaptic potential. (AVP data adapted from Albeck and Smock.[29]) Smaller spikes are taken to mean fewer pyramidal cells are firing to each test pulse and larger spikes are taken to mean more cells are firing (see text).

    The most likely explanation for the conflict is that the impaled neurons in intracellular recording behave differently than the rest of the pyramidal cell population. The way that this might come about is suggested by observation of vasopressin action on cerebral microvessels. Each pyramidal cell body is enmeshed in a network of penetrating microvessels, and these vessels constrict in response to applied vasopressin.[47] The movement of these vessel walls in the vicinity of an impaled cell can distort the cell membrane and yield an action potential discharge.[47,48] This increase in excitability is not accompanied by a measurable increase in conductance of the soma membrane, nor is there substantial depolarization in response to the mechanical stimulus.[47] In other words, the excitation produced in mechanical consequence of vasoconstriction is indistinguishable from that due to vasopressin application. Since vasopressin causes vasoconstriction in the hippocampal slice,[47] the most parsimonious explanation for the excitation seems to be that it is a secondary consequence of a primary vascular action of the peptide. In contrast to intracellular recording which involves the activity of a single neuron that is in direct contact with the electrode, field potential recording reflects the activity of a great many neurons most or all of which are not in contact with the recording electrode. Because of the vascular action of vasopressin and the confounding effect this has on the interpretation of intracellular data, we propose that the field potential results are more faithful reflections of the neural actions of this peptide.

Support for this explanation is found in the results of single unit extracellular recording. As for the studies with opioid peptides, vasopressin and oxytocin have been applied to hippocampal slices after isolation of spontaneously active cells.[34,49,50] These cells have discharge properties that identify them as inhibitory interneurons.[8,9] As would be expected from the field potential results, vasopressin excites these neurons, causing their tonic discharge frequency to increase.[50] The action of the neurohypophyseal peptides on these interneurons is exactly the opposite of the effect of opioid peptides.[34] Thus, the bulk

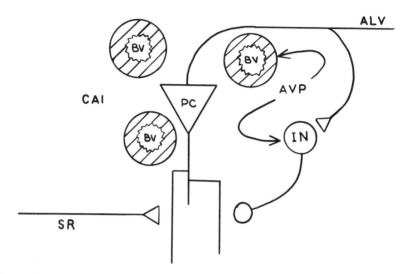

**FIGURE 5.** Microcircuitry in CA$_1$, showing site of vasopressin (AVP) action. *Large triangle* represents the pyramidal cell soma (PC) and *large circle* represents the inhibitory interneuron soma (IN). *Small triangles* represent excitatory synapses in stratum radiatum (SR) and collateral axons; *small circle* represents inhibitory contact in feedback circuit. *Hatched symbols* represent penetrating arterioles (blood vessels, BV) that surround each neuron cell body.[47] AVP has direct action in constricting microvessels and exciting interneurons and also has secondary action on pyramidal cells. ALV: alveus.

of the evidence favors vasopressin action that is inhibitory to pyramidal cells and indicates that excitation seen in intracellular recording is a unique property of impaled cells.

## CONCLUSIONS

We have reviewed research on two peptide systems projecting to the rat hippocampus; beta-endorphin from the arcuate nucleus and vasopressin from the medial amygdaloid nucleus. Use of specific antagonists together with a combination of field potential, intracellular and single unit extracellular recording has provided insight into mechanism of action of these peptides.

For the opioid peptides, field potential and intracellular results agree and support an excitation of pyramidal cells by presynaptic mechanisms. However, an increase in excitatory afferent activity cannot always be separated from disinhibition, and so there is confusion regarding the mechanism of opioid action. Direct single unit recording from the presumed inhibitory interneurons and demonstration of a decrease in their discharge frequency in response to opioids favors the disinhibition theory.

For neurohypophyseal peptides, the results of field potential recording and intracellular recording do not agree. Extracellular recording indicates an inhibition of pyramidal cell activity, and intracellular recording indicates an excitation of pyramidal cell activity. Since possible resolutions for the disparity involving changes in pyramidal cell membrane potential, input impedance or refractoriness can be excluded by the data, and since single unit extracellular recording strongly supports an action for vasopressin that is inhibitory to pyramidal cells, the best explanation appears to be that impaled pyramidal cells behave differently than the population not in direct contact with a transmembrane electrode. Constriction of microvessels surrounding each impaled cell that is induced by vasopressin most likely produces the excitation seen in response to this peptide. In the intact animal, vasopressin action should yield excitation of interneurons and inhibition of pyramidal cells.

FIGURE 5 illustrates our model for the action of neurohypophyseal peptides in the hippocampal slice. There are two direct actions; an excitation of inhibitory interneurons and a constriction of slice microvessels. There are two secondary responses; inhibition of pyramidal cells in extracellular recording and excitation of pyramidal cells in intracellular recording.

As the most likely model for the action of opioids involves a primary action on the same interneuron population that responds to vasopressin, we propose that beta-endorphin and vasopressin constitute antagonistic neuromodulatory systems for the hippocampus. When opioid-mediated transmission prevails, information should flow through the trisynaptic circuit of the hippocampus unattenuated by tonic inhibition (FIG. 1). In contrast, if vasopressin-mediated transmission prevails, such information will be attenuated, at least at the $CA_1$ stage, by an increase in tonic inhibition. Understanding of the behavioral conditions in which these peptides are released would yield great insight into the function of these peptides in the brain and, in fact, could lead to more knowledge of the function of the hippocampus itself. The fact that each of these peptides has action that can be blocked by a specific receptor antagonist suggests that this understanding could be provided if these antagonists are used to prevent the action of endogenously released beta-endorphin and vasopressin in the behaving organism.

## ACKNOWLEDGMENT

The authors would like to thank Bee Peterson for typing the manuscript.

## REFERENCES

1. BRANTON, W. D., S. ARCH, T. SMOCK & E. MAYERI. 1978. Evidence for mediation of a neuronal interaction by a behaviorally active peptide. Proc. Natl. Acad. Sci USA **75:** 5732–5736.
2. JAN, L., Y.-N. JAN & S. W. KUFFLER. 1980. Further evidence for peptidergic transmission in sympathetic ganglion. Proc. Natl. Acad. Sci. USA **77:** 5008–5012.
3. YAMAMOTO, C. & H. MCILWAIN. 1966. Electrical activities in thin sections from the mammalian brain maintained in chemically defined media *in vitro*. J. Neurochem. **13:** 1333–1343.

4.  KELLY, J. S. 1982. Intracellular recording from neurons in brain slice *in vitro*. *In* Handbook of Psychopharmacology. S. Iverson, L. Iverson & S. Snyder, Eds. Vol. **15**: 95–183. Plenum Press. New York, NY.
5.  KERKUT, G. A. & H. V. WHEAL. 1981. Electrophysiology of Isolated Mammalian CNS Preparations. Academic Press. London, England.
6.  SCHWARTZKROIN, P. A. & P. ANDERSON. 1975. Glutamic acid sensitivity of dendrites of hippocampal slices *in vitro*. *In* Advances in Neurology. G. W. Kreutzberg, Ed. **12**: 45–51. Raven Press. New York, NY.
7.  DINGLEDINE, R., J. DODD & J. S. KELLEY. 1980. The *in vitro* brainslice as a useful neurophysiological preparation. J. Neurosci. Meth. **2**: 323–362.
8.  KNOWLES, W. D. & P. A. SCHWARTZKROIN. 1981. Local circuit synaptic interactions in hippocampal brain slices. J. Neurosci. **1**: 318–322.
9.  SCHWARTZKROIN, P. A. & L. H. MATHERS. 1978. Physiological and morphological identification of a nonpyramidal hippocampal cell type. Brain Res. **157**: 1–10.
10. SAR, M. W., W. STUMPF, R. MILLER, K.-J. CHANG & P. CUATRECASAS. 1978. Immunohistochemical localization of enkephalin in the rat brain and spinal cord. J. Comp. Neurol. **182**: 17–38.
11. HERKENHAM, M. & C. B. PERT. 1980. *In vitro* autoradiography of opiate receptors in rat brain suggest loci of "opiatergic" pathways. Proc. Natl. Acad. Sci. USA **77**: 5532–5536.
12. VALENTINO, R. J., E. BOSTOCK & R. DINGLEDINE. 1982. Opioid pharmacology in the rat hippocampal slice. Life Sci. **31**: 2339–2342.
13. BLOOM, F., E. BATTENBERG, J. ROSSIER, N. LING & R. GUILLEMIN. 1978. Neurons containing beta-endorphin in rat brain exist separately from those containing enkephalin in immunocytochemical studies. Proc. Natl. Acad. Sci. USA **75**: 1591–1595.
14. ZAKARIAN, S. & D. G. SMYTH. 1982. Beta-endorphin is processed differently in specific regions of rat pituitary and brain. Nature **296**: 250–252.
15. MAINS, R., E. EIPPER & N. LING. 1977. Common precursor to corticotrophin and endorphins. Proc. Natl. Acad. Sci. USA **74**: 3014–3018.
16. SMOCK, T. & H. L. FIELDS. 1981. ACTH (1–24) blocks opiate-induced analgesia in the rat. Brain Res. **212**: 202–206.
17. SMOCK, T. 1987. Effects of ACTH (1–24) on single unit activity in the brainstem of the rat. Neuropharmacology **26**: 1771–1773.
18. NICOLL, R. A., G. SIGGINS, N. LING, F. BLOOM & R. GUILLEMIN. 1977. Neuronal actions of enkephalins and endorphins among brain regions: A comparative ionophoretic study. Proc. Natl. Acad. Sci. USA **74**: 2584–2589.
19. BORNSTEIN, J. C. & H. L. FIELDS. 1979. Morphine presynaptically inhibits a ganglionic cholinergic synapse. Neurosci. Lett. **15**: 77–82.
20. KONISHI, S., A. TSUNOO & M. OTSUKA. 1979. Enkephalins presynaptically inhibit cholinergic transmission in sympathetic ganglia. Nature **282**: 515–516.
21. JESSELL, T. M. & L. L. IVERSON. 1977. Opiate analgesics inhibit substance P release from rat trigeminal nucleus. Nature **286**: 549–551.
22. MUDGE, A. W., S. E. LEEMAN & G. D. FISCHBACH. 1979. Enkephalin inhibits release of substance P from sensory neurons in culture and decreases action potential duration. Proc. Natl. Acad. Sci. USA **76**: 526–530.
23. YAKSH, T. L., T. M. JESSELL, R. GAMSE, A. W. MUDGE & S. E. LEEMAN. 1980. Intrathecal morphine inhibits substance P release from mammalian spinal cord *in vivo*. Nature **286**: 155–157.
24. NORTH, R. A., Y. KATAYAMA & J. T. WILLIAMS. 1979. On the mechanism and site of action of enkephalin on single myenteric neurons. Brain Res. **165**: 67–78.
25. PEPPER, C. M. & HENDERSON, G. 1980. Opiates and opioid peptides hyperpolarize locus coeruleus neurons *in vitro*. Science **209**: 394–396.
26. NICOLL, R. A., B. E. ALGER & C. E. JAHR. 1980. Enkephalin blocks inhibitory pathways in the vertebrate CNS. Nature **287**: 22–25.
27. HAAS, H. L. & R. W. RYALL. 1980. Is excitation by enkephalins of hippocampal neurones in the rat due to presynaptic facilitation or disinhibition? J. Physiol. **308**: 315–330.
28. DINGLEDINE, R. 1981. Possible mechanisms of enkephalin action on hippocampal $CA_1$ pyramidal neurons. J. Neurosci. **1**: 1022–1035.

29. ALBECK, D. & T. SMOCK. 1988. A mechanism for vasopressin action in the hippocampus. Brain Res. **463:** 394–397.
30. SIGGINS, G. R. & W. ZIEGLGANSBERGER. 1981. Morphine and opioid peptides reduce inhibitory synaptic potentials in hippocampal pyramidal cells without alteration of membrane potential. Proc. Natl. Acad. Sci. USA **78:** 5235–5239.
31. LYNCH, G. S., R. A. JENSEN, J. L. MCGAUGH, K. DAVILA & M. W. OLIVER. 1981. Effects of enkephalin, morphine and naloxone on the electrical activity of the *in vitro* hippocampal slice preparation. Exp. Neurol. **71:** 527–540.
32. ZIEGLGANSBERGER, W., E. FRENCH, G. SIGGINS & F. BLOOM. 1979. Opioid peptides may excite hippocampal pyramidal neurons by inhibiting adjacent inhibitory interneurons. Science **205:** 415–417.
33. LEE, H. K., T. DUNWIDDIE & B. HOFFER. 1980. Electrophysiological interactions of enkephalins with neuronal circuitry in the rat hippocampus. II. Effects on interneuron excitability. Brain Res. **184:** 331–342.
34. RAGGENBASS, M., J. P. WUARIN, B. H. GAHWILER & J. J. DREIFUSS. 1985. Opposing effects of oxytocin and mu-receptor agonistic opioid peptide on the same class of nonpyramidal neurones in rat hippocampus. Brain Res. **344:** 392–396.
35. SWAAB, D. F., C. W. POOL & F. NIJVELDT. 1975. Immunofluorescence of vasopressin and oxytocin in the rat hypothalamo-neurohypophyseal system. J. Neural Transm. **36:** 195–215.
36. CAFFÉ, A. R. & F. W. VANLEEUWEN. 1983. Vasopressin-immunoreactive cells in the dorsomedial hypothalamic region, medial amygdaloid nucleus and locus coeruleus of the rat. Cell Tissue Res. **233:** 23–33.
37. DEVRIES, G. J., R. M. BUIJS, F. W. VAN LEEUWEN, A. R. CAFFÉ & D. C. SWAAB. 1985. The vasopressinergic innervation of the brain in normal and castrated rats. J. Comp. Neurol. **233:** 236–254.
38. CAFFÉ, A. R., F. W. VAN LEEUWEN & P. G. M. LUITEN. 1987. Vasopressin cells in the medial amygdala of the rat project to lateral septum and ventral hippocampus. J. Comp. Neurol. **261:** 237–252.
39. SOFRONIEW, M. V. 1983. Morphology of vasopressin and oxytocin neurons and their central and vascular projections. In The Neurohypophysis: Structure, Function and Control. B. A. CROSS & G. LENG, Eds. Prog. Brain Res. **60:** 101–114. Elsevier Press. Amsterdam, The Netherlands.
40. JOJART, I., F. JOO, L. SIKLOS & F. A. LASZLO. 1984. Immunoelectro-histochemical evidence for innervation of brain microvessels by vasopressin immunoreactive neurons in the rat. Neurosci. Lett. **51:** 259–264.
41. BUIJS, R. M. & J. J. VAN HEERIKHUEZE. 1982. Vasopressin and oxytocin release in the brain: A synaptic effect. Brain Res. **252:** 71–76.
42. PEARLMUTTER, A. F. & S. I. HARIK. 1985. A comparison of vasopressin binding to pig cerebral microvessels, cortex and hippocampus. Soc. Neurosci. Abstr. **11:** 80.
43. KRETSCHMAR, R., R. LANDGRAF, A. GJEDDE & A. ERMISCH. 1986. Vasopressin binds to microvessels from rat hippocampus. Brain Res. **380:** 325–330.
44. MÜHLETHALER, M., W. H. SAWYER, M. M. MANNING & J. J. DREIFUSS. 1983. Characterization of a uterine-type oxytocin receptor in the rat hippocampus. Proc. Natl. Acad. Sci. USA **80:** 6713–6717.
45. BURNARD, D. M., W. L. VEALE & Q. J. PITTMAN. 1987. Altered sensitivity to arginine vasopressin (AVP) in area $CA_1$ of the hippocampal slice following pretreatment of rats with AVP. Brain Res. **422:** 11–16.
46. MIZUNO, Y., Y. OOMURA, N. HORI & D. O. CARPENTER. 1984. Action of vasopressin on $CA_1$ pyramidal neurons in rat hippocampal slices. Brain Res. **309:** 241–246.
47. SMOCK, T., R. CACH & A. TOPPLE. 1987. Action of vasopressin on neurons and microvessels in the rat hippocampal slice. Exp. Brain Res. **66:** 401–408.
48. LIBERMAN, E. A., S. V. MINNA, O. L. MJAKOHNA, N. E. SHKLOVSKY-KORDY & M. CONRAD. 1985. Neuron generator potentials evoked by intracellular injection of cyclic nucleotides and mechanical distension. Brain Res. **338:** 33–44.
49. MÜHLETHALER, M., J. J. DREIFUSS & B. H. GAHWILER. 1982. Vasopressin excites hippocampal neurones. Nature **296:** 749–751.
50. MÜHLETHALER, M., S. CHARPAK & J. J. DREIFUSS. 1984. Contrasting effects of neurohy-

pophyseal peptides on pyramidal and nonpyramidal neurones in the rat hippocampus. Brain Res. **308:** 97–107.

51. KRUSZYNSKI, M., B. LAMMEK, M. MANNING, J. SETO, J. HALDAR & W. H. SAWYER. 1980. [1-($\beta$-mercapto-$\beta$-$\beta$-cyclopentamethylenepropionic acid) 2-(O-methyl) tyrosine] arginine vasopressin and [1-($\beta$-mercapto-$\beta$-$\beta$-cyclopentamethylenepropionic acid] arginine vasopressin, two highly potent antagonists of the vasopressor response to arginine vasopressin. J. Med. Chem. **23:** 364–368.

# The Effects of Vasopressin on Memory in Healthy Young Adult Volunteers

## Theoretical and Methodological Issues

BILL E. BECKWITH, THOMAS V. PETROS,
DEBORAH I. COUK,[a] AND TIMOTHY P. TINIUS

*Department of Psychology*
*University of North Dakota*
*Box 7187, University Station*
*Grand Forks, North Dakota 58202*
*and*
*[a]Department of Physical Medicine and Rehabilitation*
*University of California Medical Center*
*2315 Stockton Boulevard, Room 6503*
*Sacramento, California 95819*

## INTRODUCTION

Arginine vasopressin (AVP) is a nonapeptide hormone that originates from cells contained in the paraventricular, supraoptic, suprachiasmatic nuclei of the hypothalamus; the bed nucleus of the stria terminalis; medial amygdala; and the locus coeruleus.[1] Central nervous system projections from these nuclei which are believed to use AVP as a neurotransmitter/neuromodulator may be found in the spinal cord, the midbrain, and the forebrain.[2,3] In addition to its release into the general circulation, AVP is released into the cerebral spinal fluid and is transported to the median eminence of the pituitary gland where it regulates the release of ACTH. Among the many actions attributed to AVP are mediation of renal function,[4] mediation of cardiovascular function,[5] nonopioid mediation of tolerance for pain,[6] regulation of temperature,[7] and modulation of learning and memory.[8]

The belief that vasopressin influences learning and memory originated in DeWied's early demonstration that removal of the neurohypophysis resulted in disruption of avoidance behavior which was corrected after treatment with subcutaneous injections of pitressin, an extract of the posterior pituitary.[9] Subsequently, it was demonstrated that the active constituent of pitressin was lysine vasopressin (LVP) and that peripheral administration of LVP could both restore normal avoidance in hypophysectomized rats and delay extinction in intact rats.[10] DeWied and Bohus[10] interpreted this result as demonstrating that vasopressin facilitated long-term memory. Subsequent research demonstrated that treatment with vasopressin improves performance of nonhuman animals in a variety of learning paradigms.[8,11,12] However, more recent interpretations of these findings have included consolidation and retrieval of memory,[8] arousal,[12,13] and selective attention.[14,15] Despite the ultimate mechanism by which vasopressin affects performance, considerable interest arises from the possibility that it may serve as a treatment for disorders of memory in humans. Data gained from experiments with nonhuman subjects may only be suggestive regarding this issue.

Early clinical studies with humans supported the belief that peripherally administered vasopressin enhanced memory.[16–19] However, clinical tests of vasopressin's effectiveness in facilitating human memory function have not been successful.[20,21] Jolles[20] suggested that the inconsistent effects found in clinical trials resulted from vasopressin's increased effectiveness when degenerative processes in the brain are mild to moderate rather than severe. If the actions of vasopressin are more prominent in less severe memory disorders, then it seems reasonable that one may gain some understanding of its clinical potential by exploring the actions of treatment on healthy volunteers. Several laboratories have produced results demonstrating that treatment with vasopressin does enhance human memory. For example, when administered to healthy young adults vasopressin has been shown to improve the consistency, organization, and completeness of recall of structured lists of words;[22] to improve visual, spatial, and auditory memory as assessed by a variety of neuropsychological tests;[19,23] and to enhance the primacy effect and impair the recency effect in free-recall of lists of unrelated words.[24] In addition, a series of studies using acute doses of DDAVP have demonstrated enhanced visual discrimination learning,[25] memory scanning for digits,[26,27] recall of implicational sentences,[28] and recall of narrative prose.[29] Of course, there have also been failures to find an effect of treatment with vasopressin on memory in healthy human volunteers.[20,21] The conflicting results may be a consequence of critical factors that have varied among these studies: analog and dose used, route of administration, length of time during which treatments are administered, time course of testing, memory system assessed, method for assessing memory, small sample sizes.

The use of healthy young adults to determine the effects of treatment with vasopressin on memory merits more extensive consideration in light of current theories of human memory. These reflections may serve as a point of departure for the future development of a detailed understanding not only of how this neuropeptide works to modulate memory but also an understanding of which memory systems are affected. In addition, more extensive documentation of the range of variables (*e.g.*, gender, time of day, verbal ability) which mediate these effects would also clarify the mechanism(s) by which these actions occur. It is our intent to review selectively the findings regarding the effects of treatment with vasopressin on healthy volunteer adults and to suggest how these findings may fit with postulated processes underlying human memory.

### Current Models of Human Memory

Two general models have dominated the studies in human memory during the past three decades: The "pipeline" multistore model and the levels of processing model. The multistore approach was developed by Broadbent[30] and later made more explicit by Atkinson and Shiffrin.[31] This model viewed memory as a fixed set of systems which serially processed information through three major stores: sensory memory, short-term memory, and long-term memory (FIG. 1). Sensory memory is a system which stores raw sensory information long enough for pattern recognition to occur (*i.e.*, milliseconds). A subset of the information in sensory memory is then selected by means of an attentional mechanism for further processing in short-term memory, which allows brief (*i.e.*, seconds to minutes) storage of a limited amount of information. Short-term memory holds information which is currently being processed and is often described as similar to ordinary consciousness. Finally, long-term memory holds an unlimited amount of information indefinitely. Information may be retrieved from long-term memory for use by short-term memory or by encoding of new information through short-term memory.

According to the multistore model, information is conveyed from one system to the next in a fixed sequence. Furthermore, the selection of information to be processed (*i.e.*, attention) is controlled by a filter located after sensory memory and by feedback loops controlled by short- and long-term memory. Multistore models are supported by a rich and varied set of data that demonstrate that certain experimental variables differentially affect

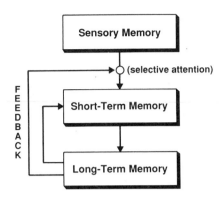

**FIGURE 1.** Discrete, linear, multistage model of memory.

memories in the various stores.[32] For example, one of the most robust effects is the so-called serial position effect. To demonstrate this effect, a subject is presented a series of words to memorize and is asked immediately to recall the words in any order he/she chooses (*i.e.*, free recall). When percent of words recalled is plotted against the position of the word in the list during presentation, a U-shaped function results. In other words, words presented first and last are better recalled than words presented in the middle of the list. The peaks at the two ends of the curve are known as the primacy and recency effects and are believed to represent processes of long-term memory and short-term memory, respectively.[33]

The levels of processing model offers an alternative to the multistore model (FIG. 2). According to this model,[34] memory is the product of the kind of analysis (*e.g.*, feature extraction versus semantic elaboration) completed during the encoding of information. This view is believed to be fundamentally different from the multistage model in that no specific stores of information are proposed. Rather, what is viewed as important is the type of analysis the subject performs on stimulus information. For example, reading serves as a model behavior for understanding this approach. The initial task for a reader is to analyze the physical structure of the letters and words (*i.e.*, feature extraction) in the text. Next, a name or label (*i.e.*, phonological analysis) must be associated with the individual words (*i.e.*, lexical access) which are recognized. Finally, the meaning (*i.e.*, semantic analysis) of the words must be placed in the context of current knowledge. This sequence, which involves three levels of analysis, is viewed as a continuum in which each level from feature extraction to semantic analysis produces "deeper" processing. The strength of a memory is determined by how elaborately information was analyzed. Accordingly, deeper analysis (*i.e.*, lexical or semantic analysis) produces more enduring memory than shallow analysis (*i.e.*, feature extraction).

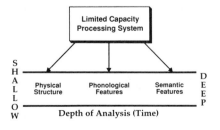

**FIGURE 2.** Levels of processing model indicating continuous analysis without discrete stages.

The next sections of this paper delineate current findings describing the effects of vasopressin on memory in healthy young adults within the context of these two approaches to memory. First, studies conducted with lists of words and studies done on the efficiency of scanning short-term memory are reviewed to illustrate findings consistent with the multistore model. Next, studies focusing upon the role of vasopressin in selective attention are reviewed. Finally, studies which arise from a levels-of-processing approach are described.

## Effects of Vasopressin on Memory for Lists of Words

There have been several studies which have examined the effects of treatment with vasopressin on memory for lists of words in healthy young adults. Weingartner found improved recall of lists of words in healthy college students.[22] Millar demonstrated improvement in immediate recall of lists of words.[35] Fehm-Wolfsdorf demonstrated an enhanced primacy effect combined with an attenuated recency effect in one study[24] and an attenuated primacy effect combined with an enhanced recency effect in a later study.[36] It is interesting to note that the first study[24] was completed during evening hours whereas the more recent study[36] was completed during morning hours. This suggests that diurnal effects of either neuroendocrine systems or memory systems may have an important relationship to the nature of the effect of vasopressin on memory (a point to which we shall return during discussion of memory scanning experiments).

However, there have also been several reported failures to demonstrate any clear effect of vasopressin analogs on free recall.[37-40] In addition to circadian rhythms, there are numerous factors which differ across these studies: number of words in the lists, relationships among words, rate of presentation, retention interval, etc. This diversity makes a simple summary of these effects impossible at the present time. As may be seen from TABLE 1, it appears that under some conditions treatment with vasopressin and its analogs do alter the processes represented by recall of lists of words. However, the specific processes and controlling variables are not clear.

## Effects of Vasopressin on Scanning Working Memory (STM)

A second method that has been used to study the effect of vasopressin on theoretically important memory processes is the Sternberg Item Recognition Task.[41] This task requires subjects to memorize a set of digits, letters, or words. Then the subject is asked to decide as quickly as possible if a probe digit is a member of the original memory set. There is a direct linear relationship between response time and memory set size on this task. The theory underlying the Sternberg Task suggests that if a treatment facilitates attentional processes (i.e., speed of encoding information into short-term memory), then the intercept of the linear function relating reaction time to memory set size would either increase (impair attention) or decrease (facilitate attention). On the other hand, the slope of the linear function relating reaction time to memory set size would decrease if a treatment facilitates the speed of scanning short-term memory and increase if a treatment impairs the speed of scanning short-term memory.

In the first study to use this methodology, Beckwith et al.[26] administered either placebo or 1-desamino-8-D-arginine vasopressin (DDAVP) to healthy young adults in a double-blind cross-over design. Subjects were presented with a memory set of one to four digits in a fixed set procedure. One week later, subjects were crossed to the converse treatment and presented with the same task. DDAVP reduced the intercept during the second session whereas it had no influence during the first session. Because DDAVP influenced the intercept rather than the slope, it was suggested that DDAVP facilitated attention. In a follow-up study in which treatment was a between-subjects factor, subjects were given either placebo, DDAVP, or AVP and assessed on the Sternberg Task.[39] Both DDAVP and AVP significantly reduced the intercept of the reaction time function, again suggesting that vasopressin facilitated attention during scanning of short-term memory. In addition, a control group was included as a control for the effects of treatment on reaction times (*i.e.*, a reaction time control group). Neither AVP nor DDAVP influenced the slope or intercept of the reaction time control group. A direct comparison of the data from the first session of the cross-over study and the second study indicated conflicting results: no effect of treatment in the first case,[26] facilitation of attentional processes in the second case.[39] This discrepancy may be accounted for by the fact that during the first study subjects were treated and tested in the late morning and during the second study subjects

**TABLE 1.** Vasopressin Studies Using Lists of Words

| Study | N | Analog | Dose | Effect of Treatment |
|---|---|---|---|---|
| Studies using multiple treatments | | | | |
| 1. Lists of related words | | | | |
| 22 | 6 | DDAVP | 30–60 μg | enhanced recall |
| 38 | 20 | DGAVP | 0.1–10 mg | no effect |
| 2. Lists of unrelated words | | | | |
| 24 | 20 | LVP | 10 I.U. | prolonged primacy effect |
| 36 | 13 | DGAVP | 1 mg | enhanced recency effect |
| 37 | 30 | LVP | 10 I.U. | enhanced recall (no interaction with serial position) |
| Studies using a single treatment (all used lists of unrelated words) | | | | |
| 35 | 36 | DDAVP | 40 μg | enhanced recall (no interaction with serial position) |
| 39 | 62 | DDAVP AVP | 60 μg | complex interaction with rate of presentation and practice (no interaction with serial position |
| 40 | 80 | DDAVP | 60 μg | complex interaction with rate of presentation and practice and rate of presentation and serial position |

were treated and tested in the evening. This possible diurnal modulation of vasopressin's effect is reminiscent of that described for lists of words and further suggests the importance of diurnal factors in the manner by which vasopressin modulates human memory.

In another recent study of the effects of vasopressin on memory scanning, Nebes *et al.*[27] investigated the effects of chronic treatment with DDAVP on healthy young (20–30 years) and old (60–70 years) adults. Treatment decreased slope and intercept on the Sternberg Task for both young and old subjects. There were no interactions between treatment and age. Thus, despite considerable methodological differences, all three studies completed on the effects of vasopressin on memory scanning suggest that treatment enhances the speed of encoding information into short-term memory (*i.e.*, attention). It also appears that treatment with vasopressin may facilitate scanning of short-term memory. This method may offer a rich arena for further exploration of the effects of vasopressin on human memory.

## Effects of Vasopressin on Selective Attention

Support for an effect of treatment with vasopressin on selective attention relies on a methodology which is believed to demonstrate similar processes in human and nonhuman tests.[42] In two studies rats were required to learn a two-choice, simultaneous brightness discrimination with black and white doors as discriminative stimuli. When they were able to consistently enter the white door, the task was altered so that entry through the black door allowed reinforcement, *i.e.*, the animals were required to reverse their initial response. If vasopressinergic peptides do enhance memory, as suggested by their ability to retard extinction of learned behaviors, then treatment with DDAVP should retard learning the reversal. Treatment with arginine vasopressin enhanced learning the reversal of the brightness discrimination.[14,15] These results were interpreted as showing that treatment with vasopressin enhanced selective attention.

According to one theoretical model of selective attention,[43] there are two behavioral requirements for mastery of a discrimination. Subjects must initially learn to attend to the relevant stimulus dimension that allows solution of the discrimination. In the present case, subjects must learn to suppress very strong position habits and learn to attend to brightness of the door (*i.e.*, to select and engage the appropriate sensory analyzer). Thereafter, they can learn appropriate response attachments based on reinforcement contingencies. Further, it is postulated that these two processes develop somewhat independently with analyzer strength accumulating at a different rate than response strength. This allows for certain treatments (*e.g.*, treatment with vasopressin) to increase the strength of the attentional response to a greater degree than the choice response.

Beckwith *et al.*[25] used a concept-learning paradigm (which was assumed to serve as a human analog of these studies with rats) to examine the effect of DDAVP on attentional processes. Subjects were randomly assigned to receive either no treatment, placebo, or DDAVP. For the visual discrimination, subjects were presented with a series of slides of colored geometric forms that differed in color and shape. Each subject was instructed to select the correct object, with color serving as the relevant dimension for making the discrimination. Following acquisition of the color response, subjects were trained on (1) a reversal shift, the opposite color was correct, (2) an intradimensional shift, a new set of stimuli were presented that differed in color and shape but color was reinforced and (3) an extradimensional shift, shape was reinforced. DDAVP enhanced subjects' performance on all discrimination problems. This facilitation of learning was interpreted as evidence that DDAVP facilitated selective attention, one of the control processes in the multistore model. This result is especially interesting because it presents a behavioral paradigm within which tests on human and nonhuman animals produce similar findings.

## Levels of Processing

The initial study conducted within the levels of processing model used implicational sentences as stimulus materials.[28] An implicational sentence is a sentence in which an inference can be drawn as a by-product of processing the sentence. For example, ''The pupil put the thumbtack on the chair'' leads most observers to infer that the student is engaging in a prank. One of two instructions was given to alter the depth to which subjects in separate groups processed sentences: (1) think about the full meaning of the event in each sentence (comprehension instructions) versus (2) listen carefully and try to learn the sentence (memorization instructions). It was assumed that the instruction to comprehend the sentences would induce deeper processing. Additionally, treatment was given to both male and female volunteers. Women were tested only during the first five days of their menstrual cycle. Previous studies had either assessed only males or not separated gender as a possible modifier of the effects of treatment with vasopressin. Males treated with DDAVP recalled more sentences than males treated with placebo under both instructional sets. Treatment with DDAVP did not influence performance in women. There were no interactions between instructional set and treatment. This sexually dimorphic influence of treatment with DDAVP is especially intriguing given the recent discovery of a sexually dimorphic, androgen-dependent innervation of vasopressin in the lateral septum and bed nucleus of the stria terminalis of rats.[1]

A second study was designed to assess a different set of questions.[44] Male subjects were asked to immediately recall sentences under the influence of either DDAVP or placebo and asked to return seven days later in a cross-over treatment. During the second session, subjects were asked to recall a new set of sentences in addition to those they had heard the week before. Furthermore, given the importance of verbal ability in mediating recall of verbal material,[45] subjects were divided into those with higher and lower verbal ability. In general, DDAVP enhanced recall during the first session, but not during the second session. However, when the subjects were separated by verbal ability, treatment with DDAVP facilitated immediate recall of subjects with lower verbal ability and facilitated delayed recall of subjects with higher verbal ability. These results suggest yet another possible mediator of the actions of treatment with vasopressin on human memory—verbal ability.

One tentative conclusion based on all of the studies reviewed so far is that vasopressin facilitates the efficiency of attentional processes in memory systems. The final experiment was conducted with highly organized verbal materials in an attempt to explore the attentional enhancing actions of DDAVP during a task that more closely matches the processes by which people are exposed to materials for learning and memory in their daily experiences. This was accomplished by testing the effect of DDAVP on the immediate recall of narrative prose passages in young adult males.[29] Subjects were treated with either placebo or DDAVP and listened to six narrative stories presented on audio tape. Immediately after listening to each story, subjects were asked to recall as much of the passage as possible. Subjects treated with DDAVP recalled a greater proportion of idea units from the passages at both high and medium levels of importance than subjects treated with placebo.

Recent evidence indicates that the effect of level of importance occurs primarily during the process of encoding prose.[46] Theoretical accounts of prose comprehension[47] suggest that rapid encoding of text while maintaining propositions from earlier portions of text in working memory is necessary for the comprehension of prose. Processing capacity is viewed as limited and must be divided between the continuous encoding of the text and maintaining the text propositions in working memory, *i.e.*, prose processing is a divided attention task. By maintaining the text propositions in working memory, the ideas should become more integrated and comprehension of the story should improve as interconnections among propositions become established. Hence, treatment with DDAVP seems to have facilitated the divided attentional processes necessary to integrate text in working memory as evidenced by the increased attention to important as opposed to less important details of the passages presented. Therefore, on a theoretical level, these results again suggest that treatment with DDAVP influences selective attention.

## SUMMARY AND FUTURE DIRECTIONS

In summary, there are a few statements that seem safe at the present time. First, exogenous administration of vasopressin enhances memory in healthy young adults. However, the questions of which mechanism modulates this action and whether the effect is also found physiologically remain unanswered. Second, treatment with vasopressin enhances the scanning of short-term memory in healthy young adults. Third, treatment with vasopressin enhances selective attention as measured in subjects' enhanced ability to engage relevant aspects of situations in certain problem solving tasks and in reading narrative prose. These effects do not appear to be large but they do appear to be consistent and reliable.

A few statements may also be warranted regarding where in terms of the multistore and levels-of-processing models vasopressin has its effect. First, it does not appear that vasopressin directly influences long-term memory. Its actions appear to come earlier in the sequence by which information is being encoded and manipulated in short-term memory for later storage into long-term memory. Second, the current evidence suggests that vasopressin may modulate memory through two processes. (1) It enhances memory by enhancing selective attention to relevant aspects of the learning environment. (2) It

**TABLE 2.** Methodological Variables Important in Delineating the Actions of Vasopressin on Human Memory

Dose of peptide
Route of administration
Frequency of administration
Duration of administration
Specific analog administered
Interval between administration and testing
Time of day (administration, testing)
Individual differences
    Trait arousal (*e.g.,* impulsivity)
    Gender
    Verbal ability
    Age
    Health
    Affect (*e.g.,* depression)
Method of testing memory
    Neuropsychological tests
    Memory scanning
    Lists of words (related, unrelated)
    Lists of sentences
    Prose (narrative, expository)

enhances the efficiency of short-term memory. It is unclear at the present time whether these two functions are complementary or independent. Third, it does not appear that vasopressin interacts directly with any of the levels of analysis postulated by the levels-of-processing approach.

Where do we go from here? There are at least two directions that seem useful for future behaviorally oriented research. First, it is apparent that there are a multitude of methodological factors which enter into the equation for determining whether an effect will be demonstrated and how large an effect may be found. As may be seen from TABLE 2, these factors include not only pharmacological variables such as dose, time course, analog, etc. but also many nonpharmacological variables. Already it appears important to consider diurnal rhythms and their impact on memory and their interaction on treatment with vasopressin. At least two discrepant findings in the literature, each in the same laboratories, may be a result of circadian influences. Furthermore, it appears important to

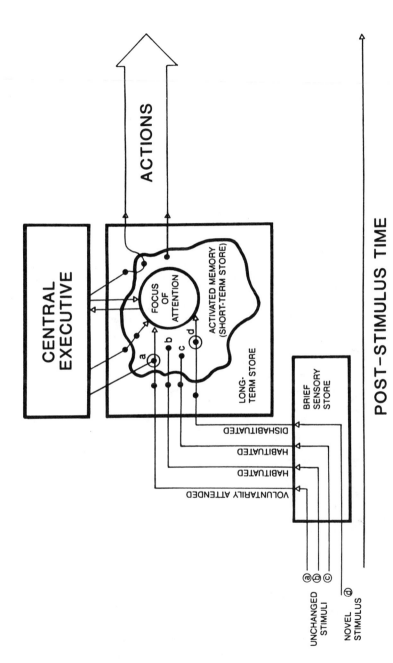

**FIGURE 3.** Cowan's revised model of the information-processing system. (Adapted from Cowan.[48])

consider the impact of individual differences in this equation. Gender and verbal ability have already been demonstrated to be important factors in determining the effects of vasopressin on memory.

Second, we need better models of human memory from which to work. One promising model has recently been presented by Cowan (FIG. 3).[48] The main advances of this model are that the distinction between short-term memory and sensory memory occurs only during the first few hundred milliseconds. Thereafter, sensory memory fades into short-term memory. In addition, short-term memory is viewed as an activated subset of long-term memory and that awareness is but one partition of short-term memory. Finally, selective attention involves habituation rather than filtering. These changes in conceptualization of human memory indicate several directions which could be taken to specify how vasopressin or other neuroactive substances affect memory. For example, the vasopressinergic enhancement of attention and scanning within short-term memory points to the need to explore in more detail the effects of vasopressin on the interface between short- and long-term memory systems. In addition, the vasopressinergic facilitation of selective attention necessitates exploration of the effects of vasopressin on habituation/ attention mechanisms. Cowan's model suggests several interesting ways to set up these tests.

As we gain a better understanding of memory systems[49] and the localization of cognitive operations in the human brain,[50] we also need to make concurrent efforts to understand the impact of behaviorally relevant variables on human memory and to develop more encompassing behavioral theories of human memory. The interaction of these variables and models is important to disentangle if we are to more clearly understand the mechanism by which vasopressin influences human memory and where to look in attempting to isolate which biological systems mediate these effects, be they central or peripheral.

## REFERENCES

1. BUIJS, R. M. 1987. Vasopressin localization and putative functions in the brain. *In* Vasopressin: Principles and Properties. D. M. Gash & G. J. Boer, Eds. 91–115. Plenum Press. New York, NY.
2. SILVERMAN, A. J. & E. A. ZIMMERMAN. 1983. Magnocellular neurosecretory system. Annu. Rev. Neurosci. **6:** 357–380.
3. SWANSON, L. W. & P. E. SAWCHENKO. 1983. Hypothalamic integration: Organization of the paraventricular and supraoptic nuclei. Annu. Rev. Neurosci. **6:** 269–324.
4. SCHRIER, R. W. & A. LEAF. 1981. Effect of hormones on water, sodium, chloride, and potassium metabolism. *In* Textbook of Endocrinology. R. H. Williams, Ed. 1033–1046. W. B. Saunders Company. Philadelphia, PA.
5. MATSUGUCHI, H., F. M. SHARAKI, F. J. GORDON, A. K. JOHNSON & P. G. SCHMID. 1982. Blood pressure and heart rate responses to microinjections of vasopressin into the nucleus tractus solitarius region of the rat. Neuropharmacology **21:** 687–693.
6. BERNSTON, G. G. & B. S. BERSON. 1980. Antinoceptive effects of intraventricular or systemic administration of vasopressin in the rat. Life Sci. **261:** 455–459.
7. KASTING, N. W., W. L. VEALE & K. E. COOPER. 1982. Vasopressin: A homeostatic effector in the febrile process. Neurosci. Biobehav. Rev. **6:** 215–222.
8. DE WIED, D., M. JOELS, J. P. H. BURBACH, E. R. DE JONG, E. R. DE KLOET, O. W. J. GAFFORI, I. J. A. URBAN, J. M. VAN REE, T. B. VAN WIMERSMA GREIDANUS, H. D. VELDHUIS, D. H. G. VERSTEEG & V. M. WIEGANT. 1988. Vasopressin effects in the central nervous system. *In* Peptide Hormones: Effects and Mechanisms of Action. A. Negro-Vilar & P. M. Conn, Eds. Vol. 1: 97–140. CRC Press. Boca Raton, FL.
9. DE WIED, D. 1965. The influence of posterior and intermediate lobe of the pituitary and pituitary peptides on the maintenance of a conditioned avoidance response in rats. Int. J. Neuropharmacol. **4:** 157–167.

10. DE WIED, D. & B. BOHUS. 1966. Long term and short term effects on retention of a conditioned avoidance response in rats by treatment with long-acting pitressin and alpha-MSH. Nature **212:** 1484–1486.
11. HOFFMAN, P. L. 1987. Central nervous system effects of neurohypophyseal peptides. *In* The Peptides. C. W. Smith, Ed. Vol. 8: 239–295. Academic Press. New York, NY.
12. GASH, D. M., J. P. HERMAN & G. J. THOMAS. 1987. Vasopressin and animal behavior. *In* Vasopressin: Principles and Properties. D. M. Gash & G. J. Boer, Eds. 517–547. Plenum Press. New York, NY.
13. SAHGAL, A. & C. WRIGHT. 1983. A comparison of the effects of vasopressin and oxytocin with amphetamine and chlordiazepoxide on passive avoidance behavior in rats. Psychopharmacology **80:** 88–92.
14. BECKWITH, B. E. & T. P. TINIUS. 1985. Vasopressin and vasotocin facilitate reversal of a brightness discrimination. Peptides **6:** 383–386.
15. BECKWITH, B. E., T. P. TINIUS & D. H. MILLER. 1987. Arginine vasopressin facilitates reversal and impairs retention of a brightness discrimination in albino rats. Psychobiology **15:** 329–335.
16. OLIVEROS, J. C., M. K. JANDELI, M. TRIMSIT-BERTHIER, R. REMY, A. BENZHEZAL, A. AUDIBERT & J. M. MOEGLEN. 1978. Vasopressin in amnesia. Lancet **1:** 42.
17. LEGROS, J. J., P. GILOT, X. SERON, J. CLAESSEUS, A. ADAMS, J. M. MOEGLEN, A. AUDIBERT & P. BERCHIER. 1978. Influence of vasopressin on learning and memory. Lancet **1:** 41–42.
18. BURISH, T. B., A. E. SLONIM, E. S. DAVIDSON, G. MORE & A. TOWER. 1982. Improved cognitive functioning in central diabetes insipidus following therapy with a vasopressin analogue. Clin. Neurophysiol. **3:** 13–15.
19. LACZI, F., Z. S. VALKRESZ, F. A. LASZLO, A. WAGNER, T. JARDANHAZY, A. SZASZ, J. SZILARD & G. TELEGDY. 1982. Effects of lysine-vasopressin and l-deamino-8-D-arginine-vasopressin on memory in healthy individuals and diabetes insipidus patients. Psychoneuroendocrinology **7:** 185–193.
20. JOLLES, J. 1987. Vasopressin and human behavior. *In* Vasopressin: Principles and Properties. D. M. Gash and G. J. Boer, Eds. 549–578. Plenum Press. New York, NY.
21. TINKLENBERG, J. R. & J. E. THORNTON. 1983. Neuropeptides in geriatric psychopharmacology. Psychopharmacol. Bull. **19:** 199–211.
22. WEINGARTNER, H., P. GOLD, J. C. BALLENGER, S. A. SMALLBERG, R. SUMMERS, D. R. RUBINOV, R. M. POST & F. K. GOODWIN. 1981. Effects of vasopressin on human memory functions. Science **211:** 601–603.
23. LACZI, F., J. M. VAN REE, A. WAGNER, Z. S. VALKUSZ, T. JARANHAZY, G. L. KOVACS, G. TELEGDY, J. SZILARD, F. A. LASZLO & D. DE WIED. 1983. Effects of desglycinamide-arginine-vasopressin (DGAVP) on memory processes in diabetes insipidus patients and in non-diabetic subjects. Acta Endocrinol. **102:** 205–212.
24. FEHM-WOLFSDORF, G., K. H. VOIGT & H. L. FEHM. 1983. Human memory and lysine vasopressin: A psychological study. *In* Neuropeptides and Psychosomatic Processes. E. Endroeczi, L. Angelucci, D. De Wied & U. Scapagnini, Eds. 81–88. Academiai Kiado. Budapest.
25. BECKWITH, B. E., T. PETROS, S. KANAAN-BECKWITH, D. I. COUK, R. HAUG & C. RYAN. 1982. Vasopressin analog (DDAVP) facilitates concept learning in human males. Peptides **3:** 627–630.
26. BECKWITH, B. E., D. I. COUK & T. S. TILL. 1983. Vasopressin analog influences the performance of males on a reaction time task. Peptides **4:** 707–709.
27. NEBES, R. D., C. R. REYNOLDS III & L. C. HORN. 1984. The effect of vasopressin on memory in the healthy elderly. Psychiatr. Res. **11:** 49–59.
28. BECKWITH, B. E., R. E. TILL & V. SCHNEIDER. 1984. Vasopressin analog (DDAVP) improves memory in human males. Peptides **5:** 819–822.
29. BECKWITH, B. E., T. V. PETROS, P. J. BERGLOFF & R. STAEBLER. 1987. Vasopressin analog (DDAVP) facilitates recall of narrative prose. Behav. Neurosci. **101:** 429–432.
30. BROADBENT, D. E. 1958. Perception & Communication. Pergamon Press. New York, NY.
31. ATKINSON, R. C. & R. M. SHIFFRIN. 1968. Human memory: a proposed system and its control processes. *In* The Psychology of Learning & Motivation: Advances in Research & Theory. K. W. Spence & J. T. Spence, Eds. 89–195. Academic Press. New York, NY.

32. WINGFIELD, A. & D. L. BYRNES. 1981. The Psychology of Human Memory. Academic Press. New York, NY.
33. GLANZER, M. & A. R. CUNITZ. 1966. Two storage mechanisms in free recall. J. Verb. Learn. Verb. Behav. **5:** 351–360.
34. CRAIK, F. I. M. & R. S. LOCKHART. 1972. Levels of processing: a framework for memory research. J. Verb. Learn. Verb. Behav. **11:** 671–684.
35. MILLAR, K., W. J. JEFFCOATE & C. P. WALDER. 1987. Vasopressin and memory: improvement in normal short-term recall and reduction of alcohol-induced amnesia. Psychol. Med. **17:** 335–341.
36. PIETROWSKY, R., G. FEHM-WOLFSDORF, J. BORN & H. L. FEHM. Effects of vasopressin on verbal memory. Peptides. In press.
37. FEHM-WOLFSDORF, G., J. BORN, K. H. VOIGT & H. L. FEHM. 1984. Human memory and neurohypopyhseal hormones: opposite effects of vasopressin and oxytocin. Psychoneuroendocrinology **9:** 285–292.
38. SNEL, J., J. TAYLOR & M. WEGMAN. 1987. Does DGAVP influence memory, attention and mood in healthy young men? Psychopharmacology **92:** 224–228.
39. COUK, D. I. 1986. Vasopressin Analogues and Their Effects upon Arousal, Attention and Memory. Unpublished Doctoral Dissertation. The University of North Dakota.
40. KNUTSON, K. K. 1987. Vasopressin's Effect on Sex Differences in Cognitive Functions: Verbal and Spatial Abilities and Verbal-Interference Tasks. Unpublished Doctoral Dissertation. The University of North Dakota.
41. STERNBERG, S. 1966. High speed scanning in human memory. Science **153:** 652–654.
42. BECKWITH, B. E. 1988. The melanotropins: learning and memory. *In* The Melanotropic Peptides: Biological Roles. M. E. Hadley, Ed. Vol. 2. 43–72. CRC Press. Boca Raton, FL.
43. SUTHERLAND, N. S. & N. J. MACKINTOSH. 1971. Mechanisms of Animal Discrimination Learning. Academic Press. New York, NY.
44. TILL, R. E. & B. E. BECKWITH. 1985. Sentence memory affected by vasopressin analog (DDAVP) in cross-over experiment. Peptides. **6:** 397–402.
45. HUNT, E. 1978. Mechanics of verbal ability. Psychol. Rev. **85:** 109–130.
46. CIRILO, R. K. & D. J. FOSS. 1980. Text structure and reading time for sentences. J. Verb. Learn. Verb. Behav. **19:** 96–109.
47. KINTSCH, W. & T. A. VAN DIJK. 1978. Toward a model of text comprehension and production. Psychol. Rev. **85:** 363–394.
48. COWAN, N. 1988. Evolving conceptions of memory storage, selective attention, and their mutual constraints within the human information-processing system. Psychol. Bull. **104:** 163–191.
49. SQUIRE, L. R. 1987. Memory and Brain. Oxford University Press. New York, NY.
50. POSNER, M. I., S. E. PETERSEN, P. T. FOX & M. E. RAICHLE. 1988. Localization of cognitive operations in the human brain. Science **240:** 1627–1631.

# Growth Hormone-Releasing Factor and Feeding

## Behavioral Evidence for Direct Central Actions[a]

FRANCO J. VACCARINO

*Departments of Psychology and Psychiatry*
*University of Toronto*
*100 St. George Street*
*Toronto, Ontario M5S 1A1, Canada*

## INTRODUCTION

In recent years growth hormone releasing factor (GRF) peptides were isolated and characterized from human pancreatic tumor[1,2] and from hypothalami of several species including rat and human.[3-6] GRF peptides have strong homology with peptides of the glucagon, vasoactive intestinal polypeptide and PHI-27 family. Many of the GRF neurons have their cell bodies in the arcuate nucleus of the hypothalamus with fibres extending into the median eminence.[7-9] GRF-containing terminals in the median eminence are located proximal to capillaries which drain into the hypophysial portal blood system. It is through this system that GRF stimulates the release of growth hormone from cells in the anterior pituitary gland.[10] The characterization and synthesis of GRF represents a very significant development and has opened important new avenues for the direct study of GRF function.

One important consequence of the characterization and synthesis of GRF was the immunohistochemical work characterizing the distribution of GRF-containing neurons in the brain. In addition to the presence of terminals in the median eminence, recent immunohistochemical results indicated that GRF terminals are present in intra- and extra-hypothalamic sites not directly associated with the median eminence and hypophysial portal blood system.[7,8] The latter results, together with electrophysiological findings demonstrating that iontophoretically applied GRF can influence neuronal membrane excitability,[11] suggested that, in addition to its hormonal actions, GRF may have neurotransmitter and/or neuromodulatory actions. This notion was consistent with the functional significance of other peptides found in the brain,[12] and raised the distinct possibility that GRF has direct central behavioral effects. The present paper reviews evidence derived from our laboratory and others which indicates that GRF has direct central actions on neural systems involved in feeding behavior.

### Effects of Intracerebroventricular GRF Treatment on Feeding

In addition to its potent endocrine action on the release of growth hormone, evidence from our laboratory has shown that centrally administered GRF has stimulatory effects on feeding behavior in rats. We have found that acute intracerebroventricular (icv) injections

[a]This work was supported by grants from the Natural Sciences and Engineering Research Council of Canada and the J.P. Bickell Foundation to FJV.

of rat hypothalamic (rh) or human pancreatic (hp) GRF, in doses ranging from 0.2 to 40.0 picomoles, enhances food intake by 25–75% in hungry and non-food-deprived rats.[13–16] Supporting the notion that the facilitatory effects of GRF on feeding are centrally mediated are the following findings. First, peripheral administration of rhGRF (in doses ranging from 0.2 to 200.0 picomoles) or growth hormone does not influence food intake.[13] Since GRF is unlikely to significantly penetrate the blood brain barrier, these results suggest that GRF-induced feeding is not due to peripheral effects of GRF or growth hormone. Second, icv administration of a structurally related but physiologically inactive peptide has no effect on food intake,[13,16] suggesting that the facilitatory effects of GRF on feeding are not due to nonspecific effects of peptide administration. Third, icv injections of rhGRF, in feeding-stimulatory doses, do not influence general locomotor activity,[13,15] indicating that the increased feeding observed following GRF treatment is not due to general behavioral activating properties of GRF. Together these findings suggest that central GRF plays a stimulatory role in feeding.

Consistent with our findings, Riviere and Bueno,[17] having investigated the effects of icv GRF treatment in sheep, found increases in food intake in doses comparable to those used in our studies. Thus, the facilitatory effects of GRF on feeding are not specific to rats.

While picomole doses of icv GRF stimulate feeding, icv treatment with higher doses has been found to suppress feeding. Imaki et al.[18] reported that icv hpGRF treatment depressed food intake at 1 and 4 nanomole doses. In an effort to replicate these findings and establish a wider dose-response curve, we tested the effects of icv GRF in doses ranging from 0.4 picomole to 4.0 nanomoles.[14] Consistent with our original report,[13] GRF was most effective at the 4.0 picomole dose. At the 40.0 and 100.0 picomole doses, however, GRF was less effective and at 1 and 4 nanomoles, GRF was either ineffective or had suppressive effects on feeding. Together with those of our original report, the above findings demonstrate that the facilitatory effects of icv GRF on feeding are most evident in doses ranging from 0.2 to 40.0 picomoles, while the suppressive effects are associated with nanomole doses (i.e., 4 nanomoles). Of special interest here is the fact that the feeding-suppressive doses of GRF are comparable to icv GRF doses which stimulate growth hormone release.[19] This raises the possibility that increased growth hormone release contributes to the suppressive effects of GRF on feeding observed with higher doses. However, findings showing that hypophysectomy does not abolish the feeding inhibitory effects of higher doses of GRF[18] suggest that the feeding inhibition is also centrally mediated.

## Photoperiod-Dependent Differences in the Feeding Effects of GRF

Rats display a circadian pattern of feeding in which the great majority of their feeding occurs during the dark phase of the light-dark photoperiod.[20] During the light phase they are relatively inactive with respect to feeding. Thus, it seems appropriate to view light and dark photoperiods as representing significantly different feeding states in the rat. The studies described thus far have examined the effects of GRF on feeding during the light photoperiod. Previous studies examining feeding effects of pharmacological agents suggest that photoperiod specificity is an important variable to consider in understanding mechanisms underlying feeding behavior.[21] The following findings indicate that GRF-induced feeding is photoperiod sensitive and raises important conceptual issues regarding the role of endogenous GRF in normal feeding.

In a recent study examining the effects of icv GRF as a function of photoperiod, we found that in contrast to its appetitive effects during the light photoperiod, GRF had either no effect or inhibitory effects at the highest dose (40.0 picomoles) when administered during the dark photoperiod.[15] Interestingly, a structurally related, but inactive peptide had no effect in the dark or the light photoperiod. The latter result suggests that both the facilitation and inhibition observed during the light and dark photoperiods, respectively, are GRF-specific.

These results indicate that GRF's central actions may be associated with two separate antagonistic feeding responses, one orexigenic (light photoperiod) and the other anorexic (dark photoperiod). To account for these light-dark differences in GRF's effects on feeding, we have hypothesized the existence of a natural circadian oscillation in endogenous levels of GRF. In the light photophase, endogeous GRF levels may be relatively low. Addition of low doses of exogenous GRF would result in raised internal GRF levels, activating a facilitatory response. During the dark, however, baseline levels of endogenous GRF may be naturally increased to the optimal facilitatory range. This would contribute to the high baseline consumption present during the dark photophase. Addition of even low doses of exogenous GRF during the dark would act to push internal levels beyond the optimal facilitatory range invoking an inhibitory response and resulting in relative suppression of feeding. This hypothesis is consistent with the fact that the doses required to produce inhibition of feeding are higher during the light photophase than during the dark photophase.[15] It should be noted that this proposed circadian oscillation in endogenous GRF levels need only be a functional one and thus may be expressed as either an actual increase in available GRF at the critical central site of action or an increased sensitivity to GRF. Interestingly, a similar photoperiod specificity has been observed with the feeding effects of central norepinephrine treatments and similar explanations have been proposed.[21]

### Central Site of Action for GRF-Induced Feeding

In an effort to localize the central site of action for GRF's facilitatory effects on feeding, we have recently tested the effects of microinjections of GRF into hypothalamic regions known to contain GRF terminals. Immunohistochemical studies examining the distribution of GRF neurons indicate that GRF neurons originating in the arcuate nucleus project to numerous hypothalamic sites other than the median eminence.[7,8] These include the anterior, periventricular, dorsomedial, paraventricular, suprachiasmatic and premammilary hypothalamic nuclei and the medial preoptic, lateral preoptic and lateral hypothalamic regions. These sites, then, represent possible sites of action for GRF's facilitatory effects on feeding.

Following a number of pilot studies examining the effects of direct intra-hypothalamic GRF microinjections on feeding it was determined that the suprachiasmatic nucleus (SCN)/medial preoptic area (MPOA) region of the hypothalamus (SCN/MPOA) was the most sensitive site for the feeding-enhancing effects of GRF. In order to examine the sensitivity of this region to GRF's appetitive effects, we tested rats for their feeding response to intra-SCN/MPOA GRF microinjections in doses of 0.0, 0.01, 0.1 and 1.0 picomole. It was found that GRF doses as low as 0.01 picomole were effective at increasing food intake, with the highest increase observed at the 1.0 picomole dose.[22] GRF microinjections into other regions which receive GRF projections, including the lateral preoptic area and anterior hypothalamus, were ineffective.

An important issue with the SCN/MPOA results deals with the fact that this hypothalamic region is located near the third ventricle. It is possible that GRF is spreading into the ventricular system and producing its stimulatory effects on feeding in some other brain region. Since the SCN and MPOA are by definition adjacent to the third ventricle this possibility is difficult to control. However, the following findings argue for a local SCN/MPOA effect of GRF. The fact that some of the extra-SCN/MPOA ineffective sites were located adjacent to the third ventricle but were nonetheless ineffective, argues against ventricular spread being a critical factor. Also, intra-SCN/MPOA microinjections of GRF doses as low as 0.01 picomole (20–40 × lower than icv doses previously found to be effective) significantly stimulated feeding. Finally, the increased feeding observed following microinjections of 0.1 and 1.0 picomole GRF into the SCN/MPOA is ca. 200–300% higher than that observed with similar doses injected icv. More recently, we have also found that GRF microinjections into the paraventricular nucleus, which receives GRF projections and is an important structure for feeding,[23] had no consistent effects on food intake.[22] Together, these observations support the notion that the SCN/MPOA is the important target region for GRF's appetitive effects. The extent to which the SCN and MPOA can be differentiated with respect to their roles in GRF-induced feeding is not yet known.

The fact that the SCN, a critical site for regulation of circadian rhythms,[24] is a sensitive site for GRF's effects on feeding is intriguing in light of the previously discussed photoperiod-sensitive differences in GRF efficacy. It is tempting to suggest that GRF may be involved in the internal mechanism regulating rats' circadian pattern of eating.

## Behavioral Characterization of GRF-Induced Feeding

In an effort to characterize the behavioral nature of GRF-induced feeding we have begun to analyze meal patterns in rats receiving central GRF microinjections.[25] Results indicate that at the moderately effective doses, GRF-induced increases in food intake are characterized by increases in the length of time spent eating a meal. Interestingly, at maximally effective doses, the meal duration does not differ from baseline, but the rate of feeding is increased. Thus, it appears that the behavioral profile of GRF-induced feeding differs as a function of dose effectiveness. These findings are consistent with those of Riviere and Bueno,[17] who reported that the GRF-induced increase in food intake in sheep is associated with increased rate of ingestion. Interestingly, we have also found that latency to meal onset is not affected by GRF treatment.[25] Taken together, these observations suggest that GRF-induced feeding is associated with meal maintenance or post-ingestional factors rather that meal initiation.

In order to investigate the extent to which the feeding effects of GRF reflect an increased motivational state, we have recently also examined GRF's ability to increase operant responding for food reward. Preliminary findings are consistent with the notion that central GRF increases the motivation to obtain food. Rats treated with icv GRF show increased bar pressing rates for food reward. Thus, it appears that GRF is not simply stimulating motor outputs required for feeding behavior, but is enhancing the animal's motivation to obtain food. This finding raises the possibility that central GRF plays a role in the maintenance of feeding during increased food-related drive states such as hunger. That GRF increases the reinforcing properties of food is also interesting in light of other findings from our laboratory[16] showing that blockade of endogenous opioids, which have been implicated in reward mechanisms, attenuates GRF-induced feeding.

## Central-Peripheral Integration of Function

The present paper has outlined findings which suggest that GRF can have direct neurotransmitter-like actions on central feeding systems. These findings, in combination with data demonstrating that systemic GRF or growth hormone do not influence feeding in the present paradigms, suggest that GRF-induced feeding is not directly associated with peripheral growth hormone actions. It is interesting to speculate that the effects of GRF on feeding are functionally associated with growth hormone actions. This possibility is based on the functional compatibility between the central effects of GRF (*i.e.*, to stimulate feeding) and the peripheral effects of GRF on growth hormone (*i.e.*, to promote growth and protein synthesis).[26] That is, GRF may underlie growth processes and metabolic changes in an integrated manner by promoting feeding through central actions and stimulating growth and protein synthesis by pituitary actions. More detailed investigations of the behavioral and physiological nature of GRF-induced feeding will be necessary in order to determine the extent to which the central feeding effects of GRF are functionally coupled with GRF's pituitary-mediated effects on growth and protein synthesis.

Indirect support for the notion that GRF may coordinate central behavioral and peripheral physiological functions comes from the finding that GRF terminals in the SCN/MPOA and the median eminence derive largely from a common anatomical source, the arcuate nucleus.[7,8] Thus, anatomical evidence is consistent with the possibility that an overlap exists between the central signals controlling GRF actions on feeding and central signals controlling GRF actions on growth hormone release. A recent report showing that the pulsatile release of growth hormone (measured in plasma) in rats is correlated with feeding behavior (independent of photoperiod) lends further support to this notion.[27] Future research will be necessary in order to further elucidate the relationship between the present behavioral effects and growth hormone function.

## ACKNOWLEDGMENTS

I thank Drs. W. Vale and J. Rivier for generously providing me with GRF and related peptides throughout the course of this work.

## REFERENCES

1. GUILLEMIN, R., P. BRAZEAU, P. BOHLEN, F. ESCH, N. LING & W. B. WEHRENBERG. 1982. Growth hormone-releasing factor from a human pancreatic tumor that caused acromegaly. Science **218**: 276–278.
2. RIVIER, J., J. SPEISS, M. THORNER & W. VALE. 1982. Characterization of a growth hormone-releasing factor from a human pancreatic islet tumor. Nature **300**: 276–278.
3. BOHLEN, P., F. ESCH, P. BRAZEAU, N. LING & R. GUILLEMIN. 1983. Isolation and characterization of the porcine hypothalamic growth hormone-releasing factor. Biochem. Biophys. Res. Comm. **116**: 726–734.
4. ESCH, F., P. BOHLEN, N. LING, P. BRAZEAU & R. GUILLEMIN. 1983. Isolation and characterization of the bovine hypothalamic growth hormone-releasing factor. Biochem. Biophys. Res. Comm. **117**: 772–779.
5. LING, N., F. ESCH, P. BOHLEN, P. BRAZEAU, W. B. WEHRENBERG & R. GUILLEMIN. 1984. Isolation, primary structure and synthesis of human hypothalamic somatocrinin: growth hormone releasing factor. Proc. Natl. Acad. Sci. USA **81**: 4302–4306.
6. SPIESS, J., J. RIVIER & W. VALE. 1983. Characterization of rat hypothalamic growth hormone-releasing factor. Nature **303**: 532–535.
7. SAWCHENKO, P. E., L. W. SWANSON, J. RIVIER & W. W. VALE. 1985. The distribution of growth-hormone-releasing factor (GRF) immunoreactivity in the central nervous system of the rat: an immunohistochemical study using antisera directed against rat hypothalamic GRF. J. Comp. Neurol. **327**: 100–115.
8. MERCHENTHALER, I., C. R. THOMAS & A. ARIMURA. 1984. Immunohistochemical localization of growth hormone-releasing factor (GHRF)-containing structures in the rat brain using anti-rat GHRF serum. Peptides **5**: 1071–1075.
9. BLOCH, B., P. BRAZEAU, N. LING, P. BOHLEN, F. ESCH, W. B. WEHRENBERG, R. BENOIT

      & F. BLOOM. 1983. Immunohistochemical detection of growth hormone-releasing factor in brain. Nature **263:** 251–257.

10. PLOTSKY, P. M. & W. VALE. 1985. Patterns of growth hormone-releasing factor and somatostatin secretion into the hypophysial-portal circulation of the rat. Science **230:** 461–463.

11. TWERY, M. J. & R. L. MOSS. 1985. Sensitivity of rat forebrain neurons to growth hormone-releasing hormone. Peptides **6:** 609–613.

12. SCHARRER, B. 1987. Neurosecretion: beginnings and new directions in neuropeptide research. Ann. Rev. Neurosci. **10:** 1–17.

13. VACCARINO, F. J., F. E. BLOOM, J. RIVIER, W. VALE & G. F. KOOB. 1985. Stimulation of food intake in rats by centrally administered hypothalamic growth hormone-releasing factor. Nature **314:** 167–168.

14. VACCARINO, F. J., D. FEIFEL, J. RIVIER, W. VALE & G. F. KOOB. 1988. Centrally administered growth hormone-releasing factor stimulates food intake in free-feeding rats. Peptides **9** (Suppl. 1): 35–38.

15. FEIFEL, D. & F. J. VACCARINO. 1989. Feeding effects of growth hormone-releasing factor in rats are photoperiod sensitive. Behav. Neurosci. **103:** 824–830.

16. VACCARINO, F. J. & K. BUCKENHAM. 1987. Naloxone blockade of growth hormone-releasing factor-induced feeding. Regul. Peptides **18:** 165–171.

17. RIVIERE, P. & L. BUENO. 1987. Influence of regimen and insulinemia on orexigenic effects of GRF (1-44) in sheep. Physiol. Behav. **39:** 347–350.

18. IMAKI, T., T. SHIBASAKI, M. HOTTA, A. MASUDA, H. DEMURE, K. SHIZUME & N. LING. 1985. The satiety effect of growth hormone releasing factor in rats. Brain Res. **340:** 186–188.

19. WEHRENBERG, W. B. & C. L. EHLERS. 1986. Effects of growth hormone-releasing factor in the brain. Science **232:** 1271–1273.

20. ROSENWASSER, A. M., Z. BOULOUS & M. TERMAN. 1979. Circadian organization of food intake and meal patterns in the rat. Physiol. Behav. **27:** 33–39.

21. MARGULES, D. L. 1972. Hypothalamic norepinephrine: circadian rhythms and the control of feeding behavior. Science **178:** 640–642.

22. VACCARINO, F. J. & M. HAYWARD. 1988. Microinjections of growth hormone-releasing factor into the medial preoptic area/suprachiasmatic nucleus region of the hypothalamus stimulate food intake in rats. Regul. Peptides **21:** 21–28.

23. LEIBOWITZ, S. F. 1977. Adrenergic stimulation of the paraventricular nucleus and its effects on ingestive behavior as a function of drug dose and time of injection in the light-dark cycle. Brain Res. Bull. **3:** 357–363.

24. RUSAK, B. & I. ZUCKER. 1979. Neural regulation of circadian rhythms. Physiol. Rev. **59:** 449–526.

25. DICKSON, P. R. & F. J. VACCARINO. 1987. Microinjections of rat hypothalamic growth hormone-releasing factor (rhGRF) into the suprachiasmatic nucleus/medial preoptic area (SCN/MPOA): behavioral characterization and effect on eating. Neuroscience **22** (Suppl.): 491.

26. WOODS, S. C., E. DECKE & J. R. VASSELLI. 1974. Metabolic hormones and regulation of body weight. Psychol. Rev. **81:** 26–43.

27. EVEN, P., J. DANGUIR, S. NICOLAIDIS, C. ROUGEOT & F. DRAY. 1987. Pulsatile secretion of growth hormone and insulin in relation to feeding in rats. Am. J. Physiol. **253:** R772–R778.

# Coexistence of Neuropeptides and "Classical" Neurotransmitters

## Functional Interactions between Galanin and Acetylcholine

JACQUELINE N. CRAWLEY

*Unit on Behavioral Neuropharmacology*
*Clinical Neuroscience Branch*
*Building 10, Room 4N212*
*National Institute of Mental Health*
*Bethesda, Maryland 20892*

### INTRODUCTION

Coexistence is the phenomenon in which two or more neurotransmitters are present within the same neuron.[1-4] The first demonstrations that neurons might have more than one transmitter came from studies of endocrine cells[5] and of invertebrate ganglia.[6] Immunocytochemical techniques have revealed at least thirty examples of coexistences in the mammalian central nervous system.[7] The majority of investigations of coexistences have identified neuropeptides within the same neurons as "classical" neurotransmitters, *e.g.*, cholecystokinin with dopamine in ventral tegmental neurons of the rat,[8] and galanin with acetylcholine in septohippocampal neurons of the rat.[9] Examples of two peptides coexisting with a "classical" neurotransmitter include substance P and thyrotropin releasing hormone with serotonin in medullary-spinal neurons of the rat,[10] and corticotropin releasing hormone and substance P with acetylcholine in dorsolateral tegmental neurons of the rat.[11] Examples of two neuropeptides coexisting in neurons without demonstrated "classical" neurotransmitters have been identified, *e.g.*, oxytocin and cholecystokinin in magnocellular hypothalamohypophyseal neurons of the rat,[12] and neuropeptide Y and somatostatin in cerebral cortex neurons of the human.[13] In addition, several examples of "classical" neurotransmitters coexisting within the same neuron have been identified, *e.g.*, serotonin and gamma amino butyric acid (GABA) in the dorsal raphe nucleus of the rat,[14] and acetylcholine (ACH) with GABA in the medial septum/diagonal band of the rat.[15] Some coexistences not normally seen have been revealed by disruption of normal afferent and efferent connections, or of altered hormonal environments, for example, the appearance of vasopressin in cholecystokinin-containing neurons of the paraventricular nucleus of the hypothalamus of the rat after adrenalectomy.[16]

Peptides may interact with "classical" transmitters at a variety of sites. Peptides could affect the synthesis, storage, release, or degradation of coexisting transmitters. Peptides could alter presynaptic reuptake sites, presynaptic receptors, postsynaptic receptors, or postsynaptic effectors. Many of these potential sites of interaction have been investigated, using both *in vitro* and *in vivo* methodologies. TABLE 1 gives selected examples of functional interactions which have been demonstrated between two or more transmitters localized within the same neuron.

### *Galanin-Acetylcholine Interactions*

The coexistence of galanin and acetylcholine in neurons of the basal forebrain illustrates many of the principles, problems, and promises of investigations of the functional

233

**TABLE 1.** Some Examples of Functional Interactions between Coexisting Neurotransmitters[a]

| Transmitters | Cell Body Location | Functional Interaction |
|---|---|---|
| **"CLASSICAL" TRANSMITTER + ONE PEPTIDE** | | |
| 1. Dopamine + cholecystokinin | Ventral tegmentum, rat[67] | Release |
| | |   CCK induces DA release from nucleus accumbens tissue slices[47,48] |
| | |   Intra-accumbens CCK induces DA release from anterior but not posterior nucleus accumbens using *in vivo* microdialysis[49] |
| | |   Intraventricular CCK induces, then inhibits, DA release from posterior nucleus accumbens using *in vivo* voltammetry[50] |
| | | Receptors |
| | |   Chronic CCK increases number of DA receptor binding sites[51] |
| | |   Chronic haloperidol, 6-OHDA lesions, or VTA lesions increase number of CCK binding sites[52] |
| | | Second messenger |
| | |   CCK potentiates DA-stimulated adenylate cyclase in posterior nucleus accumbens; CCK inhibits DA-stimulated adenylate cyclase in anterior nucleus accumbens[53] |
| | | Neurophysiology |
| | |   CCK potentiates DA-induced inhibition of VTA and SN neuronal firing[54–56] |
| | |   CCK inhibits DA-induced inhibition of neuronal firing in nucleus accumbens[57] |
| | | Behavior |
| | |   CCK potentiates DA-induced hyperlocomotion in posterior nucleus accumbens, CCK potentiates DA-induced hypolocomotion in ventral tegmentum[58–61] |
| | |   CCK potentiates intracranial self-stimulation and amphetamine-induced hyperlocomotion in posterior nucleus accumbens, CCK inhibits intracranial self-stimulation and amphetamine-induced hyperlocomotion in anterior nucleus accumbens[62–65] |
| | | Transplants |
| | |   Mesencephalic grafts into caudate nucleus demonstrate DA and CCK survival in cell bodies, but only DA in sprouting axons[66] |

*Continued*

**TABLE 1.** *Continued*

| Transmitters | Cell Body Location | Functional Interaction |
|---|---|---|
| 2. Dopamine + neurotensin | Ventral tegmentum, rat[8,68,95] | Release<br>  NT induces DA release from anterior and posterior nucleus accumbens using *in vivo* microdialysis[49]<br>  NT induces DA release from substantia nigra, using *in vivo* push-pull cannulae[69]<br>Receptors<br>  Lesions of mesencephalic DA neurons increase the number of NT binding sites in prefrontal cortex[70]<br>Behavior<br>  NT into VTA induces hyperactivity and hypothermia[71]<br>  NT into VTA decreases operant responding for food reward[72] |
| 3. Acetylcholine + vasoactive intestinal peptide | Cerebral cortex, rat[73]<br><br>Exocrine glands, rat[74] | Second messenger<br>  VIP potentiates ACH-induced phosphoinositide turnover[75]<br>Physiology<br>  Complementary actions of ACH and VIP on salivation[76]<br>Receptors<br>  VIP enhances ACH binding[77]<br>  Chronic atropine increases the number of binding sites for VIP and for ACH[78] |
| 4. Acetylcholine + substance p | Pons, rat[79] | Second Messenger<br>  Substance P inhibits carbachol-stimulated sodium flux in PC12 neuroblastoma cells[80] |
| 5. Acetylcholine + leutinizing hormone releasing hormone | Sympathetic ganglia, bullfrog[81] | Neurophysiology<br>  LHRH initiates late slow EPSPs in sympathetic neurons[81] |
| 6. Acetylcholine + calcitonin gene-related peptide | Spinal motor neurons, chick[82] | Release<br>  CGRP increases the number of ACH receptors in chick myotubes[82] |
| 7. Acetylcholine + galanin | Medial septum, rat[9] | Release<br>  GAL inhibits ACH release from ventral hippocampus, *in vitro* slices and *in vivo* microdialysis[24]<br>Second messenger<br>  GAL inhibits carbachol-stimulated phosphoinositide hydrolysis in ventral hippocampus[25]<br>Behavior<br>  GAL inhibits ACH-induced improvement of performance of a t-maze delayed alternation memory task in basal forebrain-lesioned rats[28] |

*Continued*

**TABLE 1.** *Continued*

| Transmitters | Cell Body Location | Functional Interaction |
|---|---|---|
| 8. Norepinephrine + galanin | Locus coeruleus, rat[18] | Second messenger<br>GAL inhibits NE-stimulated accumulation of cyclic AMP in cerebral cortex[83] |
| 9. Serotonin + galanin | Raphe, rat[18] | Receptors<br>GAL decreases $K_D$ for 5-HT$_{1A}$ receptors in ventral limbic cortex[84] |
| 10. Dopamine + galanin | Tuberoinfundibulum, rat[18] | Release<br>GAL inhibits DA release from median eminence[85] |
| **"CLASSICAL" TRANSMITTER + TWO PEPTIDES** | | |
| 11. Serotonin + substance P + thyrotropin releasing hormone | Bulbospinal, rat[86] | Physiology<br>TRH and 5-HT complementary on hindlimb muscle extension and flexion[87]<br>Neurophysiology<br>Complimentary excitation of spinal motoneurons by 5-HT, SP, TRH[88]<br>Behavior<br>Synergy between TRH and serotonin to inhibit male sexual behavior[89] |
| 12. Acetylcholine + substance P + corticotropin releasing factor | Dorsolateral tegmentum, rat[11] | Behavior<br>SP potentiates and CRF antagonizes carbachol-induced seizures in medial anterior cortex[11] |
| **TWO PEPTIDES** | | |
| 13. CGRP + substance P | Primary sensory neurons, rat[90] | Behavior<br>CGRP potentiates SP-induced biting and scratching[90]<br>Metabolic enzymes<br>CGRP inhibits SP metabolic degradation[91] |
| 14. Enkephalin + cholecystokinin | Periaqueductal gray, thalamus, rat[92] | Behavior<br>Intrathecal CCK blocks opiate analgesia[93] |
| 15. Oxytocin + cholecystokinin | Supraoptic nucleus and paraventricular nucleus of hypothalamus, rat[12] | Behavior<br>CCK and OXY both induce grooming[94] |

[a]Examples were chosen to illustrate the variety of approaches and techniques which are available to investigate the functional significance of coexistences, and to include cases of a peptide + a "classical" transmitter, two peptides + a "classical" transmitter, and two peptides without a "classical" transmitter. The listing herein makes no attempt to be comprehensive; a great many other excellent functional studies of coexistences are described in recent reviews.[1,7,30]

significance of peptide-transmitter coexistences. Galanin is a 29 amino acid peptide, discovered by Tatemoto and co-workers in 1983[17] from porcine small intestine. The amino acid sequence of porcine galanin 1–29 and of rat galanin 1–29 are shown in FIGURE 1. Immunocytochemical mapping of galanin-like immunoreactivity in rat brain revealed a wide distribution of galanin-containing neurons and receptors.[18-20] Coexistences of galanin with other neurotransmitters have been identified, including galanin with norepinephrine in the locus coeruleus, galanin with serotonin in the dorsal raphe, galanin with GABA in the arcuate nucleus, galanin with vasopressin in the paraventricular nucleus of the hypothalamus,[21] galanin with cholecystokinin in spinothalamic neurons,[22] and galanin with acetylcholine in basal forebrain neurons projecting to the hippocampus.[9]

Detailed mapping studies of galanin-like immunoreactivity and choline acetyltransferase-like immunoreactivity in adjacent sections of rat forebrain demonstrated that the coexistence of GAL and ACH was in neurons of the medial septum and diagonal band, but not in the nucleus basalis magnocellularis or striatum in the rat.[9] Knife cut lesions were performed in an elegant series of experiments by Melander and co-workers[23] to determine the origins of galanin-containing terminals in the hippocampus. In the rat, the GAL-ACH-containing neurons of the medial septum and diagonal band appeared to terminate predominantly in the ventral, but also to a lesser extent in the dorsal, hippocampus.[9,23] Galanin-containing terminals of the hippocampus also appeared to originate in noradrenergic neurons of the locus coeruleus.[23]

The first functional studies of GAL-ACH interactions were biochemical analyses of the release of acetylcholine from the rat hippocampus. Using tissue slices from either the dorsal or ventral hippocampus, 100 nM and 1 μM concentrations of galanin significantly

**PORCINE GALANIN 1-29**

GLY-TRP-THR-LEU-ASN-SER-ALA-GLY-TYR-LEU-
LEU-GLY-PRO-HIS-ALA-ILE-ASP-ASN-HIS-ARG-
SER-PHE-*HIS*-ASP-LYS-*TYR*-GLY-LEU-*ALA*-NH2

**RAT GALANIN 1-29**

GLY-TRP-THR-LEU-ASN-SER-ALA-GLY-TYR-LEU-
LEU-GLY-PRO-HIS-ALA-ILE-ASP-ASN-HIS-ARG-
SER-PHE-*SER*-ASP-LYS-*HIS*-GLY-LEU-*THR*-NH2

**FIGURE 1.** Amino acid sequence of galanin 1–29. The porcine galanin sequence was obtained from amino acid sequencing of purified galanin from porcine intestine.[17] The rat galanin sequence was deduced from the cDNA sequence encoding rat galanin, obtained from a cDNA library prepared from rat hypothalamic tissue.[44] The two sequences differ in three amino acids, in sequence positions 23, 26, and 29.

inhibited the potassium-stimulated release of ³H-ACH.[24] Using a microdialysis procedure *in vivo,* rats pretreated with the cholinesterase-inhibitor, physostigmine, were implanted with a microdialysis probe in the dorsal or ventral hippocampus. Galanin, 10μg/5μl intraventricularly, significantly inhibited scopolamine-induced release of acetylcholine from the ventral, but not from the dorsal, hippocampus.[24] These data suggest that galanin acts to modulate the presynaptic release of acetylcholine, at a site specific to the terminal region of the coexistence.

Further functional studies of this GAL-ACH coexistence employed second messenger assays to investigate potential postsynaptic interactions. Galanin, 1 μM, significantly inhibited carbachol-stimulated accumulation of ³H-inositol phosphate, the effector system for one subtype of muscarinic receptor in the brain.[25] These data suggest that galanin can partially block cholinergic activity, both presynaptically by inhibiting release, and postsynaptically by inhibiting the events triggered by cholinergic receptor occupation.

Behavioral studies of the GAL-ACH coexistence have focused on the well documented involvement of the septohippocampal pathway of the rat in the mediation of spatial memory tasks.[26] Rats with ibotenic acid lesions of the nucleus basalis magnocellularis medial septal area (NBM-MSA) show a reduction in cholinergic markers similar to that seen following the degeneration of cholinergic neurons in Alzheimer's disease. This lesion impairs performance on spatial tasks such as delayed alternation in a t-maze or

radial arm maze, or platform location in a Morris water maze.[26,27] In our study of
centrally administered acetylcholine and galanin, acetylcholine was found to partially
reverse the performance deficit of NBM-MSA-lesioned rats on delayed alternation in the
t-maze, at doses of 7.5 and 10 μg ACH intraventricularly, or 1 μg ACH into the ventral
hippocampus.[28] Galanin, 100 ng–1 μg, had no effect alone on performance in delayed
alternation, neither improving performance in lesioned rats nor impairing performance in
sham control rats. However, when galanin was administered in combination with acetylcholine, galanin significantly inhibited the ability of acetylcholine to improve perfor-

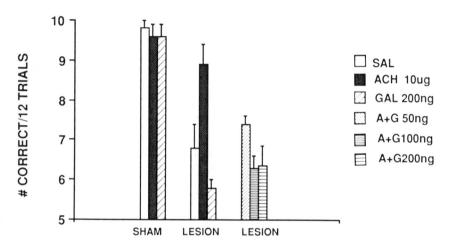

**FIGURE 2.** Galanin inhibits acetylcholine-induced improvement in performance on a t-maze delayed alternation task in ventral forebrain-lesioned rats.[28] Male Sprague-Dawley rats were lesioned
with ibotenic acid at five stereotaxic coordinates within the nucleus basalis magnocellularis-medial
septal area, or given sham surgical treatment. This lesion produces approximately a 30% decrease in
choline acetyltransferase activity in both cerebral cortex and hippocampus, and approximately 30%
decrease in galanin-like immunoreactivity in hippocampus.[45] Behavioral testing in a t-maze task, in
which the location of a food reward was alternated between the right and left arms on twelve
consecutive trials, with a 60-second delay between consecutive trials, demonstrated that lesioned rats
performed at chance levels (approximately 6 correct out of twelve consecutive trials) while sham
control rats reached the criterion of at least 9 correct out of twelve consecutive trials. Acetylcholine
(ACH or A), 10 μg/5 μl intraventricularly, significantly improved performance in lesioned rats,
while having no effect in sham control rats. Higher doses of ACH induced seizures, particularly in
lesioned rats.[46] Galanin (GAL or G), 100 and 200 ng, administered intraventricularly in combination
with ACH, significantly inhibited the improvement in performance in lesioned rats as compared to
ACH alone. GAL 200 ng had no effect alone in either sham or lesioned rats.

mance in the lesioned rats (FIG. 2), at doses of 100–500 ng intraventricularly, and 200 ng
into the ventral hippocampus.[28] These data suggest that galanin acts as an inhibitory
modulator of the behavioral actions of acetylcholine in the septohippocampal pathway,
particularly in rats with partial degeneration of cholinergic pathways from the ventral
forebrain.

A second behavioral study employed normal rats treated with galanin intraventricularly, either before training on a Morris swim maze task, or before testing for retrieval of
the Morris swim maze task.[29] Galanin significantly impaired acquisition, but not re-

trieval, of the task. This study employed substantially higher doses of galanin, 1–5 μg, than the study cited above, and a different type of task. Taken together, these two behavioral studies indicate that galanin may affect both learning and memory, and that the inhibitory effect of galanin on learning and memory may be relevant to normal, as well as to lesioned rats, depending on dose of galanin and type of task.

*Clinical Implications*

Biochemical and behavioral studies cited above suggest that galanin acts as an inhibitory modulator of cholinergic functions. Hökfelt and co-workers have proposed an intriguing hypothesis on the possible role of galanin in Alzheimer's dementia.[7] As many cholinergic neurons of the ventral forebrain degenerate during the progression of the disease, the surviving neurons may attempt to "compensate" by increasing their firing rates. Since many peptides are preferentially released at higher stimulation frequencies,[30] this compensation may result in the release of unusually high concentrations of galanin from these remaining cholinergic neurons. Released galanin may then inhibit the presynaptic release of acetylcholine from the remaining neurons, and also inhibit the postsynaptic events initiated by acetylcholine. This further inhibition of cholinergic function, in a system already substantially depleted of cholinergic transmission, could be especially deleterious in eliminating cholinergic input to brain pathways relevant to memory. Thus, galanin may act to exacerbate dementia.

In the human and monkey brain, galanin-like immunoreactivity is seen coexisting with choline acetyltransferase-like immunoreactivity in both medial septal neurons and nucleus basal of Meynert neurons.[31–35] Thus, in the primate, the coexistence of GAL and ACH may include all of the forebrain cholinergic pathways, *i.e.*, the cortical as well as the hippocampal cholinergic innervation. The hypothesis elaborated above would therefore be even more relevant to primates than to rats.

Human clinical studies with galanin have reported no differences in galanin concentrations in cerebral cortex or hippocampus in victims of Alzheimer's disease, whereas cholinergic markers were significantly reduced, as compared to age-matched controls.[36] Similarly, galanin concentrations in cerebrospinal fluid from Alzheimer's patients were not significantly different from age-matched controls.[37] These findings have many possible interpretations. 1) Concentrations of galanin in basal forebrain cholinergic neurons may be so low that their contribution to galanin levels in cortex and hippocampus is negligible, as compared to the contribution from other galanin-containing neurons such as the locus coeruleus,[21] such that loss of galanin from basal forebrain neurons would not be detectable as a significant decrease in cortex and hippocampus; 2) Galanin may degenerate so rapidly in postmortem tissue that measured levels do not accurately reflect physiologically induced changes in local concentrations of peptide; 3) The galanin-containing neurons of the ventral forebrain may be the cholinergic neurons that survive, *i.e.*, there may be a trophic function of galanin which promotes survival of the subpopulation of cholinergic neurons that contains the peptide.

Two immunohistochemical studies of galanin in human brain have been published to date, in which a short postmortem time of five hours was possible.[32,33] In samples from victims of Alzheimer's and Parkinson's disease dementias, as compared to normal controls, dendrites of galanin-containing interneurons of the basal forebrain region were found to hyperinnervate the cholinergic neurons of the nucleus basalis of Meynert region.[32] This finding suggests that other, local, non-coexisting sources of galanin may contribute to the regulation of cholinergic function in the ventral forebrain.

The primary cause of Alzheimer's disease appears to be the deposition of amyloid proteins, creating plaques and tangles that may physically block or destroy neurons.[38]

While many neurotransmitters and neuropeptides have been shown to decline during the progression of Alzheimer's disease[39] such that an effective treatment may require replacement therapy of several, carefully balanced, neurotransmitters, the loss of cholinergic neurons in the ventral forebrain is the most consistent neurochemical characteristic of advanced Alzheimer's disease.[39] Clinical trials with cholinergic drugs for alleviation of the symptoms of Alzheimer's dementia have been relatively disappointing.[40] There are many reasons that cholinergic agonists or cholinesterase inhibitors may fail to alleviate the cognitive dysfunctions associated with Alzheimer's disease. Cholinergic drug therapies presently available are nonspecific with respect to cholinergic receptor subtype. Such drugs are limited in the dose which can be administered, since every cholinergic receptor throughout the body would be activated, severely affecting respiration, heart rate, gastrointestinal function, etc. Alternatively, it is interesting to speculate that galanin may be responsible for the failure of cholinergic drugs to significantly improve memory in Alzheimer's disease. Endogenous galanin may be acting as an inhibitory "brake" on cholinergic presynaptic and postsynaptic activity. Antagonists of galanin could act to "take off the brakes," allowing the cholinergic neurons which remain in Alzheimer's patients to function more effectively. Similarly, a galanin antagonist which removes the inhibitory actions of galanin might allow cholinergic drugs to act more effectively to promote cholinergic transmission in the septohippocampal and nucleus basalis-cortical pathways relevant to memory.

The experiments described above demonstrate interactions between exogenously applied galanin and acetylcholine on cholinergic functions. Galanin inhibits the release of acetylcholine, inhibits cholinergic stimulation of a postsynaptic receptor effector system, and inhibits acetylcholine on a memory task in lesioned rats. Taken together, these several lines of evidence suggest that galanin is an inhibitory modulator of cholinergic function. The anatomical site of interaction may be restricted to the region containing the majority of the terminals of this coexistence, *i.e.*, the ventral rather than the dorsal hippocampus. More extensive studies are needed using these several techniques to further test this hypothesis, including neurophysiological studies of galanin-acetylcholine interactions in the hippocampus. However, it is important to note that actions of exogenously applied galanin do not necessarily reflect physiological actions of endogenous galanin. Specific antagonists of the hippocampal galanin receptor are required to address the question of the actions of endogenous galanin. Several laboratories are engaged in the development of galanin antagonists. Studies of fragments of the parent galanin 1–29 amino acid sequence suggest that as few as 9 C-terminal amino acids or 16 N-terminal amino acids[96] may contain the biological activity for galanin.[41–43] It therefore may be possible to target a small number of amino acids for substitutions which could modify the biological activity from agonist to antagonist. A high affinity, specific antagonist of the hippocampal galanin binding site would be critical to test the hypotheses that 1) endogenous galanin inhibits cholinergic function; 2) endogenous galanin has inhibitory effects on memory processes; and 3) elimination of endogenous galanin might prove beneficial in treating the cognitive disorders associated with dementias in humans.

## REFERENCES

1.  HÖKFELT, T., K. FUXE & B. PERNOW, Eds. 1986. Coexistence of Neuronal Messengers: A New Principle in Chemical Transmission. Elsevier. Amsterdam.
2.  CUELLO, A. C., Eds. 1982. Co-transmission. MacMillan. London.
3.  OSBORNE, N. N., Ed. 1983. Dale's Principle and Communication Between Neurones. Pergamon Press. New York, NY.
4.  CHAN-PALAY, V. & S. L. PALAY, Eds. 1984. Coexistence of Neuroactive Substances in Neurons. John Wiley & Sons. New York, NY.

5. PEARSE, A. G. E. 1969. The cytochemistry and ultrastructure of polypeptide hormone producing cells of APUD series and the embryologic, physiologic and pathologic implications of the concept. J. Histochem. Cytochem. **17**: 303–313.
6. BROWNSTEIN, M. J., J. M. SAAVEDRA, J. AXELROD & D. O. CARPENTER. 1974. Coexistence of several putative neurotransmitters in single identified neurons of Aplysia. Proc. Natl. Acad. Sci. USA **71**: 4662–4665.
7. HÖKFELT, T., D. MILLHORN, K. SEROOGY, Y. TSURUO, S. CECCATELLI, B. LINDH, B. MEISTER, T. MELANDER, M. SCHALLING, T. BARTFAI & L. TERENIUS. 1987. Coexistence of peptides with classical neurotransmitters. Experientia **43**: 768–780.
8. SEROOGY, K., S. CECCATELLI, M. SCHALLING, T. HÖKFELT, P. FREY, J. WALSH, G. DOCKRAY, J. BROWN, A. BUCHAN & M. GOLDSTEIN. 1988. A subpopulation of dopaminergic neurons in rat ventral mesencephalon contains both neurotensin and cholecystokinin. Brain Res. **455**: 88–98.
9. MELANDER, T., W. A. STAINES, T. HÖKFELT, A. RÖKAEUS, F. ECKENSTEIN, P. M. SALVATERRA & B. H. WAINER. 1985. Galanin-like immunoreactivity in cholinergic neurons of the septum-basal forebrain complex projecting to the hippocampus of the rat. Brain Res. **360**: 130–138.
10. JOHANSSON, O., T. HÖKFELT, B. PERNOW, S. L. JEFFCOATE, N. WHITE, H. W. M. STEINBUSCH, A. A. J. VERHOFSTADT, P. C. EMSON & E. SPINDEL. 1981. Immunohistochemical evidence for three putative transmitters in one neuron: coexistence of 5-hydroxytryptamine, substance P-, and thyrotropin releasing hormone-like immunoreactivity in medullary neurons projecting to the spinal cord. Neuroscience **6**: 1857–1881.
11. CRAWLEY, J. N., J. A. OLSCHOWKA, D. I. DIZ & D. M. JACOBOWITZ. 1985. Behavioral investigation of the coexistence of substance P, corticotropin releasing factor, and acetylcholinesterase in lateral dorsal tegmental neurons projecting to the medial frontal cortex of the rat. Peptides **6**: 891–901.
12. VANDERHAEGHEN, J. J., F. LOTSTRA, F. VANDESANDE & K. DIERICKX. 1981. Coexistence of cholecystokinin and oxytocin-neurophysin in some magnocellular hypothalamohypophyseal neurons. Cell Tissue Res. **221**: 227–231.
13. CHRONWALL, B. M., T. N. CHASE & T. L. O'DONOHUE. 1984. Coexistence of neuropeptide Y and somatostatin in rat and human cortical and rat hypothalamic neurons. Neurosci. Lett. **52**: 213–217.
14. BELIN, M. F., D. NANOPOULOS, M. DIDIER, M. AGUERA, H. STEINBUSCH, A. VERHOFSTAD, M. MAITRE & J. F. PUJOL. 1983. Immunohistochemical evidence for the presence of gammaamino butyric acid and serotonin in one nerve cell. A study on the raphe nuclei of the rat using antibodies to glutamate decarboxylase and serotonin. Brain Res. **275**: 329–339.
15. BRASHEAR, H. R., L. ZABORSZKY & L. HEIMER. 1986. Distribution of GABAergic and cholinergic neurons in the rat diagonal band. Neuroscience **17**: 439–445.
16. KISS, J. Z., E. MEZEY & L. SKIRBOLL. 1984. Corticotropin-releasing factor immunoreactive neurons of the paraventricular nucleus become vasopressin positive after adrenalectomy. Proc. Natl. Acad. Sci. USA **81**: 1854–1858.
17. TATEMOTO, K., A. RÖKAEUS, H. JORNVALL, T. J. MACDONALD & V. MUTT. 1983. Galanin—a novel biologically active peptide from porcine intestine. FEBS Lett. **164**: 124–128.
18. MELANDER, T., T. HÖKFELT & A. RÖKAEUS. 1986. Distribution of galanin-like immunoreactivity in the rat central nervous system. J. Comp. Neurol. **248**: 475–517.
19. SKOFITSCH, G. & D. M. JACOBOWITZ. 1986. Quantitative distribution of galanin-like immunoreactivity in the rat central nervous system. Peptides **7**: 609–613.
20. SKOFITSCH, G., M. A. SILLS & D. M. JACOBOWITZ. 1986. Autoradiographic distribution of [125]I-galanin binding sites in the rat central nervous system. Peptides **7**: 1029–1042.
21. MELANDER, T., T. HÖKFELT, A. RÖKAEUS, A. C. CUELLO, W. H. OERTEL, A. VERHOFSTAD & M. GOLDSTEIN. 1985. Coexistence of galanin-like immunoreactivity with catecholamines, 5-hydroxytryptamine, GABA, and neuropeptides in the rat CNS. J. Neurosci. **6**: 3640–3654.
22. JU, G., T. MELANDER, S. CECCATELLI, T. HÖKFELT & P. FREY. 1987. Immunohistochemical evidence for a spinothalamic pathway cocontaining cholecystokinin- and galanin-like immunoreactivities. Neuroscience **20**: 439–456.
23. MELANDER, T., W. A. STAINES & A. RÖKAEUS. 1986. Galanin-like immunoreactivity in

hippocampal afferents in the rat, with special reference for cholinergic and noradrenergic inputs. Neuroscience **19**: 223–240.

24. FISONE, G., C. F. WU, S. CONSOLO, O. NORDSTROM, N. BRYNNE, T. BARTFAI, T. MELANDER & T. HÖKFELT. 1987. Galanin inhibits acetylcholine release in the ventral hippocampus of the rat: histochemical, autoradiographic, in vivo, and in vitro studies. Proc. Natl. Acad. Sci. USA **84**: 7339–7343.

25. PALAZZI, E., G. FISONE, T. HÖKFELT, T. BARTFAI & S. CONSOLO. 1988. Galanin inhibits the muscarinic stimulation of phosphoinositide turnover in rat ventral hippocampus. Eur. J. Pharmacol. **148**: 479–480.

26. WENK, G. L. & D. S. OLTON. 1987. Animal Models of Dementia: A Synaptic Neurochemical Perspective. J. T. Coyle, Ed. *In* Neurol. Neurobiol. V. Chan-Palay & S. L. Palay, Eds. Vol. **33**: 81–101. Alan R. Liss, Inc. New York, NY.

27. GOWER, A. J. 1986. Lesioning of the nucleus basalis in the rat as a model of Alzheimer's disease. Trends Pharmacol. Sci. **7**: 432–435.

28. MASTROPAOLO, J., N. S. NADI, N. L. OSTROWSKI & J. N. CRAWLEY. 1988. Galanin antagonizes acetylcholine on a memory task in basal forebrain-lesioned rats. Proc. Natl. Acad. Sci. USA **85**: 9841–9845.

29. SUNDSTROM, E., T. ARCHER, T. MELANDER & T. HÖKFELT. 1988. Galanin impairs acquisition but not retrieval of spatial memory in rats studied in the Morris swim maze. Neurosci. Lett. **88**: 331–335.

30. BARTFAI, T., K. IVERFELDT & G. FISONE. 1988. Regulation of the release of coexisting neurotransmitters. Ann. Rev. Pharmacol. Toxicol. **28**: 285–310.

31. MELANDER, T. & W. A. STAINES. 1986. A galanin-like peptide coexists in putative cholinergic somata of the septum-basal forebrain complex and in acetylcholinesterase-containing fibers and varicosities within the hippocampus of the owl monkey (Aotus trivigatus). Neurosci. Lett. **68**: 17–22.

32. CHAN-PALAY, V. 1988. Galanin hyperinnervates surviving neurons of the human basal nucleus of Meynert in dementias of Alzheimer's and Parkinson's disease: a hypothesis for the role of galanin in accentuating cholinergic dysfunction in dementia. J. Comp. Neurol. **273**: 543–557.

33. CHAN-PALAY, V. 1988. Neurons with galanin innervate cholinergic cells in the human basal forebrain and galanin and acetylcholine coexist. Brain Res. Bull. **21**: 465–472.

34. KOWALL, N. W. & M. F. BEAL. 1989. Galanin-like immunoreactivity is present in human substantia innominata and in senile plaques in Alzheimer's disease. Neurosci. Lett. In press.

35. WALKER, L. C., V. E. KOLIATSOS, C. A. KITT, R. T. RICHARDSON, A. RÖKAEUS & D. L. PRICE. 1989. Peptidergic neurons in the basal forebrain magnocellular complex of the rhesus monkey. J. Comp. Neurol. **280**: 272–282.

36. BEAL, M. F., R. A. CLEVENS, G. K. CHATTHA, U. M. McGARVEY, M. F. MAZUREK & S. M. GABRIEL. 1988. Galanin-like immunoreactivity is unchanged in Alzheimer's disease and Parkinson's disease dementia cerebral cortex. J. Neurochem. **51**: 1935–1941.

37. BERRETTINI, W. H., W. H. KAYE, T. SUNDERLAND, C. MAY, H. E. GWIRTSMAN, A. MELLOW & A. ALBRIGHT. 1988. Galanin immunoreactivity in human CSF: studies in eating disorders and Alzheimer's disease. Neuropsychobiology **19**: 64–68.

38. COYLE, J. T., D. L. PRICE & M. R. DeLONG. 1983. Alzheimer's disease: a disorder of cortical cholinergic innervation. Science **219**: 1184–1190.

39. HARDY, J., R. ADOLFFSON, I. ALAFUZOFF, G. BUCHT, J. MARCUSSON, P. NYBERG, E. PERDAHL, P. WEBSTER & B. WINBLAD. 1985. Transmitter deficits in Alzheimer's disease. Neurochem. Int. **7**: 545–563.

40. DAVIS, K. L., R. C. MOHS, B. M. DAVIS, M. I. LEVY, T. B. HORVATH, G. S. ROSENBERG, A. ROSS, A. ROTHPEARL & W. ROSEN. 1982. Cholinergic treatment in Alzheimer's disease: implications for future research. *In* Alzheimer's Disease: A Report of Progress. S. Corkin *et al*, Eds. 483–494. Raven Press. New York, NY.

41. FISONE, G., U. LANGEL, M. CARLQUIST, T. BERGMAN, S. CONSOLO, T. HÖKFELT, A. UNDEN, S. ANDELL & T. BARTFAI. 1989. Galanin receptor and its ligands in the rat hippocampus. Eur. J. Biochem. **181**: 269–276.

42. GABRIEL, S. M., U. M. MacGARVEY, J. I. KOENIG, K. J. SWARTZ, J. B. MARTIN & M. F.

BEAL. 1988. Characterization of galanin-like immunoreactivity in the rat brain: effects of neonatal glutamate treatment. Neurosci. Lett. **87:** 114–126.
43. FOX, J. E. T., B. BROOKS, T. J. MCDONALD, W. BARNETT, F. KOSTOLANSKA, C. YANAIHARA, N. YANAIHARA & A. RÖKAEUS. 1988. Actions of galanin fragments on rat, guinea-pig, and canine intestinal motility. Peptides **9:** 1183–1189.
44. KAPLAN, L. M., E. R. SPINDEL, K. J. ISSELBACHER & W. W. CHIN. 1988. Tissue-specific expression of the rat galanin gene. Proc. Natl. Acad. Sci. USA **85:** 1065–1069.
45. WENK, G. L. & A. RÖKAEUS. 1988. Basal forebrain lesions differentially alter galanin levels and acetylcholinergic receptors in hippocampus and neocortex. Brain Res. **460:** 17–21.
46. MASTROPAOLO, J. & J. N. CRAWLEY. 1988. Behavioral evidence for increased cholinergic receptor sensitivity after nucleus basalis magnocellularis lesions in the rat. Eur. J. Pharmacol. **153:** 301–304.
47. VICKROY, T. W. & B. R. BIANCHI. 1989. Pharmacological and mechanistic studies of cholecystokinin-facilitated [3H]dopamine efflux from rat nucleus accumbens. Neuropeptides **13:** 43–50.
48. VICKROY, T. W., B. R. BIANCHI, J. F. KERWIN, H. KOPECKA & A. M. Nadzan. 1988. Evidence that type A CCK receptors facilitate dopamine efflux in rat brain. Eur. J. Pharmacol. **152:** 371–372.
49. RUGGERI, M., U. UNGERSTEDT, L. F. AGNATI, V. MUTT, A. HARFSTRAND & K. FUXE. 1987. Effects of cholecystokinin peptides and neurotensin on dopamine release and metabolism in the rostral and caudal part of the nucleus accumbens using intracerebral dialysis in the anesthetized rat. Neurochem. Int. **10:** 509–520.
50. LANE, R. F., C. D. BLAHA & A. G. PHILLIPS. 1986. In vivo electrochemical analysis of cholecystokinin-induced inhibition of dopamine release in the nucleus accumbens. Brain Res. **397:** 200–204.
51. DUMBRILLE-ROSS, A. & P. SEEMAN. 1984. Dopamine receptor elevation by cholecystokinin. Peptides **5:** 1207–1212.
52. CHANG, R. S. L., V. J. LOTTI, G. E. MARTIN & T. B. CHEN. 1983. Increase in brain 125-I-cholecystokinin (CCK) receptor binding following chronic haloperidol treatment, intracisternal 6-hydroxydopamine or ventral tegmental lesions. Life Sci. **32:** 871–878.
53. STUDLER, J. M., M. REIBAUD, D. HERVE, G. BLANC, J. GLOWINSKI & J. P. TASSIN. 1986. Opposite effects of sulfated cholecystokinin on DA-sensitive adenylate cyclase in two areas of the rat nucleus accumbens. Eur. J. Pharmacol. **126:** 125–128.
54. HOMMER, D. W., G. STONER, J. N. CRAWLEY, S. M. PAUL & L. R. SKIRBOLL. 1986. Cholecystokinin-dopamine coexistence: electrophysiological actions corresponding to cholecystokinin receptor subtype. J. Neurosci. **6:** 3039–3043.
55. FREEMAN, A. S. & B. S. BUNNEY. 1987. Activity of A9 and A10 dopaminergic neurons in unrestrained rats: further characterization and effects of apomorphine and cholecystokinin. Brain Res. **405:** 46–55.
56. BRODIE, M. S. & T. V. DUNWIDDIE. 1987. Cholecystokinin potentiates dopamine inhibition of mesencephalic dopamine neurons in vitro. Brain Res. **425:** 106–113.
57. WHITE, F. J. & R. Y. WANG. 1984. Interactions of cholecystokinin octapeptide and dopamine on nucleus accumbens neurons. Brain Res. **300:** 161–166.
58. CRAWLEY, J. N., D. W. HOMMER & L. R. SKIRBOLL. 1985. Topographical analysis of nucleus accumbens sites at which cholecystokinin potentiates dopamine-induced hyperlocomotion in the rat. Brain Res. **335:** 337–341.
59. CRAWLEY, J. N., J. A. STIVERS, L. K. BLUMSTEIN & S. M. PAUL. 1985. Cholecystokinin potentiates dopamine-mediated behaviors: evidence for modulation specific to a site of coexistence. J. Neurosci. **5:** 1972–1983.
60. CRAWLEY, J. N. 1988. Attenuation of dark-induced hyperlocomotion by a cholecystokinin antagonist in the nucleus accumbens. Brain Res. **473:** 398–400.
61. CRAWLEY, J. N. 1989. Microinjection of cholecystokinin into the rat ventral tegmental area potentiates dopamine-induced hypolocomotion. Synapse **3:** 346–355.
62. WEISS, F., D. J. TANZER & A. ETTENBERG. 1988. Opposite actions of CCK-8 on amphetamine-induced hyperlocomotion and stereotypy following intracerebroventricular and intra-accumbens injections in rats. Pharmacol. Biochem. Behav. **30:** 309–317.
63. VACCARINO, F. J. & J. RANKIN. 1989. Nucleus accumbens CCK can either attenuate or

potentiate amphetamine-induced locomotor activity: evidence for rostral-caudal differences in accumbens CCK function. Behav. Neurosci. **103:** 4: 831–836.

64. DE WITTE, P., C. HIEBREDER, B. ROQUES & J. J. VANDERHAEGHEN. 1987. Opposite effects of cholecystokinin octapeptide (CCK-8) and tetrapeptide (CCK-4) after injection into the caudal part of the nucleus accumbens or into its rostral part and the cerebral ventricles. Neurochem. Int. **10:** 473–479.

65. VACCARINO, F. J. & A. L. VACCARINO. 1989. Antagonism of cholecystokinin function in the rostral and caudal nucleus accumbens: differential effects on brain stimulation and reward. Neurosci. Lett. **97:** 151–156.

66. SCHULTZBERG, M., S. B. DUNNETT, A. BJORKLUND, U. STENEVI, T. HÖKFELT, G. J. DOCKRAY & M. GOLDSTEIN. 1984. Dopamine and cholecystokinin immunoreactive neurons in mesencephalic grafts reinnervating the neostriatum: evidence for selective growth regulation. Neuroscience **12:** 17–32.

67. HÖKFELT, T., L. SKIRBOLL, J. F. REHFELD, M. GOLDSTEIN, K. MARKEY & O. DANN. 1980. A subpopulation of mesencephalic dopamine neurons projecting to limbic areas containing a cholecystokinin-like peptide: evidence from immunohistochemistry combined with the retrograde tracing. Neuroscience **5:** 2093–2124.

68. HÖKFELT, T., B. J. EVERITT, E. THEODORSSON-NORHEIM & M. GOLDSTEIN. 1984. Occurrence of neurotensin-like immunoreactivity in subpopulations of hypothalamic, mesencephalic and medullary catecholamine neurons. J. Comp. Neurol. **222:** 543–559.

69. MYERS, R. D. & T. F. LEE. 1983. In vivo release of dopamine during perfusion of neurotensin in substantia nigra of the unrestrained rat. Peptides **4:** 955–961.

70. HERVE, D., J. P. TASSIN, J. M. STUDLER, C. DANA, P. KITABGI, J. P. VINCENT, J. GLOWINSKI & W. ROSTENE. 1986. Dopaminergic control of 125-I-labeled neurotensin binding site density in corticolimbic structures of the rat brain. Proc. Natl. Acad. Sci. USA **83:** 6203–6207.

71. KALIVAS, P. W. 1984. Neurotensin in the ventral mesencephalon of the rat: anatomical and functional considerations. J. Comp. Neurol. **226:** 495–507.

72. KELLEY, A. E., M. CADOR, L. STINUS & M. LE MOAL. 1989. Neurotensin, substance P, neurokinin-a, and enkephalin: injection into ventral tegmental area in the rat produces differential effects on operant responding. Psychopharmacology **97:** 243–252.

73. ECKENSTEIN, F. & R. W. BAUGHMAN. 1984. Two types of cholinergic innervation in cortex, one co-localized with vasoactive intestinal polypeptide. Nature **309:** 153–155.

74. LUNDBERG, J. M. 1981. Evidence for coexistence of vasoactive intestinal polypeptide (VIP) and acetylcholine in neurons of cat exocrine glands. ACTA Physiol. Scan. **112**(Suppl. 496): 1–57.

75. RAITERI, M., M. MARCHI & P. PAUDICE. 1987. Vasoactive intestinal polypeptide (VIP) potentiates the muscarinic stimulation of phosphoinositide turnover in rat cerebral cortex. Eur. J. Pharmacol. **133:** 127–128.

76. LUNDBERG, J. M., A. ANGGARD, J. FAHRENKRUG, T. HÖKFELT & V. MUTT. 1980. Vasoactive intestinal polypeptide in cholinergic neurons of exocrine glands: functional significance of co-existing transmitters for vasodilation and secretion. Proc. Natl. Acad. Sci. USA **77:** 1651–1655.

77. LUNDBERG, J. M., B. HEDLUND & T. BARTFAI. 1982. Vasoactive intestinal polypeptide enhances muscarinic ligand binding in cat submandibular salivary gland. Nature **295:** 147–149.

78. HEDLUND, B., J. ABENS & T. BARTFAI. 1983. Vasoactive intestinal polypeptide and muscarinic receptors: supersensitivity induced by long-term atropine treatment. Science **220:** 519–521.

79. VINCENT, S. R., K. SATOH, D. M. ARMSTRONG & H. C. FIBIGER. 1983. Substance P in the ascending cholinergic reticular system. Nature **306:** 688–691.

80. SIMASKO, S. M., J. R. SOARES & G. A. WIELAND. 1985. Structure-activity relationship for substance P inhibition of carbamylcholine-stimulated 22-Na$^+$ flux in neuronal (PC12) and non-neuronal (BC3H1) cell lines. J. Pharmacol. Exp. Ther. **235:** 601–605.

81. JAN, Y. N. & L. Y. JAN. 1983. A LHRH-like peptidergic neurotransmitter capable of 'action at a distance' in autonomic ganglia. Trends Neurosci. **6:** 320–325.

82. FONTAINE, B., A. KLARSFELD, T. HÖKFELT & J. P. CHANGEUX. 1986. Calcitonin gene-related

peptide, a peptide present in spinal cord motoneurons, increases the number of acetylcholine receptors in primary cultures of chick embryo myotubes. Neurosci. Lett. **71:** 59–65.

83. NISHIBORI, M., R. OISHI, Y. ITOH & K. SAEKI. 1988. Galanin inhibits noradrenaline-induced accumulation of cyclic AMP in the rat cerebral cortex. J. Neurochem. **51:** 1953–1955.

84. FUXE, K., G. VON EULER, L. F. AGNATI & S. O. ÖGREN. 1988. Galanin selectively modulates 5-hydroxytryptamine 1A receptors in the rat ventral limbic cortex. Neurosci. Lett. **85:** 163–167.

85. NÖRDSTROM, O., T. MELANDER, T. HÖKFELT, T. BARTFAI & M. GOLDSTEIN. 1987. Evidence for an inhibitory effect of the peptide galanin on dopamine release from the rat median eminence. Neurosci. Lett. **73:** 21–26.

86. HELKE, C. J., K. B. THOR & C. A. SASEK. 1989. Distribution and coexistence of neuropeptides in bulbospinal and medullary autonomic pathways. This volume.

87. BARBEAU, H. & P. BEDARD. 1981. Similar motor effects of 5-HT and TRH in rats following chronic spinal transection and 5,7-dihydroxytryptamine injection. Neuropharmacology **20:** 477–481.

88. WHITE, S. R. 1985. Serotonin and co-localized peptides: effects on spinal motoneuron excitability. Peptides **6**(Suppl. 2): 123–127.

89. HANSEN, S., L. SVENSSON, T. HÖKFELT & B. J. EVERITT. 1983. 5-Hydroxytryptamine-thyrotropin releasing hormone in the spinal cord: effects on parameters of sexual behaviour in the male rat. Neurosci. Lett. **42:** 299–304.

90. WIESENFELD-HALLIN, Z., T. HÖKFELT, J. M. LUNDBERG, W. G. FORSSMANN, M. REINECKE, F. A. TSCHOPP & J. A. FISCHER. 1984. Immunoreactive calcitonin gene-related peptide and substance P coexist in sensory neurons to the spinal cord and interact in spinal behavioural responses of the rat. Neurosci. Lett. **52:** 199–204.

91. LE GREVES, P., F. NYBERG, L. TERENIUS & T. HÖKFELT. 1985. Calcitonin gene-related peptide is a potent inhibitor of substance P degradation. Eur. J. Pharmacol. **115:** 309–311.

92. GALL, C., J. LAUTERBORN, D. BURKS & K. SEROOGY. 1987. Co-localization of enkephalin and cholecystokinin in discrete areas of rat brain. Brain Res. **403:** 403–408.

93. FARIS, P. L., B. R. KOMISARUK, L. R. WATKINS & D. J. MAYER. 1983. Evidence for the neuropeptide cholecystokinin as an antagonist of opiate analgesia. Science **219:** 310–312.

94. KALTWASSER, M. T. & J. N. CRAWLEY. 1987. Oxytocin and cholecystokinin induce grooming behavior in the ventral tegmentum of the rat. Brain Res. **426:** 1–7.

95. STUDLER, J. M., P. KITABGI, G. TRAMU, D. HERVE, J. GLOWINSKI & J. P. TASSIN. 1988. Extensive co-localization of neurotensin with dopamine in rat mesocortico-frontal dopaminergic neurons. Neuropeptides **11:** 95–100.

96. FISCONE, G., M. CHRISTENSON, K. BEDECS, A. UNDEN, T. BARTFAI, R. BERTORELLI, S. CONSOLO, J. CRAWLEY, B. MARTIN, S. NILSSON & T. HÖKFELT. 1989. The N-terminal galanin fragment 1–16 is an agonist at the hippocampal galanin receptor. Proc. Natl. Acad. Sci. USA. In press.

# Nonradioactive Detection of Vasopressin and Somatostatin mRNA with Digoxigenin-Labeled Oligonucleotide Probes

MICHAEL E. LEWIS, ELAINE ROBBINS, DEBRA GREGA,[a] AND
FRANK BALDINO, JR.

*Cephalon, Inc.*
*145 Brandywine Parkway*
*West Chester, Pennsylvania 19380*
*and*
*[a]Boehringer Mannheim Biochemistry R & D*
*Indianapolis, Indiana 46250-0100*

## INTRODUCTION

*In situ* hybridization histochemistry has become a powerful tool to study the regulation of selected mRNA species in various regions of the central nervous system (CNS). Several laboratories have successfully used this technology to localize relatively rare mRNAs within the cytoplasm of individual neurons.[1-4] In the main, hybridization studies are performed with radiolabeled oligonucleotide, cDNA or cRNA probes. Although high resolution autoradiographic images have been successfully produced with these radiolabeled probes, the level of background, and the prolonged autoradiographic exposure time (6–10 weeks) required with $^{35}$S- and $^{3}$H-labeled probes has often limited their utility. Although autoradiography has permitted the identification of cellular profiles, the degree of resolution achieved with radiolabeled probes has never approached that normally obtained with enzyme-generated signals (*e.g.*, immunohistochemistry).

In recent years, several nonradioactive markers have been developed to detect specific nucleotide sequences under a variety of hybridization conditions. Several different classes of enzymes or haptens can be directly conjugated to nucleotides using conventional chemical techniques. Histochemical studies in the nervous system have focused on the use of alkaline phosphatase or horseradish peroxidase for the detection of antigen and hybridization signals. A few laboratories have utilized these enzymes conjugated to streptavidin to detect biotinylated probes.[5,6] However, the successful use of biotinylated probes to detect rare mRNAs has been limited. One laboratory has published an alternative method which chemically incorporates modified bases with functionalized "linker arms" into synthetic oligonucleotides.[7] These linker arms can be conjugated to several different enzymes. Although we have successfully used this method for high resolution detection of arginine vasopressin mRNA in rat CNS,[8] the sensitivity of these probes is limited by the addition of only a single enzyme (*e.g.*, alkaline phosphatase) into the nucleotide sequence. Moreover, it is not a routine procedure for histochemical laboratories to conjugate alkaline phosphatase to nucleotides by this method.

Recently, we developed a new method for nonradioactive *in situ* hybridization histochemistry.[9] This method, based on the conjugation of digoxigenin with dUTP[10] (Boehringer Mannheim Biochemicals) provides a higher degree of resolution than radio-

246

labeling and other nonradioactive methods. We successfully labeled synthetic oligonucleotide probes for somatostatin mRNA and arginine vasopressin mRNA with digoxigenin-dUTP. The purpose of this study is to establish the degree to which we can resolve
single neurons synthesizing these neuropeptide mRNAs in tissue sections from the rat
CNS.

## METHODS AND MATERIALS

### *Tissue Preparation*

Sprague Dawley rats (150–200 g) were obtained from Hilltop Labs (Scottsdale, PA).
Brains were removed and quickly frozen in powdered dry ice. Sections were cut on a
cryostat at 12 μm, thaw-mounted onto gelatin-coated slides, and stored at −80°C until
used.

### *Labeling of Oligonucleotides*

Nonradioactive labeling of 35 picomoles of both a 24-mer arginine vasopressin oligonucleotide and a 39-base somatostatin oligonucleotide at their 3′ end was accomplished
using the Boehringer Mannheim Biochemicals DNA tailing kit (catalogue #1028-707).
The reaction involves the incorporation of digoxigenin-11-dUTP (dig-dUTP) and a small
amount of dATP. Incubation at 37°C was completed after 5 minutes. Each tailed oligonucleotide was purified from the labeling reaction by ethanol precipitation. One-tenth
volume of 3 M sodium acetate, 1 μl of glycogen (Boehringer Mannheim Biochemicals)
and 3 volumes of 100% ethanol were added followed by incubation in a dry ice ethanol
bath for 30 minutes. Each tube was centrifuged at full speed in a microcentrifuge for 15
minutes and the supernatant removed. The pellet was then air dried and resuspended in
water. This method yields a 2–3-fold increase in sensitivity over previously described
tailing methods.

### In Situ *Hybridization Histochemistry*

Detailed methods for using synthetic oligonucleotide probes for *in situ* hybridization,
as applied in our laboratory, have been previously reported.[2,10] Briefly, tissue sections
were quickly dried and warmed to room temperature with a blow dryer set on "cool,"
fixed in buffered 3% paraformaldehyde for 5 minutes, rinsed 3 times in phosphate-
buffered saline, and incubated for 10 minutes in 2× SSC at room temperature. Slides
were then placed in a humidified chamber and 500 μl of prehybridization buffer (containing 0.6 M sodium chloride, 10 mM Tris-HCl, pH 7.5, 0.02% Ficoll, 0.02% polyvi-
nylpyrrolidone, 0.02% BSA, 1 mM EDTA, 0.05% yeast tRNA, 0.05% salmon sperm
DNA, 10% (w/v) dextran sulfate and 50% formamide) was pipetted onto each slide and
allowed to incubate at room temperature for one hour. After removal of excess prehybridization buffer the digoxigenin-labeled probe was diluted in 1 ml of prehybridization
buffer and 30 μl/section was applied. Sections were covered with Parafilm coverslips and
incubated at 37°C overnight.

Coverslips were removed in 2× SSC and sections rinsed in decreasing concentrations
of SSC to a final rinse of 0.5× SSC at 37°C. Immunological detection was preceded with
a 30-minute incubation in 2% normal sheep serum and 0.3% Triton-X 100 in 100 mM

Tris-HCl, pH 7.5 and 150 mM NaCl. Dilute antidigoxigenin antibody-enzyme conjugate (1:500; Boehringer Mannheim Biochemicals) in the same buffer containing 1% normal sheep serum and 0.3% Triton X-100 was pipetted onto each section and allowed to incubate at room temperature for 3–5 hours. Sections were washed for 5 minutes in the same buffer followed by a 10-minute incubation in 100 mM Tris-HCl, pH 9.5, 100 mM NaCl, 50 mM $MgCl_2$, also at room temperature. Slides were then placed in a light-tight box and 200 μl of chromogen was pipetted onto each section and allowed to incubate overnight. Chromogen was prepared by the addition of 0.34 mg/ml Nitroblue tetrazolium salt (Boehringer Mannheim) and 0.18 mg/ml of 5-bromo-4-chloro-3-indolyl phosphate toluidinium salt (Boehringer Mannheim) and levamisol in preceding magnesium buffer. Sections were then dipped in distilled water, dehydrated, cleared briefly in xylene, and coverslipped.

## RESULTS

The resolution achieved with probes labeled with dig-dUTP was sufficient to permit the detection of single cell profiles in several regions of the CNS. Individual perikarya containing somatostatin or vasopressin mRNA were clearly resolved. In this study the anatomical distribution of these neuropeptide mRNAs was consistent with that reported in previous *in situ* hybridization studies using radiolabeled probes.

Neurons containing somatostatin transcripts were found widely distributed throughout many regions of the rat brain. There was a marked correspondence between the distribution of this nonradioactive hybridization signal and previous studies which have localized peptide immunoreactive material in morphologically distinct regions of the nervous system.[11] In the telencephalon, somatostatin mRNA-containing neurons were localized mainly in layers 3 and 5 of the neocortex (FIGS. 1A,1B) and piriform cortex. In the hippocampus, labeled cell profiles were limited to layers outside the pyramidal and granule cell layers. In the CA1 and CA2 regions of the hippocampus, labeled perikarya were observed in the stratum oriens extending into the alveus, but were rarely observed in the stratum radiatum. In CA3, hybridization-positive neurons were distributed throughout all strata. In the dentate, labeled neurons were limited to the hilus. In the striatum, where somatostatin neurons are scattered throughout the caudate-putamen, single hybridized parvocellular neurons were clearly resolved positioned around the fiber fascicles (FIG. 1B).

In the diencephalon, labeled neurons were mainly found in the hypothalamus. The hybridization signal was most dense in the periventricular hypothalamus (PIV) at the level of the paraventricular nucleus (PVN). These neurons were magnocellular and fully occupied the dorsoventral extent of the PIV. Labeled neurons were also observed in the PVN (FIG. 2) suprachiasmatic nucleus (SCN), medial preoptic nucleus, ventromedial nucleus, and the arcuate nucleus. In general, the distribution and type of alkaline-phosphatase-labeled neurons for somatostatin mRNA was consistent with previous studies using an [35]S-labeled oligonucleotide probe.[12]

In contrast to the wide distribution of somatostatin neurons, cells containing arginine vasopressin transcripts were largely localized to the hypothalamus. Similar to previous hybridization studies with radiolabeled probes,[1,13–16] both parvocellular and magnocellular neurons were avidly labeled in the PVN. Neurons in the posterior magnocellular subdivision of the PVN were the most prominently labeled cells (FIG. 3). Although a few parvocellular profiles were noted in this subdivision, parvocellular neurons were routinely observed in the accessory PVN and the SCN.

Densely labeled magnocellular neurons were observed throughout the rostral-caudal

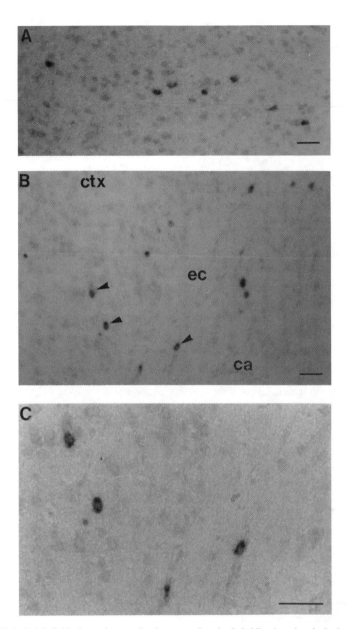

**FIGURE 1.** Brightfield photomicrographs demonstrating the hybridization signal obtained with a dig-dUTP-labeled 39-base oligonucleotide probe for somatostatin mRNA. (**A**) Photomicrograph of a section illustrating labeled perikarya in layer III of the cingulate cortex. (**B**) Photomicrograph taken more ventrally in a similar section showing layer V of the parietal cortex and the dorso-lateral portion of the caudate. (**C**) Higher magnification (200×) of the alkaline-phosphatase-labeled neurons indicated by *arrows* in panel B. ec = external capsule; ca = caudate; ctx = cortex. Bar = 100 μm.

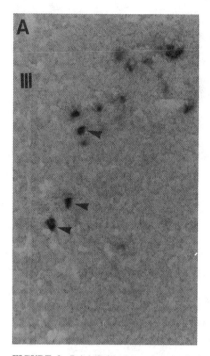
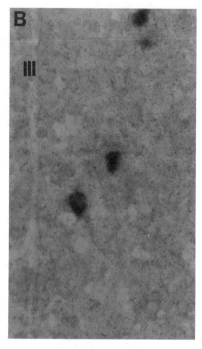

**FIGURE 2.** Brightfield photomicrograph demonstrating the distribution of somatostatin mRNA containing neurons in the paraventricular nucleus. **(A)** Small diameter labeled neurons were found extending dorsolaterally from the third ventricle. **(B)** Higher magnification (400×) of neurons highlighted by the *arrows* in panel A. III = third ventricle. Bar = 50 μm.

extent of the supraoptic nucleus (SON). This region is characterized by an extremely dense population of magnocellular vasopressinergic neurons (FIG. 4). Individual hybridization positive somata were easily resolved in the SON with this dig-dUTP-labeled probe.

In all regions of the CNS, labeled somatostatin or vasopressin perikarya were characterized by a dense particulate labeling in the cytoplasm of the soma. In several neurons the nucleus appeared prominent and unlabeled. However, the position and ability to detect the nucleus varied with the plane of the tissue section.

## DISCUSSION

Over the last several years, autoradiographic analysis has permitted the identification of a single species of mRNA within single neurons in the CNS. However, resolution with this technology has been limited by several factors which are intrinsic to the use of radiolabeled probes. The prolonged exposures required with low energy beta emitters (*i.e.*, $^{35}$S and $^{3}$H) on emulsion-coated slides has been cumbersome, costly, and difficult to serially reproduce in tissue sections. In this study, we demonstrate that the cellular resolution obtained with dig-dUTP-conjugated probes is greater than that previously observed with probes labeled with $^{35}$S-dATP.[2]

We previously showed that the oligonucleotide probes used in this study satisfy several criteria applied to test their specificity.[17] Pretreatment of tissue sections with RNase A resulted in a total loss of the specific hybridization signal. In addition, thermal stability of the probe determined empirically was within 5°C of the theoretical melting temperature (Tm) calculated from the probe length, G + C content, and salt concentration. Moreover, in Northern blot analysis, each oligonucleotide probe hybridized to a single species of rat brain RNA,[17] and the size was consistent with that previously reported (vasopressin, 760 base pairs;[18] somatostatin, 650 base pairs[19]). These data demonstrated that the sequences of the DNA probes utilized in this study specifically recognize somatostatin and vasopressin mRNA.

The distribution of perikarya containing either somatostatin or vasopressin mRNA corresponded directly to previous *in situ* hybridization studies using radiolabeled probes[1,12–17] and immunocytochemistry.[11,20] In general, alkaline-phosphatase-labeled somatostatin (mRNA) neurons were widely distributed throughout the CNS, whereas neurons containing vasopressin mRNA were largely limited to diencephalic regions.

The degree of cellular resolution obtained with dig-dUTP labeling is far superior to radiolabeled probes. Individual cell profiles were easily defined, and multiple cells could be distinguished within deeper layers of the tissue section. Hybridization signal was characterized by dense particulate labeling within the cytoplasm and a clear unlabeled nucleus (note arrows in FIG. 3). Little if any hybridization signal extended beyond the soma with either of these probes. The nonspecific (*i.e.*, background) labeling was also considerably less than that observed with radiolabeled oligonucleotides. Moreover, hybridization and detection of these probes was obtained within 48 hours compared to the weeks required to detect single cell profiles with [35]S- or [3]H-labeled oligonucleotide probes.

One advantage of this particular nonradioactive method is that since several substrates are presently available for alkaline phosphatase, it should be possible to detect multiple mRNAs within a single cell. It is also possible to detect two different species of mRNA

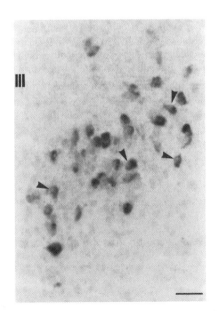

III

**FIGURE 3.** Brightfield photomicrograph demonstrating the hybridization signal achieved with a 24-base oligonucleotide probe complementary to arginine vasopressin mRNA. These labeled neurons are shown distributed in the rostral portion of the PVN approximately 200 μm past the columns of the fornix. Magnocellular neurons are clearly labeled throughout this region. *Arrows* point to neurons where an unlabeled nucleus is evident. III = third ventricle. Bar = 100 μm.

by combining an enzyme-labeled probe with a radiolabeled probe.[21] Future studies in our laboratory will focus on identifying multiple mRNAs within the same tissue sections, perhaps even the same neuron. Another interesting feature inherent to the use of the digoxigenin-dUTP system is amplification. The enzymatic addition of multiple digoxigenin-dUTPs, when coupled with standard double or triple bridging techniques with alternate species antisera, should permit the detection of rarer mRNA species. Presently, studies are underway to optimize the incorporation of dig-dUTP into olignucleotide probes and to establish the use of this hapten with RNA probes.

In summary, this study has demonstrated that high resolution *in situ* hybridization histochemistry can be readily performed with alkaline-phosphatase-dig-dUTP-labeled oligonucleotide probes. The ease of performance, safety, and rapidity of detection render this methodology a useful alternative to that employing radiolabeled probes for the detection of mRNAs in the CNS or any organ system where cellular resolution is essential.

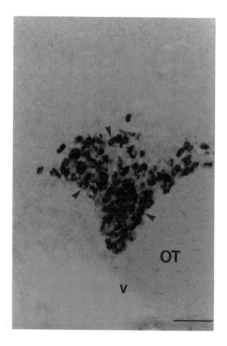

**FIGURE 4.** Brightfield photomicrograph of labeled perikarya containing arginine vasopressin mRNA within the supraoptic nucleus. Note that individual magnocellular neurons (*arrows*) are easily resolved in this figure. OT = optic tract; v = ventral surface of the brain. Bar = 200 μm.

## ACKNOWLEDGMENTS

The authors gratefully acknowledge the technical assistance of Kathleen Callison and the secretarial help of Linda Morrison. The contributions of Dr. Joseph Springer and Dr. Rick Martin are also appreciated. We thank Dr. W. Scott Young III for providing a copy of his manuscript.

## REFERENCES

1. BALDINO, F., JR. & L. G. DAVIS. 1986. *In In Situ* Hybridization in Brain. G. R. Uhl, Ed. 97–116. Plenum Press. New York, NY.

2. BALDINO, F., JR., M. F. CHESSELET & M. E. LEWIS. 1989. Methods Enzymol. **168:** 761–777.
3. LEWIS, M. E., R. G. KRAUSE II & J. M. ROBERTS-LEWIS. 1988. Synapse **2:** 308–316.
4. YOUNG, W. S. III, T. I. BONNER & M. R. BRANN. 1986. Proc. Natl. Acad. Sci., USA **83:** 9827–9831.
5. ARAI, H., P. EMSON, S. AGRAWAL, C. CHRISTODOULOU & M. GAIT. 1988. Mol. Brain Res. **4:** 63–69.
6. GUITTENY, A. F., B. FOUQUE, C. MOUGIN, R. TEOULE & B. BLOCH. 1988. J. Histochem. Cytochem. **36:** 563–511.
7. JABLONSKI, E., E. W. MOOMAW, R. H. TULLIS & J. L. RUTH. 1986. Nucleic Acids Res. **14:** 6115–6128.
8. BALDINO, F., JR., J. L. RUTH & L. G. DAVIS. 1989. Exp. Neurol. **104:** 200–207.
9. BALDINO, F., JR. & M. E. LEWIS. 1989. Methods Neurosci. In press.
10. SEIBL, R., H.-J. HÖLTKE, J. BURG, K. MÜHLEGGER, R. MATTES & C. KESSLER. 1988. Freserius Z. Anal. Chem. **330:** 305.
11. JOHANSSON, O., T. HÖKFELT & R. P. ELDE. 1984. Neuroscience **13:** 265–339.
12. FITZPATRICK-McELLIGOTT, J. P. CARD, M. E. LEWIS & F. BALDINO, JR. 1988. J. Comp. Neurol. **273:** 558–572.
13. WOLFSON, B., R. W. MANNING, L. G. DAVIS, R. ARENZEN & F. BALDINO, JR. 1985. Nature **315:** 59–61.
14. DAVIS, L. G., R. ARENTZEN, J. REID, R. W. MANNING, B. WOLFSON, K. L. LAWRENCE & F. BALDINO, JR. 1986. Proc. Natl. Acad. Sci. USA **83:** 1145.
15. LEWIS, M. E., R. ARENTZEN & F. BALDINO, JR. 1986. J. Neurosci. Res. **16:** 117–124.
16. UHL, G. R., H. H. ZINGG & J. F. HABENER. 1985. Proc. Natl. Acad. Sci. USA **82:** 5555–5559.
17. CARD, J. P., S. FITZPATRICK-McELLIGOTT, I. GOZES & F. BALDINO, JR. 1988. Cell Tissue Res. **252:** 307–315.
18. MAZJOUB, J. A., A. RICH, J. VAN BOOM & J. F. HABENER. 1983. J. Biol. Chem. **258:** 14061.
19. GOODMAN, R. H., J. W. JACOBS, P. C. DEE & J. F. HABENER. 1982. J. Biol. Chem., **257:** 1156–1159.
20. ZIMMERMAN, E. A., K. C. HSU, A. G. ROBINSON, P. W. CARMEL, A. G. FRANTZ & M. TANNENBAUM. 1973. Endocrinology **92:** 931–940.
21. YOUNG, W. S. III. 1989. Neuropeptides **13:** 271–275.

# Molecular Biological Studies on the Diversity of Chemical Signalling in Tachykinin Peptidergic Neurons[a]

JAMES E. KRAUSE, ANDREW D. HERSHEY,
PHILIP E. DYKEMA, AND YASUO TAKEDA

*Department of Anatomy and Neurobiology*
*Washington University School of Medicine*
*660 South Euclid Avenue*
*St. Louis, Missouri 63110*

## INTRODUCTION

The recent advances in peptide and protein biochemistry, and especially in molecular biology, have allowed molecular neurobiologists the opportunity to understand the physical basis of cell-cell communication in the nervous system. Within the past twenty years, it has been generally recognized that peptide-secreting neurons comprise a significant portion of the communicative neurons involved in chemical neurotransmission throughout the neuraxis. With regard to peptide-secreting and peptide-receptive neuronal systems, the technical advances have resulted in many applications toward the understanding of 1) the specific ligands involved in cell-cell communication, 2) the physiological receptors with which the ligands interact, and 3) how the processes of ligand production and receptor recognition and activation are regulated at both cellular and molecular levels.

Our interest for the past several years has been focused upon neurons that secrete the class of peptide neurotransmitters called tachykinins, and the cells that respond to the tachykinin peptides. The tachykinins represent a family of neuropeptides so named because of their ability to rapidly stimulate the contraction of gut tissue, though by no means does this represent their sole biological activity. Peptides that belong to this family are distributed differentially throughout the nervous system, as are the receptors with which they interact. In this article we use the tachykinin peptide neurotransmitter system to illustrate how some uses of recently developed molecular biological techniques and strategies, coupled with the use of peptide and protein biochemical methods, have resulted in a greater appreciation of the diversity of chemical signalling within these peptide-secreting neurons.

### *Preprotachykinin Genes That Encode the Multiple Tachykinin Peptides*

The mammalian tachykinin peptides isolated to date include Substance P (SP), Neurokinin A (NKA), Neuropeptide K (NPK), Neuropeptide $\gamma$ (NP$_\gamma$), and Neurokinin B (NKB).[1,2] Their primary structures are shown in FIGURE 1. As a result of cDNA and genomic cloning experiments,[3,4] it is now established that SP, NKA, NPK, and NP$\gamma$ are derived from the first preprotachykinin (PPT) gene isolated (called the PPT I or PPT A

[a]This work was supported in part by National Institutes of Health Grant NS21937 and a grant from the Pew Memorial Trust. JEK is a Pew Scholar in the Biomedical Sciences.

gene). Three different SP-encoding mRNAs are produced from the PPT I gene as a consequence of differential RNA splicing in which the 6th exon sequence is excluded from γ-PPT mRNA, all 7 exon sequences are present in β-PPT mRNA, and the 4th exon sequence is excluded from γ-PPT mRNA. SP is encoded in part of exon 3, whereas NKA is encoded as a discrete genomic entity as exon 6. These differentially spliced substance P-encoding mRNAs differ in their protein coding sequences, and thus have the ability to encode different peptide products. As shown in FIGURE 2, different peptides can be produced from the NKA portion of β- and γ-PPT precursors. Thus, either NKA and/or NPK can be produced from β-PPT, and either NKA and/or NPγ can be produced from γ-PPT.

| Gene | Peptide | Sequence |
|------|---------|----------|
| PPT I gene (PPT A gene) | Substance P | Arg-Pro-Lys-Pro-Gln-Gln-Phe-Phe-Gly-Leu-Met-NH₂ |
| | Neurokinin A Substance K | His-Lys-Thr-Asp-Ser-Phe-Val-Gly-Leu-Met-NH₂ |
| | Neuropeptide K β-PPT-(72-107)-NH₂ | Lys-Arg-His-Lys-Thr-Asp-Ser-Phe-Val-Gly-Leu-Met-NH₂  His-Ser-Ile-Gln-Gly-His-Gly-Tyr-Leu-Ala-Lys  Asp-Ser-Ser-Ile-Glu-Lys-Gln-Val-Ala-Leu-Leu  Ala-Asp |
| | γ-PPT-(72-92)-NH₂ (Neuropeptide γ) | Lys-Arg-His-Lys-Thr-Asp-Ser-Phe-Val-Gly-Leu-Met-NH₂  His-Ser-Ile-Gln-Gly-His-Gly-Ala-Asp |
| PPT II gene (PPT B gene) | Neurokinin B | Asp-Met-His-Asp-Phe-Phe-Val-Gly-Leu-Met-NH₂ |

**FIGURE 1.** Primary structures of the naturally-occurring mammalian tachykinin peptides. The multiple names for the genes and peptides presented represent the various nomenclature used by various authors. Two genes have been identified which encode the precursor sequences of the displayed peptides. Note that neuropeptide K [β-preprotachykinin(72–107)-peptide amide] and neuropeptide γ [γ-preprotachykinin(72–92)-peptide amide] are amino-terminally extended derviatives of neurokinin A. Neurokinin A has also been referred to as neurokinin α or neuromedin L. Neurokinin B has also been referred to as neurokinin β or neuromedin K.

The mammalian tachykinin peptide NKB is produced from a distinct PPT gene called either the PPT II or PPT B gene. NKB represents the only known tachykinin peptide derived from this gene, and in rat its unprocessed sequence within its PPT precursor encompasses residues 82 to 91.

### Regulation of Preprotachykinin Gene Expression

Aside from differential splicing of the primary transcript derived from the PPI I gene, little information is available regarding the molecular details of specific regulation of tachykinin gene expression. Species differences have been observed for differential RNA splicing of the PPT I gene transcript. Thus, in the rat, the pattern of splicing is essentially the same in all tissues where the gene is expressed in that the relative abundance of each mRNA is γ-PPT mRNA > β-PPT mRNA >> α-PPT mRNA.[4,6] On the other hand, in the bovine, where α- and β-PPT mRNA levels have been quantitated there exists tissue-specific splicing of the PPT I gene primary transcript.[7] In the CNS, the α-PPT mRNA is more abundant than the β-PPT mRNA, whereas in the gastrointestinal tract and thyroid the β-PPT mRNA is more abundant than the α-PPT mRNA. The significance of splicing of the PPT I primary transcript is not understood, particularly in light of the species differences mentioned. One possibility for the significance of differential splicing relates to the formation of NKA and its two N-terminally extended derivatives NPK and NPγ.

Although both PPT genes are expressed primarily in the nervous system, the overall distribution of RNA transcripts derived from the PPT I and PPT II gene differ significantly. Using RNA probes specific for SP-encoding mRNAs[6] and NKB-encoding mRNAs (Krause, Dykema, and Hershey, manuscript in preparation), we quantified these transcripts in a variety of neural and nonneural tissues. The tissue distribution in rat of RNA transcripts derived from the PPT I and PPT II gene are shown in TABLE 1. Within the central nervous system, PPT I gene-derived RNAs are most abundant in striatum, trigeminal ganglia, and hypothalamus, and these RNAs are not detectable in kidney and liver. As mentioned above, the γ-PPT mRNA predominates. On the other hand, PPT II gene-derived mRNA is most abundant in hypothalamus, striatum, retina, hippocampus, cortex, and spinal cord, and is not detectable in liver, kidney, and trigeminal ganglia. Recent *in situ* hybridization experiments with probes for both PPT genes have carefully

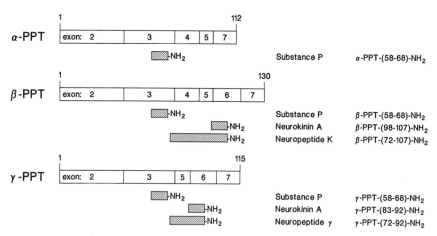

**FIGURE 2.** The three substance P precursors are polyproteins in which multiple biologically-active peptides may be derived. Displayed are the three preprotachykinin precursors that are translated from α-, β- and γ-preprotachykinin mRNA. The various exon-encoded regions are displayed within each precursor displayed. The α-preprotachykinin precursor lacks the sequences encoded by exon 6, whereas the γ-preprotachykinin lacks the sequences encoded by exon 4. Shown at the *right* are the specific locations of the processed peptides within their respective precursor sequence.

**TABLE 1.** Expression of Preprotachykinin Genes in the Rat[a]

| | PPT I (substance P, Neurokinin A) Gene Products | | | | PPT II (Neurokinin B) Gene Products |
|---|---|---|---|---|---|
| | Relative Abundance | mRNA Type α | β | γ | Relative Abundance |
| CNS | | | | | |
| Olfactory bulb | 0.03 | 1% | 21% | 78% | 0.41 |
| Cortex | 0.05 | <1 | 27 | 73 | 0.52 |
| Striatum | 1.00 | 1 | 27 | 72 | 0.77 |
| Hypothalamus | 0.29 | <1 | 25 | 75 | 1.00 |
| Hippocampus | 0.03 | <1 | 20 | 80 | 0.57 |
| Midbrain | 0.13 | <1 | 24 | 76 | 0.26 |
| Cerebellum | 0.01 | <1 | 20 | 79 | ND |
| Medulla/pons | 0.09 | <1 | 25 | 75 | 0.11 |
| Spinal cord | 0.09 | <1 | 22 | 78 | 0.47 |
| Other tissue | | | | | |
| Kidney | ND | — | — | — | ND |
| Liver | ND | — | — | — | ND |
| Anterior pituitary | <0.01 | ND | 26 | 74 | ND |
| Retina | 0.05 | <1 | 20 | 79 | 0.64 |
| Stomach | <0.01 | <1 | 34 | 65 | 0.10 |
| Large intestine | <0.01 | <1 | 10 | 89 | 0.11 |
| Small intestine | <0.01 | <1 | 9 | 90 | 0.05 |
| Trigeminal ganglia | <0.71 | <1 | 27 | 72 | ND |
| Thyroid | <0.01 | — | — | — | ND |

[a]ND, not detectable.

documented the anatomical nature of these neuronal systems. The expression of the PPT I gene is largely nonoverlapping with the PPT II gene.[8,9]

With regard to intercellular signals and intracellular mediators that regulate PPT gene expression, research is only beginning in this area and published reports relate only to substance P gene expression. *In vivo* and organ culture experiments have been performed by several investigators with the aim of understanding the intercellular factors involved in regulation of the PPT I gene with an initial focus on stimuli-induced changes in the steady-state levels of either peptide (*i.e.*, SP), mRNA, or both. Evidence has been presented for the involvement of nerve growth factor,[10] dopamine neurotransmitter systems,[11-13] thyroid hormone[14] and estrogen[15,16] in the regulation of SP-mRNA levels in these peptidergic neurons.

### *Posttranslational Processing of Substance P Polyprotein Precursors*

The distribution of SP in rat central and peripheral nervous system tissues is widespread and has been studied extensively.[17] With the isolation of NKA from porcine CNS,[18,19] its subsequent characterization in rat,[20,21] and along with the elucidation of the structure for α-PPT and β-PPT by cDNA cloning,[3] it became tempting to explain the distribution of tachykinins in the rat central and peripheral nervous system by the relative amounts of the different mRNAs present.[20,21] The relative ratios of SP and NKA in various rat nervous system structures have been studied by combined reverse-phase HPLC and radioimmunoassay,[20-22] and in general it has been found that the molar amounts of SP are consistently greater than the molar amounts of NKA.

In the past few years, N-terminally extended forms of NKA have been isolated from

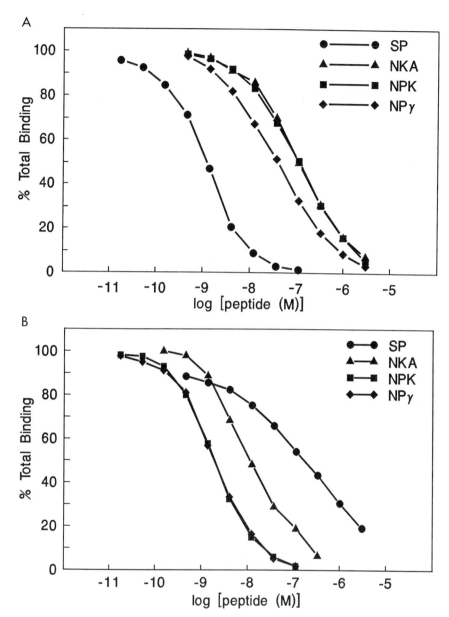

**FIGURE 3.** Displacement of specific tachykinin receptor sites by naturally occurring tachykinin peptides. (**A**) Displacement of $^3$H-substance P binding to rat submandibular gland membranes by substance P, neurokinin A, neuropeptide K, or neuropeptide $\gamma$. Membranes were prepared and a filter-binding assay was performed with 0.5 nM $^3$H-substance P as previously described. Note that the IC$_{50}$ for displacement of $^3$H-substance P bound by authentic substance P is some 50- to 100-fold lower than that observed for neurokinin A and related peptides. (**B**) Displacement of $^{125}$I-neuropeptide binding to rat duodenum membrane by substance P, neurokinin A, neuropeptide K, or neuro-

*(continued on facing page)*

tissues where the SP gene is expressed. NPK, an N-terminally extended form of NKA derived from β-PPT, was first isolated in high levels from porcine brain[23] and is diagrammed in FIGURE 2. The analagous form derived from γ-PPT, designated NPγ, was first isolated from rabbit intestine.[24] The discovery of these immunologically similar tachykinins, some of which have been found to co-migrate in HPLC systems used in earlier studies,[24] indicates that the NKA portion of β-PPT and γ-PPT precursors may be differentially processed posttranslationally. In studies examining the relative amounts of NKA and N-terminally extended forms of NKA, quantitative extraction of the peptides, resolution of these peptides by HPLC, and precise determination of their relative amounts as well as their cross-reactivity with the antisera used are critical for analyzing possible differences in patterns of posttranslational processing. To date, no published study adequately controls for these various problems inherent in the quantification of these tachykinin peptides.

Despite the problems inherent with the methods used in determination of tachykinin levels in tissue extracts, several lines of evidence indicate the existence of tissue-specific posttranslational processing of the PPTs. In one study, NPK levels were found to be greater than NKA levels only in hippocampus and cerebral cortex[25] compared to other CNS regions, which might be explained by differential posttranslational processing of β-PPT. The presence of large amounts of NPK with little or no detectable NKA in porcine brain,[23] with NKA predominating in the spinal cord[18,19] suggests differential processing. It appears also that in rabbit intestine there is differential posttranslational processing of β- and γ-PPT, since NKA, NPγ, and the N-terminal 24 residues of NPK were isolated, with no detectable NPK. In addition, human carcinoid tumors have been found to produce tachykinins, and NPK has been found to be a major tachykinin present in patient plasma and tumor tissues.[26,27] In one study plasma samples from patients during a flush reaction were examined and some were found to contain increased levels of SP and NKA>NPK, with others showing increases in NPK>NKA with no detectable SP.[26] In addition, these tumors have been found to contain NKA(3–10) and NKA(4–10).[28] Based upon these observations the NKA portion of β- and γ-preprotachykinin appears to be differentially processed.

## *Functional Significance of Differential Posttranslational Processing of β- and γ-Preprotachykinin*

The functional significance of differential posttranslational processing of the preprotachykinin precursors appears to be related to specific receptor interaction by NKA and related peptides. Though the extent of physiological receptors for the tachykinins is perhaps not well appreciated at present, it is clear that there exist at least three classes of binding sites that appear to correspond to these specific subtypes of receptors (see discussion below).

At the present time, this functional significance of differential processing appears to be related to NKA and its N-terminally extended peptides NPK and NPγ. However, these ligands (NKA, NPK, and NPγ) have only been evaluated in a few systems, and more

---

peptide γ. The ligand, $^{125}$I-neuropeptide γ, was prepared by chloramine T catalyzed iodination, and was purified by HPLC prior to use. Membranes were prepared and the filter-binding assay was performed with 0.1 nM $^{125}$I-neuropeptide γ similar to that described for part A. Note that the $IC_{50}$ value for displacement of $^{125}$I-neuropeptide γ bound by authentic neuropeptide γ or neuropeptide K are some 10-fold lower than that observed with neurokinin A.

investigation of both the biological activities and receptor binding activities is necessary for a full appreciation of their biological significance. It appears that, whereas SP is the most potent natural ligand at submandibular NK-1 receptor sites, NPK and NPγ are the most potent ligands at duodenal NK-2 receptor sites (FIG. 3), where the NK-2 receptor is involved in the contraction of the longitudinal muscle and peristalsis.[29] Also, *in vivo* NPK and NPγ have potent sialogogic effects, and in fact both of these tachykinins potentiate substance P-stimulated salivation responses.[30,31] Tachykinin NK-1 receptors are believed to mediate the SP-stimulated physiological salivation response.[32] More studies on a variety of NK-1, NK-2, and NK-3 receptor systems will be necessary to categorize the NPK and NPγ effects into similar or different classes of tachykinin receptors than those currently characterized.

### Receptor Mechanisms for Tachykinin Peptide Action

Research related to tachykinin peptide receptors has been reviewed in the past few years,[33,34] and much of the extensive research performed will only be summarized here. The biochemical and pharmacological characterization of individual tachykinin receptors has been hindered by the lack of highly selective pure antagonists. Additionally, two other problems have hampered research in this area. First, the naturally occurring mammalian tachykinins, especially SP, NKA, and NKB, all appear to interact to varying degrees with each of the currently characterized receptors. Secondly, many tissues preparations have been used for both bioassays and ligand binding studies in which more than one receptor subtype exists. However, significant progress has been made on receptor characterization since 1980, the first time in which a high affinity substance P binding site had been demonstrated in the mammalian CNS.[35]

There is now good evidence for the existence of at least three specific types of high affinity binding sites that appear to be physiological receptors for the peptides. Based upon a nomenclature scheme proposed and accepted at the Montreal tachykinin peptide symposium,[36] the receptor subtypes have been named NK-1 (SP-P), NK-2 (SP-E), and NK-3 (SP-E and SP-N). A classification of the various receptor subtypes is presented in TABLE 2, and includes for each subtype: 1) model tissues in which the receptor is selectively expressed, 2) characteristics of ligand (agonist) binding, 3) the second messenger system that appears to be involved in the signal transduction process, and 4) some biological correlates of each receptor subtype.

As displayed in TABLE 2, the three tachykinin receptor subtypes interact to varying degrees with the multiple mammalian tachykinin peptides. Selective ligands for binding studies, as well as selective agonists for biological studies, have been established for the various subtypes. It is of interest that the labeling of NKA with $^{125}$I-Bolton-Hunter reagent results in a significant structural change of the NKA molecule such that it now binds to NK-3 receptor sites.[37,38] This was an important observation since this ligand had been used to identify NK-2 receptor sites in mammalian brain. With the use of other labeled ligands, NK-2 sites have been identified in peripheral tissues that are responsive to NKA. However, few NK-2 sites have been observed in the CNS with these other NK-2 ligands. Quirion and co-workers and others have shown that NK-2 sites are present only in low amounts in the CNS,[39] and indeed these sites appear to be selectively present in the cerebral cortex in the first two weeks of postnatal life in the rat. This is surprising since there exist substantial amounts of β- and γ-PPT mRNA and NKA immunoreactive peptides in the rat CNS, and one might expect the NK-2 receptor subtype to be more abundant.

Evidence has been presented for all three receptor subtypes that GTP or GTP analogues modulate ligand binding affinity (see REFS. 2, 33, and 34 for review). Also,

TABLE 2. Classification of Mammalian Tachykinin Receptors

| Subtype | Model Tissue | Ligand | Ligand Binding Specificity | | Second Messenger | Biological Correlates |
|---|---|---|---|---|---|---|
| | | | Natural Agonist Potency | Selective Agonist | | |
| NK-1 | Dog carotid artery<br>Rat salivary gland<br>Rat cerebral cortex<br>(layers II, III) | $^3$H-SP<br>$^{125}$I-BH-SP<br>$^{125}$I-Phy | SP>NP$\gamma$ $\geq$<br>NKA = NPK>NKB | SP-OMe<br>[Sar$^9$,Met(O$_2$)$^{11}$]SP<br>[Pro$^9$,Met(O$_2$)$^{11}$]SP<br>[Cys$^{3,6}$,Tyr$^8$,Pro$^9$]SP | PLC/PI-Ca$^{2+}$ | capillary permeability<br>hyperalgesia<br>hypotension<br>salivary secretion |
| NK-2 | Rat vas deferens<br>Rabbit pulmonary artery<br>Rat cerebral cortex<br>(layer VI during first<br>postnatal two weeks) | $^3$H-NKA<br>$^{125}$I[iodohistidyl$^1$]NKA<br>$^{125}$I-BH-NKA<br>$^{125}$I-BH-Ele<br>$^{125}$I-NP$\gamma$ | NPK = NP$\gamma$ $\geq$<br>NKA>NKB>SP | [Nle$^{10}$]NKA(4–10) | PLC/PI-Ca$^{2+}$ | tachycardia<br>peristalsis |
| NK-3 | Rat portal vein<br>Guinea pig myenteric plexus<br>Rat cerebral crotex<br>(layers IV, V) | $^3$H-NKB<br>$^{125}$I-BH-NKA<br>$^{125}$I-BH-senktide<br>$^{125}$I-BH-Ele | NKB>NKA>SP | [MePhe$^7$]NKB<br>senktide<br>[Pro$^7$]NKB | PLC/PI-Ca$^{2+}$ | analgesia<br>capillary permeability |

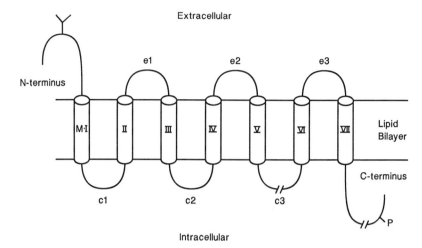

**FIGURE 4.** A schematic illustration of the relationship of the primary structure of a G-protein-linked receptor to transmembrane topology. The nomenclature of Lefkowitz and co-workers is used.[46] The amino terminal and domains e1, e2, and e3 are extracellular, and the C1, C2, C3, and carboxyl terminal domains are intracellular. The seven putative membrane spanning domains are M-I to M-VII. Potential N-linked glycosylation sites are often observed on the amino-terminal region, and potential phosphorylation sites are often observed on the carboxyl-terminal domain.

phosphatidyl inositol turnover has been observed to occur upon activation of the receptor subtypes, presumably as a result of the activation of phospholipase C.[35,40–42] This information, coupled with the extensive knowledge accumulated over the past eight years concerning GTP modulation of ligand binding for a variety of neurotransmitter and other receptors (*i.e.*, G-protein coupling),[43,44] indicated that the tachykinin receptor subtypes may be functionally and/or structurally related to the G-protein coupled superfamily of receptors.

Recently, Nakanishi and co-workers[45] isolated a stomach cDNA clone based upon an oocyte expression system that responded to NKA. The potency of the mammalian tachykinin peptides examined was NKA > NKB > SP. The sequence of the deduced protein demonstrated that it was homologous to other G-protein linked receptors; thus it was concluded that the "substance K" receptor was cloned. That this clone corresponds to the NK-2 receptor subtype has not been proved, though the use of selective agonists in the response assay or a binding assay should establish definitively whether this clone represents the NK-2 or perhaps another previously unidentified tachykinin receptor subtype.

## Structural Features of Receptors Linked to G-Regulatory Binding Proteins

G-protein-coupled receptors are a superfamily of receptors whose action is linked to the activation of G-proteins. Upon binding ligand—whether it is an amino acid derivative, a peptide, or a specific wavelength of light—the ligand-receptor complexes activate G-proteins by catalyzing the exchange of bound GDP to GTP. Binding of GTP to the G-protein $\alpha$-subunit causes it to dissociate from the $\beta\gamma$-subunits, allowing the subunits to stimulate ($G_s$, $G_o$, Tn) or inhibit ($G_i$, $G_o$) a cascade of reactions. Examples of members of this superfamily include $\alpha_1$, $\alpha_2$, $\beta_1$, and $\beta_2$-adrenergic receptors,[46] bacteriorho-

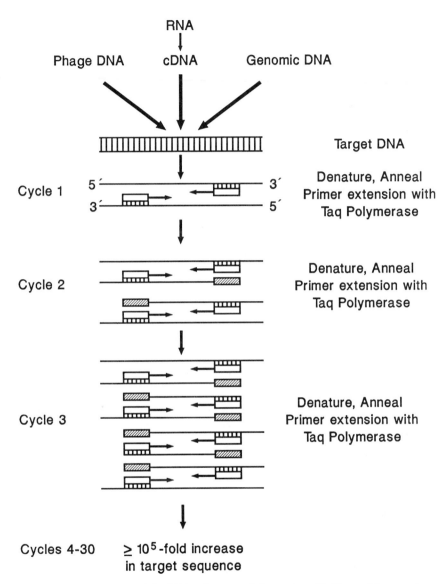

**FIGURE 5.** An illustration of the DNA polymerase chain reaction with Thermophilus aquaticus DNA polymerase. Either phage DNA, RNA reverse transcribed into cDNA, or genomic DNA can be used as the target DNA. In the polymerase chain reaction as shown here, target DNA is denatured, oligonucleotide probes are annealed to the target DNA, and DNA polymerization is carried out with Thermophilus aquaticus DNA polymerase. The cycle is repeated up to 30 times, whereby a $\geq$ $10^5$-fold increase in target sequence can be achieved.

dopsin,[47] rhodopsin,[48] color opsins,[49] serotonin $5HT1_a$,[50] and $5HT1_c$[51] receptors, muscarinic receptors,[52,53] yeast mating type receptors (STE-2, STE-3),[54,55] $D_2$ receptor[56], mas oncogene/angiotensin II receptor,[57,58] and the substance K receptor[45]. The coupled G-proteins for some of these receptors have also been determined, though the precise nature of their linkage is only beginning to be determined. Although the diversity of ligands that interact with this superfamily of receptors is great, the similarity of putative structural features indicates that common mechanisms may exist for the activation of intracellular responses.

The most evident structural feature of the members within this superfamily of receptors is their common seven $\alpha$-helical membrane spanning domains. X-ray crystallography of bacteriorhodopsin has shown the existence of these membrane spanning domains,[59] whereas homology comparisons among members of this superfamily and hydrophobicity plots of their amino acid sequence have supported the existence of these domains among the members of this superfamily. The homology comparison of these 20–28 hydrophobic amino acids allows for classifying a sequence as a member of this superfamily and permits the sequence to be aligned with other members of the family. As shown in FIGURE 4, these membrane spanning domains divide the receptor into discrete cellular domains. Using the nomenclature of Lefkowitz and co-workers,[46] these include an N-terminal extracellular region, three extracellular loops called e1, e2, e3, three cytoplasmic loops called c1, c2, c3, and a C-terminal cytoplasmic region. In addition to the highly conserved nature of the membrane spanning domains among the members of this superfamily, c1 and c2 show a high degree of conservation, while all of the extracellular domains, c3, and the C-terminal tail are much more divergent. Various parts of the receptor domains appear to have conserved sequences for posttranslational modifications. These include N-linked glycosylation site(s) in the amino terminal domain, site(s) for palmitic acid esterification of the C-terminal domain, and phosphorylation site(s) in c3 and the C-terminal region.

Only recently has the functional role of some of these structural features been investigated. For those receptors with small ligands, the membrane core appears to be the part of the molecule involved with ligand binding. Retinal in rhodopsin and bacteriorhodopsin has been shown to involve membrane spanning regions. The retinal is bound to a lysine residue in M-VII with M-III, M-IV, M-V, and M-VI contributing sites for interaction as indicated by site-directed mutagenesis.[60] For the $\beta_2$-adrenergic receptor various membrane spanning domains of the receptor are apparently involved in epinephrine binding. This is based on studies of site-directed mutagenesis,[61] deletion,[62] and chimeric receptors with the $\alpha_2$-adrenergic receptor.[63] All of these have suggested that the membrane spanning regions form a binding pocket, especially the M-II and M-VII domains. By this model the membrane spanning regions—and possibly to some extent the extracellular regions—could provide the specificity of the receptor for ligand. With regard to the interaction of peptide with specific receptors of the superfamily, the nature of the binding site for these ligands (which may be from 3 to 50 times the size of the biogenic amine ligands) is not currently appreciated. Perhaps extracellular as well as membrane spanning domains contribute to both the specificity and avidity of peptide ligand binding.

The cytoplasmic domain, on the other hand, seems to involve G-protein activation. Some interesting observations about these regions are that c1 and c2 seem to be quite conserved, they may provide a specific binding site for certain classes of proteins—either G-protein(s) or possibly kinase(s). The c3 and C-terminal regions could then provide the more specific binding to the individual members within these classes of proteins. This is supported by the general observation[46] that the subgroup within this receptor superfamily that resemble $\beta$-adrenergic receptor—those activating $G_s$—have short c3 segments and long C-terminal regions, whereas those receptors involved with activation of $G_i$ ($\alpha_2$-adrenergic and $M_2$ muscarinic receptors) and phospholipase C ($M_1$ muscarinic receptor) have long c3 regions and short C-terminal regions. What purpose these size variations

PUTATIVE MEMBRANE SPANNING REGION II

```
                   75                              80                    85                      90
Bovine Protein     Leu Ala Leu Ala Asp Leu   Cys Met Ala Ala Phe   Asn  Ala Ala Phe Asn

Bovine cDNA                                   TGC ATG GCT GCC TTC   AAC  GCT

PCR II.pr                                     TGᵀc ATG GCI GCI TTᵀc AAᵀc GC

Rat "cDNA"                                    TGC ATG GCG GCG TTT   AAC  GC
```

PUTATIVE MEMBRANE SPANNING REGION VII

```
                   295                               300                       305                      310
Bovine Protein     Leu Ala Met Ser Ser Thr Met Tyr  Asn Pro   Ile Ile Tyr Cys Cys Leu

Bovine cDNA                                          ACC ATG TAC AAT CCC ATC

PCR VII.pr                                           ACN ATG TAᵀc AAᵀc CCI AT

Rat "cDNA"                                           ACC ATG TAC AAC CCG AT
```

FIGURE 6. Design of degenerate synthetic oligonucleotides based on bovine "substance K" receptor sequence for the amplification of homologous rat sequences with the polymerase chain reaction. The nucleotide and deduced protein sequence of the bovine "substance K" receptor is shown for putative membrane spanning regions II and VII. The potential homologous sequences are shown below of the bovine (called PCR II.pr and PCR VII.pr). These oligonucleotides were used to amplify a specific rat sequence from small intestine cDNA, as discussed in the text. The rat "cDNA" sequence is that primer sequence obtained by nucleotide sequence analysis of the specifically primed and cloned cDNA.

```
                                                                              30                                            60                                       90
         M-II
Rat cDNA TGC ATG GCG GCG TTT AAC GCG GTG GTG AAC TTC ACC TAC GCA GTC CAC AAT GTG TGG TAC TAC GGC CTC TTC TAT TGC AAG TTT CAC AAC
Rat Prot Cys Met Ala Ala Phe Asn Ala Val Val Asn Phe Thr Tyr Ala Val His Asn Val Trp Tyr Tyr Gly Leu Phe Tyr Cys Lys Phe His Asn
Bov Prot Cys Met Ala Phe Ala Ala Phe Asn Ala Phe Val Phe Tyr Ala Ser His His Ile Trp Tyr Phe Gly Arg Ala Phe Cys Tyr Tyr Phe Gln Asn
                                         10                                      20                                     30

                                                        120                                       150                                       180
Rat cDNA TTC TTC CCC ATC GCT GCT CTC TTC GCC TAC AGT ATC TAC TCC ATG ACA GCC GGG GCC TTG GAC AGA TAC ATG GCC ATC ATC CAC CCT CTC CAG
Rat Prot Phe Phe Pro Ile Ala Ala Leu Phe Ala Tyr Ser Ile Tyr Ser Met Thr Ala Gly Ala Leu Asp Arg Tyr Met Ala Ile Ile His Pro Leu Gln
Bov Prot Leu Phe Pro Ile Thr Ala Leu Met Phe Val Ser Ile Tyr Ser Met Thr Ala Ala Ala Tyr Arg Tyr Met Ala Ile Ile Val His Pro Phe Gln
         40                                              50                                        60

                           210                                        240                                       270
         M-IV
Rat cDNA CCC CGG CTC TCA GCC ACG GCT ACC AAA GTG GTC ATC TTT GTC ATC TGG GTC CTC CTG GCT CTC CTG TTT CCA CAA GGC TAC TAC TCC
Rat Prot Pro Arg Leu Ser Ala Thr Ala Thr Lys Val Val Ile Phe Val Ile Trp Val Leu Leu Ala Leu Leu Phe Pro Gln Gly Tyr Tyr Ser
Bov Prot Pro Arg Leu Ser Ala Pro Gly Thr Arg Ala Val Ile Ala Gly Ile Trp Leu Val Ala Leu Ala Leu Ala Phe Pro Gln Cys Phe Tyr Ser
         70                                        80                                        90

                           300                                        330                                       360
         M-V
Rat cDNA ACC ACA GAG ACC ATG AGC AGA GTC TGC GTG ATC ATG GAG TGG CCG GAG CAT CCC AAC AGG ACT TAT GAG AAA GCG TAC CAC ATC TGC
Rat Prot Thr Thr Glu Thr Met Ser Arg Val Cys Val Ile Met Glu Trp Pro Glu His Pro Asn Arg Thr Tyr Glu Lys Ala Tyr His Ile Cys
Bov Prot Thr Ile Thr Thr Glu Asp Gly Glu Ala Thr Val Cys Val Val Ala Trp Ile Asp Pro Glu Pro Gly Ser Gly Lys Met Leu Leu Tyr His Leu Ile
         100                                       110                                       120
```

```
                                       390                                             420                                             450
GTG ACT GTA CTG ATC TAC TTC CTG CCT CTA CTG GTG ATC GCG TAC GCG TAC ACT GTG GTG GGG ATT ACA CTG TGG GCC AGT GAG ATC CCC
Val Thr Val Leu Ile Tyr Phe Leu Pro Leu Leu Val Ile Ala Tyr Ala Tyr Thr Val Val Gly Ile Thr Leu Trp Ala Ser Glu Ile Pro
 |           |   |   |   |   |   |   |   :   |   :           |   |   :   |   :   |   :   |   |   |               :   |
Val Ile Ala Leu Ile Tyr Phe Leu Pro Leu Val Val Met Phe Val Ala Tyr Ser Val Ile Gly Leu Thr Leu Trp Arg Arg Ser Val Pro
                                    130                                     140                                     150

                                          480                                         510     M-VI
GGC --- GAC TCC TCT GAC CGC TAC CAT GAG CAA GTC TCT GCC AAA CGC AAG GTG GTC AAA ATG ATG ATC GTG GTT GTG TGT ACC TTC GCC
Gly --- Asp Ser Ser Asp Arg Tyr His Glu Gln Val Ser Ala Lys Arg Lys Val Val Lys Met Met Ile Val Val Val Cys Thr Phe Ala
 |       :   :                           :       |   |   :   |       |   |       |   :   :   |   |       |   |   |
Gly His Gln Ala His Gly Ala Asn Leu Arg His Leu Gln Ala Lys Lys Lys Phe Val Lys Thr Met Val Leu Val Val Val Thr Phe Ala
                                        160                                     170

 540                                     570                                     600
ATC TGC TGG CTG CCC TTC CAC GTC TTC TTC CTC CTG CCC TAC ATC AAC CCA GAT CTC TAC CTG AAG AAG TTC ATC CAG CAG GTC TAC CTG
Ile Cys Trp Leu Pro Phe His Val Phe Phe Leu Leu Pro Tyr Ile Asn Pro Asp Leu Tyr Leu Lys Lys Phe Ile Gln Gln Val Tyr Leu
 |   |   |   |   |   :   |   :   :   |   :   |   :           :       |   :   |       :   |   |   |   |   |   |   |   |
Ile Cys Trp Leu Pro Tyr His Leu Tyr Phe Ile Leu Gly Thr Phe Gln Glu Asp Ile Tyr Cys His Lys Phe Ile Gln Gln Val Tyr Leu
180                                     190                                     200

 630    M-VII                            660
GCC AGC ATG TGG CTG GCC ATG AGT TCT ACC ATG TAC AAC CCC AT
Ala Ser Met Trp Leu Ala Met Ser Ser Thr Met Tyr Asn Pro
 |           |   |   |   |   |   |   |   |   |   |   |
Ala Leu Phe Trp Leu Ala Met Ser Ser Thr Met Tyr Asn Pro
210                                     220
```

**FIGURE 7.** Primary structure of a partial rat small intestine cDNA that displays a high degree of homology to the bovine ''substance K'' receptor. The rat sequence is aligned to that of the bovine. Homologous residues are indicated by (|) and conservative changes are indicated by (:). The regions corresponding to membrane spanning domains are underlined and labeled M-II to M-VII. The rat nucleotide sequence numbering is presented above the sequence, and the rat deduced protein sequence numbering is presented below the sequence.

have will not be known until a more detailed study of G-protein receptor/G-protein interactions can be made and a more specific determination of which G-proteins are used is established, but it may be used as a way of further classifying receptors. In addition, c3 and the C-terminal region show areas of potential controlled phosphorylation. This phosphorylation may result in desensitization of the receptor. This may come about by the phosphorylation causing decreased binding of G-proteins by blocking interaction, or by marking the receptor for sequestration and internalization. This may result from heterologous or homologous phosphorylation as described by Lefkowitz[46]. Phosphorylation may represent an interesting control mechanism of the receptor-initiated cascade, but recombination of the individual components either *in vivo* or *in vitro* in combination with mutagenesis studies will be necessary to establish its general relevance.

### Use of the Polymerase Chain Reaction to Generate a Putative Rat Tachykinin Receptor cDNA

We have made use of the DNA Polymerase Chain Reaction (PCR) method[64] to amplify the DNA sequence for tachykinin receptors. FIGURE 5 shows the general procedure that we used for PCR. A template DNA (*e.g.*, genomic DNA, phage DNA, 1st strand cDNA from mRNA) is denatured and strand separated, where specific oligonucleotides of choice can then anneal. These oligonucleotides provide the priming sequence for DNA polymerization 3' to the primer. Using two primers of opposite orientation and repetition of the denaturation, annealing, and synthesis cycle can result in a tremendous amplification ($\geq 10^5$) of the DNA sequence between the primers. Automation and the use of a heat stable DNA polymerase (*Taq* polymerase from *Thermus aquaticus* YT1) have greatly simplified this process, allowing for target DNA amplification and subsequent subcloning of this fragment.

We designed tachykinin receptor probes as shown in FIGURE 6. We selected regions of the bovine NK-2 receptor cloned by Masu *et al.*[45] that we reasoned would be conserved between species. The probes were made as degenerate probes, taking into account the various codons possibly used to represent the amino acids found in the area we selected. In addition, the probes were selected for PCR by their ability to melt and anneal efficiently. As described below, these probes were used to amplify and clone a cDNA fragment from rat that displays a high degree of homology to the bovine "substance K" receptor.

### Structural Features of a Putative Rat Tachykinin Receptor

The probes described above were used in a PCR reaction in which the first strand of cDNA that was reverse transcribed from Poly(A)$^+$ RNA and was used as the template. Both rat intestine and bovine intestine mRNA produced a single fragment of amplified cDNA of approximately 700 base pairs. This 700-base-pair band was not seen when cDNA from rat of bovine salivary gland was used but could also be seen when rat cortex cDNA was used. The 700-base-pair fragment derived from rat intestinal cDNA was made blunt ended with *E. coli* DNA polymerase I, and synthetic Eco RI linkers were added. The fragment was then subcloned and the resulting plasmid was purified and used directly for sequencing. The resulting sequence is shown in FIGURE 7.

The rat cDNA nucleotide sequence and the deduced protein sequence show a high degree of homology with the bovine "substance K" receptor. Using the nomenclature described above, the membrane spanning regions, M-III to M-VI, are 81% homologous— in general the most conserved areas within the superfamily. In addition, the regions of the extracellular and cytoplasmic domains also show homology ranging from e2 being 35% homologous to e3 being 79% homologous for the extracellular domains and ranging from c3 being 58% homologous to c2 being 95% homologous. There are also several specific regions within these domains that show sequence conservation throughout the superfamily (*e.g.*, the M-III/c2 border, with a highly conserved Asp-Arg-Tyr, and the series of basic residues at the c3/M-VI border), although their structural or functional significance is not currently appreciated. Further analysis of these areas by molecular biological methods (*i.e.*, deletion, mutagenesis) will be required to specifically determine their importance.

This partial cDNA can be used to isolate a full length cDNA for this receptor for further expression studies. Screening cDNA libraries with the cDNA fragment have not been successful, probably as a result of the low copy number of this receptor. Currently, we are isolating the 5' and 3' ends independently employing both the RACE technique[65] and the technique of using λ-phage libraries as target DNA and λ-primers as one of the PCR primers.[66] These studies are a prerequisite for further functional (*i.e.*, expression) studies, as well as for studies related to an analysis of the regulation of tachykinin receptor gene expression.

## CONCLUSIONS

We have described various applications of molecular biology to an understanding of tachykinin peptidergic neurons. Specifically, we have focused an mechanisms responsible for the production of tachykinin peptides, as well as on our initial studies on the isolation of a putative rat tachykinin receptor cDNA clone. These studies have documented the existence of four tachykinin peptides derived from the PPT I gene, namely SP, NKA, NPK, and NPγ. Moreover, we have isolated a cDNA with a high degree of homology to a bovine "SK receptor" cDNA. As a result of these and related, complementary studies on both the peptide ligands and their receptors, it should be possible to understand further the complexity of chemical signalling mechanisms in tachykinin neuronal systems.

### *Note Added in Proof*

The tachykinin receptor cDNA sequence shown in FIGURE 7 is that of the substance P receptor. We have recently generated a complete coding region cDNA that, when expressed in Cos-7 cells, displays ligand binding characteristics expected of the substance P receptor (Hershey and Krause, submitted).

## REFERENCES

1. MAGGIO, J. E. 1988. Tachykinins. Ann. Rev. Neurosci. **11:** 13–28.
2. KRAUSE, J. E., M. R. MACDONALD & Y. TAKEDA. 1989. The polyprotein nature of substance P precursors. Bioessays **10:** 62–69.
3. NAWA, H., T. HIROSE, H. TAKASHIMA, S. INAYAMA & S. NAKANISHI. 1983. Nucleotide sequences of cloned cDNAs for two types of bovine substance P precursor. Nature **306:** 32–36.
4. KRAUSE, J. E., J. M. CHIRGWIN, M. S. CARTER, Z. S. XU & A. D. HERSHEY. 1987. Three rat preprotachykinin mRNAs encode the neuropeptides substance P and neurokinin A. Proc. Natl. Acad. Sci. USA **84:** 882–885.
5. BONNER, T. I., H. U. AFFOLTER, A. C. YOUNG & W. S. YOUNG. 1987. A cDNA encoding the precursor of the rat neuropeptide, neurokinin B. Mol. Brain Res. **2:** 243–249.
6. KRAUSE, J. E., J. D. CREMINS, M. S. CARTER, E. R. BROWN & M. R. MADDONALD. 1989.

Solution hybridization-nuclease protection assays for sensitive detection of differentially spliced substance P- and neurokinin A-encoding messenger RNAs. Methods Enzymol. **168:** 634–652.

7. NAWA, H., H. KOTANI & S. NAKANISHI. 1984. Tissue-specific generation of two preprotachykinin mRNAs from one gene by alternative RNA splicing. Nature **312:** 729–734.

8. WARDEN, M. K. & W. S. Young. 1988. Distribution of cells containing mRNAs encoding substance P and neurokinin B in the rat central nervous system. J. Comp. Neurol. **272:** 90–113.

9. HARLAN, R. E., M. M. GARCIA & J. E. KRAUSE. 1989. Cellular localization of substance P- and neurokinin A-encoding preprotachykinin mRNA in the female rat brain. J. Comp. Neurol. In press.

10. LINDSAY, R. M. & A. J. HARMAR. 1989. Nerve growth factor regulates expression of neuropeptide genes in adult sensory neurons. Nature **337:** 362–364.

11. YOUNG, W. S., T. I. BONNER & M. R. BRANN. 1986. Mesencephalic dopamine neurons regulate the expression of neuropeptide mRNAs in the rat forebrain. Proc. Natl. Acad. Sci. USA **83:** 9827–9831.

12. BANNON, M. J., J. M. LEE, P. GIRAUD, A. YOUNG, H. U. AFFOLTER & T. I. BONNER. 1986. Dopamine antagonist haloperidol decreases substance P, substance K, and preprotachykinin mRNAs in rat striatonigral neurons. J. Biol. Chem. **261:** 6640–6642.

13. SIVAM, S. P., G. R. BREESE, J. E. KRAUSE, T. C. NAPIER, R. A. MUELLER & J. S. HONG. 1987. Neonatal and adult 6-hydroxydopamine-induced lesions of rat nigrostriatal dopamine system differentially alter tachykinin and enkephalin gene expression. J. Neurochem. **49:** 1623–1633.

14. JONASSEN, J. A., D. MULLIKEN-KILPATRICK, A. McADAMS & S. E. LEEMAN. 1987. Thyroid hormone status regulates preprotachykinin-A gene expression in male rat anterior pituitary. Endocrinology **121:** 1555–1561.

15. JONASSEN, J. A., D. MULLIKEN-KILPATRICK, J. HOOGASIAN & S. E. LEEMAN. 1988. Sex differences in regulation of SP, NKA and preprotachykinin gene expression in anterior pituitary. Regul. Peptides **22:** 99.

16. BROWN, E. R., R. E. HARLAN & J. E. KRAUSE. 1988. Differential effects of estrogen on substance P mRNA levels in the rat anterior pituitary and hypothalamus. Soc. Neurosci. Abstr. **14:** 1191.

17. NICOLL, R. A., C. SCHENKER & S. E. LEEMAN. 1980. Substance P as a transmitter candidate. Annu. Rev. Neurosci. **3:** 227–268.

18. KIMURA, S., M. OKADA, Y. SUGITA, I. KANAZAWA & E. MUNEKATA. 1983. Novel neuropeptides, neurokinin αa and β, isolated from porcine spinal cord. Proc. Jap. Acad. **59:** 101–104.

19. MINAMINO, N., K. KANGAWA, A. FUKUDA & H. MATSUO. 1984. Neuromedin L: a novel mammalian tachykinin identified in porcine spinal cord. Neuropeptides **4:** 157–166.

20. KANAZAWA, I., T. OGAWA, S. KIMURA & E. MUNEKATA. 1984. Regional distribution of substance P, neurokinin α and neurokinin β in the rat central nervous system. Neurosci. Res. **2:** 111–120.

21. MINAMINO, N., H. MASUDA, K. KANGAWA & H. MATSUO. 1984. Regional distribution of neuromedin K and neuromedin L in rat brain and spinal cord. Biochem. Biophys. Res. Comm. **124:** 731–738.

22. BRODIN, E., LINDEFORS, N., DALSGAARD, C. J., THEODORSSON-NORHEIM, E. & S. ROSELL. 1986. Tachykinin multiplicity in rat central nervous system as studied using antisera raised against substance P and neurokinin A. Regul. Peptides **13:** 252–272.

23. TATEMOTO, K., J. M. LUNDBERG, H. JORNVALL & V. MUTT. 1985. Neuropeptide K: isolation, structure and biological activities of a novel brain tachykinin. Biochem. Biophys. Res. Commun. **128:** 947–953.

24. KAGE, R., G. P. McGREGOR, L. THIM & J. M. CONLON. 1988. Neuropeptide γ: a peptide isolated from rabbit intestine that is derived from γ-preprotachykinin. J. Neurochem. **50:** 1412–1417.

25. ARAI, H. & P. C. EMSON. 1986. Regional distribution of neuropeptide K and other tachykinins (neurokinin A, neurokinin B, and substance P) in rat central nervous system. Brain Res. **399:** 240–249.

26. NORHEIM, I., E. THEODORSSOR-NORHEIM, E. BRODIN & K. OBERG. 1986. Tachykinins in carcinoid tumors: their use as a tumor marker and possible role in the carcinoid flush. J. Clin. Endocrinol. Metab. **63:** 605–612.

27. CONLON, J. M., C. F. DEACON, G. RICHTER, W. E. SCHMIDT, F. STCKMAN & W. CREUTZ-FELDT. 1986. Measurement and partial characterization of the multiple forms of neurokinin A-like immunoreactivity in carcinoid tumors. Regul. Peptides **13:** 183–196.

28. THEODORSSON-NORHEIM, E., H. JORNVALL, M. ANDERSSON, K. BERG & G. JACOBSSON. 1987. Isolation and characterization of neurokinin A, neurokinin A(3–10) and neurokinin A(4–10) from a neutral water extract of a metastatic ileal carcinoid tumor. Eur. J. Biochem. **166:** 693–698.

29. MAGGI, C. A., S. GIULIANI, S. MANZINO, P. SANTICIOLI & A. MELI. 1986. Motor effect of neurokinins on the rat duodenum: evidence for involvement of substance K and substance P receptors. J. Pharmacol. Exp. Ther. **238:** 341–351.

30. TAKEDA, Y. & J. E. KRAUSE. 1989. Neuropeptide K potently stimulates salivary secretion and potentiates substance P-induced salivation. Proc. Natl. Acad. Sci. USA **86:** 392–396.

31. TAKEDA, Y. & J. E. KRAUSE. 1989. Neuropeptide γ potentiates substance P-induced saliva-tion. Eur. J. Pharmacol. **161:** 267–271.

32. GALLACHER, D. V. 1983. Substance P is a functional neurotransmitter in the rat parotid gland. J. Physiol. **342:** 483–498.

33. QUIRION, R. & T. V. DAM. 1988. Multiple neurokinin receptors: recent developments. Regul. Peptides **22:** 18–25.

34. REGOLI, D., G. DRAPEAU, S. DION & R. COUTURE. 1988. New selective agonists for neu-rokinin receptors: pharmacological tools for receptor characterization. Trends Pharmacol. Sci. **9:** 290–295.

35. HANLEY, M. R., B. E. B. SANDBERG, C. M. LEE, L. L. IVERSEN, D. E. BRUNDISH & R. WADE. 1980. Specific binding of 3H-substance P to rat brain membranes. Nature **286:** 810–812.

36. HENRY, J. L. 1987. Substance P and Neurokinins. Springer-Verlag. New York, NY.

37. QUIRION, R. & T. V. DAM. 1985. Multiple tachykinin receptors in guinea pig brain: high densities of substance K (neurokinin A) binding sites in the substantia nigra. Neuropeptides **6:** 191–204.

38. SAFFROY, M., J. C. BEAUJOUAN, Y. TORRENS, J. BESSEYRE, L. BERGSTROM & J. GLOWINSKI. 1988. Localization of tachykinin binding site (NK1, NK2, NK3 ligands) in the rat brain. Peptides **9:** 227–241.

39. DAM, T. V., E. ESCHER & R. QUIRION. 1988. Evidence for the existence of three classes of neurokinin receptors in brain. Differential ontogeny of neurokinin-1, neurokinin-2, and neu-rokinin-3 binding sites in rat cerebral cortex. Brain Res. **453:** 372–376.

40. WATSON, S. P. 1984. The action of substance P in contraction, inositol phospholipids and adenylate cyclase in rat small intestine. Biochem. Pharmacol. **33:** 3733–3737.

41. BRISTOW, D. R., N. R. CURTIS, N. SUMAN-CHAUHAN, K. J. WATLING & B. J. WILLIAMS. 1988. Effects of tachykinins on inositol phospholipid hydrolysis in slices of hamster urinary bladder. Br. J. Pharmacol. **90:** 211–217.

42. GUARD, S., K. J. WATLING & S. P. WATSON. 1988. Neurokinin 3 receptors are linked to inositol phospholipid hydrolysis in the guinea pig ileum longitudinal muscle-myenteric plexus preparation. Br. J. Pharmacol. **94:** 148–154.

43. GILMAN, A. G. 1987. G proteins: transducers of receptor-generated signals. Annu. Rev. Biochem. **54:** 615–650.

44. NEER, E. J. & D. E. CLAPHAM. 1988. Roles of G protein subunits in transmembrane signal-ling. Nature **332:** 129–134.

45. MASU, Y., K. NAKAYANA, H. TAMAKI, Y. HARADA, M. KUNO & S. NAKANISHI. 1987. cDNA cloning of bovine substance K receptor through oocyte expression system. Nature **329:** 836–838.

46. LEFKOWITZ, R. J. & M. G. CARON. 1988. Adrenergic receptors. J. Biol. Chem. **263**(11): 4993–4996.

47. DUNN, R. J., N. R. HACKETT, K.-S. HUANG, S. JONES, H. G. KHORANA, D.-S. LEE, M.-J. LIAO, K. M. LO, J. MCCOY, S. NOGUCHI, R. RADHAKRISHNAN & U. L. RAJBHANDARY.

1983. Studies on the light-transducing pigment bacteriorhodopsin. Cold Spring Harbor Symp. Quant. Biol. **48:** 853–862.

48. NATHANS, J. & D. S. HOGNESS. 1983. Isolation, sequence analysis, and intron-exon arrangement of the gene-encoding bovine rhodopsin. Cell **34:** 807–814.

49. NATHANS, J., D. THOMAS & D. S. HOGNESS. 1986. Molecular genetics of human color vision: the genes encoding blue, green, and red pigments. Science **232:** 193–202.

50. KOBILKA, B. K., T. FRIELLE, S. COLLINS, T. YANG-FENG, T. S. KOBILKA, U. FRANCKE, R. J. LEFKOWITZ & M. G. CARON. 1987. An intronless gene encoding a potential member of the family of receptors coupled to guanine nucleotide regulatory proteins. Nature **329:** 75–79.

51. JULIUS, D., A. B. MACDERMOTT, R. AXEL & T. M. JESSEL. 1988. Molecular characterization of a functional cDNA encoding the serotonin 1c receptor. Science **241:** 558–564.

52. PERALTA, E. G., J. W. WINSLOW, G. L. PETERSON, D. H. SMITH, A. ASHKENAZI, J. RAMACHANDRAN, M. I. SCHIMERLIK & D. J. CAPON. 1987 Primary structure and biochemical properties of an $M_2$ muscarinic receptor. Science **236:** 600–605.

53. BONNER, T. I., N. J. BUCKLEY, A. C. YOUNG M. R. BRANN. 1987. Identification of a family of muscarinic acetylcholine receptor genes. Science **237:** 527–532.

54. NAKAYAMA, N., A. MIYAJIMA & K. ARAI. 1985. Nucleotide sequences of STE2 and STE3, cell type-specific sterile genes from *Saccharomyces cerevisiae*. EMBO J. **4:**(10): 2643–2648.

55. BURKHOLDER, A. C. & L. H. HARTWELL. 1985. The yeast α-factor receptor: structural properties deduced from the sequence of the STE2 gene. Nuclecic Acids Res. **13**(23): 8463–8475.

56. BUNZOW, J. R., H. H. M. VAN TOL, D. K. GRANDY, P. ALBERT, J. SALON, M. CHRISTIE, C. A. MACHIDA, K. A. NEVE & O. CIVELLI. 1988. Cloning and expression of a rat $D_2$ dopamine receptor cDNA. Nature. **336:** 783–787.

57. YOUNG, D., G. WAITCHES, C. BIRCHMEIER, O. FASANO & M. WIGLER. 1986. Isolation and characterization of a new cellular oncogene encoding a protein with multiple potential transmembrane domains. Cell **45:** 711–719.

58. JACKSON, T. R., L. A. C. BLAIR, J. MARSHALL, M. GOEDERT & M. R. HANLEY. 1988. The *mas* oncogene encodes an angiotensin receptor. Nature **335:** 437–440.

59. HENDERSON, R. & P. N. T. UNWIN. 1975. Three-dimensional model of purple membrane obtained by electron microscopy. Nature **257:** 28–32.

60. KHORANA, H. G. 1988. Bacteriorhodopsin, a membrane protein that uses light to translocate protons. J. Biol. Chem. **263**(16): 7439–7442.

61. CHUNG, F.-Z., C.-D., WANG, P. C. POTTER, J. C. VENTER & C. M. FRASER. 1988. Site-directed mutagenesis and continuous expression of human β-adrenergic receptors. J. Biol. Chem. **263:**(9): 4052–4055.

62. DIXON, R. A. F., I. S. SIGAL, M. R. CANDELORE, R. B. REGISTER, W. SCATTERGOOD, E. RANDS & C. D. STRADER. 1987. Structural features required for ligand binding to the β-adrenergic receptor. EMBO J. **6**(11): 3269–3275.

63. KOBILKA, B. K., T. S. KOBILKA, K. DANIEL, J. W. REGAN, M. G. CARON & R. J. LEFKOWITZ. 1988. Chimeric $\alpha_2$-, $\beta_2$-adrenergic receptors: delineation of domains involved in effector coupling and ligand binding specificity. Science. **24:** 1310–1316.

64. SAIKI, R. K., S. SCHARF, F. FALOONA, K. B. MULLIS, G. T. HORN, H. A. ERLICH & N. ARNHEIM. 1985. Enzymatic amplification of β-globin genomic sequences and restriction site analysis for diagnosis of sickle cell anemia. Science **230:** 1350–1354.

65. FROHMAN, M. A., M. K. DUSH & G. R. MARTIN. 1988. Rapid production of full-length cDNAs from rare transcripts: amplification using a single gene-specific oligonucleotide primer. Proc. Natl. Acad. Sci. USA **85:** 8998–9002.

66. FRIEDMAN, K. D., N. L. ROSEN, P. J. NEWMAN & R. R. MONTGOMERY. 1988. Enzymatic amplification of specific cDNA inserts form λgt11 libraries. Nucleic Acids Res. **16:**(17): 8718.

# Differential Cloning Approaches to the Nervous System[a]

ROBERT J. MILNER

*Department of Neuropharmacology*
*Research Institute of Scripps Clinic, BCR1*
*10666 North Torrey Pines Road*
*La Jolla, California 92037*

The physiological properties of any tissue are largely determined by the set of protein molecules made by the cells of that tissue. Functions that are unique to a particular tissue or organ may therefore depend on proteins that are expressed only in that tissue or organ. Because many of the properties and functions of the nervous system are unique, we may expect the cells of the nervous system—neurons and glia—to express a wide variety of neural-specific proteins. Furthermore, neurons display a variety of forms and functions and these phenotypic differences probably also result from a heterogeneity of protein expression. To dissect the complexity of the nervous system and approach an understanding of its function, it will be essential to characterize the proteins that are uniquely or predominantly expressed by neural cells and to identify the phenotypic differences between neural cell types.

Over the past decade our knowledge of the proteins that constitute the nervous system has expanded considerably, although the current list is far short of the estimated 30,000 genes that may be active in the brain.[1,2] Many proteins have been identified by characterizing the molecules that mediate a particular function, using that function as an assay for protein isolation. Thus, corticotrophin releasing factor was isolated and identified by its ability to cause ACTH release from pituitary cells.[3] This approach has been tremendously powerful, particularly when augmented by molecular cloning techniques, and has led to the identification of many neuronal proteins. Studies of neuropeptides and their precursors in particular have been well served by recombinant DNA technology.[4,5] But this approach is limited in that it can only be applied to functions that are known and are adaptable to testing during protein isolation.

One alternative approach has been to identify molecules of interest by means of specific antibodies, particularly monoclonal antibodies. An advantage of the monoclonal antibody technique is that it is possible to generate hybridomas using cells immunized against an antigenically complex mixture, such as a tissue extract, and then to screen for individual hybridomas secreting monoclonal antibodies that recognize antigens with an interesting tissue or cellular distribution. This procedure has been extremely effective in dissecting the complexity of the immune system, which, like the nervous system, consists of populations of cells that are largely similar in their properties except for distinct and functionally important differences in the expression of certain gene products. In the nervous system, monoclonal antibodies[6] have been used with considerable success to advance the characterization of known proteins as well as to identify antigens expressed on neural cells in the adult and during neuronal development.

[a]Studies from our laboratories described here were supported in part by grants from the National Institutes of Health (NS 20728, NS 21815, NS 22347). This is publication number BCR-5891 from the Research Institute of Scripps Clinic.

A third experimental strategy is to conduct the search for tissue or cellular specificity of gene expression at the level of mRNA. Because each protein is encoded by its corresponding mRNA, the collection of mRNAs in a cell is more or less equivalent to the proteins expressed by that cell. If the mRNAs in a tissue are converted to a form that is experimentally manipulable—a cDNA library—they can be screened for molecules of interest. Here we exploit the ability of nucleic acids to bind to their complementary sequences: for example, a cDNA library can be screened for the clone of a known mRNA by using a single hybridization probe designed to be complementary to that cDNA. Alternatively, cDNA libraries can be screened with probes derived from mRNA preparations from cells or tissues, in order to identify mRNAs that are differentially or uniquely expressed in those cells or tissues. In this report I will discuss the various modifications and extensions of this approach and describe the results that have been obtained.

## Cloning Tissue-Specific cDNAs

The goal is to identify cDNA clones of mRNAs that are expressed in one tissue source but not in another. The most straightforward, but also most laborious, method would be to determine the tissue distributions of the mRNAs corresponding to individual clones taken from an appropriate cDNA library. For example, Greg Sutcliffe and I hybridized cDNA clones, taken at random from a rat brain library, to mRNA preparations from different rat tissues. Clones that hybridized to brain mRNA but not to liver or kidney mRNA were operationally defined as "brain-specific."[1,7] Approximately 30% of almost 200 clones tested in this fashion gave this pattern of hybridization. In this case the screen was quite efficient in detecting cDNA clones with the desired properties, largely because of the divergence in gene expression between the tissues tested. But this method would not be appropriate where the tissues are more closely related, such as a comparison of different brain regions.

### Plus-Minus Screening

Plus-minus screening or differential colony hybridization is a more efficient method for detecting clones of mRNAs that are selectively expressed in different cell types or tissues. A cDNA library is plated out and the bacterial colonies or bacteriophage plaques, each containing an individual cDNA, are transferred to duplicate nitrocellulose or nylon filters. One filter is hybridized with a radioactively-labelled probe derived from mRNA of tissue A, while the second, duplicate filter is hybridized with a probe made from tissue B mRNA (FIG. 1). Most usually, the probes are single-stranded cDNAs generated from the mRNA populations by the enzyme reverse transcriptase. Following hybridization and washing, autoradiograms of the filters are compared to identify colonies that have hybridized with one probe but not with the other.

One of the earliest uses of this technique was by Dworkin and Dawid,[8] who screened cDNA libraries from *Xenopus laevis* tadpoles with probes derived from mRNAs expressed at different stages of embryogenesis. Several of the selected clones corresponded to mRNAs that first appeared at the onset of neurulation and displayed "tissue-specific" patterns of expression detected by in situ hybridization. One such mRNA was expressed specifically in the nervous system and encoded a "neural-specific" isotype of β-tubulin.[9] This technique has been used extensively to reveal tissue- or cell-specific cDNAs, but it is limited by its sensitivity to detect cDNA clones of mRNAs with an abundance of 0.06% or greater.[8]

## Subtractive Hybridization

In subtractive cloning methods the mRNAs present in preparations from two different tissue sources are compared directly, by hybridization of one to the complement of the other. Most simply, single stranded cDNAs derived by reverse transcription of mRNA from tissue A are hybridized with an excess of mRNA from tissue B. For mRNAs that are common to both tissues, the cDNAs from tissue A will hybridize to their complementary mRNAs in tissue B to form double stranded cDNA-RNA hybrids. However, the cDNAs that correspond to mRNAs uniquely expressed in tissue A will not find a partner and will remain single stranded. Chromatography on hydroxyapatite will separate single from double stranded nucleic acid hybrids. The single stranded cDNA population, which represents mRNAs uniquely expressed or highly abundant in tissue A, can then be used to screen an appropriate cDNA library (a "subtracted probe") (FIG. 1) or may be converted into cDNA clones directly (a "subtracted library"). Subtractive cloning has been used to

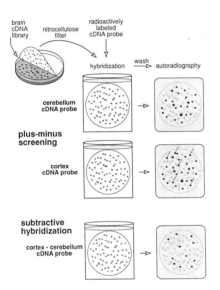

**FIGURE 1.** Illustration of differential screening procedures. Multiple nitrocellulose filters carrying plasmids from the same bacterial plate are hybridized in parallel with labelled cDNAs from cortex and cerebellum (plus-minus screening) or with a cortex-cerebellum subtracted probe (subtractive hybridization). Clones (*marked*) of putative cortex-specific mRNAs are detected by the cortex cDNA but not the cerebellum cDNA; the subtracted probe reveals these clones as well as additional "cortex-specific" clones.

identify cDNA clones of mRNAs whose expression may be related to functions displayed by one set of cells but not another, as illustrated by one of the original uses of this approach to isolate cDNA clones for the T cell receptor, which is expressed on T but not B lymphocytes.[10] Further modifications have refined the technique so that it is now possible to compare gene expression in any two cell populations in a systematic fashion using relatively small amounts of mRNA.[11,12] The advantage of subtractive hybridization is its sensitivity: in one of these studies[11] it was estimated that clones corresponding to mRNAs of 0.001% abundance could be detected. It is also possible to combine subtractive and positive selections: for example, to select for rat brain cDNAs corresponding to mRNAs absent from liver but expressed in the immune system.[13]

### Clones of Neurobiological Interest

In practice none of these strategies is perfect: hybridization of mixed cDNA probes to a cDNA library typically generates many false positives. To weed these out and to focus on the most interesting clones, it is common to employ a series of sequential screens, often involving both differential hybridization and subtracted probes. Finally, the mRNAs corresponding to the selected clones are characterized, usually by Northern blotting and in situ hybridization, to demonstrate that the cloned mRNAs have the desired properties. Using these general approaches, several laboratories have isolated clones encoding proteins specific to the nervous system or to particular brain regions, proteins expressed following treatment of cells with growth factors, proteins expressed during development that may mark developing cell populations, and proteins that are implicated in disease processes. These examples will illustrate how differential cloning procedures might be applied to other problems in neuroscience.

*Nervous System-Specific Proteins*

The simplest strategy has been to select cDNA clones for nervous system-specific mRNAs,[1,7,14] on the assumption that these would encode proteins with neural-specific functions. Several of the selected brain-specific cDNA clones were found to encode known proteins: the myelin components proteolipid protein[14,15] and myelin-associated glycoprotein[16] and the neuronal proteins neuron-specific enolase[17] and secretogranin.[18] A cDNA clone encoding a novel, and virtually neural-specific, calcium-binding protein, calretinin, was identified in chick retina cDNA library screened by differential hybridization with cDNA probes from chick retina and wingbud mRNA.[19] Differential cloning procedures can also be a valuable means to identify cDNA clones of a known protein if that protein has a well-defined tissue distribution. For example, cDNA clones encoding the myelin protein $P_0$, which is expressed only in peripheral nervous system myelin, were selected by screening a sciatic nerve cDNA library for clones that hybridized with a cDNA probe from sciatic nerve mRNA but not with cDNA probe from brain mRNA.[20]

*Specific Expression in Brain Regions*

Regionally expressed proteins in the nervous system have also been a popular target, particularly with subtractive cloning techniques. For example Travis and Sutcliffe[21] have isolated clones of mRNAs that are highly enriched in primate neocortex by screening a cortex cDNA library with a cortex cDNA probe subtracted with cerebellum mRNA. An excellent validation of the method was the isolation of clones encoding the neuropeptides cholecystokinin and somatostatin, both highly enriched in cortex with respect to cerebellum. A forebrain-enriched cDNA probe was also used to identify clones of rare mRNAs with regionally distinct patterns of expression in canary brain.[22] Other laboratories have identified cDNAs for mRNAs enriched in cerebellum using plus-minus screening: one such mRNA was specifically expressed in cerebellar granule cells,[23] while a second was found only in Purkinje cells and encoded a protein with sequences similar to platelet-derived growth factor.[24]

*Neural Development*

The unique properties of neurons and their heterogeneity of form and function are generated during the process of neuronal development. Molecular markers for developing neural cells have been investigated extensively by monoclonal antibody-based approaches[6] but similar markers can also be identified by cloning approaches. For example, to generate markers for neural crest development, Anderson and Axel used differential hybridization to select cDNA clones of mRNAs expressed in adult superior cervical ganglion cells but not in adrenal chromaffin cells.[25] We have also attempted to identify such markers by selecting cDNA clones of mRNAs that are enriched in the embryonic rat brain, using subtractive cloning techniques.[26] These studies were based on the premise that there are mRNA species that are specific to, or highly enriched in, the embryonic vs adult nervous systems. The results suggest that such mRNAs do exist and that they may encode proteins of several types, including those, such as the T$\alpha$1 isotype of $\alpha$-tublin, that mark particular stages (neurite extension) of the terminal differentiation of neural cells,[27] as well as those products that are involved in the processes of development. Interestingly, several "embryonic" mRNAs appear to be reexpressed during axonal regeneration in the adult nervous system, including those encoding the T$\alpha$1 isotype of $\alpha$-tubulin,[28] the class II isotype of $\beta$-tubulin,[29] and the growth-associated protein GAP-43,[30] all of which show increases in expression. Together these studies suggest that there is a recapitulation of embryonic gene expression during this process, at least of those genes whose products are components of growing axons.

## Studies with Cultured Cells

Cultured cells, with their ease of manipulation and responsiveness to growth factors, have been an attractive subject for differential cloning. Several laboratories have investigated the short- and long-term changes that occur following nerve growth factor (NGF) stimulation of PC12 (rat pheochromocytoma) cells, using differential hybridization to identify clones of mRNAs that increase in expression at different times. At three hours following NGF treatment, several mRNAs increase dramatically in abundance: two of these encode putative gene regulatory factors, one with the "zinc finger" sequence motif characteristic of DNA-binding proteins[31] and a second with sequence similarities to glucocorticoid receptors.[32] A similar set of mRNAs were identified from mouse 3T3 cells after induction with phorbol ester (TPA);[33] these were also shown to have increased expression on NGF treatment of PC12 cells.[34] Another early mRNA, encoding a 90,000-dalton protein, was identified by screening a cDNA library made from PC12 cells at 24 hours following induction.[35] A different set of cDNA clones were identified following long-term (24 h) treatment with NGF:[36] among these were cDNAs encoding tyrosine hydroxylase, thymosin $\beta_4$, and a new type of intermediate filament.[37]

## Applications to Disease

A potentially powerful application of these techniques is to the study of disease. Thus, differential cloning could be used to identify mRNAs whose expression is altered in the diseased cells. For example, a comparison of uninfected brains with brains from hamsters infected with scrapie by subtractive cloning methods identified several clones of mRNAs that were increased in expression following infection.[12] Alternatively, a disease that affects a particular brain region or cell type can be investigated using cDNA clones of mRNAs enriched in or specific to that region or cell type. Of the mRNAs identified as "cortex-specific" in the studies described above, several show decreases in expression in cortex samples from human patients with Alzheimer's disease.[11]

Genetic mutations, particularly those causing loss of a specific cell type, are also appropriate for this type of analysis. The recent identification[38] of the gene defect in mice carrying the mutant gene *rds,* which causes a slow degeneration of photoreceptor cells, is a spectacular demonstration of the power of subtractive cloning techniques. A set of cDNA clones encoding retina-specific mRNAs was identified by subtractive cloning techniques using retinal mRNA preparations from wild type animals and from mice carrying the related mutation *rd,* which causes a more rapid loss of photoreceptor cells. One of these cDNAs was shown to be encoded by a gene located on the same chromosome (17) as the *rds* gene. The mRNA corresponding to this cDNA was aberrant in both size and abundance in *rds* mice, due to a large insertion in the gene. These studies therefore demonstrated the gene defect in *rds* mice and identified the product of the *rds* gene, a hitherto uncharacterized photoreceptor-specific protein.

## *From Clone to Function*

Once a clone has been selected for study, much can be learnt about its corresponding mRNA and the protein that it encodes. An advantage of cDNA cloning is that the amino acid sequence of the encoded protein can be determined rapidly from the nucleotide sequence of the cDNA. Comparisons of a new sequence with databases of known protein sequences often reveal identities or similarities with other proteins. Antibodies can be generated against synthetic peptide fragments of the protein sequence[7] or against all or part of the protein expressed in bacteria. These antibodies can be used to characterize the protein and its anatomical distribution by conventional protein chemical and immunocytochemical techniques. Similarly, the expression of the mRNA can be analysed by RNA blotting and in situ hybridization.

The ultimate goal is to place each protein in its functional context within the neuron or glial cell. One strategy is to provide a basic description of the structure of each protein of interest. From this information, together with the detailed neuroanatomical mapping of the protein and its mRNA, one can hope to predict the possible functions of the protein. These hypotheses can then be tested with appropriate assays. An alternative and potentially powerful approach[5] is to generate experimental animals that carry genetically engineered alterations in the expression of the gene encoding the protein of interest. Most exciting, but not yet fully realized experimentally, will be the ability to produce animals carrying a designed mutation in a particular gene. Finally, it will be possible to bridge the gap between clone and function and to explore systematically the relationships between genes and behavior.

## ACKNOWLEDGMENTS

I thank Greg Sutcliffe, Floyd Bloom, and their colleagues for their contributions to these studies.

## REFERENCES

1. MILNER, R. J. & J. G. SUTCLIFFE. 1983. Gene expression in rat brain. Nucleic Acid Res. **11:** 5497–5520.
2. SUTCLIFFE, J. G. 1988. mRNA in the mammalian central nervous system. Annu. Rev. Neurosci. **11:** 157–198.
3. VALE, W., J. SPIESS, C. RIVIER & J. RIVIER. 1981. Characterization of a 41-residue ovine hypothalamic peptide that stimulates secretion of corticotrophin and β-endophin. Science **213:** 1394–1397.

4. SCHWARTZ, J. P. & E. COSTA. 1986. Hybridization approaches to the study of neuropeptides. Annu. Rev. Neurosci. **9:** 227–304.
5. MAYO, K. E., R. M. EVANS & G. M. ROSENFELD. 1986. Genes encoding mammalian neuroendocrine peptides: strategies toward their identification and analysis. Annu. Rev. Physiol. **48:** 431–446.
6. VALENTINO, K. L., J. WINTER & L. F. REICHARDT. 1985. Applications of monoclonal antibodies to neuroscience research. Annu. Rev. Neurosci. **8:** 199–232.
7. SUTCLIFFE, J. G., R. J. MILNER, T. M. SHINNICK & F. E. BLOOM. 1983. Identifying the protein products of brain-specific genes using antibodies to chemically synthetized peptides. Cell **33:** 671–682.
8. DWORKIN, M. B. & I. B. DAWID. 1980. Use of a cloned library for the study of abundant polyA⁺ RNA during *Xenopus laevis* development. Dev. Biol. **76:** 449–464.
9. DWORKIN-RASTL, E., D. B. KELLEY & M. B. DWORKIN. 1986. Localization of specific mRNA sequences in Xenopus laevis embryos by in situ hybridization. J. Embryol. Exp. Morphol. **91:** 153–168.
10. HEDRICK, S. M., D. I. COHEN, E. A. NIELSEN & M. M. DAVIS. 1984. Isolation of cDNA clones encoding T cell-specific membrane-associated proteins. Nature **308:** 149–153.
11. TRAVIS, G. H. & J. G. SUTCLIFFE. 1988. Phenol emulsion-enhanced DNA-driven subtractive cDNA cloning: isolation of low abundance monkey cortex-specific mRNAs. Proc. Natl. Acad. Sci. USA **85:** 1696–1700.
12. DUGUID, J. R., R. G. ROHWER & B. SEED. 1988. Isolation of cDNAs of scrapie-modulated RNAs by subtractive hybridization of a cDNA library. Proc. Natl. Acad. Sci. USA **85:** 5738–5742.
13. ERICSSON, A., D. LARHAMMAR, K. R. MCINTYRE & H. PERSSON. 1987. A molecular genetic approach to the identification of genes expressed predominantly in the neuroendocrine and immune systems. Immunol. Rev. **100:** 261–277.
14. BRANKS, P. L. & M. C. WILSON. 1986. Patterns of gene expression in the murine brain revealed by *in situ* hybridization of brain-specific mRNAs. Mol. Brain Res. **1:** 1–16.
15. MILNER, R. J., C. LAI, K.-A. NAVE, D. LENOIR, J. OGATA & J. G. SUTCLIFFE. 1985. Nucleotide sequences of two mRNAs for rat brain myelin proteolipid protein. Cell **42:** 931–939.
16. LAI, C., M. A. BROW, K.-A. NAVE, A. B. NORONHA, R. H. QUARLES, F. E. BLOOM, R. J. MILNER & J. G. SUTCLIFFE. 1987. Two forms of 1B236/myelin-associated glycoprotein MAG, a cell adhesion molecule for postnatal neural development, are produced by alternative splicing. Proc. Natl. Acad. Sci. USA **84:** 4337–4341.
17. FORSS-PETTER, S., P. DANIELSON & J. G. SUTCLIFFE. 1986. Neuron-specific enolase: complete structure of rat mRNA, multiple transcriptional start sites, and evidence suggesting post-transcriptional control. J. Neurosci. Res. **16:** 141–156.
18. FORSS-PETTER, S., P. DANIELSON, E. BATTENBERG, F. BLOOM & J. G. SUTCLIFFE. 1989. Nucleotide sequence and cellular distribution of rat chromogranin B secretogranin I mRNA in the neuroendocrine system. J. Mol. Neurosci. **1:** 63–75.
19. ROGERS, J. H. 1987. Calretinin: a gene for a novel calcium-binding protein expressed principally in neurons. J. Cell Biol. **105:** 1343–1353.
20. LEMKE, G. & R. AXEL. 1985. Isolation and sequence of a cDNA encoding the major structural protein of peripheral myelin. Cell **40:** 501–508.
21. TRAVIS, G. H. & J. G. SUTCLIFFE. 1988. Phenol emulsion-enhanced DNA-driven subtractive cDNA cloning: isolation of low abundance monkey cortex-specific mRNAs. Proc. Natl. Acad. Sci. USA **85:** 1696–1700.
22. CLAYTON, D. F., M. E. HUECAS, E. Y. SINCLAIR-THOMPSON, K. L. NASTIUK & F. NOTTEBOHM. 1988. Probes for rare mRNAs reveal distributed cell sets in canary brain. Neuron **1:** 249–261.
23. SCHAAL, H., D. GOLDOWITZ, U. A. HEINLEIN, A. UNTERBECK, C. RUPPERT, T. PAPENBROCK, B. MULLER-HILL, W. VIELMETTER & W. WILLE. 1987. A highly abundant transcript in adult murine cerebellar granule cells contains repetitive sequences homologous to L1. J. Neurosci. **7:** 2041–2048.
24. OBERDICK, J., F. LEVINTHAL & C. LEVINTHAL. 1988. A Purkinje cell differentiation marker

shows a partial DNA sequence homology to the cellular *sis/PDGF2* gene. Neuron **1**: 367–376.

25. ANDERSON, D. J. & R. AXEL. 1985. Molecular probes for the development and plasticity of neural crest derivatives. Cell **42**: 649–662.

26. MILLER, F. D., C. C. G. NAUS, G. A. HIGGINS, F. E. BLOOM & R. J. MILNER. 1987. Developmentally regulated rat brain mRNAs: molecular and anatomical characterization. J. Neurosci. **7**: 2433–2444.

27. MILLER, F. D., C. C. G. NAUS, M. M. DURAND, F. E. BLOOM & R. J. MILNER. 1987. Isotypes of α-tubulin are differentially regulated during neuronal maturation. J. Cell Biol. **105**: 3065–3073.

28. MILLER, F. D., W. TETZLAFF, M. A. BISBY, J. W. FAWCETT & R. J. MILNER. 1989. Rapid induction of the major embryonic α-tubulin mRNA, Tα1: during neuronal regeneration in adult rats. J. Neurosci. In press.

29. HOFFMAN, P. N. & D. W. CLEVELAND. 1988. Neurofilament and tubulin expression recapitulates the developmental program during axonal regeneration: induction of a specific beta-tubulin isotype. Proc. Natl. Acad. Sci. USA **85**: 4530–4533.

30. BASI, G. S., R. D. JACOBSON, I. VIRAG, J. SCHILLING & J. H. SKENE. 1987. Primary structure and transcriptional regulation of GAP-43: a protein associated with nerve growth. Cell **49**: 785–791.

31. MILBRANDT, J. 1987. A nerve growth factor-induced gene encodes a possible transcriptional regulatory factor. Science **238**: 797–799.

32. MILBRANDT, J. 1988. Nerve growth factor induces a gene homologous to the glucocorticoid receptor gene. Neuron **1**: 183–188.

33. LIM, R. W., C. VARNUM & H. R. HERSCHMAN. 1987. Cloning of tetradecanoyl phorbol ester-induced 'primary response' sequences and their expression in density-arrested Swiss 3T3 cells and a TPA non-proliferative variant. Oncogene **1**: 263–270.

34. KUJUBU, D. A., LIM, R. W., C. VARNUM & H. R. HERSCHMAN. 1987. Induction of transiently expressed genes in PC-12 pheochromocytoma cells. Oncogene **1**: 257–262.

35. LEVI, A., J. D. ELDRIDGE & B. M. PATTERSON. 1985. Molecular cloning of a gene sequence regulated by nerve growth factor. Science **229**: 393–395.

36. LEONARD, D. G. B., E. B. ZIFF & L. A. GREENE. 1987. Identification and characterization of mRNAs regulated by nerve growth factor in PC12 cells. Mol. Cell. Biol. **7**: 3156–3167.

37. LEONARD, D. G., J. D. GORHAM, P. COLE, L. A. GREENE & E. B. ZIFF. 1988. A nerve growth factor-regulated messenger RNA encodes a new intermediate filament protein. J. Cell Biol. **106**: 181–193.

38. TRAVIS, G. H., M. B. BRENNAN, P. E. DANIELSON, C. A. KOZAK & J. G. SUTCLIFFE. 1989. Identification of a photoreceptor-specific mRNA encoded by the gene responsible for retinal degeneration slow (*rds*). Nature **338**: 70–73.

# Index of Contributors